W9-DFK-190

AGRICULTURAL POLICY ANALYSIS

Award-Winning Books by Harold G. Halcrow

Food Policy for America, McGraw-Hill, 1977.
Economics of Agriculture, McGraw-Hill, 1980.

AGRICULTURAL POLICY ANALYSIS

Harold G. Halcrow

Professor Emeritus of Agricultural Economics
University of Illinois, Urbana-Champaign

McGRAW-HILL BOOK COMPANY

New York   St. Louis   San Francisco   Auckland   Bogotá
Hamburg   Johannesburg   London   Madrid   Mexico   Montreal   New Delhi
Panama   Paris   São Paulo   Singapore   Sydney   Tokyo   Toronto

This book was set in Times Roman by University Graphics, Inc. (ECU).
The editor was Mary Jane Martin;
the production supervisor was Marietta Breitwieser.
The cover was designed by Kao & Kao Associates.
Project supervision was done by The Total Book.
Halliday Lithograph Corporation was printer and binder.

AGRICULTURAL POLICY ANALYSIS

1 2 3 4 5 6 7 8 9 0   HALHAL   8 9 8 7 6 5 4

ISBN 0-07-025562-8

Library of Congress Cataloging in Publication Data

Halcrow, Harold G.
   Agricultural policy analysis.

   Bibliography: p.
   Includes indexes.
   1. Agriculture and state—United States.
2. Agriculture and state.   I. Title.
HD1761.H349   1984   338.1′873   83-14952
ISBN 0-07-025562-8

CONTENTS

PREFACE

Agricultural Policy Analysis is designed as a comprehensive text for the first general course in agricultural policy or agricultural and food policy. The reading level is for advanced undergraduate students, because this is the level at which the course is usually taught. Prerequisites include principles of economics, basic economics of agriculture, and appropriate courses in agricultural production, marketing, price analysis, and the like.

An Exciting Subject

Agricultural policy is an exciting subject because it deals with the public measures that can be taken to improve the competitive structure, operation, and performance of one of our largest industries. American agriculture has been growing faster than almost any other major industry; yet, it has policy problems that are as challenging as anyone may care to imagine. The challenge in studying agricultural policy is to build a broad vision of the agricultural industry, and to bring the discipline of economics and other social sciences to bear on the policy issues. The goal is to learn how to visualize and how to analyze so that these skills will be useful throughout life.

Organization of Study

Agricultural policy deals with two broad sets of markets: those for products and those for inputs. The approach is from the general to the specific, dealing first in Part One with the concepts of values and goals, the setting for policy, and the general methodology that is used. Part Two develops the foundations for policy in the product markets and the alternative choices for the three economies of crops, livestock, and marketing. Part Three covers policy in the input markets—the financial, natural resource, agribusiness input, and human resource markets.

ACKNOWLEDGMENTS

Many people over many years have contributed to this subject through their research, writing, and teaching, and in other ways. This is acknowledged in part in references to the literature. More specifically, this book has benefited from comprehensive reviews by the following scholars: Larry L. Bauer, Clemson University; Harold F. Breimyer, University of Missouri, Columbia; Earl H. Brown, University of Maryland; Harold O. Carter, University of California at Davis; H. B. Clark, University of Florida; M. C. Hallberg, The Pennsylvania State University; Dale M. Hoover, North Carolina State University; Randall Kramer, Virginia Polytechnic Institute and State University; Dean Linsenmeyer, The University of Nebraska at Lincoln; Marshall A. Martin, Purdue University; William H. Meyers, Iowa State University.

My colleagues at the University of Illinois continue to be most generous in giving me both assistance and encouragement. I couldn't ask for a friendlier and more helpful place to work. I wish to acknowledge specifically Wesley D. Seitz, Head of Department, who has given me every encouragement; Harold D. Guither and Stephen C. Schmidt, who gave me comprehensive reviews and advice; and Gail Metheny, who helped me greatly with her excellent secretarial work. The work has also benefited from the help of my son, Ronald, at Colgate University, and from many discussions with students at Illinois. Finally, the pictures in the book that are not otherwise credited have been supplied by University of Illinois photographers Paul Hixon and Larry Baker.

With all of this excellent help and advice, there should not be many errors of omission or commission. But to the extent that there are, the author accepts responsibility.

Harold G. Halcrow

AGRICULTURAL POLICY ANALYSIS

PART ONE

FOUNDATIONS FOR POLICY ANALYSIS

BASIC CONCEPTS AND GOALS OF POLICY

All recommendations of policy involve judgments of value concerning what shall or shall not be done, and why. Values depend on beliefs that people hold about what is good, and on the strengths of their beliefs. Beliefs and values provide the foundation on which the goals of policy are built.

IN THIS CHAPTER

1 You can learn some of the basic concepts of policy and sharpen your vision concerning the scope of agricultural policy.

2 You can learn to visualize the system of beliefs, values, and creeds that provides the foundation for agricultural policy, and you can learn the usefulness of this system in agricultural policy analysis.

3 You can learn to identify the major goals of agricultural policy, and develop an understanding concerning how they relate to policy-making groups and to the beliefs and values that underlie them.

DEFINITIONS AND SCOPE OF POLICY

What is agricultural policy? What is its range, or scope? To answer these questions, let us first consider some of the basic concepts of policy, and distinguish what we mean by public policy. Then we can define and visualize the scope of agricultural policy, explain why we have an agricultural policy, and consider our reasons for studying such policy.

Definition and General Concept of Policy

Policy is defined as a deliberate course of action, as contrasted with a haphazard or capricious type of activity followed by a public body, private firm, family, or individual. Policy generally implies wisdom or prudence in managing affairs, based on a definitive plan or program created through a process of thought and reason. It is a universal activity of rational individuals, families and firms, political movements, organized groups, governments, and agencies of government.

Elements of Policy

Policy involves planning based on certain beliefs, values, and goals, taking into account the resources that may be available for reaching the goals, and the benefits and costs of using one plan or another. The elements of policy involve the *goals* that may be established, the *means* that may be used to reach these goals, the *implements* such as agents or agencies that activate and control the means, and the *constraints* that are applied to the plan or program. The basic concept of policy is that of deliberate action or activity involving these four elements.

Distinguishing Public Policy

Public policy, as contrasted with a private policy of an individual, family, or firm, involves individuals in their roles as citizens; groups and organizations with a political objective or goal; and government on a local, state, national, or international level. Through actions of government, public policy affects us all. A study of policy does not cover the full disciplines of political services, but it involves the political systems on which governments are based, and on this basis we may draw sharp distinctions among different systems for making policy.

In a democracy, such as the United States, numerous individuals and interest groups are involved in making policy, as contrasted with an authoritarian government, run by one individual or a single interest group, such as a military dictatorship or a one-party state. Hence, in the United States, making public policy involves innumerable compromises by many individuals and political interest groups, represented by various organizations, political parties, and government agencies. Public policy involves action based on expected results, as we act through government to solve collectively selected problems experienced by many individuals.

The Process of Making Policy

We can distinguish a number of steps that are typically involved in making public policy in a democracy. First, the process generally starts with a feeling that a change in the current state of affairs is desired. This may be a feeling of hurt or dissatisfaction, or dissent from what is being done or not done. Second, there must be development of public awareness that something should be and can be done. Third, there must be public acceptance of some proposed policy or policies, and associated political action to get one or another of these policies adopted. Fourth, there is evaluation and analysis or review, which may take place at any stage in the process of making policy, or as an additional step in reappraisal of policy. Making public policy involves the concept of *incrementalism,* as each new decision is added to the old. Policy is built, step by step or decision by decision. Both the wise decisions of the past, as well as the mistakes, are the foundation for current and future action, or policy.

Defining Agricultural Policy

Agricultural policy, which is regarded as an important area of public policy, may be defined as a course of public action directed primarily but not exclusively toward the farm and agribusiness sectors of society. Broadly speaking, it involves the full range of public decisions that influence individuals and firms to decide what products shall be produced, how they shall be produced, and for whom.

Agricultural policy applies to two broad sets of markets: the agricultural input markets, through which the resources and commodities used in farming (and ranching) are made available for production; and the agricultural product markets, through which farm food products are marketed and processed for consumption at home and abroad. Policy in the input markets applies to the use of land and other natural resources, agricultural credit, industrial products used by agriculture, and the human resources employed in all sectors of agriculture. Policy in the product markets involves a broad range of laws, government rules and regulations that apply to these markets. For instance, it deals with issues such as free markets, or price supports with production and marketing controls; relatively free international trade in farm food products (or trade agreements), and subsidies, tariff and nontariff barriers to trade; consumer food subsidies, such as food stamps and school lunch programs, and concerns how such issues are to be handled.

Why We Have Agricultural Policy

Both the input and product markets are characterized by a significant amount of government involvement, and the policy choices that are made affect us all in more ways than we can imagine. For instance, over the first 300 years of United States history, from the colonial settlements at Jamestown and Plymouth through the second decade of this century, agricultural policy was dominated by what may be called developmental policy. Government policy, directed primarily at development and settlement of family farms, determined the economic structure of agriculture, and the conditions under which it would develop and grow. The Morrill Act of 1862, which initiated the land-grant college system, was the first in a long series of acts which have developed the policy of public support for agricultural research and education. This policy has provided the foundation for the scientific and technological revolution that has transformed traditional agriculture into its modern industrial state.

The increase in output of this modern industrial system has tended to force down the prices of agricultural products relative to the index of prices of all inputs used in production. Returns to farm labor have tended to be depressed. Although the farm population has declined, primarily as a result of reduced entry, there has been considerable pressure from farm and agribusiness interests for government to aid farmers.

So the farm sector, which traditionally has been the model of free enterprise under pure competition, involves government and public policy for at least three reasons. First, increasing the productivity of agriculture is essential for meeting the growing world demand for food, and government is widely and deeply involved in helping almost all sectors of agriculture to increase their productivity. Second, economic stability is important, too, and this is largely the responsibility of policy. Third, government policy greatly influences income distribution. And, since income distribution is not satisfactory, as we have just said, there is a continuing interest in policy.

We have agricultural policy for the same reason that we have government. It is a necessary part of public order. A particular policy has been chosen and followed because citizens wanted it, voted for political candidates who favored it, and formed organizations to work through the political process until they could get it. This is why we have an agricultural policy and why it is worthwhile to study this policy.

Why Studying Agricultural Policy Is Worthwhile

Because of the importance of agricultural policy in influencing our lives, self-interest alone may be sufficient reason to make studying it worthwhile. The choices that are made affect our lives and well-being every single day. How we react to some of these choices will have a great deal to do with our prosperity, health, and happiness. Study of agricultural policy is—or should be—worthwhile because of our current and future roles in the political process. One way or another, through these roles we each help determine what choices are made.

The two parts of policy study involve vision and analysis of possible policy choices. Vision and analysis are both important, and we study policy to broaden and sharpen our vision, and to improve our competence in analysis. You can learn a great deal by studying agricultural policy, which will benefit you throughout life. Just how much you learn and how you will benefit depends on how well the subject is presented, and on how diligently and effectively you apply yourself to it. Let us consider the beliefs and values underlying agricultural policy.

BELIEFS AND VALUES UNDERLYING POLICY

As we said in the first sentence, all recommendations of policy involve judgments of value concerning what shall or shall not be done, and why. These judgments are based on beliefs about what is good, or thought to be good and hence of value, and involve judgments as to what should or should not be done to try to achieve that which is deemed good. Such beliefs differ from those dealing simply with what is true in an empirical sense, to which no particular values may be attached.

From Beliefs to Values

People often share the same beliefs about what is and is not good, but they may act differently because of differences in the strengths of their beliefs, or in the relative importance they attach to their beliefs. In principle, there is no single correct answer to the question of what values and weights shall be accepted, and consequently no uniquely correct concept of the social benefits and costs of a particular policy or program. This means that all public policy is subject to comment and criticism from one standpoint or another, or subject to valuation in terms of individual and group preferences. The market gives us some measures of the values that people place on material goods, and some policies can be judged in terms of whether they increase or decrease market values. But, beyond this, there is the very large question of non-market costs, such as pollutants; there is the question of what is good for society in terms of a desired economic structure and distribution of income, its economic growth rate, its political organization, and the relationships among major industries. Since we do not have a unique way for approaching these questions, an early step in studying policy is to review what beliefs and values people attach to policy.

What are some of the more important beliefs and values underlying agricultural policy?

General Beliefs and Values

What are the fundamentals of what is good and worth struggling to achieve? Certainly freedom is fundamental, as we should be aware, in every passing day. Economic progress and rising standards of living are universally desired. Economic stability is an important goal; we are reminded especially of this in periods of instability. And equitable distribution of the fruits of production is generally recognized as desirable, even though we have had great difficulty in defining what is equitable.

Studying policy will help us understand what consequences one policy choice or another may have, and from this we can decide whether the result is good, or not. Among the foundations of this country is a strong belief in the rights of the individual and the family, with government action limited or constrained by consent of the governed. This requires free speech and free press; free assembly, and the accompanying basic right to dissent; freedom of religion, with groups and organizations bound by certain codes of morality, and with separation of church and state.

These beliefs are balanced by certain concepts of justice and equity, those applied to the distribution of resources being quite important for agricultural policy. As a nation, we have always argued that government plays a positive role in seeing that resources are made available to individuals and families in some just and fair manner. In respect to agriculture, one of the basic concepts is that of the family farm, viewed as a unit large enough to support a family but not too large for a family to manage or farm. Value judgments concerning the worth of the family farm provided a guide for land settlement policy over some 300 years. Since then certain concepts of equity and justice, such as fair prices and distribution, are guiding principles in the value judgments underlying U.S. agricultural policy.

The 4-H program is part of the cooperative extension program in agriculture and home economics, which is supported by federal, state, and local funds, including donations. The 4-H pledge highlights the important policy goals and suggests some of the reasons for public support of the program.

Equity and Justice

These concepts are fundamental. The concept of democracy in the United States emphasizes learning and active mastery of the world, in contrast to the more ascetic concept found in parts of the Eastern world, which emphasizes self-denial, self-discipline, and abstinence. American concept and practice involves participatory democracy. It allows for a pluralism of ideas and actors in the process of policy making. Government is of the people and for the people, and by the people in the sense that it is carried out through their elected representatives and executives. The roots of these concepts may be traced to the antiquity of Greek democracy, to the dialogues of Plato and the logic of Aristotle, through the upheavals of the Middle Ages, to the Magna Carta, the Reformation, and the evolution of English democracy. These concepts have provided a framework for evolution of economics as well as for development of agricultural policy.

During the eighteenth and nineteenth centuries the policy of free land and support for public services encouraged development through freedom of opportunity. A policy of laissez faire in markets for farm products was consistent with the concept of perfect competition that generally applied to these markets.

Economic conditions of the twentieth century created a new role for government with respect to agriculture. Early in the 1920s, a sharp and hard fall in prices of farm products ignited an intense political campaign to get the federal government to raise these prices. Farm people argued that prices set by the government were ruin- and unfair. These prices were not low by prewar standards, but they were low in relation to the prices farmers had to pay for other goods. This disparity was, and most of the time has continued to be, at the heart of government involvement in agricultural policy making (Figure 1-1).

Government involvement with agriculture comes from the concepts of justice and equity, and beliefs concerning what is beneficial and worthwhile. This does not nec- essarily require heavier and heavier involvement, however. The real questions are: What is worthwhile? What policy alternatives shall be supported, and why? How shall a given program be limited, or constrained? This is the essence of democratic thought as applied to policy. What beliefs and values are relevant?

FIGURE 1-1
Prices received and paid by farmers and the parity ratio. In comparison with the base period, if the change in prices received just matches the change in prices paid, the parity ratio is 100. If prices received are half of what they were in the base period, while prices are still at 100, the parity ratio is 50. In the early 1980s, the ratio tended to slide below 70 as prices of major farm inputs continued to rise. (*Source: USDA,* Agricultural Statistics, *and* 1982 Handbook of Agricul- tural Charts, *p. 10.*)

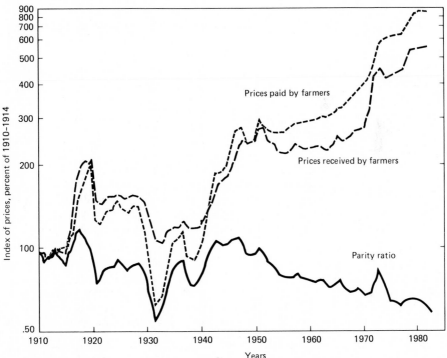

The Democratic Creed[1]

Among the beliefs and values underlying agricultural policy, as well as democracy in general, are two relating to what is called the *democratic creed:* (1) that all persons, no matter how wise or good, are of equal worth and dignity; and (2) that no person, again no matter how wise or good, is wise or good enough to have dictatorial power over another. This creed has led to the separation of powers in the three branches of the U.S. government, in which all elected officials are responsible to the electorate, and all persons holding public appointments are constrained by the rules and customs of their office. Policy affecting the public welfare and the various economic sectors of our economy evolves from the democratic creed.

Agricultural policy is based on the democratic creed. Farmers have been enfranchised to vote on program proposals that will affect them all, but generally individual farmers have been left free to participate in a given program, or not. Powers are delegated to government to operate a program. But programs that are mandatory for producers of certain commodities, such as marketing agreements and order programs, which are designed to regulate marketing of specified commodities, are not instituted without a favorable vote of producing or marketing firms. Even then, a farmer or a marketing firm has the option of deciding whether or not to produce or market the commodity or commodities covered under the program.

The Enterprise Creed

A concept concerning the role of managers or entrepreneurs, known as the *enterprise creed,* also has implications for agricultural policy. This is based on at least four distinguishable beliefs or value judgments: (1) Members of a family bear a mutual responsibility to each other, the mainstream of which flows at least initially from parents to their children, and then branches out in various ways. (2) The primary function of government is to prevent the lazy or imprudent from pressing governments, businesses, or other institutions and individuals into sharing the burden of their imprudence. (3) Within the general laws of the state, proprietors deserve exclusive rights to prescribe the rules under which they operate. (4) It is a prime function of government to prevent any one individual or institution, including the government itself, from infringing on the managerial freedom of proprietors.

Wide acceptance of the enterprise creed tends to limit governments at all levels in acting to infringe on the agricultural sector's freedom to manage. Participation in agricultural programs, such as farm price supports and production controls, has generally been of a voluntary nature based on economic incentives. Most infringements on the proprietor's rights to use resources have occurred only when the rights of other individuals are threatened, or when there is an overriding public interest among other

---

[1]The following discussion draws most importantly on the work of John M. Brewster, "Society Values and Goals in Respect to Agriculture," in *Goals and Values in Agricultural Policy,* Iowa State University Press, Ames, 1961; and *A Philosopher Among Economists, Selected Works of John M. Brewster,* J. Patrick Madden and David E. Brewster (eds.), T. J. Murphy Co., Philadelphia, 1970. See especially Part III, chapters 5–8.

individuals. Controls on pesticides is one example. Strict adherence to the enterprise creed prevents government from adopting mandatory or compulsory programs that restrict managers yet allows managers to use the powers of government to help themselves.

The Creed of Self-integrity

Within a democratic state, the *creed of self-integrity* deals specifically with the status of dissent, and this has played and continues to play a crucial role in making agricultural policy. The early colonists dissented from the feudal land systems of the European states. Land-grant colleges and universities, a primary resource in agricultural research and education, arose out of dissent with more traditional systems. Federal farm credit programs were started and have grown as a result of farmers' protests aimed at getting cheaper and more adequate sources of credit. Protests over low farm prices, appearing as dissent, have involved the federal government in farm price-support programs.

The goals of agricultural policy grow out of this system of beliefs, creeds, and value judgments. What are the major goals, and how are they formed?

GOALS OF AGRICULTURAL POLICY

Goals of policy are defined as the ends of objectives toward which activity may be directed. *Means* are the ways in which goals are achieved. *Values* are the standards or preferences, based on beliefs, that guide behavior. But values, as feelings of what is desirable, or thought to be desired, can often be interpreted as goals; goals may be interchangeable with means. A soil conservation goal, for example, may be visualized as the means to preserve soil productivity and increase crop yields over a certain planning horizon. A specific target price in a price-support program may be visualized as the goal of a farm organization, for instance, or as the means to reach a certain farm-income goal. Hence, it is true that a clear-cut distinction among values, goals, and means is frequently difficult to arrive at, and as such not necessary to policy study.

Yet it is essential to have definable goals that can be supported as guides for policy activity; these can be described in terms of productivity, stability, income distribution, and welfare.

Productivity and Development

General goals of increasing productivity and development can be defined in terms of the public interest. This is best understood by imagining that it is the goal of policy to make everyone as well off as possible. Being "better off" means having increased command over material goods, or immaterial sources of satisfaction, such as more leisure time, cultural advantages, or political and religious freedom. In the context of agriculture, it means having more or higher-quality food, or more goods produced jointly with food, under a given level of resource use. With an increasing use of

TABLE 1-1
INDEXES OF TOTAL FARM OUTPUT, INPUT, AND PRODUCTIVITY
1967 = 100

Year	Output	Input	Productivity[a]	Year	Output	Input	Productivity[a]
1910	43	86	50	1947	69	101	68
1911	42	88	48	1948	76	103	74
1912	47	90	53	1949	74	105	71
1913	43	90	47	1950	74	104	71
1914	47	92	51	1951	76	107	71
1915	49	92	53	1952	79	107	74
1916	44	92	48	1953	79	106	75
1917	47	93	51	1954	80	105	76
1918	47	95	49	1955	82	105	78
1919	47	95	50	1956	82	103	80
1920	50	98	52	1957	81	101	80
1921	45	95	47	1958	87	100	87
1922	49	96	51	1959	88	102	87
1923	50	97	51	1960	91	101	90
1924	49	99	50	1961	91	100	91
1925	51	99	51	1962	92	100	92
1926	52	101	52	1963	96	100	96
1927	52	99	52	1964	95	100	95
1928	54	101	53	1965	98	98	100
1929	53	102	52	1966	95	98	97
1930	52	101	51	1967	100	100	100
1931	57	101	56	1968	102	100	102
1932	55	97	57	1969	102	99	103
1933	51	96	53	1970	101	100	102
1934	43	90	48	1971	110	100	110
1935	52	91	57	1972	110	100	110
1936	47	93	50	1973	112	101	111
1937	57	98	59	1974	106	101	105
1938	57	96	60	1975	114	100	115
1939	58	98	59	1976	117	103	115
1940	60	100	60	1977	119	105	114
1941	62	100	62	1978	122	105	116
1942	70	103	68	1979	129	108	119
1943	69	104	66	1980	122	106	115
1944	71	105	67	1981	140	106	132
1945	70	103	68	1982	139[b]	n.a.[c]	n.a.[c]
1946	71	101	71	1983	119[b]	n.a.[c]	n.a.[c]

[a]Data computed from unrounded index numbers.
[b]Preliminary, interpolated from 1977 base.
[c]Not available.
Source: U.S. Department of Agriculture, Economic Research Service, *Economic Indicators of the Farm Sector, Production and Efficiency Statistics, 1980,* Statistical Bulletin 678, January 1982, p. 77; *Ibid., 1981,* ECIFS 1–3, January 1983, p. 73; and *Agricultural Outlook,* October 1983 / AO-92, p. 27.

resources, being better off means total output will increase more, relative to total input (Table 1-1).

The productivity goal is quite evident in public investment in research and agricultural education and extension programs. Education increases the productivity of people, and provides for broad advances in science and technology. This has made modern agriculture a high-technology, capital-intensive industry. Changes in agriculture are still rapid, and productivity continues to rise. Major farm inputs have involved more and more agricultural chemicals as fertilizers and pesticides, more and more productive mechanical power and machinery, and a steady downtrend in use of farm labor. The amount of farm real estate or land has changed relatively little (Figure 1-2). The goals for productivity, or for development and growth based on increasing productivity, are not self-evident, however. Currently, increasing productivity, made possible by more chemicals and mechanical equipment with more intensive use of natural resources, tends to have some adverse effects on the environment; there are worrisome questions about how long increases in productivity can be sustained. The apparently rising world demand for food suggests a strong long-term outlook for market growth, however, which suggests that productivity and development will continue to be important.

FIGURE 1-2
Trends in use of selected farm inputs. *(Source: USDA,* 1982 Handbook of Agricultural Charts, *p. 11.)*

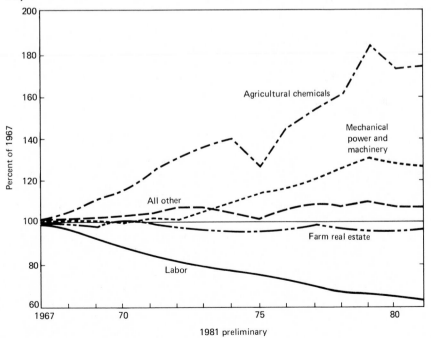

Stability

Of all the economic goals of government, that of obtaining stability in the economy may be regarded as most universally accepted. Much of agricultural policy is aimed at increasing stability—price supports and storage programs, trade agreements, supplementary payments to farmers, crop insurance, credit programs, and others. Variability in both prices and crop yields is a major cause of instability in agriculture, and well-designed policy can do much to counteract or offset this variability.

Income Distribution

Two aspects of income distribution are involved in the goals of agricultural policy. One is the comparative income levels between farm and nonfarm families, with the lower average income of farm families often invoked as a justification for aid to agriculture. The other is the skewness in income distribution among farm families, which is greater than that among people employed in most other industries. A larger percentage of farm families are poor than is the case for those outside of agriculture. Also, the most productive farmers generally have very good incomes.[2]

The skewness in farm incomes complicates the problem of giving aid to agriculture. Our beliefs and values are generally consistent with the idea of helping poor people. But most farm programs help well-off farmers much more than poor farmers. From the standpoint of welfare, this is ridiculous.

Frequently, economists argue that prices are inappropriate as goals of agricultural policy, because this tends to distort agricultural incentives, as we have just mentioned. But the public has an interest in trying to stabilize agricultural income, and farmers tend to gain in the short run from programs that raise and stabilize their prices and incomes. So, aid to agriculture commands considerable public support, even though programs may not be consistent with public interests. There is no a priori basis for judgment and, although farmers may gain in the short run, the long-term effect of price supports on agriculture is unclear. Theoretically, in the long run, under pure or perfect competition, the average cost of production will equal the product price. Hence, it is dangerous if not wrong to make sweeping generalizations about price-support policy, and we will reserve our judgment until we study the product markets. In the meantime, let us also acknowledge, in a more general view, some of the broader welfare goals related to agricultural policy.

Welfare Goals Related to Agricultural Policy

People generally, both individually and collectively, attempt to maximize something that may be called welfare, utility, satisfaction, or well-being. This depends on productivity and equity in distribution, security of person and property, and certain concepts of liberty and justice. The importance of recognizing these as values or goals

---

[2]For current data see the U.S. Department of Agriculture's annual *Handbook of Agricultural Charts.*

Children in 4-H clubs learn rules of conduct and safety while enjoying outdoor recreation.

of policy cannot be overemphasized, because if we do not have a certain degree of equity or fairness, liberty and security, then we cannot benefit from rising productivity or more income. Maintaining individual freedom is one of the important considerations in deciding how far to go with a production-control or income-support program. Maintaining world peace and democratic freedoms are primary goals without which all else may be lost.

Economic policy cannot guarantee peace, freedom, and security, but an unwise public policy can make their attainment or preservation difficult, if not impossible. It is the function of policy to create the conditions in which peace, freedom, and security can continue to be realized. Policy cannot be directed toward the maximization of any particular goal. Rather it is a process for maximizing the general welfare, as conceived, which involves innumerable compromises among a wide variety of goals.

Conflict and Compromise in Policy Making

Policy compromises are reached through the political process, even though the major goals remain essentially in conflict. The crux of this conflict is found in comparing goals of agricultural producers and the general public, which are summarized in the following paragraph.

The general public wants from agriculture an abundance of farm food products at reasonable cost, which means, over time, with economic progress or growth, real prices will decrease. As Figure 1-1 shows, this goal is being met, to some degree at least.

Agriculture, however, wants from society measures to at least partially compensate producers for economic losses resulting from the national policy of development and growth based on increasing efficiency, because this tends to result in declining real prices for farm food products. Agricultural producers generally want what may be called fair prices, and equality of opportunity to share in the fruits of national economic growth with publicly supported measures to educate, train, and assist them to be productive. They want publicly supported schools, roads, hospitals, etc., without paying more than their fair share for these services. As demonstrated in the last several decades, hired farm laborers as well as farmers want the right to organize to achieve equal opportunity and a fair return for their work. In short, the political policy struggle of agricultural producers is for equal opportunity and a fair return, or distributive and commutative justice, as we have said. But both farm and agribusiness leaders want a minimum of government intervention in their affairs.

Policy Process and Participants[3]

In recent years, these conflicts have erupted not as direct confrontations between producers and consumers, but as part of the process in policy making. This shows most clearly in conflicts between Congress and the White House over farm legislation, and in struggles for power within Congress, where elected representatives try to accommodate to the demands of competing political groups. How is this process carried out, and who are the most direct participants?

The making of agricultural policy is importantly influenced, some may say even uniquely influenced, by the competing and sometimes conflicting goals of farm organizations and related policy-oriented groups. In 1933, when the first Agricultural Adjustment Act established the first farm price-support program, the agricultural policy-making establishment was a relatively uncomplicated affair. It consisted basically of the major farm organizations, agriculture committees of Congress, the U.S. Department of Agriculture, and land-grant universities. These groups didn't always agree on a course of action, but they did agree that it was up to them to decide what the goals should be, and what issues should be brought before Congress and the administration.

Since then, this establishment has expanded greatly. In the last two decades, especially since the early 1970s, hundreds of organizations and groups concerned with some aspect of agricultural and food policy have clamored to be heard. In addition to producers, these groups represent agricultural and food firms, industry, consumers, environmentalists, public institutions and agencies, and research organizations.

---

[3]This section is based on an article by Harold D. Guither and Harold G. Halcrow, "The Politics of Food," *Illinois Research,* College of Agriculture, University of Illinois at Urbana-Champaign, vol. 24, no. 3, Summer 1982, pp. 5–7.

Producer Groups   Producer organizations trying to influence agricultural policy have proliferated over the years. Five general farm organizations, representing all types of producers, draw members from almost all states and regions. The American Farm Bureau Federation is by far the largest, with more than three million family members. The National Grange, the oldest of the five, has 450,000 farm and rural family members. The National Farmers Union stands at 275,000 members, mainly from the Great Plains and the midwest. The National Farmers Organization, begun in 1955, and the American Agriculture Movement, organized in 1979, are smaller and more militant and their membership figures are not reported.

Commodity organizations, most of which have representatives in Washington, D.C., have developed legislative and lobbying activities. Among the most active groups are the milk producers and marketing cooperatives; wheat, cotton, and tobacco growers; pork producers; cattle producers and feeders; and soybean and corn growers. Organizations in individual states are usually affiliated with a national organization, which concentrates on problems and concerns of the producers.

Farmer-owned cooperatives influence policy that affects their business. Often of special interest to them are transportation, energy, taxes, and marketing practices.

Two national organizations of farm women are active in efforts to protect family farms and financial interests of farm families, and to represent agriculture to nonfarm groups. American Agri-Women has more than 20 affiliated state and commodity-oriented farm women's groups. Women Involved in Farm Economics, an independent organization concentrated in the Great Plains, generally supports the positions of the major farm organizations to which men belong.

Business and Industry   Agricultural and food firms and industrial organizations support the largest number of lobbyists in agricultural and food policy. Groups represented include trade organizations whose members manufacture and sell farm inputs such as fertilizers, seed, feed, petroleum products, chemicals, and machinery. Also represented are agribusiness firms and organizations that process and market farm food products for domestic use and for export. Often enough their interests are in line with those of farm producer groups, but occasionally they may oppose farmers or have common interests with consumers.

Agribusiness groups are usually highly specialized. Practically every major farm input and farm food product industry has a Washington representative attempting to influence policy in Congress and federal agencies. Highly trained, well-financed, and skillful in dealing with Congress and officials in the executive branch, these representatives often provide important and useful information as they try to influence policy according to the positions of their organizations.

Consumer and Citizen Groups   More and more, consumer and citizen groups, sometimes referred to as public-interest groups, have become active in making agricultural and food policy. Advocacy groups support food assistance and rural development programs for the poor to help them obtain food stamps and other benefits. Legislation on migrant farm workers has led to organizations that help these workers use the government assistance provided. More attention to the needs of the hungry and malnourished has stimulated religious groups and others to improve food assistance programs both at home and overseas. Antipoverty and rural housing programs have encouraged groups in helping to implement these programs.

Wildlife and environmental groups actively promote policies for controlling the use of pesticides and for encouraging organic farming. With the growing concentration of large farms, organizations are now advocating increased support for small and medium-sized farms, social justice for farm workers, direct marketing of farm products, and increased land ownership among minority-group members.

Membership funding of citizen and consumer groups is limited, so these organizations must seek contracts and grants from foundations and federal and state agencies. As the budgets of government agencies are cut back, however, these groups face financial stress, and many have ceased or greatly reduced their activities.

Other Organizations   Many public institutions and agencies form professional associations and often maintain representation in Washington, D.C. Although they may not lobby, they do communicate with policy makers and take part in legislative hearings. Included in this category are the National Association of Conservation Districts, the National Association of State Universities and Land Grant Colleges, the Association of Veterinary Medical Colleges, the National Association of Counties, and the American Public Welfare Association.

Professional associations with a continuing concern in policy include the American Veterinary Medical Association, American Dietetic Association, American Society of Professional Farm Managers and Rural Appraisers, and the American School Food Service.

Although not necessarily involved directly in legislation and lobbying, certain organizations engage in research and information activities that provide support for activist, lobbying, and legislative groups. Examples of such organizations are the Council for Agricultural Science and Technology (CAST), the Agriculture Council of America, the Conservation Foundation, the American Enterprise Institute for Public Policy Research, Resources for the Future, and the Brookings Institution. Some have specific interests in agricultural and food-related topics, while others have a much broader policy interest that includes some related aspect of the national or international economy.

Strategies and Methods   Efforts to influence policy take several forms, such as: *direct contact* between professional lobbyists and members of Congress or agency heads who make policy decisions; *letter-writing campaigns* organized by the national office and directed to members during critical periods of mark-up (bill writing) and roll call; *group visits* of constituents to the members of Congress who represent the constituents' state or district; and *testimony of organization officers* at committee hearings on issues of special concern.

Some organizations keep a low profile. Their legislative activities may involve publishing an educational newsletter and urging members to voice their concerns about certain laws to congressional representatives. Other groups serve as Washington contact points for members who want information that is unavailable elsewhere. A group that cannot afford to rent office space and keep a full-time staff in Washington, D.C., may hire one person who represents other groups as well.

To be more effective on a single issue, one group may form a coalition with other organizations having similar policy positions on that issue. Coalitions tend to come and go. Once a decision has been made on a bill or regulation, the coalition usually disbands. It may form again when issues of common interest appear in the future.

Another form of mutual assistance is the practice known as networking that is prevalent among citizen and consumer groups with small memberships and limited funds. Networking involves publicizing the other groups' activities, having the same board member on their respective boards, and having members of one organization serve as consultants or committee members for activities of the other groups. Through networking, groups form coalitions, testify jointly at congressional hearings, and meet at conferences to develop plans for future activities.

Political Action Committees Agricultural and food organizations have organized political action committees (PACs) to raise funds and contribute to the campaigns of candidates for Congress, the presidency, and state legislatures. Compared with contributions collected by other business, professional, and labor groups, these funds are relatively modest, but some are large enough to be very significant. In the 1978 congressional campaign, the five largest PACs were sponsored by the Dairymen, Inc., the Chicago Mercantile Exchange, the Associated Milk Producers, Inc., the Mid-America Dairymen, Inc., and the National Rural Electric Cooperative Association. Since 1978, the level of contributions has increased substantially in real terms, and in almost every area of policy making. Most groups that sponsor PACs do not always expect to influence the votes of those candidates they support who are elected. They do expect their contributions to give them some recognition and to make communication of their views possible during future legislative activities.

Diversity of Interests The growing numbers of organizations concerned with goals of agricultural and food policy provide diverse input into the policy-making process. Along with this growth, traditional farm organizations face increasing competition for attention from congressional committees and members of Congress.

Increased numbers of producer organizations, as well as business, citizen, institutional, and professional groups, make it difficult for Congress to reach a consensus. The long, drawn-out process of writing and passing recent agricultural acts demonstrates this. Even so, dissatisfaction with final decisions is not uncommon.

With the increasing diversity of interests, the dominance or control of some issues by specific commodity groups is sometimes weakened. Attacks on the dairy, sugar, peanut, and tobacco programs during the debate on the 1981 Agriculture and Food Act reflects this development. In this case, the commodity groups were able to compromise and retain some special advantages. But future farm policy-making efforts could see greater influence by consumer groups and less control by the special commodity interests.

All of the groups discussed here have considerable influence. Yet individuals can also make significant contributions to the process of agricultural and food policy making. As citizens we should understand how policy decisions affect us and our communities and businesses. We also have a responsibility to vote, and opportunities to influence policy.

SUMMARY

We have studied some of the basic concepts and goals of agricultural policy, or agricultural and food policy. It has been stressed that all recommendations of policy depend on value judgments concerning what shall be done, or not done, and why. Certain beliefs and creeds have been identified, such as the work ethic, the democratic creed, the enterprise creed, and the creed of self-integrity. These are important in establishing our values, and the goals for policy.

Major policy goals have been related to concepts of increasing productivity, income distribution, and the general welfare. We have identified the elements of policy as goals, means, implements, and constraints; and we have noted that elements, such as goals and means, are interchangeable, but nevertheless meaningful in policy analysis. Conflicts in goals are settled through the political process, and a general outline of organization and process in agricultural policy making has been presented. We must realize that there are many reasons for studying agricultural policy, and these reasons must be made meaningful for our study to be worthwhile.

IMPORTANT TERMS AND CONCEPTS

Definition of policy

Elements of policy

Distinguishing public policy from private policy

Distinguishing public policy in a democracy

The process of policy making and steps in the process

Definition of agricultural policy

Concept of policy in the agricultural input markets

Concept of policy in the agricultural product markets

Concept of beliefs and values

Relationships between beliefs and values

General beliefs and values underlying agricultural policy

Concept of the work ethic and its application to policy

Commutative and distributive justice as values in the work ethic

The democratic creed and beliefs underlying it

The enterprise creed: beliefs and value judgments

The creed of self-integrity: the status of dissent

Goals of policy based on beliefs and value judgments

Economic development and growth based on maximizing efficiency

Goals of compensation and distribution

Goals of the public interest and general welfare as constraints on agricultural policy

Concepts of conflict and compromise in policy making

LOOKING AHEAD

In order to visualize more clearly where policy comes from and to gain a broader perspective or vision of the problems of policy making, it is essential to have an overview of the agricultural industry and its major components. A conceptual overview of agriculture that will be useful in policy study and analysis is presented in the next chapter. This is followed in Chapter 3 by an overview of the markets for agricultural products, which provide the underpinnings of the agricultural industry, and link it to the broader national and international economy. Then we conclude this first major part in Chapter 4 with a study of how supply and demand, and related concepts, are used in policy analysis.

The second major part of our study deals with analysis of policy in the agricultural product markets. In Chapter 5, we study the foundation and evolution of policy in these markets, limiting ourselves to the events that are most significant for studying current and future policy alternatives. Chapters 6 and 7 deal respectively with policy alternatives in the crops and the livestock economy, and with the markets for these products. Chapter 8 covers the marketing economy more specifically, especially at the wholesale and retail, or consumer, levels.

The third major part concludes with analysis of policy in the agricultural input markets. This will help us learn how to visualize and analyze policy in the financial markets that serve agriculture, the natural resource markets, the agribusiness input markets, and in human capital as related to employment and income alternatives.

QUESTIONS AND EXERCISES

1 What is policy? What are the elements of policy? How is public policy distinguished from private policy? How is public policy in a democracy distinguished from policy in a dictatorship, or a one-party state? What are the steps in making policy?

2 How is agricultural policy defined, or distinguished from other areas of public policy? To what two major sets of markets does it apply? How are these markets limited or defined?

3 Why do we have an agricultural policy? It is sometimes said that agricultural policy is primarily developmental, or that it is compensatory. Do you agree, or not? Why?

4 Explain why agriculture, which traditionally has been the model of free enterprise under pure or perfect competition, invites so much government policy intervention. Is this inherent in agriculture's economic structure, its set of beliefs and values, or its political organization and power structure, compared with these factors in another major industry, such as the steel industry, the automobile industry, or the housing industry?

5 Why do we study agricultural policy? Specifically, what are the major choices that we face in agricultural policy? In general, what will be the economic benefits and costs of following one or another of the choices that we have mentioned?

6 As used in public policy, what is a belief? How does it differ from a fact? What is a value? Why do people who may share similar beliefs sometimes act differently in respect to their recommendations for policy? Give an example to illustrate.

7 What are the general beliefs and values underlying the development of agricultural policy in the United States? How has the concept of the family farm influenced agricultural

policy? Does the priority given to the family farm involve a value judgment? If so, what is it? If not, why not?

8 What is classical economics? What is the meaning of laissez faire? What is commutative justice? Distributive justice? Did the policy of free land, emphasizing family farms, contribute to commutative justice? To distributive justice? Why or why not?

9 In what ways did the policy of family farms tend to break down in the 1920s? What policy remedies were proposed?

10 What are the major beliefs and value judgments underlying the democratic creed? In what general ways do these judgments tend to affect agricultural policy?

11 What are the beliefs and value judgments underlying the enterprise creed? What are the practical implications of this creed for agricultural policy?

12 Explain what is meant by a status for dissent. How is this concept related to the creed of self-integrity? Name at least four major programs in agricultural policy that have evolved from dissent. Do these programs support the concept of the creed of self-integrity? Explain your answer.

13 What are the general goals of agricultural policy? Can these be expressed as values or means as well as goals? Explain your answer.

14 Do you believe that any of the goals listed in your answer to question 13 have been fulfilled, or are being fulfilled? Explain.

15 Although a particular goal for agricultural productivity and growth may not be apparent, we may recognize that the public interest may be served by high productivity, or maximum economic efficiency. Define maximum economic efficiency, and give an illustration.

16 What income and compensatory goals have been used to guide agricultural policy? Why is there a conflict between these goals and the goal concept of maximizing the public interest?

17 What are some of the broader welfare goals that may be influenced by agricultural policy? Why is it important to recognize these as values or goals of policy?

18 It has been said that the major goals of agricultural policy are essentially in conflict. Do you agree, or not? Explain your answer.

19 What evidence do we have of conflicts in goals of agricultural policy? In what ways are these conflicts expressed? In what ways are the goals compromised?

RECOMMENDED READINGS

Breimyer, Harold F., *Farm Policy: 13 Essays,* Iowa State University Press, Ames, 1977, especially pp. 35–42, 105–117.

Guither, Harold D., *The Food Lobbyists,* Lexington Books, D.C. Heath and Company, Lexington, Mass., 1980, pp. 1–16, 173–180.

Madden, J. Patrick and David E. Brewster (eds.), *A Philosopher Among Economists, Selected Works of John M. Brewster,* T. J. Murphy Co., Philadelphia, 1970, Chapters 5–8.

Stucker, T. A., J. B. Penn, and R. D. Knutson, "Agricultural-Food Policymaking: Process and Participants," *Agricultural Food Policy Review,* Economic Research Service, U.S. Department of Agriculture, ERS A-FPR-1, January 1977, pp. 1–11.

CHAPTER 2

OVERVIEW OF AGRICULTURE FOR POLICY ANALYSIS

Competence in policy analysis requires that we develop a comprehensive vision of the economy covered by our subject. In this chapter, we develop an overview of agricultural production, which is followed in the next chapter by an overview of agricultural markets.

IN THIS CHAPTER

1 You can learn how to visualize the basic economic organization of agriculture in terms of its major sectors, involving separate and distinct economies.

2 You can learn how to visualize growth in agriculture in terms of two alternative economic models, visualizing how the traditional model is transformed into the industrial model.

3 You can learn how the unique characteristics of agriculture may be viewed as a foundation for policy analysis. These characteristics include agriculture's unique biological and geographical orientation, the large number of independent producers, the importance of economic structure as a policy issue, and the effects of inflation on the economic organization of agriculture.

ECONOMIC ORGANIZATION OF AGRICULTURE

Agriculture has been defined as an industry covering the organization of resources, such as land and minerals, capital in a wide variety of forms, and management and labor, for the production and marketing of food and fiber. It is organized in three major economic sectors, which we identify primarily by resource use and economic function, as farming; agribusiness; and a publicly supported sector of research, edu-

Modern large-capacity field equipment favors large-scale farming. What major policy problems does this create? What are the alternative policy solutions to these problems?

cation, and service.[1] Within each sector there are separate and distinct subsectors, or economies. Let us consider them.

The Farm Sector

Farming, which also includes ranching, is subdivided for purposes of policy analysis into two separate but interrelated economies: crops and livestock.[2] The crops economy uses a variety of resources to produce primary products from the soil; it, and it alone, is dependent on the unique resource of soil. The livestock economy uses feedstuffs and bulky raw materials from the crops economy, combined with other resources, to produce animals and animal products, including poultry and poultry products. Since it uses the commodities from the crops economy to produce other finished and semifinished commodities, it may be viewed as a secondary economy

[1]Harold G. Halcrow, *Economics of Agriculture*, McGraw-Hill Book Company, New York, 1980, pp. 6–16.

[2]This concept of the farm sector is based on Harold F. Breimyer, "The Three Economies of Agriculture," *Journal of Farm Economics*, vol. 44, no. 3, August 1962, pp. 679–699. This article received the award of Outstanding Journal Article for 1962.

within agriculture, no less than is milling wheat, crushing soybeans, or processing fruits and vegetables. Each economy also buys and uses products and commodities from agribusiness, and the commodities that each produces are processed and marketed through other agribusiness firms or industries. The interrelationships between and among these economies provide a major part of the substance of policy analysis (Table 2-1 and Figure 2-1).

TABLE 2-1
SUMMARY OF THE FARM SECTOR'S FINANCIAL STATUS, PRODUCTION TRANSACTIONS, AND OPERATOR INCOME (EXCLUDING FARM HOUSEHOLDS), 1978–81

Item	1978	1979	1980	1981
	Thousands			
Farms	**2,436**	**2,430**	**2,428**	**2,436**
	Billion dollars			
Financial summary				
Farm				
Assets on January 1	655.3	781.8	904.6	983.3
Debt (including CCC loans), January 1	111.3	127.2	147.5	163.1
Equity, January 1	544.1	654.6	757.1	820.1
Change during year in:				
Farm assets	126.5	122.8	78.7	.3
Farm debt	16.0	20.3	15.7	18.4
Farm equity	110.5	102.5	63.0	− 18.1
Transactions summary				
Gross receipts	119.2	141.8	139.5	154.3
Intermediate product expenses	56.5	68.0	72.5	76.0
Capital consumption and business taxes	18.2	20.4	22.4	24.2
Factor payments	44.6	53.4	44.6	54.0
Interest	9.5	12.2	15.1	19.0
Wages to hired labor	7.5	8.5	9.4	10.0
Net rent to all landlords	5.5	6.1	6.5	7.4
Returns to operators	22.0	26.7	13.6	17.7
Farm operators' income summary				
Total operator income	55.4	66.1	56.7	64.4
Farm sources	26.7	32.3	20.1	25.1
Returns to operators	22.0	26.7	13.6	17.7
Net rent to operator landlords	.7	.7	.8	.9
Imputed net rental value of operator dwellings	4.0	4.9	5.8	6.6
Off-farm sources	28.7	33.8	36.6	39.3
	Dollars			
Income per operator (assume one per farm)				
Total income	22,730	27,214	23,352	26,458
Farm sources	10,941	13,312	8,289	10,312
Off-farm sources	11,789	13,902	15,062	16,146

Source: Economic Indicators of the Farm Sector: Income and Balance Sheet Statistics, 1981. National Economics Division, Economic Research Service, U.S. Department of Agriculture, ECIFS 1-1, August 1982, p. 9.

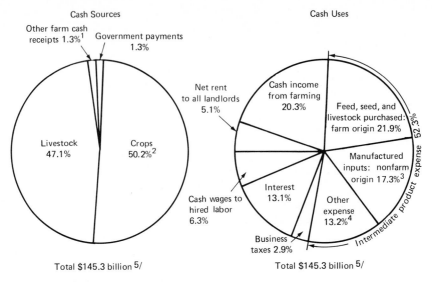

FIGURE 2-1
Sources and uses of cash income from farming (excluding farm households), 1981. (Economic Indicators of the Farm Sector: Income and Balance Sheet Statistics, 1981, *National Economics Division, Economic Research Service, United States Department of Agriculture, ECIFS 1-1, August 1982, pp. 13 and 14.*)

The Agribusiness Sector

Agribusiness is also divided into two separate economies for purposes of policy analysis: the farm input supply economy and the marketing processing economy. Whether the input economy is included in a formal definition of agriculture or not, its selling prices and economic performance are a crucial factor in visualizing the economic organization and functioning of agriculture. In any given year (as shown in Table 2-1 and Figure 2-1), about one-half of the gross receipts from farming are paid out as intermediate product expense for inputs of farm and nonfarm origin, and about one-fourth are business taxes, interest, and wages for hired labor. The remaining one-fourth is rent to landlords and returns to operators. The net income from farming is most significantly affected by the interaction of the market for inputs with the markets for farm products. How policy can be used to influence or affect the input markets may be as important as policy in the product markets.

The farm input supply economy includes the farm machinery and equipment industry, the commercial fertilizer industry, the pesticide industry, and the commercial seed and feed industries. Although these have been in the forefront of agricultural development and growth, the economic structure of the economy generally conforms to the oligopsony-oligopoly model of imperfect competition. The aggregate demand for the individual classes of products is generally highly inelastic because there is no close substitute for each class of product used as a farm input. Usually a small number of farm input supply firms are in oligopolistic competition to meet demands of a relatively large number of purely competitive farm firms. Since the individual input firms produce products that may have close substitutes, however, each firm generally faces a more elastic demand, which it attempts to influence through advertising, product differentiation, and services to buyers.

The agricultural marketing processing economy embraces the long and complicated system of assembling, transforming, storing, conveying, and distributing the

The modern self-propelled combine tends to favor farms that are larger than were optimum just a few years ago. What are the policy implications of the new technology? What kinds of political pressures does this tend to create for policy makers?

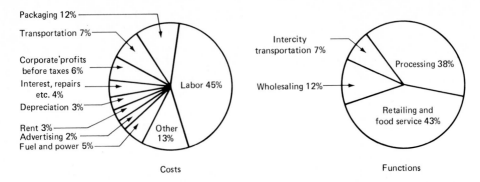

Preliminary 1981 data. Based on foods marketed through foodstores as well as away-from-home eating places. Other includes promotion, professional services, property taxes, local hired transporation, and insurance.

FIGURE 2-2
Components of the farm-food marketing bill. *(Source: USDA,* 1982 Handbook of Agricultural Charts *p. 34.)*

commodities produced in the crops and livestock economies through to retail levels. Large economic values are created in this economy, which vary from year to year, depending on the interactions of supply and demand at the farm and the retail levels. Generally, these values—which are identified in accounts of the U.S. Department of Agriculture (USDA) as the farm food marketing bill, or more simply the marketing bill—will constitute about two-thirds of the value of farm food products at retail (Figure 2-2). Similar data can be calculated for the nonfood products of agriculture, such as cotton, wool, and tobacco.

The Publicly Supported Sector

Agricultural production depends on a large number of services that are in large part publicly supported. This includes agricultural research and education, market regulation, transportation and communication facilities, food inspection and grading, and a number of other services. A study of agricultural policy must take account of these services, because they are of vital importance to agriculture and its transformation into a modern industrial-type industry.

ECONOMIC TRANSFORMATION OF AGRICULTURE

In the long history of the human race, the development of agriculture has been spurred by necessity and deliberate design, rather than accident of technology.[3] Traditionally, shortages of food have been met by people increasing their efforts to get more food. Stages of hunting and gathering have given way to growing crops and

[3]Ernest W. Grove, "Present and Prehistoric Problems of Natural Resources," *American Journal of Agricultural Economics,* vol. 61, no. 4, November 1979, pp. 612–619.

domesticating animals. Shortages of resources—land and labor—have also led to war, slavery, genocide, and other evils, besides efforts to transform agriculture by more peaceful means to more productive systems. To generalize about transforming agriculture, it is helpful to visualize two distinct models, which we shall call the traditional and the industrial models of agriculture.

Two Economic Models[4]

As a reference point for review and interpretation of the economies of agriculture and the process of transforming agriculture, it is expedient to concentrate on three economies—the crops, livestock, and marketing economies—and on the two economic models just mentioned. The traditional model may be visualized in its most primitive stage as consisting almost entirely of land and labor. Markets do not exist, or are poorly developed, and almost all efforts are directed toward survival. For some three to four million years on earth the human race survived this way. Then fifteen to ten thousand years ago agriculture began to be transformed slowly to more advanced stages. But, until just a few decades ago, land and labor were the major resources in farm production. Even in the United States, as late as 1940, land and farm-resident labor constituted 66 percent of the total inputs used in farm production, while the other 34 percent was composed of machinery, fuel, fertilizer, pesticides, feed supplements and mixing, and many other goods and services, including nonfarm labor and management.[5] Then, with innovations of modern technology, under the pressures of war and its aftermath, agriculture was transformed more swiftly, into what we now call the industrial model.

The industrial model of agriculture emphasizes commodities from the scientifically advanced agribusiness farm input industries, and education and training of labor. The industrial model is essentially dynamic, rather than static (as is the traditional model), because, in its pure form, all resources may be produced to order. If perfect divisibility of resources is assumed, then there will be neither increasing nor decreasing returns to scale. Farm firms will appear in a wide variety of sizes and types, rather than in a uniform standard size or type, as in the traditional family farm. Agribusiness firms will also vary widely in size and type, depending on experience, and in factors such as financing, managerial goals and expertise, and the timing of business decisions. A wide variety of sizes and types of firms is evident in both the farm and agribusiness sectors of agriculture in the United States.

Transforming Traditional Agriculture

In 1964, Theodore Schultz, who later became the first agricultural economist to be honored as a Nobel laureate, developed the thesis that transforming traditional agri-

---

[4]This discussion also draws on some of the concepts developed by Harold F. Breimyer, "The Three Economies of Agriculture," *Journal of Farm Economics,* vol. 44, no. 3, August 1962, pp. 679–699.
[5]Ralph A. Loomis and Glen T. Barton, *Productivity of Agriculture,* United States, 1870–1958, U.S. Department of Agriculture Technical Bulletin no. 1238, 1961.

culture into the more productive industrial model requires prices for farm inputs and products to be set at levels that make it profitable for the necessary investments to be made. But this alone may not be sufficient. Advances in science and technology that reduce the real prices of industrial inputs are crucial, as are investments in human resources, or human capital, to reduce the real cost of organizing and managing.[6]

If transformation is to proceed apace, then increases in saving and investment must apply to all the economies of agriculture. Where agriculture is poor or depressed, more resources must come from the public sector outside of traditional agriculture. Efforts of governments in poor countries to hold down food costs by fixing prices at low levels to appease their urban populations tend to slow down the transformation, and are therefore counterproductive. Efforts in rich countries, such as the United States, to support farm prices above their competitive equilibrium levels, tend to stimulate the industrial model to greater investment and increase in output. Development of this thesis drew on some of the earlier work by Schultz,[7] and was followed by a more general study of economic growth in agriculture, which confirmed and expanded on these generalizations.[8]

A General Model to Fit the United States

Over many decades, agriculture in the United States has been evolving or transforming from the traditional to the industrial model; and, as is generally recognized, this process is still going on.[9] Progressively, through each decade, agricultural growth has depended on expanding use of the industrial products based on advances in science and technology, improving managerial expertise, and making growth-oriented policy decisions.

Although the total amount of inputs used in farming was practically constant for many years up to the early 1970s and has increased by only 5 to 6 percentage points since then (as shown in Table 1-1), the input mix has changed dramatically. In economic terms, increased use of scientific and industrial products implies declining real costs for them, relative to other inputs. Decreased use of farm labor implies relatively higher opportunity costs for this input, which is reflected primarily in reduced entry. Fairly stable use of land implies a rather constant real price for this input, relative to the average for total inputs. When land and labor are combined and viewed against all other inputs, a growth curve or expansion path for American agriculture may be visualized (Figure 2-3).

Figure 2-3 portrays hypothetical equal-product curves for 1940, 1960, 1980, and

---

[6]Theodore W. Schultz, *Transforming Traditional Agriculture,* Yale University Press, New Haven, 1964.

[7]Theodore W. Schultz, *The Economic Organization of Agriculture,* McGraw-Hill Book Company, New York, 1953.

[8]Theodore W. Schultz, *Economic Growth in Agriculture,* McGraw-Hill Book Company, New York, 1968.

[9]Lyle P. Schertz and others, *Another Revolution in U.S. Farming?,* U.S. Department of Agriculture, Washington, D.C., 1979.

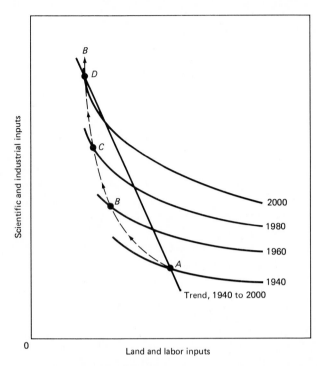

Note: The growth curve running from A to B, and B to C, approximates the resource mix for 1940, 1960, and 1980; while the curve from C to D is projected, or hypothetical. As shown in Table 1-1, for 1940, 1960 and 1980 (with 1967 = 100), the respective input levels are 100, 101, and 105, and the output levels are 60, 91, and 125.

FIGURE 2-3
Using hypothetical equal product curves to visualize development and growth of agriculture in the United States from 1940 to 2000.

2000; with points A through D representing the actual resource mix for 1940, 1960, and 1980; and conjecturally for 2000. The shifts in these curves have recurred, and are expected to continue to recur, primarily as a result of increasing productivity and continued shift in the resource mix, rather than by use of more resources. The equal-product curves are spaced to represent the increases in output, which (based on 1967 = 100) increased from 60 in 1940 to 91 in 1960, and to 125 in 1980 (Table 1-1). The equal-product curve for 2000 is, of course, conjectural for both the level of output and the resource mix.

Potentials for Growth in the Industrial Model

The growth of agriculture by industrialization has come largely from lower real costs of inputs, rather than higher prices of products. This being so, its potential for growth depends on the future costs of these inputs, including, most importantly, energy and technology, labor and government, and the limits imposed by land, or natural resources.

Energy as a Resource   Energy is most crucial; and currently, under the broadest definition of agriculture (taken to include the entire food processing and distribution system), agriculture uses only about 15 percent of the total energy consumed in the United States.[10] Projections of total energy use tend to suggest that at current growth rates this percentage will tend to drop, or at least not increase during the 1980s.[11] Moreover, only about one-fourth of the total energy used in agriculture is used on the farm and in the manufacture and delivery of farm inputs. The rest is used in marketing, processing, cooking, and refrigerating. Only about 3 percent of the total is used in transporting.

If the increases in farm output were to be used primarily to increase exports, which is the only way in which large increases will be absorbed in the next few decades, then exports could be increased several times with only small increases in total use of energy in all industrial sectors. That is, shifts of more energy and industrial inputs primarily to the crops economy would be of minor significance in the total industrial complex of the United States.

Labor and Management   Labor-saving mechanical technology is responsible for the growth of agriculture with constantly declining labor, and this also clearly implies that sufficient human resources are available for much greater growth. As a result of increasing use of labor-saving mechanical technology, the total quantity of resident-farm-family and hired labor has declined practically every year. But this decline may be coming to an end, and the presence of a very inexpensive migrant work force, in the southern half of the country especially, will tend to offset declines elsewhere, if not increase the total farm work force. Even so, clearly there is an adequate total supply of labor to allow further growth in agriculture.

Limits Imposed by Land   Although energy is important, land is the major input limiting long-term growth of agriculture. Most of the advances in biology, fertilizer, and pesticides have tended to compensate for the limited land supply. Although land is the most fixed of agricultural resources, it is surprisingly difficult to project an accurate picture of future supply and demand for land, and to visualize the competitive structure of future land markets. This is true in part because land-use classifications are cultural as well as economic variables. New uses arise (wilderness, wildlife, and recreation areas), old uses acquire new meaning (rivers or lakes become reservoirs or flowage areas), land shifts from one use to another (cropland to timber, and timberland to crop), and the boundaries separating land uses become blurred.

---

[10]John S. Steinhart and Carol E. Steinhart, "Energy Use in the U.S. Food System," in Philip H. Abelson (ed.), *Food: Politics, Economics, Nutrition and Research,* American Association for the Advancement of Science, Washington, D.C., 1975, pp. 33–42.

[11]Michael Rieber and Ronald Halcrow, *U.S. Energy Use and Fuel Demand to 1985,* Center for Advanced Computation, University of Illinois, Urbana-Champaign, CAC Document no. 108, 1974.

The category of most significance for agricultural policy, cropland used for crops, has been remarkably stable for more than 70 years. But enormous changes have been made in intensity of use. Stability of annual use, which has been between 363 and 387 million acres (except from the late 1950s to the early 1970s, when soil bank and land retirement programs were in effect), masks regional shifts of critical magnitude. In aggregate terms, the most important losses of cropland have been timberland gains (mainly east of the Mississippi River), and the most important gains have come through more intensive use of existing cropland (mainly west of the Mississippi).

Between 1956 and 1975, about 1.8 million acres of land were acquired as right-of-way in building the interstate highway system, and more uncounted millions of acres were given access values that can be likened to near-instantaneous conversion from agricultural use to urban use. The associated urbanization which has followed, stimulated by this conversion and other factors, has generated demands for green space, recreation, and residential land uses that are inextricably combined with largely unplanned expansion of private, noncommercial forest land. Some of the most urban and industrial areas in the United States have become the most heavily forested, as cropland has been converted to trees. But the continuing loss of prime farmland to city use, which amounts to about $\frac{1}{3}$ of 1 percent of U.S. cropland annually, will be almost insignificant, at least for the next decade or two. According to a number of studies,[12] total U.S. cropland could be increased by 25 percent if the demand were there. Still, the problem of soil conservation remains acute,[13] and the conversion of much more land to cropland will necessitate conservation measures with costs that, to date, we have not been prepared to accept.

Hence, although the industrial model of American agriculture contains great potential for growth, the future is clouded with uncertainty. There are a number of important characteristics of the economies of agriculture that must be taken into account when overviewing agriculture for purposes of policy analysis. Let us continue by considering some of these.

CHARACTERISTICS IMPORTANT FOR POLICY

Agriculture is unique among the major industries because of the combination of economic, physical, and biological factors that determine supply. The biological nature of production in the crop and livestock economies, set against relatively stable domestic but less stable export demand, leads to both random and cyclical fluctuations in price. Inelastic supply and demand for total output in the short run exaggerate these price fluctuations; and lags in production, in respect to price signals, result in the classic cobweb models of alternating cyclical fluctuations in output and price, which fit many agricultural situations.[14]

---

[12]See, for example, *Perspectives on Prime Lands, Background Papers for Seminars on Retention of Prime Lands,* U.S. Department of Agriculture, July 16–17, 1975.

[13]See *Soil Conservation Policies, Institutions, and Incentives,* Harold G. Halcrow, Earl O. Heady, and Melvin L. Cotner (eds.), Soil Conservation Society of America, Ankeny, Iowa, 1982.

[14]For further discussion of the cobweb theorem applied to agriculture, see Harold G. Halcrow, *Economics of Agriculture,* McGraw-Hill Book Company, 1980, pp. 219–221.

The current policy emphasis on farm price supports and production controls, farm income payments, storage programs, and other measures has its foundation in the biology of agricultural production and in the economics of the markets served by agriculture. The biology of cultivating crops and raising animals is a high-risk operation in terms of both output and price. The risks and uncertainties of disease, pests, and unfavorable weather fall most heavily on the individual farmer. This burden accounts for measures taken by individual operators to avoid risk or reduce their uncertainty, through the use of pesticides to protect crops and livestock, diversification to reduce effects of both price and output variations, and use of hail and all-risk crop insurance, for example. Risks also extend beyond the farm into the food processing and marketing system. Food firms go to considerable expense to protect themselves from product spoilage and loss, and to avoid losses related to changes in markets.

Entrepreneurs in each of the farm economies might like to transfer the major burdens of risk and uncertainty to the public sector, but for the large part they have been unable to do so. Farming remains an unusually risky and uncertain business. Still, some of this risk and uncertainty is alleviated by policy measures such as price supports, credit programs, and crop insurance. More measures may be taken in the future as needs arise.

Land as a Factor in the Crops Economy

The crops economy is essentially land-based, as nearly all plant life requires soil, in which roots are anchored and from which nutrient-laden water is absorbed for growth. A very limited amount of crops are based on hydroponics, which uses water cultures without soil. But for practical purposes, crops cannot grow without land. Although the growth of industrial agriculture, based increasingly on certain industrially produced inputs, relegates land to a relatively decreasing economic role (land declines in relative economic importance), land is still essential and important for policy.

The natural limits to land imbue it with an economic and social status that magnify its role in policy. Whenever food shortages or high population pressures are felt, policy proposals arise to protect and preserve land for farming, whether or not this is the most economical way to ensure future productivity. Similarly, whenever policy is proposed to limit and control farm output, farm leaders may turn to land as the means for implementing a program.

Why is land assigned this role and status in policy? Briefly, this is because farmers have demanded it. Limiting land use tends to make the land that is cropped more valuable and creates a windfall, or capital gain, for land owners. If government payments are made to encourage farmers to set aside or retire their land from production, this of course also enhances their cash flow. If, in addition, prices are raised or stabilized, then the direct returns from crop production are increased still more.

The crucial economic role of land is one of the distinguishing characteristics of agriculture, and it often accounts for the dominance of the crops economy in policy making. Land also provides agriculture with its strong geographic orientation. What is the significance of this for policy?

Geographic Orientation of Agriculture

The extensive nationwide geographic orientation of agriculture leads to regional specialization based on comparative advantage. Different regions of the country develop dominating interests in one or more commodities, and this interest is reflected especially in Congress, as individual members of Congress vie for the support of their constituents by voting for legislation that favors their region. Southern senators and representatives support strong cotton and tobacco programs, for instance. Those from the corn belt reflect the interests of corn and soybean growers, as well as those of livestock farmers. Congressional members from the plains states support a strong wheat program. Nearly all members of Congress are involved in the political activity of supporting one anothers' interests in order to further their own. The broad geographic orientation develops a political strength for agriculture that far exceeds what might be assumed solely on the basis of the number of people in farming.

The political strength of geographic orientation is furthermore greatly enhanced by the fact that farm producers are also large-scale consumers of other goods and services. In 1981, for instance, more than half of the $145.3 billion gross receipts from farming were disbursed to pay for manufactured inputs and other expenses of nonfarm origin (Figure 2-1). Although this fraction might not be as high in other years of the 1980s, it is evident that a large number of merchants, bankers, laborers, and others in the labor force are at least partially dependent on the prosperity of farmers. Hence, the political power of farmers may be strengthened by a variety of widely dispersed and politically powerful groups. This power is reinforced further by the existence of a large number of independent producers in the farm sector.

Large Numbers of Independent Producers

Geographic scatter and the absence of pronounced technical or internal economies of large scale, particularly in the crops economy, account for the large number of farm firms, a factor that influences policy and is characteristic of agriculture. At their peak in the mid 1930s, there were some 6.8 million farms. By 1940, the number had dropped to about 6.0 million; by 1960, to around 4.0 million; and by 1978, to about 2.4 million (Figure 2-4).

The picture presented by USDA data is one of a technological revolution superimposing an industrial type of farm unit on a traditional agrarian land base. In 1981, a small number of large farms, with annual sales ranging well over $100,000, produced the bulk of the total farm output. A group of medium-sized farms, with sales of $20,000 to $100,000 annually, produced about 28 percent of the total. Some 1.5 million small farms, more than two-thirds of the total number of farms, contributed very little to the total output, and got only a small proportion of the total income from farm marketings (Figure 2-5).

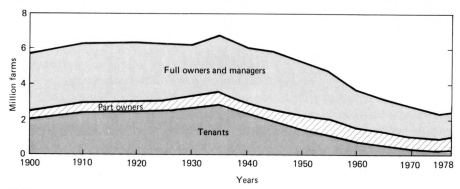

FIGURE 2-4
Number of farms in the United States by tenure of operator. *(Source: USDA,* 1982 Handbook of Agricultural Charts, *p. 15.)*

But the economic picture of farm size and income is a complicated mosaic. Large farms are getting larger. Many units once operated by a single family have expanded into multiple units, or superfarms. Middle-sized farms, traditionally the backbone of the family-farm concept, are a shrinking component of all agriculture. At the same time, the number of small, subfamily units remains large. Small farms have been tending to hold their own in many parts of the country, disappearing in other regions, and actually increasing in other areas.[15]

A major reason for these mixed trends and the complicated mosaic is the variety of types of farms and the growing importance of off-farm income to farm families. In 1981, almost three-fifths of the total income of all farm families came from off-farm sources, and this was most important for small farms. This has done a great deal to reduce the skewness of incomes of farm families, despite the growth of large farms through the transformation of traditional agriculture to the industrial model (Figure 2-6).

The still-growing trend by farm families toward receiving an increasing amount of their income from off-farm sources indicates that the small farm will continue to be a socially important part of the rural scene. An Illinois study, for example, has shown that small farms of 5 to 100 acres in size, under the day-to-day control of a resident family, and selling at least $1,000 annually, often offer the best of two worlds: an attractive and comfortable place in the country to live and raise a family, combined with the advantages of a steady and adequate income from urban-oriented employment, business, or profession.[16]

The growth of large farm and agribusiness firms, and the decline of small units, apart from those dominated by substantial off-farm income, have tended to raise

[15]Emily B. Harper, Frederick C. Fliegel, and J. C. van Es, "Growing Numbers of Small Farms in the North Central States," *Rural Sociology,* vol. 45, Winter 1980, pp. 608–620.
[16]J. C. van Es, F. C. Fliegel, C. Erickson, H. Backus, and E. Harper, *Choosing the Best of Two Worlds: Small, Part-time Farms in Illinois,* University of Illinois, Department of Agricultural Economics, Agricultural Economics Research Report no. 185, 1982.

Cash Receipts, Net Income, and Farms
by Sales Class

Cash Receipts and Farms by Sales Class

	Cash receipts	Net income	Farms
	Million dollars		*Thousands*
Farms with annual sales of:			
$200,000 and over	72,583	16,961	112
$100,000-$199,999	28,150	2,949	186
$ 40,000-$ 99,999	27,983	1,509	396
$ 20,000-$ 39,999	9,042	-244	278
Under $20,000	9,574	-1,586	1,464
All farms	147,332	19,589	2,436
	Percentage of total sales		
$200,000 and over	49.3	86.6	4.6
$100,000-$199,999	19.1	15.1	7.6
$ 40,000-$ 99,999	19.0	7.7	16.3
$ 20,000-$ 39,999	6.1	-1.2	11.4
Under $20,000	6.5	-8.2	60.4
All farms	100.0	100.0	100.0

1981 data. Net income before adjustment for inventory change.

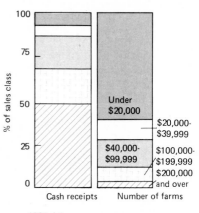

1981 data.

FIGURE 2-5
Distribution of farms in the United States in 1981, by sales classes and net income from farming. *(Source: USDA, 1982 Handbook of Agricultural Charts, p. 4.)*

questions of economic structure to a more prominent level. The question is what kind of economic structure is consistent with the major goals of policy, and are the benefits of getting it greater than the cost?

Economic Structure as a Policy Issue

Determining what goals shall be pursued in respect to the economic structure of agriculture has long been an important policy issue. The issue was highlighted in a

FIGURE 2-6
Average income of farm families in the United States in 1981 from all sources. *(Source: USDA, 1982 Handbook of Agricultural Charts, p. 4.)*

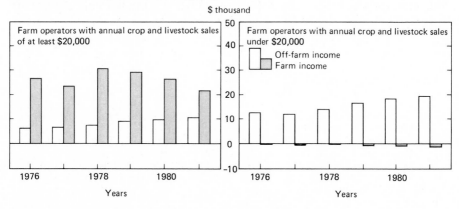

study published in 1981 by the U.S. Department of Agriculture[17] that was based on several research papers by members of the Department staff.[18] The study was undertaken to research structural issues, to determine the impact of market forces and policy on agriculture, and to recommend policy alternatives. It signaled that the public interest in agriculture had broadened from the traditional two-pronged concern of ensuring equitable returns to farmers and adequate supplies of food at affordable prices, to encompass issues of economic and social concern. It concluded that the changing economic structure of agriculture will continue to be an important policy issue. Let us use some of the study's conclusions to develop a number of propositions for future policy, as follows.

Federal Tax Policies Favor Large Farms Specifically, treatment of capital gains and investment credits has a significant effect on farm structure, favoring large farms, wealthy investors, and corporations. For many years, farmers have been provided the unique advantage of being able to report income from sale of breeding stock as capital gain, a provision that favors large-scale farms and ranches. Because of investment credits against taxes, investment in farmland and certain related improvements are favored, with high-income taxpayers generally benefiting more than individuals with lower incomes. As a result, prices of farmland tend to be higher, and some products are in greater supply and lower in price than they would be otherwise. Large-scale farms and absentee ownership have been encouraged by these trends.[19]

Modern Technology Favors Economic Concentration as Well as Growth Although economic growth made possible by advancing technology benefits consumers and increases export potentials, advancing technology also has been recognized as probably the most important contributing factor to structural change and concentration. Such technology, although founded in publicly supported research, has been furthered through the competition of agribusiness firms. Although the initial goals might not have been to favor large farm and agribusiness firms, continuing public emphasis on technology has tilted the benefits.[20]

Development of the Marketing Economy Favors Concentration Growth and modernization of the marketing system have tended to favor large firms because economies of large scale are associated with advances in both technology and management. Growth of the agribusiness farm input industries, which accounts for an increased supply of these inputs relative to the supply of land and labor, favors inno-

---

[17]U.S. Department of Agriculture, *A Time to Choose: Summary Report on the Structure of Agriculture,* Washington, D.C., January 1981.

[18]U.S. Department of Agriculture; Economics, Statistics, and Cooperatives Service, *Structure Issues of American Agriculture,* Agricultural Economic Report 438, November 1979.

[19]For further discussion, see "U.S. Tax Policy and Agricultural Structure," in ibid., pp. 152–167.

[20]For further discussion see papers by Thomas A. Miller, George W. Coffman, Yao-Chilu, and Donn Reimund, in ibid., pp. 108–133.

vations in farming that contribute to economies of large scale.[21] Standardization of farm food products favors large-scale farming, manufacturing, and food retailing.[22] Specialization, automation, and improvements in transportation have tended to favor large marketing firms, which in turn tend to promote specialization and capital-intensive technology in farming, and thus growth of large-scale farms.[23]

Farm Commodity Programs Encourage Concentration   Although farm commodity programs are intended to be neutral in respect to farm size, they actually favor large farms.[24] This is because reduced risk and less uncertainty, which are major beneficial effects of such programs, encourage specialization and large-scale operations. In addition, direct price-support benefits and payments are highly skewed by size of farms and this has been true for a long time. For instance, in the 1964 price-support programs for wheat, cotton, feed grains, rice, peanuts, and tobacco, the lower 60 percent of the farmers in terms of gross farm income received in total less than 20 percent of the total benefits. The top 20 percent of farmers received over half of the direct benefits.[25] Under the 1969 program, the largest farms in terms of sales accounted for about 7 percent of all farms, but they received more than 40 percent of the direct benefits from commodity programs.[26] A 1981 study showed that in 1978 some 10 percent of the participants in commodity programs for wheat, feed grains, cotton, and rice received 47 percent of the payments. The smallest farms, amounting to 50 percent of the total participants, received 10 percent. A $40,000 ceiling on payments to individuals had a negligible effect on distribution of payments. Proposals to prohibit payments to corporations would not have a significant impact on structure, because most farm corporations are involved in livestock, fruits, and vegetables, and few grow the commodities covered by the programs.[27] Also there was essentially no informatttion on how marketing orders for fluid milk and fresh fruits and vegetables have affected farm structure.[28]

Federal Farm Credit Programs Tend to Favor Concentration   Increasing credit availability, through expansion in federal farm credit programs and increased credit offered by other lenders, encourages structural change and concentration in both the

---

[21]See L. G. Hamm, "Farm Input Industries and Farm Structure," in ibid, pp. 218–226.

[22]John M. Connor, "Manufacturing and Food Retailing," in ibid, pp. 226–234.

[23]William G. Tomek and Allen B. Paul, "Coordination and Exchange Influences on Farm Structure," ibid., pp. 235–240.

[24]James D. Johnson, Milton H. Ericksen, Jerry A. Sharples, and David H. Harrington, "Price and Income Policies and the Structure of Agriculture," ibid., pp. 174–184.

[25]James T. Bonnen, "The Distribution of Benefits from Selected U.S. Farm Programs," in *Rural Poverty in the United States,* a report by the President's National Advisory Commission on Rural Poverty, Washington, D.C., May 1968, pp. 461–505; especially p. 505.

[26]Charles L. Schultze, *The Distribution of Farm Subsidies: Who Gets the Benefits?,* Brookings Institution, Washington, D.C., February 1971.

[27]William Lin, James Johnson, and Linda Calvin, *Farm Commodity Programs: Who Participates and Who Benefits?,* National Economics Division, Economic Research Service, U.S. Department of Agriculture, Agricultural Economic Report no. 474, September 1981.

[28]E. M. Babb and Robert Bohall, "Marketing Orders and Farm Structure," in ibid., pp. 249–254.

farm and agribusiness sectors.[29] This has been found to be especially important since the early 1970s.

Effects of Inflation on Agriculture

The effects of policies favoring large-scale industrial agriculture were greatly strengthened by the long-term inflation of the 1970s and early 1980s. Inflation provided opportunities for windfall gains which could be exploited to best advantage by wealthy investors, corporations, and large-scale farm firms. For several years the appreciation in land values exceeded the standard rates of interest charged by agricultural lenders. Investors with good credit ratings, who were not solely dependent on cash income from agriculture, could consistently realize important capital gains by borrowing heavily to invest in farmland. This favored more concentration in ownership of farmland, while the growing economies of large scale favored farm mergers and consolidations.

The declining real prices for farm products (as shown in Figure 1-1) made the situation more difficult for the family farmer who was depending mainly on cash income from farming. Some were forced to borrow heavily, but were unable to use the proceeds from loans to finance technological advances or to develop larger operating units. Many farmers, therefore, have not benefited from inflation, and the rising costs of inputs relative to the prices of farm products have limited the growth of a rather high percentage of family-sized farms. While inflation has probably contributed to concentration, it is unlikely that many farmers will benefit from it in the future either. If the family farm survives, its average size will be larger, but not all farms will be able to grow. Any increase in foreclosure rates will tend to lead to further concentration, whether inflation persists or not. The family farmer will continue to wield important political influence, however. But if the past is a portent of the future, much of this influence will not be used to benefit family farms, but will encourage programs that will continue to induce concentration.

The General Issue for Policy

The general policy issue is what kind of economic structure and income distribution is wanted for agriculture. It has been concluded that commodity programs have contributed to the inequality of farm income while supporting overall farm income in the short run, as we have discussed. But the longer-term effects of the programs are less clear with regard to growth, size of farm, and a number of other factors. Even if the results become clearer, the issues of economic structure and income distribution will not fade from the policy agenda. Questions will remain about what to do about people on the fringe of the farm economy—the rural poor, unorganized hired farm labor, poorer ethnic groups, and child laborers.

[29]David A. Lins, "Credit Availability Effects on the Structure of Farming," in ibid., pp. 134–142.

The rise of new political groups—consumer, special-interest, and others—has already expanded the agenda for agricultural policy, and will generate new issues in the future. How these issues can be approached, what the policy alternatives are for them, and how choices can be made in the future, is the essence of our further study.

SUMMARY

In this chapter, we have studied the economic organization of agriculture, identifying two economies in the farm sector, two agribusiness economies, and a publicly supported sector. We have considered the magnitudes of these sectors.

Two economic models of agriculture have been discussed as a way of making the organization functional, and to visualize the process of development and growth. We have attempted to visualize the potentials for growth of the industrial model in the United States, emphasizing the crucial role of land and the implications of this growth model for future policy.

We have identified some of the characteristics of agriculture that account for the great importance of policy. These include unique biological and geographic characteristics, the unique role of land in policy, the large numbers of independent producers in the crops and livestock economies, the importance of economic structure as a policy issue, and the effects of inflation on agriculture.

A specific hierarchy determining which of these issues will be most important in the future cannot be established, because the importance of individual issues will depend on the beliefs, values, and goals that people bring to policy. But we can assume that these issues will be important, and we will be studying policy alternatives for the future.

IMPORTANT TERMS AND CONCEPTS

Economic organization of agriculture
The crops economy
The livestock economy
Agribusiness farm input industries
Agricultural marketing economy
Agriculture's publicly supported sector
Magnitudes of the sectors
Traditional and industrial models of agriculture
Transforming traditional agriculture
Industrial model of agriculture in the United States
Declining economic importance of land
Crucial role of land in models of economic growth

Biological nature of agriculture
Geographic organization of agriculture
Status of land in agricultural policy
Implications of large numbers of producers
Economic structure as a policy issue
Effects of inflation on agriculture
Importance of growth as a policy issue
Policy issues related to compensation
Growing importance of environmental issues
Economic structure and income distribution

LOOKING AHEAD

To develop a broader vision for policy analysis, it is necessary to complement the overview of agriculture with an overview of markets for agricultural products. In Chapter 3, you can learn how these markets have developed and grown, with emphasis on development in the last two decades. You can learn that the domestic market has grown very slowly, by less than $\frac{1}{3}$ of 1 percent annually since 1967, and that the major growth has been in exports. You can learn why this has happened, and how to analyze prospects for the future. You can learn how the growth of world population and real income in other countries will tend to affect the export markets for agricultural products of the United States. You can learn some of the policy alternatives for the United States in dealing with domestic and export markets, and some of the major prospects or scenarios for policy over the next two or three decades.

QUESTIONS AND EXERCISES

1 What is meant by vision in an economic or social study? How is vision related to economic analysis?

2 What are the major economic sectors of agriculture? What is distinguishing or unique about the crops economy? The livestock economy? Explain why such a large portion of agricultural policy is centered on the crops economy.

3 Characterize the traditional and industrial models of agriculture in terms of their economic characteristics. Explain the process by which traditional agriculture is transformed into the industrial model. What are the necessary conditions? The sufficient conditions?

4 What has been the general growth path for agriculture in the United States, assuming there are only two categories of inputs: (1) land and labor, and (2) all other scientific and industrial inputs? It has been said that land is of declining economic importance, but still crucial and marked with a unique status in agricultural policy. Why?

5 What are the major characteristics of agriculture that account for the unique importance of agricultural policy in the nation's economy? Can you say which of these characteristics will be most important in the future? Give reasons for your answer.

6 Do you believe that the economic structure of the two farm economies will be a more important economic issue in the future than it has been in the past? Why, or why not? Note that, in discussing this issue, we wish to separate the fact of economic concentration from the question of the importance of the issue.

7 What has been the effect of inflation on economic concentration in the farm sectors? Has it had the same effect in the livestock economy as in the crops economy? Explain your answer.

8 Why is the economic growth of American agriculture considered an important policy issue for the future? Should international trade policy be considered part of this issue? Public support for research and education? Why?

9 The big commodity programs have tended to dominate agricultural policy in the past. Why? How will this issue tend to change in the future? Why?

10 Do you expect agriculture to lose its claim to special compensation or its unique ability to claim special compensation? Why? What are the general implications of your answer for future agricultural policy?

11 Why do we expect certain agriculturally related environmental issues to grow in importance? Which ones do you expect to become of greatest importance? Why?

12 Economic concentration has increased in almost all of the economic sectors, or economies, of agriculture. In view of this, might we expect economic structure to be a more important policy issue in the future? Why? Apart from economic structure, do you expect issues of income distribution to become of greater or of lesser importance? Explain.

RECOMMENDED READINGS

Breimyer, Harold F., "The Three Economies of Agriculture," *Journal of Farm Economics,* vol. 44, no. 3, August 1962, pp. 679–699.

Campbell, Keith O., *Food for the Future, How Agriculture Can Meet the Challenge,* University of Nebraska Press, Lincoln and London, 1979, Chapter 3.

Grove, Ernest W., "Present and Prehistoric Problems of Natural Resources," *American Journal of Agricultural Economics,* vol. 61, no. 4, November 1979, pp. 612–619.

Schultz, Theodore W., *Transforming Traditional Agriculture,* Yale University Press, New Haven, Connecticut, 1964.

Schertz, Lyle P., et al., *Another Revolution in U.S. Farming?,* U.S. Department of Agriculture, Washington, D.C., 1979.

U.S. Department of Agriculture, *A Time to Choose: Summary Report on the Structure of Agriculture,* Washington, D.C., January 1981.

CHAPTER 3

OVERVIEW OF MARKETS FOR POLICY ANALYSIS

Although agricultural policy is largely national in terms of its elements (goals, means, implements, and constraints), it is local, regional, national, and international in terms of the markets to which it applies. To have a good foundation for policy analysis, it is essential to learn how to visualize these markets and appraise their potentials in both the long view and the short.

IN THIS CHAPTER

1 You can learn how to identify factors underlying the comparative growth of domestic and foreign markets.

2 You can learn how to appraise world population growth and real income as factors in the growth of the total market for agricultural products of the United States.

3 You can learn some of the policy implications of the market projections and prospects.

GROWTH OF AGRICULTURAL MARKETS

The growth of agricultural markets depends mainly on (1) population growth and its distribution; (2) real income or per capita purchasing power and its distribution; and (3) the terms of trade. By the last we mean the value of the dollar relative to other currencies, and the conditions of trade; that is, whether free or not. In addition, changes in tastes and in programs designed to improve nutritional standards are influential and government subsidies, such as food stamps and foreign aid programs, contribute in a supplementary way. How shall we appraise these factors?

Recent Changes in Market Shares

Let us review how domestic and export markets have grown over the past two or three decades. This will help us to visualize the future.

Conditions in the 1960s   Throughout most of the 1960s, the domestic market was absorbing about 83 to 84 percent of the total farm output in terms of value. After allowing for year-to-year changes in inventory, the balance of 16 to 17 percent was being exported. With a new program for feed grains in 1961, and for wheat and cotton in 1964, the United States shifted from a policy of high price supports, which restricted exports even with substantial export subsidies, to lower price supports, with increased payments from the federal treasury to help compensate producers and get their compliance with programs intended to control production. Largely as a result of these policies, the nation's farm food prices continued to decline in real terms, while consumer expenditures for food declined to an all-time low as a percentage of total expenditures on all consumer goods. But even with these bargain prices, the export market failed to grow.

One reason for low exports was the strength of the U.S. dollar. Since 1933, it had been fixed in terms of gold at $35 an ounce. This established the dollar as the key monetary unit against which other currencies could be traded around the world. But as other currencies generally depreciated, it took more of another country's currency to buy a certain number of dollars. Or, it would take more of the other currency to buy a certain quantity of exports valued in dollars. This tended to increase the cost to foreign purchasers of agricultural imports from the United States. So, in spite of declining real prices for agricultural products in the United States, and substantial export subsidies costing as much as a billion dollars or more annually, agricultural exports increased very little, if at all.

Changes in the 1970s   The decade of the 1970s brought substantial changes. Early in the 1970s an increasingly unfavorable balance of trade forced the United States to abandon the fixed-rate gold standard, and the dollar declined in value. Then in 1972, the Soviet Union abandoned its traditional policy of refusing to import grain in large quantity even in years of shortage, and began to buy grain in substantial quantities from the United States and other countries—but mostly from the United States, because this was where the excess grain was stored. In addition, in the 1970s, practically all of the other nations in the communist bloc, one after another, became net grain importers.

With flexible exchange rates, many important countries outside of the communist bloc tended to find American agricultural products increasingly attractive. This included Japan, most countries in the European community, the petroleum-exporting countries of the Middle East, and a number of newly developing countries, such as Mexico, Taiwan, and South Korea. By the end of the 1970s, the domestic market was absorbing about two-thirds of the total farm output and one-third was being exported.

In many countries, expanding populations created a growing pressure on local food-producing capacity. This did not necessarily require buying from the United States, but it was a factor. What is the policy significance of this change in market shares?

Slow Growth of the Domestic Market

For almost a quarter of a century the domestic market for farm output has grown by about one-half of 1 percent anually, and an extremely important question for agricultural policy is whether such a slow growth rate will continue in the future. From the early 1960s to near the mid 1980s, farm output increased by about one-third (Table 1-1). But the domestic market grew by less than half this, relatively; as exports grew to take as much as one-third of the total farm output.[1]

The slow growth in the domestic market with stable or declining real prices for food tends to imply increasingly efficient use of food by American consumers, rather than a deterioration in the average diet of the typical consumer. The average level of food consumption per capita in the United States is still close to the highest of all nations'; as many, if not more, health problems arise from overeating as from the inability of a percentage of the population to get enough food. Nutritional studies have revealed that obesity is the major diet-related health hazard of as many as one-fourth to one-third of the total U.S. population. Many health problems result from overeating, that is, too high a consumption of total calories even in a well-balanced diet, as well as from consuming certain types of food too freely (sugar, fats, and alcohol), and there is increased incidence of diseases associated with obesity, such as diabetes, high blood pressure, and heart disease. Studies also show that about 30 percent of the total population shows some evidence of malnutrition from inadequate intake of food nutrients (especially iron, calcium, vitamin A, vitamin C, and ribo-flavin—vitamin B_2). This appears in the form of anemia, obesity, or other diseases closely associated with poor nutrition, such as the circulatory diseases (heart disease, high blood pressure, and stroke), diabetes, severe dental and periodontal disease, and alcoholism. Altogether, it has been concluded that appropriate nutrition intervention activities could reduce morbidity and mortality from heart disease by 25 percent, respiratory and infectious diseases by 20 percent, cancer by 20 percent, and diabetes by 50 percent.[2] This does not require an increase in average per capita consumption of food.

The emphasis on dietary improvements and other health-related activities that has developed in the United States apparently has not resulted in an increase in the total food demanded by the average consumer. Increases in real income of low-income consumers and improvement in their diets could result in significant increases in the quantities of food they demand. But for the majority of the remaining population, dietary education would not increase total demand per capita, and might result in

---

[1] For current data, see U.S. Department of Agriculture, *Handbook of Agricultural Charts.*

[2] Helen Andrews Guthrie, *Introductory Nutrition,* 3rd ed., The C. V. Mosby Company, St. Louis, 1975, p. 8.

future modest reductions in quantities demanded per capita. This could come as a result of the increasing attention being paid to nutritional planning, and weight-control diets and programs.[3]

Future Growth of Domestic Markets

Domestic demand will probably increase in accordance with population growth, neither much faster nor much slower, except insofar as farm products displace industrial materials, particularly industrial energy. Unless governments increase subsidies to support use of corn for ethanol (which would be uneconomic), by the turn of the century the domestic market will be using only one-fifth to one-fourth more of the total farm output than it was using a third of a century before. Since the rate of population increase is decreasing, with the largest increases in older-age groups, population growth will play a progressively smaller role. Increases in real income among more affluent consumers will have a limited effect because of the low income elasticity of demand for food.

Slow growth of the domestic market for total farm output may be projected as a basis for planning and policy making. This leaves the export market as the major factor for future growth in the demand for total agricultural output. Let us consider this factor.

WORLD POPULATION GROWTH AND REAL INCOME

Population growth and increasing real income per capita are the two major factors in the future growth of world markets. Of the two, population growth has been the major factor for the world as a whole, and this is expected to continue. But increases in export markets for agricultural products of the United States may depend as much on increasing real income as on population growth. Let us consider why.

Transitional Growth of World Population

The world population has experienced a great era of rapid transitional growth. At the beginning of the Christian era, there were about 250 million people on earth. By 1650, world population had doubled, to reach 500 million. Then, despite the thousands of centuries required to reach the first half billion people, it took less than two centuries to add the next half billion. The one billion mark was reached just before 1850. Then, one billion more people were added in just 80 years, to reach two billion by 1930. It took just 30 years—to 1960—to add the third billion; and, in 1975, just 15 years later, the fourth billion was added.[4]

---

[3]For further discussion see Harold G. Halcrow, *Food Policy for America,* McGraw-Hill Book Company, New York, 1977, pp. 493–525.

[4]Data for 1950 to 1979 are from U.S. Bureau of the Census, *World Population 1979—Recent Demographic Estimates for the Countries and Regions of the World,* Washington, D.C., 1980.

The great transitional growth came from rapid declines in mortality rates and subsequent unprecedented sharp increases in life expectancy. The first modern surge of growth could be seen in Western Europe near the beginning of the Industrial Revolution. Among the factors that led to the gradual reductions in mortality rates (advances which in modern times are aptly described as "death control") were (1) sanitary and medical advances that brought increasing control over the deadly contagious diseases that had decimated populations throughout the Middle Ages, (2) improving living standards, (3) a series of agricultural innovations, (4) increases in food supplies from the new world based on declining costs of both land and ocean transportation, (5) migration of people out of Europe, and (6) a spreading of optimism about development and growth that made large families popular. In scarcely two centuries, from the mid 1700s to the mid 1900s, crude death rates for the world as a whole fell from about 45 people per 1,000 to about 12 to 15 per 1,000.

Although one may question why it took so long for death rates to fall, birth rates were even slower to fall. In most countries, high birth rates, which had been necessary for societies to survive in preindustrial economies, persisted because they were entrenched in customs, religious values, and long-standing traditions. Indeed, large families were officially encouraged in most advancing societies, as required for national development and growth. Birth rates continued high through World War II, and a few years beyond. Then a new era emerged.

The Deceleration of Population Growth

The rate of population increase did not begin to decelerate until people began to control their birth rates sufficiently to bring them into line with the lower death rates that modern societies have been able to achieve. Then, lower birth rates were a rational decision of people in all walks of life, not a condition forced on people by conditions beyond their control. What has happened, and why?

Although birth rates had been falling in most countries for a hundred years or more, the modern deceleration of population growth can be visualized in terms of the changing projections of future world population that have been issued since 1970. At that time, there were about 3.7 billion people on earth—about 1.1 billion in developed regions, 0.9 billion in communist Asia (chiefly China and Siberia), and 1.7 billion in the balance of less developed regions. In 1970, the most commonly accepted projection was 6.7 billion by the year 2000, based on studies in the United Nations published by the U.S. Department of State.[5] This 6.7 billion, an increase of 3.0 billion over 1970, was regarded as the best medium variant projection, taking account of the growth rates current at that time and possible future trends. Because of already declining birth rates in developed countries, however, more than seven-eighths of this total growth was projected for the less developed countries and regions, including communist Asia. But then rapid change set in, as some demographers had suggested.

Since 1970, projections of world population have been moving down rapidly, and

[5] *World Food-Population Levels,* Report to the President, U.S. Department of State, April 1970.

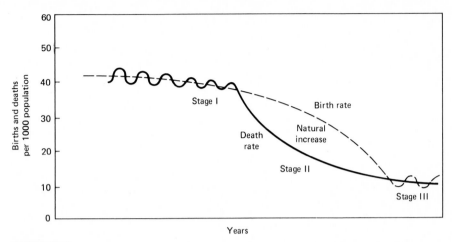

FIGURE 3-1
The three stages of demographic transition. Hypothetical: Stage I is slow growth with high birth and death rates, such as existed prior to the industrial revolution. Stage II is rapid transition growth, with death rates declining prior to birth rates, such as began with the industrial revolution and continued to recent times. State III is slow growth or zero growth, based on low birth and death rates, which is characteristic of the modern era.

the end of this trend is not yet in sight. A United Nations study, which was started in 1973, used a medium projection of 6.3 billion for 2000.[6] Soon the World Bank began to use a projection of 6.0 billion for 2000 as a basis for its plans and programs. In 1978, a new projection of 5.8 billion by 2000 was offered as an appropriate estimate, based on assumptions that family-planning programs would continue to be supported to the end of the century, especially in the world's most populous countries.[7]

In contrast with the transitional growth model of the world's population, the world was now entering a third stage of low birth and low death rates. This contrasted with a long first stage of high birth and death rates, which had existed for three to four million years, up to the beginning of the Industrial Revolution, and with the second stage of rapid transitional growth of the eighteenth and nineteenth centuries (Figure 3-1).

Alternative Projections of World Population

Now it is possible to make a number of alternative projections of world population, each one of which has important implications for agricultural policy, and for society at large. Figure 3-2 shows the trend in world population from 1850 to 1975, and

[6]Wassily Leontief, Anne P. Carter, and Peter A. Petri, *The Future of the World Economy: A United Nations Study,* Oxford University Press, New York, 1977.
[7]Amy Ong Tsui and Donald J. Bogue, "Declining World Fertility: Trends, Causes, Implications," *Population Bulletin,* vol. 33, no. 4, 1978.

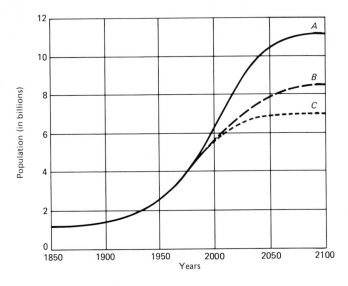

Note: All projections are hypothetical. Curve *A* is based on actual data to 1975, a United Nations medium variant projection from 1975 to 2000, and an assumption of the net reproduction rate reaching 1.0 between 2020 and 2025. (*Source: Thomas Frejka,* **The Future of Population Growth,** *Wiley, New York, 1973, p. 224.*) Curve *B* is based on actual data to 1975, the projection of Tsui and Bogue (see text) of 5.8 billion in 2000, and a net reproduction rate reaching 1.0 between 2020 and 2025. Hypothetical, based on assumptions made by author. Curve *C* is based on actual data to 1975, the projection of Tsui and Bogue of 5.8 billion in 2000, and a net reproduction rate reaching 1.0 between 2000 and 2005. Hypothetical, based on assumptions made by author.

FIGURE 3-2
Growth of world population to 1975, with projections to 2100, based on assumptions stated in the text.

alternative growth curves to the year 2100. These projections assume no third world war, which would make the curves obsolete. The upper curve in Figure 3-2, labeled *A*, shows the world population reaching 6.2 billion by 2000, and leveling off at about 11 billion sometime before 2100. This appeared to be the best estimate available in 1973. Curve *B* is based on the projection of 5.8 billion by 2000, and world population leveling off at about 8.3 billion before 2100. Curve *C* is the same as *B*, except that a net reproduction rate of 1.0 is reached at an earlier date. Hence, projections of world population depend on assumptions made about net reproduction rates, and a number of factors—including future public policy—that will affect the rates.

Some Policy Implications

It is not necessary for students of policy to agree on what the population growth rate will be in the future, because any rate selected is apt to be proven wrong, one way or another. But it is important to ask what difference it will make if one rate or another is achieved, and how future rates may be affected by policy.

For about 100 years, birth rates have dropped steadily in most developed countries, with the exception of higher birth rates following most major wars, so that now birth rates in developed countries are far below those of less developed countries. In 1974, for instance, the average crude birth rate among the 1.1 billion people living in developed countries was 16.6 per thousand, as compared with 39.5 per thousand for the 2.0 billion people in developing countries (excluding the People's Republic of China).[8] But between 1960 and 1974, the crude birth rate in these developing countries had declined from 45.1 to 39.5 per thousand, a result generally attributed to the spread of educational and family-planning programs sponsored by various governments, which were supported in part by the governments, and in part by some major foundations and by organizations of the United Nations.

By 1981, in countries with a population of 10 million or more (which made up about 92 percent of the world's population), birth rates were down to 15 to 16 per thousand in the more developed countries, and to 34 to 37 per thousand in the less developed (excluding the People's Republic of China).[9] The birth rates for Africa were still very high, about 45 to 47 per 1,000 population, while rates for Latin America, at 32 to 33 per 1,000 population, were slightly above the world average. Asia's birth rate approximated the world average of 26 to 29 per thousand, while the rates in the developed regions of North America, Europe, and Oceania were at a level of about half of the combined rate for the world as a whole. By 1981, death rates in the more developed countries were down to about 10 to 11 per thousand, and appeared to be stabilizing around this level.

Except for Latin America, the levels of mortality have tended to follow the fertility levels rather closely. Following this trend, the death rate in Africa is still high. The rate in Asia is about average. Death rates in the more developed countries have been below the world average, but these can be expected to rise as the increased life span in these countries begins to take more of a toll. The crude death rates in Latin America have tended to approximate those in more developed regions because of the combination of rapid mortality declines and a relatively young age structure. Because of the relatively large percentages of people of child-bearing age in Latin America, the crude birth rates in the region will remain high for at least the rest of this century, and it will be several decades before the crude death rates in Latin America rise to substantially higher levels.

With a world population growth rate of around 1.8 percent annually in the first half of the 1980s, the world would reach a population of five billion in 1986, and, continuing at this rate, six billion by 1996; with the latter figure being reached about two years earlier than predicted by curve *A* in Figure 3-2.[10] In other words, the net growth rate in the world must drop below 1.8 percent annually to meet growth curve *A,* and it must drop still lower to conform to *B* or *C.*

---

[8]Robert S. McNamara, *The Population Problem,* World Bank, Washington, D.C., 1977.

[9]U.S. Bureau of the Census, *Demographic Estimates for Countries with a Population of 10 Million or More: 1981,* Washington, D.C., 1981, p. 15.

[10]This results from extrapolating the compound growth rate of 1.8 percent annually based on an estimated world population of 4.575 billion in 1981. Basic data from U.S. Bureau of the Census, *Demographic Estimates for Countries with a Population of 10 Million or More: 1981,* p. 15.

Can lower rates be achieved? Among the very poorest people, population growth may be constrained according to the Malthusian doctrine, that is, that there is a tendency for population to increase until it presses against the physical means of subsistence.[11] But for the great majority of the world's population the rate of growth is more a function of peoples' desire for children, family planning, and government policy. It is not certain that governments in developing countries will adopt policies that will result in a growth rate such as B or C in Figure 3-2. But it is possible that they will. In country after country, in all stages of economic development, birth rates have fallen as levels of living have risen. The demand for large families weakens and the number of children is limited by rising opportunity costs of raising a large family. If governments adopt tax and other policies that favor smaller families, as a number have done, it is possible that population growth rates in developing countries will continue to drop somewhat, as projected in curves B or C.

How will decelerating growth rates affect agricultural markets? More specifically, what will be the effect on agricultural markets if the developed countries generally reach zero population growth (ZPG), and birth rates in the less developed countries continue to drop to the extent that a growth curve such as B or C in Figure 3-2 is achieved? The increases in demand caused by population growth alone will gradually come to a halt. This will be felt first in the demands from the primary markets now served by United States agriculture—the United States itself, Western Europe, and Japan; and second in demands from other countries. The effects will not tend to be those affected by population growth rates alone, however. The question of real income and purchasing power must be taken into account. Let us consider why.

Real Income as a Factor in Export Demand

If the developed countries that currently provide the major markets for United States farm food exports reach ZPG, and if they are at a high level of real income when this occurs, then their total demand for farm food products will stabilize, rather than grow. In addition, if some of them continue to increase their agricultural production, which they are capable of doing, then their demand for imports will not stabilize, but will tend to decline. Western Europe, especially, has the potential to be a major net exporter of grain. By the twenty-first century it may cease to be a major market for wheat and feed grains from the United States.

Increasingly, or so it appears, the United States will have to find new markets for its agricultural exports, and this emphasizes the critical importance posed to agricultural interests in the United States by economic development of other countries. Increases in the per capita demands for food that might arise out of economic growth in developing countries would come from two sources—increases in average calorie availabilities and shifts to a diet containing a higher percentage of animal products. For many years, the average calorie availabilities in less developed countries has been

---

[11]See Thomas Robert Malthus, *On Population,* edited and introduced by Gertrude Himmelfarb, The Modern Library of the World's Best Books, New York, 1960.

TABLE 3-1
COMPARISON OF CALORIE REQUIREMENTS AND AVAILABILITIES BY REGIONS: 1961–63 and 1972–74

Region	Energy requirements— kilocalories per person per day	Average calorie availabilities per person per day	
		1961–63	1972–74
Developed countries with market economies			
North America	2,642	3,320	3,530
Western Europe	2,565	3,200	3,390
Oceania	2,656	3,300	3,370
Other	2,363	2,570	2,850
Total	2,555	3,130	3,340
Developing countries with market economies			
Africa	2,335	2,070	2,110
Latin America	2,383	2,400	2,540
Near East	2,456	2,290	2,440
Asia and Far East	2,223	2,010	2,040
Total	2,284	2,110	2,180
Countries with centrally planned economies			
Asian countries with centrally planned economies	2,355	1,960	2,290
U.S.S.R. and Eastern Europe	2,570	3,240	3,460
All countries			
World	2,385	2,410	2,550

Source: United Nations World Food Conference, *Assessment of the World Food Situation,* Food and Agriculture Organization, Rome, 1974; and Food and Agriculture Organization, *Fourth World Food Survey,* Rome, 1977.

only about two-thirds that in developed countries (Table 3-1). Significant increases could occur without changing the traditional dietary mix.

Some increases in total food demand could arise out of relative increases in use of animal products. Some of the possibilities for this are suggested by the data in Figure 3-3. Rapid increases in demand are suggested for all countries in transitional stages of economic growth and rising per capita incomes. Some countries in these stages of growth will increase their demands for food imports, and exports from the United States can be expected to shift in this direction. Increasing exports from the United States to third world countries that are not experiencing economic growth are much more difficult to imagine, however. Many third world countries are not experiencing real gross income gains per capita. Nothing on the horizon indicates that they will do so in the next decade or two. Most of the signals now evident indicate there would be financial obstacles to their buying food from the United States or other major world food exporters.

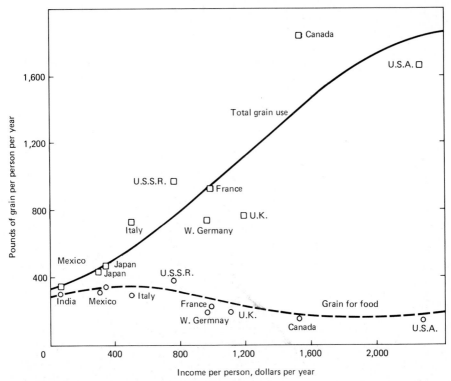

FIGURE 3-3
General relationship between income per person and pounds of grain per person per year in
selected countries. As income per person increases, smaller and smaller amounts are consumed
directly as human food, and more is consumed in the form of animal and other products.
(Source: Orville L. Freeman, "Malthus, Marx, and the North American Bread Basket," Foreign
Affairs, *July 1967, p. 582; copyright 1967 by the Council on Foreign Relations, Inc.)*

    All this does not add up to a great surge in demand for agricultural exports. Since
the beginning of the 1960s, there have been slow increases in the world production
of food per capita (Table 3-2). The developed countries have added to their already
high standards, and many developing countries have increased production per capita
significantly. Again, most of the less developed countries have fallen behind in food
production per capita. These countries do not have the buying power for more food
imports, and this draws attention to what has popularly been called "the world food
problem." Let us consider some of its dimensions, as something to take into account
in building the foundation for agricultural policy.

Some Dimensions of the World Food Problem

During the last 30 years, according to annual reports of the World Bank, the average
per capita real income in developing countries has doubled. But 750 million people
in these countries, about one out of three, get barely enough food to keep themselves

TABLE 3-2

FOOD AND AGRICULTURE ORGANIZATION (FAO) INDEX NUMBERS OF WORLD AND REGIONAL FOOD PRODUCTION

Region	Production in 1981 as a percentage of 1969–71 average production (%)*	Average annual rate of change in production 1971–80 (%)	Average annual rate of change in production per capita (%)	
			1961–70	1971–80
Developing market economies	139	3.3	0.3	0.6
Africa	123	1.8	0.4	−1.2
Far East	142	3.6	0.2	0.9
Latin America	146	3.8	0.3	1.2
Near East	141	3.5	0.7	0.6
Asian centrally planned economies	141	3.2	1.1	1.6
Total developing countries	140	3.3	0.6	1.0
Total least developed countries (LDC)†	122	2.2	n.a.‡	−0.4
Total developed countries	121	1.9	1.6	1.1
World	129	2.5	0.9	0.6

*Preliminary.

†The category of least developed countries (LDC) was adopted by the United Nations General Assembly in 1971 to represent the poorest countries which deserve special international assistance. In 1981, there were 31 countries in the LDC category, with a total population of 270 million (1977 estimate), and their economies have typically grown at very low rates.

‡Not available.

Source: The State of Food and Agriculture (Reports from 1976 and 1981), FAO Agriculture Series, no. 9, 1977, and no. 14, 1982. Food and Agriculture Organization, Rome.

alive from one week to the next. Living standards among them are very low—intolerably low as compared with conditions in most developed countries. Malnutrition, which is a lack of or deficiency in one or more of the protective nutrients, is widespread among this 750 million. Undernourishment, which is a deficiency in total calories such that a person cannot maintain bodily activity without losing weight and eventually dying, affects a large percentage of those who are malnourished. Untold millions of young children are stunted and retarded, and many die prematurely. Life and death under these circumstances are grim, indeed.

Why does this deplorable situation exist, even in the midst of economic development and growth? It is not because of a worldwide shortage of food. Indeed, it may not be due to a general shortage of food even in countries where malnutrition and undernourishment are most prevalent. The U.S. Department of Agriculture has estimated that between 1961 and 1979 world per capita grain production increased by 17 percent.[12] But the fact is that very little of the increased per capita supply has gone to the 750 million people who are most in need. Instead, it has been used mainly

---

[12]Can We End World Hunger?, U.S. Department of Agriculture. Prepared by the Office of Governmental and Public Affairs in cooperation with the Office of International Cooperation and Development and the Economic Research Service, September 1981, p. 4.

to produce more animal and poultry products for more affluent consumers. Most of the world's malnourished people live in about 65 countries, primarily in Africa and southern and southeast Asia. These nations have about one-third of the world's population, and at least 50 percent of them live in abject poverty, compared with about 3 percent in poverty in the more affluent developed nations. With low productivity, the people are unable to produce or purchase a regular and dependable supply of food.[13]

Some General Answers to the World Food Problem

Economic development and growth and reductions in the rate of population increase are the general answers to raising living standards around the world. No country would be poor if it were able to feed itself adequately, either directly or externally by trade, through the work and efforts of a small fraction of its labor force. Poor countries are poor because it takes too many people too much time to feed the population, and because—partly as a result of this diversion of effort—they also have little or nothing to export in exchange for food imports.

Increasing agricultural productivity and higher food output per capita is a necessary condition for improvement in these countries, but this alone is not sufficient. Governments in these countries must adopt policies for employment and income distribution that will provide the poorest with a means of livelihood. Unless these governments do this, there is no imaginable increase in world food production that could solve their problem. Food aid can help on an emergency basis. In fact, it may be urgent. But the more fundamental need is internal structural reform, combined with broader programs of economic development, based on more comprehensive international planning and cooperation. As one study has said, "Without new institutions and policies specifically designed to improve the lot of the poor, there is no realistic chance of social justice in the underdeveloped world of our time."[14]

Required Basic Policies to Solve the World Food Problem

There are at least four basic policies required for significant improvements in per capita food supplies, and for more equitable distribution in the developing countries:

1 It is necessary to expand agricultural research and education through long-term programs in the countries where the food deficiencies exist. Only about 10 to 11 percent of the world's publicly supported agricultural research has been undertaken in the poorer developing areas of the world, which contain at least half of the world's population.

2 The recommended research should not be limited to improving crop and live-

---

[13]U.S. Department of Agriculture, ibid., p. 5.

[14]Irma Adelman and Cynthia Taft Morris, *Economic Growth and Social Equity in Developing Countries,* Stanford University Press, Stanford, California, 1973, pp. 192 and 202.

Government inspectors sample grain for certification prior to clearing a ship for departure from the United States. However, deterioration of grain during ocean transit or unloading has caused some lowering of grades. As a general policy, how much should our government be involved in regulating this trade? *(Larry Wood Studio, Perrysburg, Ohio.)*

stock production, but should also aim at developing the marketing processing economy.

3 Perhaps of most importance for the poorest people is the need for more equitable income distribution, either through land reform, tax reform, or development of other income opportunities.

4 Achieving adequate food reserves to meet emergencies arising out of poor crops or other natural disasters is an important part of policy. Where people depend primarily on crops rather than livestock products, there is generally little food reserve to carry them through a year of bad crops.

Three Suggested Policy Goals

Three goals of policy must be coordinated: (1) increased production, (2) changes in income distribution, and (3) slower population growth.

First, as shown in Table 3-2, total world food production has increased about 2.5 percent annually. But this rate of growth barely balances projected population growth rates. A general increase in the growth rate of food production is required.

Second, it may be said that the major reason people are hungry is not that there is not enough food in the world; it is because people are poor. Chronic hunger and malnutrition result from a lack of purchasing power of poor countries and poor families when they compete for the available food supplies. The major policy strategies for improving the lives of people in the less developed countries are through aid programs, supported by the governments of the United States and other more developed countries, designed to encourage the economic development of the less developed and developing countries. A broader base for employment and income in these countries is required, and a more equitable income distribution is a necessary part of the answer.

Third, a continuing decline in birth rates is required in most developing countries. Fortunately, the record over the last two or three decades shows that this is occurring, but further declines will be required in the future.

Until some of these policies are implemented, the poorest countries cannot become comfortably self-sufficient, or enter in more important ways into world trade. In the meantime, the hunger of the 750 million poorest people—one-sixth of the total world population—will remain a moral and ethical issue of major magnitude. Efforts to aid them can be intensified. But foreign aid is only a second-best solution to their continuing needs.

What are the policy implications of this overview?

POLICY IMPLICATIONS OF PROJECTIONS AND PROSPECTS

The overview of markets that we present for policy analysis is not one of overwhelming population growth such as existed some 15 to 20 years ago, nor is it one of great resource stringency, a popular theme throughout much of the 1970s. It is, rather, a view of some countries' developing increasingly large food export potentials, and some others' developing larger and larger food deficits, which means increasing demands for imports only if there is more trade and economic development in these countries.

In the domestic market, the vision is one of continuing slow growth in demand, dependent in part on domestic policy. Exports from the United States will face declining rates of growth in the major markets of Western Europe and Japan; increasing demands in the markets of developing countries that are in transitional stages of industrial development, as well as in the communist countries where the growth of agriculture has been stagnant; and continuing weak demand from the poorest less developed countries, coupled with periodic needs for emergency aid.

Projecting Market Growth

It is possible to be rather optimistic about the overall growth of markets, however, as a basis for agricultural policy. For instance, it has been projected that between 1978-79 and 2005, with appropriate emphasis on world markets and under constant real prices, there will be a 52 to 69 percent increase in world grain production/consumption, and a 91 to 95 percent increase in world grain exports.[15] World coarse grain exports would increase from 95 million metric tons (mmt) in 1978-79 to 185 mmt in 2005, while world wheat exports would increase from 76 mmt in 1978-79 to 145 mmt in 2005. The United States would provide 78 percent (145 mmt) and 42 percent (61 mmt) of world exports of coarse grains and wheat, respectively. Based on projections of domestic population growth, known current income elasticities of demand, and a continuing trend by consumers to substitute poultry for some beef and pork, constant prices would require increases in cattle, hog, chicken, and turkey production of 45, 8, 84, and 93 percent, respectively.

Increased growth in demand for exports of soybeans, feed grains, and wheat would depend on improvements in economic conditions in the various importing countries and on their relaxation of tariffs and nontariff barriers (NTBs) to trade. These barriers are formidable, and the course of future events regarding such barriers depends importantly on further progress being made in reducing barriers to trade in general. The future world markets for United States farm products will depend on whether there is more freedom or restriction in world trade over the next two or three decades. No matter how the trade issues are settled, we must regard uncertainty as a continuing problem for policy, as we may continue to be faced with highly erratic ups and downs that will be the focus of policy.

Three Alternative Scenarios for Policy

We may visualize three alternative scenarios for policy. In the first, the United States will be fortunate indeed if supply and demand grow at an even pace over the next two or three decades. Constant real prices for agricultural prices would make government involvement in the product markets largely unnecessary. Markets could clear at prices that would be acceptable from the standpoint of policy. Trade could become more free. Competitive prices would allocate resources most efficiently.

In the second, if supply grows more rapidly than demand, real prices of farm food products will decline, and there will be more political pressure for government to control and subsidize agriculture. This has been the general experience for more than 60 years, since the early 1920s.

Finally, if supply fails to keep pace with domestic and world demand, the real prices of agricultural products will rise. In this event, there could be pressure for government to intervene on behalf of consumers. The United States could be entering an era where productivity will be increasing at a decreasing rate. If so, then real prices of domestic food could rise, and there would be a tendency for exports to be curtailed. More farm food products might be imported duty free.

We do not know which of the three scenarios will tend to dominate over the next two or three decades. As we have noted, there is a great potential for growth in the

---

[15]Martin E. Abel, "Growth in Demand for U.S. Crop and Animal Production by 2005," in Pierre R. Crosson (ed.), *The Cropland Crisis: Myth or Reality?*, published for Resources for the Future by The Johns Hopkins University Press, Baltimore and London, 1982, pp. 63–88.

industrial model of agriculture. But there is also a perception that the pattern of technical change induced by declining energy prices, which so dramatically dominated agricultural productivity over the 50 years leading to the early 1970s, is no longer sustainable. An implication is that costs of agricultural production could rise rather substantially in response to further growth in domestic and international export demand. There is no longer any great reservoir of cheap land to draw on, as was the case during the nineteenth century. To get further large increases in agricultural output, there appears to be no substitute for more energy, nor for more fertilizers and pesticides, which also require energy. In the absence of energy increases and with constraints on use of more land, we could be entering an era somewhat similar to the 30 years that followed the close of the land frontier in the United States, from the early 1890s to the early 1920s. During this period, the real prices of agricultural products rose substantially (by about 50 percent from 1895 to 1914), while, in the 1920s and 1930s, agricultural exports were fewer than imports. By 1940, exports were practically zero.

Because of the large current capacity of agriculture and the large export base, we do not expect this scenario to be repeated. But the magnitude of the export surplus over the next two or three decades is not exactly predetermined, and it will be influenced by policy. Those who advocate higher levels of public expenditure for research and development of U.S. agriculture are probably right, however; not because we know which of the scenarios will emerge, but because the rate of return is generally high. This will lead to still lower real costs of production, and to more general prosperity.

SUMMARY

In this chapter, we have undertaken an overview of markets for policy analysis, emphasizing comparative growth of domestic and export markets, and the factors underlying this growth.

We have found that the domestic market for agricultural output has been growing very slowly, by about $\frac{1}{2}$ of 1 percent annually. This slow growth is related to decreasing rates of population growth and to the low income elasticity of demand that prevails among the more affluent sectors of society. Somewhat more rapid growth in the future has been projected. But this is dependent on use of more farm products for nonfood uses, such as corn for ethanol (which may be uneconomic, requiring large subsidies), and on improving real incomes among low-income consumers.

The export market has provided the major source of growth, and this may continue to be the case for at least the next two or three decades. Whether the export market continues to grow depends on both supply and demand. That is, American agriculture must be price-competitive with other exporting industries if it is to maintain a given share of the nation's export market. More importantly, it must be price-competitive with agriculture in other exporting countries; or, alternatively, the U.S. government will have to subsidize exports. The growth of the export market will depend on population growth and increasing real income in other countries.

Although the above propositions may follow logically from the discussion in this chapter and Chapter 2, the major policy alternatives for the United States may be visualized more precisely by studying the use of supply and demand in policy analysis. This will be the subject of our next chapter.

IMPORTANT TERMS AND CONCEPTS

Comparative growth of domestic and export markets

Factors underlying changes in market shares

Strength of the dollar as a factor in export markets

Reasons for slow growth of the domestic market

Basis for future growth of the domestic market

World population growth as a market factor

Basis for rapid transitional growth of world population

Basis for deceleration of world population growth

Basis for alternative projections of world population

Increasing real income as a factor in demand for food

Nature and magnitude of the world food problem

Required basic policies to solve the world food problem

Policy implications of market projections and prospects

Three alternative scenarios for policy, and their implications

LOOKING AHEAD

Vision and analysis are the two sides of policy study, and since we have concentrated on building a vision of agriculture and its markets, the next step is to develop more competence in using the tools of policy analysis. Supply and demand are the most powerful tools, and consequently they are used most frequently in policy analysis. In the next chapter, we will review the characteristics of supply and demand for agricultural products, identify some of the elasticities of supply and demand, and consider some of the policy implications of these concepts. This will provide a foundation for more specified policy analysis of agricultural markets in the chapters that follow.

QUESTIONS AND EXERCISES

1 How has market growth affected the domestic and export markets for agriculture? Why has the export market grown faster than the domestic market?

2 What factors have accounted for the slow growth of the domestic market? How might these factors be changed in the future?

3 Account for the rapid transitional growth of the world population. Which of the factors were most important? Why?

4 What are the causal factors in the recent deceleration of world population growth? What conditions are necessary for this deceleration to continue?

5 How have projections of world population changed since the beginning of the 1970s? Does a lower world population necessarily mean a lower world demand for food? Why?

6 How does per capita meat consumption tend to vary in relation to income? What are the major implications of this for demand? For agricultural policy?

7 Why has economic development in developing countries generally not solved the so-called world food problem? In answering this question, what is your concept of the problem? What measures are necessary for a satisfactory solution? Is increasing agricultural output a necessary part of the solution? Is it sufficient for a solution? Why?

8 What are the required basic policies for solution of the world food problem? Why are they required?

9 What are the major policy implications of (1) approximately equal growth in supply and demand, (2) more rapid growth in supply than in demand, and (3) more rapid growth in demand than in supply?

10 In view of your study, which of the three scenarios mentioned in question 9 do you expect to be most dominant in the future? Why? If you cannot decide which will be most dominant, what implication does this have for policy?

RECOMMENDED READINGS

Abel, Martin E., "Growth in Demand for U.S. Crop and Animal Production by 2005," in Pierre R. Crosson, *The Cropland Crisis: Myth or Reality?*, published for Resources for the Future by The Johns Hopkins University Press, Baltimore and London, 1982, pp. 63–88.

Campbell, Keith O., *Food for the Future,* University of Nebraska Press, Lincoln, 1979, pp. 6–21.

National Planning Association, *Feast or Famine: The Uncertain World of Food and Agriculture and Its Policy Implications for the United States,* Washington, D.C., 1974.

Paarlberg, Robert L., "Food as an Instrument of Foreign Policy," in Don F. Hadwiger and Ross B. Talbot (eds.), *Food Policy and Farm Programs,* Proceedings of the Academy of Political Science, vol. 34, no. 3, The Academy of Political Science, New York, 1982, pp. 25–39.

Polopolus, Leo, "Agricultural Economics Beyond the Farm Gate," *American Journal of Agricultural Economics,* vol. 64, no. 5, December 1982, pp. 803–810.

CHAPTER 4

USE OF SUPPLY AND DEMAND IN POLICY ANALYSIS

Most of the problems in agricultural policy and the alternatives for their solution can be analyzed in terms of supply and demand. It is important therefore to gain more understanding of how to use supply and demand in policy analysis, and this is the purpose of this chapter. It emphasizes the factors that determine the level of agricultural supply and demand, the elasticity of supply and demand, and some of the implications of these topics for policy.

IN THIS CHAPTER

1 You can learn more about applications of supply and demand, factors determining agricultural supply and demand, and the effects of changes in supply and demand on agricultural output and price.

2 You can learn how the concepts of elasticity of supply and demand apply to agriculture, how to measure elasticity, and how these concepts apply to policy in domestic and export markets for farm commodities.

SUPPLY AND DEMAND OF AGRICULTURAL PRODUCTS

The theory of supply and demand as applied to agricultural policy seeks to provide an explanation of the level and fluctuations of prices in agricultural input and product markets. This explanation consists of an analysis of the factors determining the quantities of commodities supplied and the quantities demanded under given conditions. The analytical methods that are used in developing such an explanation are the same for agricultural markets as for other economic sectors. But there are many organizational differences in production and marketing of agricultural products that are important for policy, and a number of the assumptions used must be made explicit.

Definition and Determination of Agricultural Supply

Supply may be defined as a schedule showing the various amounts of a product that will be produced and offered for sale in a market at each specified price in a set of possible prices during some specified period of time. Such a schedule portrays a series of alternative possibilities in which the quantity supplied depends on the price. Supply should always be considered as a schedule or a curve, rather than a stock or flow.

There is an infinite number of supply schedules in agriculture, as schedules exist at all market levels, such as farm, wholesale, and retail markets. Supply schedules exist for individual commodities; for groups of commodities, such as meat or grains; and for classes or grades of a commodity, such as no. 1 dark hard northern spring wheat or no. 2 yellow corn. There are supply schedules for agricultural inputs, such as fertilizer and pesticides, as well as supply schedules for products.

Determinants of Supply   In constructing a supply curve, the economist assumes that price is the most significant determinant of the quantity supplied of any product.

The efficiency of beef production is limited by the fact that most cows have just a single calf each year. If research results in more twins and triplets, would this be a gain in net social income? Who might gain from such a change? Who might lose?

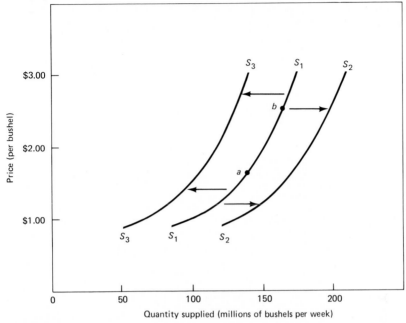

FIGURE 4-1
Changes in the supply of corn under given physical and biological conditions, a change in one or more of the determinants of supply—the technology of production, prices of resources used in production, prices of other products, expectations concerning prices, the number of sellers, taxes, and subsidies—all will cause a change in the supply. An increase in supply causes the curve to shift to the right from S_1S_1 to S_2S_2. A decrease causes it to shift from S_1S_1 to S_3S_3. A change as from point *a* to *b* on S_1S_1 is not a change in supply, but a change in quantity supplied, which involves a change in the price of corn, all other things being equal.

This is because the supply curve is anchored on the concept of given conditions (ceteris paribus, or the "other things being equal" assumption). That is, the supply curve is drawn on the supposition that certain nonprice determinants of the amount supplied are given and do not change.

In visualizing agricultural supply, if there is a change in physical or biological conditions, such as the weather, the supply schedule will change. But given these changeable conditions, the basic economic nonprice determinants of agricultural supply are (1) the technology of production, (2) prices of resources used in production, (3) prices of products that may be substituted for the given products in production, (4) expectations concerning prices, (5) the number of sellers in a market, and (6) taxes and subsidies. A change in any one or more of these determinants will cause the supply curve for a product to shift either to the right or the left. A shift to the right (from S_1 to S_2 in Figure 4-1) designates an increase in supply: producers are now willing to offer more of a product at each possible price. A shift to the left (from S_1 to S_3) is a decrease: producers now offer less at each price.

Changes in Supply Let us consider the effect of changes in each of the determinants of supply, with some applications to agricultural policy.

1 and 2 The first two determinants of supply—technology and resource prices—are the two components of production costs. Increases in agricultural supply have depended on many advances in technology, such as hybrid corn; and on reductions in the prices of inputs, such as occurred with growth of the fertilizer industry. Sometimes it has been impossible to separate neatly the effect of a specific advance in technology and the effect of an organizational improvement, or the discovery and use of a new resource with given technology. Fortunately, we usually don't need to try. The important point for policy analysis is to recognize that increases in agricultural supply arise out of advances in technology, as well as out of declines in resource prices that are caused by other factors.

3 Changes in the prices of other products can shift the supply curve for a given product. A decline in the price of corn may cause farmers to shift to soybeans, thus increasing the supply of soybeans. Conversely, an increase in the price of corn can cause farmers to plant fewer soybeans, thus decreasing the supply of soybeans. One of the major problems in agricultural policy analysis is to determine the effects that a specific commodity program may have on other commodities. A program to control

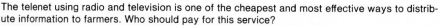

The telenet using radio and television is one of the cheapest and most effective ways to distribute information to farmers. Who should pay for this service?

wheat production, for example, may have undesired consequences for other commodities.

4 Expectations concerning the future price of a product can affect a farmer's willingness to produce that product. It is difficult, however, to generalize about the effects that the expectation of, say, a higher price, will have on current supply schedules. Usually, the expectation of a higher price will cause supply to increase, even though the current price stays the same. However, if hog producers expect a higher price in the next year or two, they may keep more sows for farrowing, which will reduce the current market supply. Expectations of a lower price may bring more sows to market, thus increasing current supply. Yet expectations of a lower price for wheat may not affect the current supply, but instead cause farmers to plant less wheat, thus reducing future supply. The physical and biological nature of agricultural production makes us wary of generalizing about the effects of expectations, but it is nevertheless important to be able to analyze the effects specific programs will have on expectations, as well as on current prices.

5 Given the scale of each firm, the more firms there are in an industry, the greater will be the market supply. As more firms enter an industry, the supply will increase, or the curve will shift to the right. In the nineteenth century, the dominant factor in increasing agricultural supply in the United States was the increase in the number of farm firms. In the twentieth century, since the 1920s at least, the dominant factor has been technology and declining resource prices, with a great decrease in the number of both farm and agribusiness firms. Today one of the big issues in agricultural policy concerns the setting of goals for size, number, and distribution of firms, and what policy to follow, assuming there can be agreement on goals. It appears that these issues are far from settled.

6 Finally, we can say that certain taxes, such as sales taxes, add to production costs and therefore reduce supply. Hence, rebates of sales taxes on fuel used for farming increase agricultural supply. But other taxes will not affect supply unless they affect marginal cost. A change in property taxes, for example, will not affect supply in the short run because they are levied on a fixed resource and marginal cost is not affected. In the long run, however, any tax or subsidy will affect supply.

Changes in Quantity Supplied   The distinction between a change in supply and a change in the quantity supplied is important in economic analysis. A *change in supply* is involved when the entire supply schedule shifts. It is caused by a change in one or more of the determinants of supply. A *change in the quantity supplied,* however, may arise either from a change in supply or from a shift from one point to another on a supply curve.

A farm price support or government payment based on production does not change the supply curve for the commodity to which it applies. But it will increase the quantity supplied if it increases the return per unit produced. If this is not desired, then production controls such as a land retirement program may be used to force production back to a lower supply curve. Because the price support tends to offset the production effect of land retirement, total output may be the same, higher, or lower than before (Figure 4-2).

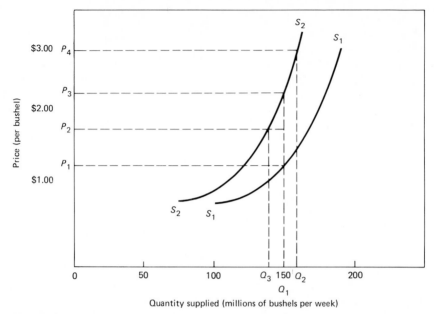

FIGURE 4-2
If land retirement or any other type of production control reduces the supply from S_1S_1 to S_2S_2, then the quantity supplied depends on the level of price support. If the initial price is P_1, then quantity supplied is Q_1. When supply is reduced from S_1S_1 to S_2S_2: If the support price is P_2, then Q_3 will be the quantity supplied, which is a reduction from Q_1. If the support price is P_3, then the quantity supplied will not change. If the support price is P_4, then the quantity supplied will be Q_2, which is an increase from Q_1 (hypothetical).

Definition and Determination of Demand for Agricultural Products

Demand may be defined as a schedule showing the various amounts of a product that consumers are willing and able to purchase at each specific price in a set of possible prices during a specified period of time. We say "are willing and able to" instead of "will," because a demand may exist without a product's being available, and the product must be available at a price on the curve before a transaction will occur. We may view demand from the standpoint of price—as indicating the various amounts that consumers will offer to buy at various prices. Or, we may view it from the standpoint of quantity—as indicating the various prices that can be collected for various amounts of a product.

When these concepts are applied to agriculture, we must recognize that there are many demand curves. There is a demand for total farm output; for groups of commodities, such as meat or vegetables; for individual commodities, such as potatoes or fluid milk; and for specific grades, classes, or even brands of a given commodity. There are also many demands by producers for resources, or inputs, and these demands are derived from the demands for products. In the product market, there is what we call a *primary demand* at the retail or consumer level, from which the demand at the farm level is derived.

In short, demand is a tabular statement of buyers' plans or intentions with respect to a product, or a resource. The quantities demanded at each price relate to a specific time period. The relationship between price and quantity on a given demand curve is generally inverse, a characteristic economists sometimes call "the law of demand." Again, as in the case of supply, a *change in demand* refers to a shift of the demand curve, while the *quantity demanded* usually refers to a point on a given curve. As in supply, there can be a change in quantity demanded when the price changes, without there being a change in the demand curve itself.

Determinants of Demand The slope and location of the demand curve are determined by (1) the size of the population, both domestic and foreign, (2) the per capita incomes, (3) the prices of other goods, (4) advertising, (5) taxes and subsidies, and (6) various sociological and demographic factors such as living conditions, tastes, habits, and customs. These determinants apply to all agricultural products, but for convenience, food will be used as an example.

Changes in Demand A change in demand occurs as a result of change in one or more of these determinants: (1) population growth, (2) per capita income, (3) prices of other goods, (4) advertising, (5) taxes and subsidies, and (6) sociological and demographic factors, as described below.

Population growth has been a major factor in causing a change in demand for farm products, as we discussed in Chapter 3. Since the rate of population growth has slowed down in the United States and most other developed countries, it may be expected that this factor will have a relatively smaller effect on demand in the future than it has had in the past. In most of the developing countries, population growth will have a relatively greater effect on demand, at least for the next generation or so.

Per capita income and its rate of change has a more subtle effect on food demand. In the United States, where per capita income is high, further increases in real income will have a relatively small effect on demand. This can be measured in terms of the *income elasticity of demand,* which is defined as the increase in expenditure on a commodity when there is an increase in income per capita, other things remaining the same. For instance, when per capita income increases by 10 percent, if expenditure increases by 10 percent, the income elasticity of demand is 1.0. If expenditure increases by 5 percent, income elasticity is 0.5; if by 2 percent, income elasticity is 0.2; and so on.

Studies of the United States economy have revealed very low income elasticities for all food, as might be expected in the case of affluent, or relatively high-income, consumers. In Table 4-1, for instance, the income elasticity for all food is 0.176, meaning that a 10 percent increase in income spread evenly over the domestic population will result in a 1.76 percent increase in expenditure on food, other things being equal. Hence, even if there is a general increase in per capita income, there will be relatively small increases in the per capita demand for food. But, as income elasticity is higher among low-income consumers, transfers of income to low-income

TABLE 4-1

ESTIMATED INCOME AND PRICE ELASTICITIES OF DEMAND, AND UNITED STATES PER CAPITA CONSUMPTION OF SELECTED FOOD COMMODITIES

	Estimated elasticities of demand at retail		Per capita consumption (weight in pounds at retail)		
	Income	Price	1962–66	1971–75	1976–81
Beef	0.290	−0.644	72.1	85.2	84.2
Pork	0.133	−0.413	57.8	60.1	60.5
Chicken	0.178	−0.777	32.2	41.3	47.7
Fish	0.004	−0.230	10.7	12.2	13.0
Eggs	0.055	−0.318	40.3	37.6	34.3
Cheese	0.249	−0.460	14.0	13.6	17.0
Butter	0.318	−0.652	6.6	4.8	4.4
Margarine	0.000	−0.847	9.8	11.2	11.4
Apples, fresh	0.140	−0.720	17.0	15.9	17.2
Potatoes	0.117	−0.309	106.2	114.2	118.9
Wheat flour	0.083	−0.300	108.2	108.2	116.8
Rice, milled	0.055	−0.320	7.2	7.3	8.4
Sugar, refined	0.032	−0.242	96.8	98.6	88.6
All foods	0.176	−0.237	1,373.7	1,385.7	1,403.1
Nonfoods	1.243	n.a.	n.a.	n.a.	n.a.

Source: P. S. George and G. A. King, *Consumer Demand for Food Commodities in the United States with Projections to 1980,* Giannini Foundation Monograph no. 26, University of California, Berkeley, March 1961; and *Food Consumption Prices, Expenditures, 1960–1981,* Statistical Bulletin 694, Economic Research Service, U.S. Department of Agriculture, Washington, D.C., 1982.

consumers and special food programs such as food stamps could increase the average per capita demand for food.

As shown in Table 4-1, income elasticity is generally higher for beef and most other animal products than it is for the crop products. We may infer that the per capita consumption of products such as beef, cheese, and butter is relatively higher among high-income consumers, and that increases in per capita income tend to favor the livestock economy over the crops economy. During the 1950s and 1960s, the livestock economy grew more rapidly than the crops economy, which, we may infer, was due mainly to rising per capita income in the United States and increasing per capita consumption of beef, pork, and chicken. In the 1970s, the consumption of beef and pork stabilized, while the revival of exports favored the crops economy, grains and soybeans especially.

It is harder to generalize about the other determinants of demand mentioned above. Certainly we know that the demand for food will be affected by the prices of other goods. But since other goods do not substitute for food, a general change in their prices has an effect similar but inverse to a change in per capita income. That is, an increase in the index of nonfood prices would have an effect similar to a decrease in per capita income, while a general decrease in the cost of nonfood items would be similar to an increase in per capita income, other things being the same.

The low income elasticity of demand for all food would tend to lessen the impact on demand for food.

Advertising is believed to have a greater effect on the demand for individual food products, or classes and brands of products, than on the demand for all food. Advertising performs a useful informational service but also tends to entice people to buy more expensive "luxury" foods, which increases the total expenditure on food.

Taxes and subsidies may be said to have a rather small effect, except for the growth, largely since the early 1960s, of food stamps and other food-aid programs. These programs have the effect of shifting income from the general population to people who have low incomes, and therefore higher income elasticities of demand for food. This tends to increase the average per capita demand for food. Requiring that the subsidy transferred be spent on food increases this effect somewhat more. It is believed, however, that the net increase in demand brought about by food stamps and other low-income subsidies is relatively small, and that the programs must be judged primarily in terms of their effects on nutrition and the needs of the recipients.[1]

The sociological and demographic factors of living conditions, tastes, habits, and customs have a powerful effect on food demand, but influencing these is generally outside the scope of agricultural policy. It is more pertinent for us to turn to the important topic of the price elasticity of supply and demand.

PRICE ELASTICITY OF SUPPLY AND DEMAND

Price elasticity of demand (supply) is the percentage change in the quantity demanded (supplied) of a product or service in response to a given change in the price of that product or service, ceteris paribus.[2] It depends primarily on percentage changes and is independent of the units used to measure quantities and prices.

Often, in economic discussions, reference is made to simply the elasticity of supply or demand. When this is done, we should understand that the reference is to price elasticity, rather than to income elasticity.

Coefficient of Elasticity of Supply and Demand

Precise measurement of the elasticity of supply and demand, which is expressed in terms of the "coefficient of elasticity," is important in agricultural policy analysis. This is true even though we often do not have an accurate measurement to go on and must make assumptions about the elasticities.

The coefficient of the elasticity of demand (supply) is the percent change in the quantity demanded (supplied) divided by the percent change in price, ceteris paribus.

---

[1]For further discussion, see Harold G. Halcrow, *Food Policy for America,* McGraw-Hill Book Company, New York, 1977, pp. 58–71 and 493–525.
[2]Other things being equal.

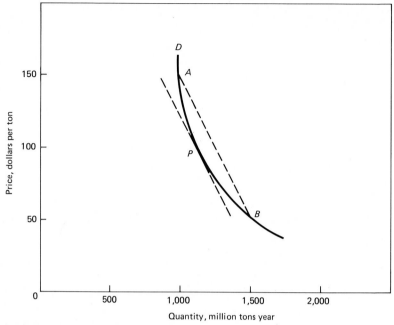

FIGURE 4-3
Demand curve for an agricultural commodity (hypothetical).

Hence, the coefficient of the elasticity of demand (E_d), and the elasticity of supply (E_s), may be written as follows:

$$E_d = \frac{\% \text{ change in quantity demanded}}{\% \text{ change in price}}$$

$$E_s = \frac{\% \text{ change in quantity supplied}}{\% \text{ change in price}}$$

Coefficients of elasticity can be measured either (a) at a point on the curve *(point elasticity);* or (b) between two points on the curve *(arc elasticity).* In Figure 4-3, the slope of the tangent to the demand curve at point *P* indicates the elasticity at that point, which corresponds to the formula:

$$\frac{dQ}{dP} \cdot \frac{P}{Q}$$

In practice, in dealing with marketing or policy problems, however, we are generally dealing with finite changes; for example, the price falls from $150 to $50, and the quantity demanded increases from 1,000 million to 1,500 million tons in a year. In Figure 4-3, the straight line AB joins these two points, and the elasticity calculated from it is an average of the point elasticities along the curve between these two points. The general formula is then:

$$\frac{\Delta Q}{\Delta P} \cdot \frac{P_1 + P_2}{Q_1 + Q_2}$$

where ΔQ = change in quantity
   ΔP = change in price
   P_1 = first price
   P_2 = second price
   Q_1 = first quantity
   Q_2 = second quantity

In the example mentioned above the coefficient of the elasticity of demand is:

$$E_d = \frac{500}{-100} \cdot \frac{150 + 50}{1,000 + 1,500} = -5 \cdot \frac{200}{2,500} = -0.4$$

This is equivalent to another formula, which is sometimes preferred, where:

$$E_d = \frac{\Delta Q}{(Q_1 + Q_2)/2} \div \frac{-\Delta P}{(P_1 + P_2)/2}$$

Calculating the coefficent of the elasticity of demand for the same example:

$$E_d = \frac{500}{(1,000 + 1,500)/2} \div \frac{-100}{(50 + 150)/2}$$
$$= \frac{500}{1,250} \div \frac{-100}{100}$$
$$= .4 \div -1 = -0.4$$

(Note: The suggested use of $(Q_1 + Q_2)/2$ and $(P_1 + P_2)/2$, instead of $Q_1 + Q_2$ and $P_1 + P_2$, is to confirm the fact that we are dealing in percentage changes. The divisor 2 in the denominator may be dropped. Two prices and two quantities are used, so that elasticity is the same in the illustration whether the price rises or falls.)

The monetary value of expenditure at any point on a demand curve is equal to price times quantity. Hence, it is possible, on the basis of any curve, to construct a receipts curve, showing total receipts from marketing in relation to either price or quantity. When the price elasticity of demand is 1, the receipts remain constant as price and quantity change; the change in price exactly offsets the change in quantity. When elasticity is less than 1, receipts fall as the quantity increases. Since the relationship between price and quantity is generally inverse, E_d is normally negative; however, in practice, the minus sign is sometimes omitted as a matter of convenience.

Theoretically, the elasticity of supply can be measured in the same way as that of demand. Supply curves are generally upward sloping, corresponding to the slope of producers' marginal cost curves above minimum average variable cost for farm firms in perfect competition. Economists sometimes refer to this characteristic as the "law of supply." Because of diminishing returns, supply curves are more inelastic at high prices than at low prices. But elasticity increases as the time available for adjustment increases. Also, there exists a direct relationship to the closeness of the supply curve of a commodity's substitutes in production. Hence, the elasticity of supply of an individual commodity, such as corn or soybeans, will be much greater than that for total grains, or for total farm output.

Elasticity of Agricultural Supply

The supply of total agricultural output tends to be very inelastic in the short run (taken to be two years), or between two harvest seasons, which is a fact that has been confirmed in many studies. Luther Tweeten and Leroy Quance, for instance, have estimated short-run (two-year) elasticities for 1921 to 1941, and for 1948 to 1966, by three methods.[3] (1) By the method of least squares, their best single estimate was 0.155. (2) By using separate yield and production components for crops and livestock, they estimated short-run elasticities of 0.17 for crops; 0.38 for livestock; and 0.25 for aggregate crops and livestock. (3) By using eight separate categories of inputs, with each weighted according to its relative importance in contributing to total output, the short-run (two-year) elasticity was 0.26 for periods of rising prices, and 0.10 for periods of falling prices.

These results have been generally useful for policy analysis, except that the difference in elasticity between years of rising prices and years of falling prices may or may not be generally significant. In a later study, Mike Woods, Tweeten, Daryll Ray, and Greg Parvin concluded that supply response (elasticity) is low in the short run, for both rising *and* falling prices, and that the null hypothesis of equal price response coefficients for falling and rising prices could not be rejected.[4] This is because short-run response of output to price depends on variable inputs such as fertilizer and pesticides, and these inputs are readily reversible (as quickly reduced as increased). Some other inputs, such as farm machinery and land, are more fixed in cost in the two-year short run, which suggests that supply may be more inelastic when prices fall, but recent statistical tests have raised doubts about this being the case.[5]

For our purposes, we may conclude that the aggregate agricultural supply func-

---

[3]Luther G. Tweeten and C. Leroy Quance, "Positivistic Measures of Aggregate Supply Elasticities: Some New Approaches," *American Journal of Agricultural Economics,* vol. 51, no. 2, May 1969, pp. 342–352.

[4]Mike Woods, Luther Tweeten, Daryll E. Ray, and Greg Parvin, "Statistical Tests of the Hypothesis of Reversible Agricultural Supply," *North Central Journal of Agricultural Economics,* vol. 3, no. 1, January 1981, pp. 13–19.

[5]For a review of more studies, see Harold G. Halcrow, *Food Policy for America,* McGraw-Hill Book Company, New York, 1977, pp. 133–141.

tion is very inelastic in the short run, while the supply of individual commodities tends to be more elastic, especially where commodities can be most easily substituted for one another in the agricultural production process. A general implication for policy is that the aggregate production function will respond rather slowly to either very high or very low agricultural prices. Strong increases in demand from poor crops in other countries may result in relatively high prices for two or three years or longer, while good weather, or rapid introduction of new production technologies, in the absence of equivalent demand increases, can result in relatively low product prices. In the absence of farm commodity programs these may last for several years.

These conclusions are also greatly dependent on assumptions concerning the elasticity of demand. To clarify related concepts, let us consider the separate demands in the domestic and export markets.

Elasticity of Demand for Food in the Domestic Market

Table 4-1 presents price elasticities of demand in the domestic market for all food, and selected food commodities, at retail. As has been concluded also in many other studies, demand for total food is highly inelastic, in the case of Table 4-1 − 0.237. This indicates that a 10 percent increase or decrease in price will result in a 2.37 percent change in the opposite direction in quantity demanded. Or, a 2.37 percent change in quantity supplied will result in a 10 percent change in price in the opposite direction.

The quantity demanded or supplied is measured in terms of index numbers weighted by value. Therefore, in cases of general price increases, low-value commodities may be substituted for high-value commodities, and with general price decreases, the reverse substitution may be made. In other words, people are not so apt to change the total calories consumed as they are to substitute one commodity for another. This suggests that when prices fall, people shift to a more luxurious diet. However, when prices rise faster than their incomes, consumers seek to substitute more economical foods.

Elasticity of Demand for Individual Commodities

The extent to which one commodity is substituted for another depends on the closeness of substitutes; the possibilities for substitution differ from one food to another. Because pork and chicken are fairly close substitutes, there is a fairly rapid switch when one or the other becomes comparatively cheaper; this is reflected in relatively high elasticities of demand. Beef is also a close substitute for other meats, and the demand for it is more elastic than for most other foods. Cheese, butter, and margarine may be substituted for one another. Apples are close substitutes for some other fruits and, as a result, the demand for apples is more elastic than individual demands for potatoes, wheat flour, rice, or sugar. Among the important commodities not shown in Table 4-1 is fluid milk; having no close substitute, it is highly inelastic in demand.

When demand is inelastic, any change in supply will result in relatively greater changes in price than in quantity demanded, other things being equal. The commodities that are most inelastic in demand generally experience the widest price fluctuations, unless there are effective programs to stabilize supply, or to offset random changes in output due to weather or other factors. The inelasticity of demand for major crops—such as wheat, sugar, rice, and tobacco—has provided a strong impetus for programs to stabilize supply and to take surplus commodities off the domestic market, by subsidizing exports or through other means. A highly inelastic demand for fluid milk has been the basic economic factor accounting for the unique program of federal and state milk-marketing orders to regulate the price and market flow of fluid milk. The generally less inelastic demands for meat, chicken, and dairy products other than milk are factors helping to account for there being less emphasis on efforts to control these commodities.

The demand for total farm output and for each farm commodity is more inelastic at the farm level than at the retail level. This is because the marketing margin—the difference between farm and retail prices—tends to change relatively much less than prices at the farm level. So a price fluctuation at retail generally results in a relatively greater—not absolutely greater—fluctuation at the farm level. Although no completely reliable rule applies, the normal fluctuations are relatively greatest for the major crops, which adds to the political pressure on government to support these crops' prices in times of large supply. Prices at the farm level result from the interaction of supply and demand in this market, while another set of supply and demand curves, which are not so inelastic, interacts at the retail level.

These concepts of elasticity, combined with the projection of slow growth in the domestic market, tend to create a setting for policy that magnifies the importance of the elasticity of demand for exports. The recent expansion of agriculture into the export market makes the elasticity of export demand a crucial factor in considering alternatives in production and price policy. Let us consider why.

Elasticity of Demand for Agricultural Exports

Changes in the way trading is done suggest that the export demand for agricultural products is not as elastic as it once was. Some years ago, the most statistically accurate studies suggested that the elasticity of demand for exports of food and feed from the United States could be as high as −1.91 in the short run of three years, and −6.42 in the long run of four or more years.[6] This would mean that the United States could increase these exports by some 64 percent in the long run with only a 10 percent reduction in export price, other things remaining the same. But due to the imposition of new tariffs, and nontariff barriers to trade (NTBs), such as quotas, it began to appear that the demand for exports was not so elastic.[7] Most importing

[6]Luther G. Tweeten, "The Demand for United States Farm Output," *Food Research Institute Studies,* Food Research Institute, Stanford University, Stanford, California, vol. 7, no. 3, 1967, pp. 343–369.

[7]Paul R. Johnson, "The Elasticity of Foreign Demand for U.S. Agricultural Products," *American Journal of Agricultural Economics,* vol. 59, no. 4, November 1977, pp. 735 and 736; and Luther Tweeten, "The Elasticity of Foreign Demand for U.S. Agricultural Products: Comment," ibid., pp. 737 and 738.

countries were providing a degree of protection for their own farmers so that the effective prices within these countries would not fluctuate freely with the prices received for exports from the United States and other countries.

Under these circumstances, the *elasticity of price transmission,* which is the importing country's price response to the price received by exporters, would be less than one. Under a free-trade model, if there were perfect price transmission, it would be one; where protection was complete, so that the exporter's price was not reflected at all in the importing country, it would be zero. Where elasticity of price transmission was zero, the elasticity of export demand would be zero, or near zero, depending on the policy of the importing country. Hence, the real elasticity of export demand faced by the United States could vary from high elasticity when trade was relatively free, to nearly zero elasticity where export prices were not transmitted to those of the importing country.

Elasticity of Export Demand Related to Policies of Importing Countries

The trade policies of most major importing countries involve a mixture of price insulation, or protection against imports of some products, and free trade or relatively free trade in other products.

The European Community (EC), for example, insulates or protects its prices for feed grains and wheat by means of a variable import levy. This is designed to fill the gap between the fixed-target support price within the EC and the world price, which is generally lower. The levy increases as world market prices fall relative to internal target prices, and decreases as world prices rise relative to the internal prices. As long as world prices do not rise above the internal EC target price, the EC's demand for imports will be very inelastic for those commodities covered by the variable import levy, because the prices received by exporting countries will not influence the prices paid by consumers in the EC. The EC has maintained free trade for soybean imports, however, and a mixture of free trade combined with a trade agreement on cotton.

In contrast to the EC, Japan has had limited free trade in feed grains, soybeans, and cotton, but state trading and a fixed resale price for wheat. Because of these arrangements, the demands faced by countries shipping to Japan will tend to be inelastic for wheat, as changes in export prices are not reflected in consumer prices for wheat. (A low and fluctuating price for wheat in Japan would tend to be unsettling to the market for rice.) Japan's demands for feed grains, soybeans, and cotton are also inelastic, however, because imports are controlled by a government agency under the general policy goal of stabilizing domestic prices.

Western European countries not in the EC, Eastern Europe, and the Soviet Union generally insulate domestic prices by controlling imports through government monopoly of trade. The rest of the world varies from free trade to highly restricted trade, with internal prices insulated, to varying degrees, from external export prices.

The general effect of insulating internal prices in major importing countries is to make them insensitive to changes in world prices or to changes in world supplies. For instance, as long as the EC maintains a fixed-support price for feed grains and wheat above world market prices it will regulate imports so as to keep its own internal market in equilibrium at the support levels. Imports will fluctuate, not according to world market prices, but according to changes in production within the Community and changes in its internal demands. Japan controls its imports of wheat, so that its market is in equilibrium at the fixed resale price, regardless of world market prices. This may make Japan's demand for wheat imports very inelastic, but Japan may still be very sensitive to small differences in quality or price among the three or four major exporters. This would tend to make the demand faced by each exporter considerably more elastic within a narrow price range.

Elasticity of Export Demand Related to Policies of Exporting Countries

In most years, the United States typically has served as the residual export supplier of feed grains and soybean products. Principal competing exporters of feed grains and soybeans have been able to export a desired quantity of their production by varying their own prices and exchange rates, export taxes, and incentives. Nearly all of the competing exporters have been able to insulate their internal production and consumption prices from fluctuations in world market prices, which is of critical importance. In most instances, this is done by use of marketing boards or by direct government intervention.

The situation for wheat is much more complicated, however. The United States exports more than 40 percent of the world total, and as much as 50 percent in some years. Because of such large volumes, the United States plays a dominant role in world prices. But the price elasticity of export supply of the United States is obscured by traditionally high price supports, production controls, and large stocks, and use of export subsidies to achieve a desired export volume. Alex F. McCalla hypothesized that, until the mid 1960s, the United States and Canada largely divided the world market, and their policies largely established the world price.[8] Production and marketing controls in these two countries tended to limit production, and stable (strong dollar) exchange rates tended to limit exports. Since the early 1970s, increasing grain exports, fluctuating exchange rates, and plunging grain prices have been unsettling. Exporting countries have generally conformed to a competitive market model, while importers have been cast as exerting monopsony power over the competitive exporters. This has led to the proposal of organizing grain export cartels, from which exporters could gain, a policy that would capture some of the monopsony gains that may have gone to importers, or would push importers toward free trade.[9]

Under an ideal producer cartel, producer welfare might be maximized by setting export prices above the free-trade price for all users, assuming the import demand elasticities are generally low. But little is known about what the response of importers

---

[8]Alex F. McCalla, "A Duopoly Model of World Wheat Pricing," *Journal of Farm Economics,* vol. 48, no. 3, part 1, August 1966, pp. 711–727.
[9]Andrew Schmitz, Alex F. McCalla, Donald O. Mitchell, and Colin A. Carter, *Grain Export Cartels,* Ballinger Publishing Co., Cambridge, Massachusetts, 1981.

would be to a cartel, what changes would occur in foreign cropland bases, and what the elasticities of import demand would be under sustained higher prices. In addition, little is known about what kinds of production controls would be required in exporting countries, most especially in the United States, to maintain the degree of control over supply that is required to capture the possible monopoly gains of a cartel.[10] Since the early 1970s, the United States has tended to be the reserve supplier of wheat on world markets, as the excess supply of other exporters—Canada and Australia, especially—has not been very price responsive. Their internal market prices, like those of most importers, have been insulated from the world market, and they have maintained a rather stable export volume. This means that their wheat export-supply curves tend to be very inelastic, while exports of wheat from the United States are regulated by the residual demands of importers under more freely fluctuating export prices.

Cotton production is influenced in most countries by government-controlled producer prices that are insulated to some degree from fluctuations in world prices. There is a very close correlation between cotton prices in the United States, northern Europe, and the Soviet Union, but export subsidies and taxes and exchange rate manipulations are important policy features of almost all major cotton-producing countries, insulating producer prices from world markets. Since 1933, production controls, price supports, and deficiency payments have been important features of the cotton program in the United States, which greatly limits the responsiveness of cotton production to world prices, thus tending to decrease the elasticity of export supply. All this influences our view of the elasticity of export demand.

Policy Implications of the Elasticity of Export Demand

By taking account of the policies of importers and exporters, it is possible to calculate the elasticity of export demand for individual commodities existing at a given time.[11] Although the elasticities tend to change when world trade conditions change, it may be correct to conclude that the real elasticity is neither as elastic as it would be if trade were free or as inelastic as it would be if trade were controlled by importing countries without regard to price. Hence, some sample elasticities of export demand faced by United States exporters, under restricted trade, with maximum transmission of prices, have been cited, as follows: corn: -1.31; sorghum: -2.36; wheat: -1.67; soybeans: -0.47; and cotton: -0.65.[12]

If these elasticities were accepted as a basis for export policy, then it might be concluded that the United States will be best advised to be very price-competitive for exports of corn, grain sorghum, and wheat. This assumes that earnings from

[10]Keith J. Collins, review of Schmitz et al., *Grain Export Cartels, American Journal of Agricultural Economics,* vol. 64, no. 3, August 1982, pp. 606 and 607.

[11]For a discussion of a suggested methodology, see Maury E. Bredahl, William H. Meyers, and Keith J. Collins, "The Elasticity of Foreign Demand for U.S. Agricultural Products: The Importance of the Price Transmission Elasticity," *American Journal of Agricultural Economics,* vol. 61, no. 1, February 1979, pp. 58–63.

[12]Bredahl et al., ibid., p. 62.

exports of these commodities are to be maximized and that other exporters do not, or are not able to, retaliate; or that other exporters program their own exports independently of the policy followed by the United States. In the case of soybeans, although the United States might gain in the short run by restricting exports, it may gain much more in the longer term by increasing world demand for soybeans at prices competitive with other high-protein and oil crops. In the case of cotton, although export demand is not as inelastic as that for soybeans, export earnings also could be increased in the short run by restricting exports. But again, as should be evident from the experience since 1933, such a policy would tend to result in further increases in cotton production in other countries, and over the longer term lose export markets for the United States.

There is no simple solution to the problems of trade policy faced by the United States. There are measures that can be taken to further expand agricultural trade, and to stabilize prices in world markets. But these will take continuing negotiations and a generally broader commitment on the part of the United States toward world economic development and cooperation. It will be important to understand what has been proposed and what has been accomplished before we turn to the more specific alternatives for agricultural policy.

Trade Negotiations and Prospects

Ever since passage of the Reciprocal Trade Agreements Act of 1934, the United States has been intermittently involved in trade negotiations, the primary policy goal of which is to get freer international trade, especially for exports from the United States. Although the results for agricultural exports may be regarded as generally disappointing, we do not know how much greater the restrictions on trade would have been in the absence of these negotiations. General access to most markets has been maintained. Some important reductions in tariffs and nontariff barriers (NTBs) have been achieved. Since the early 1970s, exports from the United States have increased, as we have seen, primarily through a combination of increasing demand from importing countries, increased sales efforts by United States farm organizations and marketing firms, dollar devaluation as a result of the adverse trade balances of the United States, and some relaxation of trade restrictions by food-importing countries.

General Agreement on Tariffs and Trade   In 1947, bilateral (two-nation) negotiations under the 1934 act gave way to a broader approach, when 23 nations, including the United States, signed the General Agreement on Tariffs and Trade (GATT). This agreement contained three cardinal principles: (1) equal, nondiscriminatory treatment for all member nations, (2) reduction of tariffs by multilateral (several-nation) negotiations, and (3) elimination of quotas for imports, a feature especially important for agricultural exports from the United States. More than 100 nations now belong to GATT, and in general it has been an important force for liberalizing international trade. Under its sponsorship seven "rounds" of negotiations to reduce trade barriers have been completed. In addition, the United States has been involved in efforts to get the countries of the European Community to reduce their subsidies on exporting dairy, wheat, and other agricultural products. Negotiations have been undertaken with Japan in efforts to reduce the Japanese restrictions on imports of beef, citrus fruits, and other products from the United States. A number of agreements have been reached with other countries to get them to import more agricultural products from the United States.

Prospects for the Future   Even though economists have long emphasized that nations can gain from an expanded volume of world trade based on comparative advantages in all countries, there is an inherent tendency in both developed and developing countries to become more protectionist. In most developed countries, advances in agricultural productivity combined with declining birth rates and slower population growth are tending to increase per capita food supplies. The political pressures for freer trade from the major exporters of agricultural products are being offset to a degree by the pressures for more protection from producers in importing countries. Consumers in both importing and exporting countries will be generally better off with freer trade, so the political struggle for freer trade is continually being revived and extended, with support not only from exporting countries, but from importing countries as well.

Theoretically, if a unanimous decision were required for trade to be permitted, or to be expanded under restrained conditions, it would always be possible for those desiring trade to buy off those opposed to trade, with the result that all would be made better off financially.[13] This is the basic concept under which further expansion of agricultural trade may be achieved. In the future, as the potential demand by developed countries for exports of more agricultural products tends to be fulfilled, the United States and other exporting countries may find it increasingly advantageous to negotiate with developing countries for freer trade, combined with aid for projects of economic development. The feasibility of such policy will depend on the general approach of the United States to major world problems as well as on policy alternatives followed in the agricultural input and product markets. The latter will be the subject of the next eight chapters.

SUMMARY

In this chapter, we have studied how supply and demand may be used in policy analysis. We have defined supply and demand as schedules of quantities that will be supplied or demanded at each price within a set of possible prices, under given conditions during a specified period of time. We have summarized the factors that determine agricultural supply and demand. Because of its importance in policy we have

---

[13]For further discussion and expansion of this concept and principle, see Vernon L. Sorenson, *International Trade Policy: Agriculture and Development,* Michigan State University, East Lansing, 1975, pp. 75–81; and Robert G. Chambers, John M. Letiche, and Andrew Schmitz, "The Gains from International Trade," in Jimmye S. Hillman and Andrew Schmitz (eds.), *International Trade and Agriculture: Theory and Policy,* Westview Press, Boulder, Colorado, 1979, pp. 61–90.

given some special attention to income elasticity of demand, and to the joint effects of substitution and income on demand.

Price elasticity of supply and demand has been treated as a major topic because this is a crucial concept in practically all agricultural policy analysis. The method for deriving the coefficient of elasticity is an important concept for students to master. Aggregate agricultural supply is highly inelastic in the short run, while supply curves for commodities that are easily substituted in production are more elastic. The domestic demand for total food is also highly inelastic, while the elasticities of demands for individual commodities are directly related to the closeness of substitutes. Major policy implications of these concepts have been summarized.

The elasticity of export demand has also been treated as a major topic because major alternatives in production and price policy depend on export stability and growth. Over the next 20 or 30 years, major increases in demand will depend on exports. New knowledge concerning the inelasticity of the export market tends to suggest that the United States has somewhat limited alternatives for growth, unless there is a broader, more comprehensive approach to world economic development and growth.

IMPORTANT TERMS AND CONCEPTS

Agricultural supply and demand

Factors determining agricultural supply

Factors determining demand for agricultural products

Income elasticity—concepts and estimates

Substitution effect and income effect on demand

Price elasticity of supply and demand

Coefficient of elasticity—concept and measurement

Policy implications of inelastic agricultural supply

Differences in supply elasticity in the short and the long run

Elasticity of demand in the domestic market

Policy implications of inelastic domestic demand

Elasticity of export demand for agricultural output

Elasticity of price transmission—concept and measurement

Elasticity of export demand related to policies of importers and exporters

Concept of producer grain export cartel

Methodology for calculating elasticity of export demand

Policy implications of export demand elasticities

LOOKING AHEAD

In the next chapter we shall study some of the major policy proposals that have been advanced over many years aimed at the major goals of agricultural policy. Emphasis will be placed on the economic rationale, the fundamental reasons for the proposals, and the possible consequences of following one proposal or another. This in turn will provide a foundation for studying the evolution of policy and analysis of more specific alternatives for the future.

QUESTIONS AND EXERCISES

1 Define agricultural supply and demand. Why do we specify given conditions, a range of prices, and a specific period of time?

2 What factors have determined the growth of agricultural supply in the United States? Explain why supply may increase either from increases in amounts of resources, or in productivity.

3 If output increases purely as a result of increase in the price of the product (ceteris paribus), does this constitute a change in supply? Why?

4 In your judgment, what are the most significant technological advances in agriculture over the past 25 years? Explain why you consider these to be the most significant.

5 Under what conditions will a tax or a subsidy change agricultural supply? Illustrate with use of supply and demand curves. Explain, in terms of supply and demand, why a land retirement program may or may not decrease the quantity of farm products produced.

6 What are the factors determining the demand for total farm food products? Given such a demand curve, what additional information is needed to determine the quantity of food demanded?

7 Define income elasticity of demand. Does the income elasticity of demand for food tend to increase or decrease as real incomes rise, ceteris paribus? Explain.

8 How is the income elasticity of demand for farm food products generally determined? Is income elasticity generally higher or lower for foods such as steak and shrimp than for bread and potatoes? Why?

9 Define price elasticity of supply (and of demand). What is the elasticity of demand if the price changes by 10 percent when output increases by 2 percent, ceteris paribus? Show your method of computation. What is the elasticity of supply if an increase in demand results in a 10 percent increase in price when the quantity demanded increases by 1 percent?

10 Why is supply more elastic in the long run than in the short run? Why is the supply of corn more elastic than the supply for total farm output, and what is the importance of this for policy?

11 What is the policy significance of inelastic demand for total farm output? Does demand tend to be more inelastic in the domestic market or the export market? Explain.

12 What is meant by the term "elasticity of price transmission"? How is this elasticity affected by import regulations? By controls over exports?

13 What is the policy significance of a low elasticity of price transmission? A high elasticity? How may each affect export policy for the United States?

14 What factors must be taken into account in measuring the elasticity of export demand? Which factors tend to be most important in world trade in agricultural products? Why?

15 What are the general policy implications of the current elasticities of price transmission? Of the current elasticities of export demand for agricultural products? Give examples to illustrate your comments.

RECOMMENDED READINGS

Bredahl, Maury E., William H. Meyers, and Keith J. Collins, "The Elasticity of Foreign Demand for U.S. Agricultural Products: The Importance of the Price Transmission Elasticity," *American Journal of Agricultural Economics,* vol. 61, no. 1, February 1979, pp. 58–63.

Chambers, Robert G., and Richard E. Just, "Effects of Exchange Rate Changes on U.S. Agriculture: A Dynamic Analysis," *American Journal of Agricultural Economics,* vol. 63, no. 1, February 1981, pp. 32–46.

Chambers, Robert G., John M. Letiche, and Andrew Schmitz, "The Gains from International Trade," in Jimmye S. Hillman and Andrew Schmitz (eds.), *International Trade and Agriculture: Theory and Policy,* Westview Press, Boulder, Colorado, 1979, pp. 61–90.

Gardner, Bruce L., "Determinants of Supply Elasticity in Interdependent Markets," *American Journal of Agricultural Economics,* vol. 61, no. 3, August 1979, pp. 463–475.

Woods, Mike, Luther Tweeten, Daryll E. Ray, and Greg Parvin, "Statistical Tests of the Hypothesis of Reversible Agricultural Supply," *North Central Journal of Agricultural Economics,* vol. 3, no. 1, January 1981, pp. 13–19.

PART TWO

POLICY ANALYSIS OF THE PRODUCT MARKETS

FOUNDATIONS OF POLICY ANALYSIS IN THE PRODUCT MARKETS

Now that we have studied the beliefs, values, and goals underlying agricultural policy; viewed agriculture and its markets in broad perspective; and discussed the use of supply and demand in policy analysis; let us build on this knowledge to study the foundation and evolution of policy making in the product markets, including the economic thought underlying this policy. This will help us visualize the range of policy that can be applied to the product markets, and the results of choosing specific alternatives. This also provides a background for the more specific analysis of policy in these markets in the three chapters that follow.

IN THIS CHAPTER

1 You can learn why the early foundation of policy in the product markets was concerned primarily with goals of raising and stabilizing farm incomes, what programs were used as a means of trying to accomplish this, and what economic thought underlay these efforts.

2 You can learn how policy evolved in the era following the close of World War II, why policy in the product markets came under increasing criticism, and what alternatives were proposed by economists and others.

3 You can learn how and why the policy has tended to change since the beginning of the 1970s, and some of the implications of these changes for the future.

THE EARLY FOUNDATIONS: 1920 TO 1940

Since the early 1920s, in contrast to the preceding 300 years of land settlement, the federal government has been directly involved in the agricultural product markets. Generally, the chief motivation for this involvement, or market intervention, has been

Adequate facilities for grain marketing are of concern to many farmers. Even though country elevators may have excess capacity for several months of the year, during the harvest season farmers may have to wait some time to get unloaded, or the elevator may run out of space to take more grain. This increases the costs of marketing. The upkeep of country roads and other facilities presents a problem for public policy, which is of important interest to farmers as well as consumers.

what is called "the farm problem": low prices for farm products, instability and uncertainty in farm prices and incomes, and associated elements of distress in the farm sector. The early foundation for this policy was laid to cope with the economic distress of farm people that resulted from the collapse of farm prices after World War I. Although prices recovered from the collapse, they never regained a level that allowed farmers to think they were sharing in the industrial prosperity of the 1920s. Therefore, farm policy issues stayed alive throughout the decade, as farm groups proposed various solutions.

The proposals, in some cases based on the work of economists, can be grouped around three main ideas for action: (1) Concerning the domestic market, first to improve the efficiency of the marketing system, and then, going beyond this, to establish a nationwide system of farm cooperatives that would regulate the flow of farm food products so as to achieve more orderly marketing with fair and stable farm prices. (2) To reestablish the export market to achieve farm prices that would be in the same ratio to nonfarm prices as such prices had been just before the war. (3) To withdraw farmland from crop production to balance the total farm output with market demand. These three ideas have been important ever since their proposal in the 1920s.

The growth of export markets depends on the increasing productivity of American agriculture, increases in export demand, and large-scale ocean transport systems. How to achieve continuing growth in exports is a major issue in agricultural policy analysis.

Improving the Marketing System

One of the basic concepts underlying agricultural policy in the product markets has been the idea that improvements in the marketing system would benefit both producers and consumers. In 1921, largely in response to efforts of livestock producers, Congress passed the Packers and Stockyards Act, which provided for government inspection and regulation of livestock commission firms and packers in public stockyards. Next, as a result of political efforts by farmers to gain more control over marketing, Congress passed the Capper-Volstead Act of 1922. This act, sometimes called the Magna Carta of cooperative marketing, authorized farmers' cooperatives to issue capital stock and engage in interstate trade, providing they did not violate anti-trust laws by combining or conspiring in restraint of trade. This was sought by perfectly competitive farmers as a way of grappling with the more imperfectly competitive agribusiness input and marketing industries. The Grain Futures Act of 1922, later amended and expanded in a number of acts, provided the foundation for government regulation of commodity exchanges. The act prohibited manipulation of prices, or attempts to manipulate prices, a measure thought to be most important for grain, cotton, and other commodities traded on futures markets. Commission merchants and floor brokers, as well as boards of trade, were made subject to regulation under the broad jurisdiction of the secretary of agriculture.

Cooperatives as Bargaining Agents

In addition, several farm groups had the idea, arising out of the experience of fruit and nut cooperatives in California, that farm cooperatives should be developed on a nationwide basis, as national bargaining associations organized on commodity lines, to control the supply of major farm commodities and get higher prices for farm products. The American Farm Bureau Federation (AFBF), which had been organized on a national basis in 1919, put considerable effort into organizing national cooperatives, among them the U.S. Grain Growers, the National Livestock Producers Association, the American Cotton Growers' Exchange, and the Federated Fruit and Vegetable Growers, Inc. Although many of the state and local cooperatives succeeded as marketing firms, none was able to develop national bargaining power and, except for some intermittent developments in more recent years, cooperatives generally have failed as national bargaining associations.

Export Subsidy as National Policy

Programs involving export subsidy have been of major interest to producers for a long time, as a means of getting higher prices for exportable crops in the domestic market than would exist under free trade. The basic concept is one of price discrimination, which will increase total market receipts if demand is more elastic for exports than it is for the same commodity in the domestic market. Very early in the 1920s, a number of bills were considered in Congress for buying certain crops at prices that would assure farmers "cost of production" plus a reasonable profit, but none received general farm support. In 1921, however, Professor George Warren of Cornell University published a study showing that the index of prices received by farmers, relative to prices paid, was about 20 percent lower than it had been in 1913.[1]

Soon thereafter the Department of Agriculture began publishing a "purchasing power index" which generally confirmed these adverse terms of trade and, early in 1922, the secretary of agriculture convened a large conference of farm and Congressional leaders to discuss what could be done. George N. Peek of the Moline Plow Company in Illinois presented a resolution, which was adopted by the conference, calling for the Congress and the President to take immediate steps to reestablish a "fair exchange value" for farm products. Then, Peek and Hugh S. Johnson (a World War I general who was later named by President Roosevelt to head the National Recovery Administration) published a bulletin defining their interests, which was widely distributed.[2] Fair exchange value was defined as a price "which bears the same ratio to the current general price index as a ten-year pre-war average crop price bore to the average price index for the same period." As an example, wheat should have been $1.60 a bushel instead of $1.02. To get such a price, it was proposed that

---

[1]George F. Warren, *Prices of Farm Products in the United States,* U.S. Department of Agriculture, Bulletin 999, August 1921.

[2]George N. Peek and Hugh S. Johnson, *Equality for Agriculture,* privately published, Moline, Illinois, 1922.

an "ample" portion of any crop included in a program be fed into the domestic market only in such amounts as would meet domestic demand at the fair exchange value. Any quantity produced in excess of this would be sold abroad, and losses in selling abroad at the lower price would be spread evenly among all producers through a general sales tax on the commodity.

These proposals attracted wide attention and became the basis for a bill, introduced in 1924 by Senator Charles McNary of Oregon and Representative Gilbert N. Haugen of Iowa, to get fair exchange value in the domestic market for the portion of exportable crops used domestically, with the balance sold abroad at world prices. This was the first of five bills introduced in Congress in each session from 1924 to 1928. Although the details of the five bills differed somewhat, each adhered to a goal of fair exchange value in the domestic market and export sales at world prices. The first three bills failed to pass Congress, and the fourth and fifth passed but then were vetoed by the President.

The final McNary-Haugen bills received strong political support from farm groups, even though the production stimulant of higher prices could have made the benefits only temporary. Weaknesses of the proposed program were pointed out in a number of studies.[3] President Coolidge's vetoes of the fourth and the fifth bills included an argument that the bills were unconstitutional, and listed six additional objections: (1) the attempted price fixing, (2) the tax characteristics of the equalization fee, (3) the widespread bureaucracy that would be set up, (4) the probable encouragement to profiteering and wasteful distribution, (5) the stimulation to overproduction, and (6) the aid to foreign agricultural competitors.[4]

Although the second Coolidge veto brought the policy struggle over export subsidy to a close for the time being, the idea became a major policy issue again in the early days of the Roosevelt New Deal. Again it was rejected by the administration, this time as being inconsistent with reciprocal trade agreements begun under the Reciprocal Trade Agreements Act of 1934. This act was aimed at lowering, rather than increasing, tariffs, the latter being implied in export subsidy programs. In the late 1930s and 1940s, modest export subsidies were financed out of tariff receipts. In 1954, under the Agricultural Trade Development and Assistance Act, more popularly known as Public Law 480, or P.L. 480, the foundation was laid for food aid to developing countries on a concessional basis, and for export subsidies sufficient to keep American farm products, wheat and feed grains especially, competitive in commercial exports markets. Hence, the idea of export subsidy, vigorously sought in the 1920s, but rejected then and again in the mid 1930s, expanded greatly in the post–World War II era, to become imbedded in agricultural policy, both as a means of increasing returns to producers and as a program for providing aid to people in other countries.

---

[3]See, for example, Joseph S. Davis, "The McNary-Haugen Plan as Applied to Wheat," *Wheat Studies of the Food Research Institute,* Stanford University, February 1927, pp. 177–234, and March 1927, pp. 235–264.

[4]United States President, *Veto Message Relating to Agricultural Surplus Control Act,* 70th Cong., 1st Sess., S. 141, May 3, 1928.

The Foundation of Storage Programs

The vetoes of the McNary-Haugen bills brought a halt to the efforts to develop an export-subsidy program, and the election of Herbert Hoover in 1928 forced those concerned with the farm problem to turn in another direction. In his campaign, Hoover had expressed himself as deeply concerned about the economic condition of agriculture but unalterably opposed to export subsidy in any form. The Senate, however, which had come within four votes of overriding the second veto, had demonstrated strong support for aid to agriculture. It was clear to the President and congressional leaders that something had to be done to try to support farm prices and keep campaign promises.

The Federal Farm Board was established by the Agricultural Marketing Act of 1929 in June in a special session called to consider farm and tariff legislation. It received an initial appropriation of $500 million to be used as a revolving fund by cooperatives to finance storage operations at relatively low rates of interest.[5] The board was directed to use this money to accomplish four things: (1) to minimize speculation, (2) to prevent inefficient and wasteful methods of distribution, (3) to help producers organize cooperative marketing associations, and (4) to aid in preventing and controlling surpluses. The board moved quickly to establish new cooperative associations and soon allotted nearly all of the $500 million appropriated, most for stocks of wheat and cotton, and lesser amounts for other commodities. The idea was to have cooperatives hold these stocks until markets improved and the commodities could be sold at a profit. But, with the beginning of the great depression prices fell hard. By 1931, the average price of wheat was about 39 cents a bushel, as compared with $1.04 in 1929. The 1931 cotton crop sold for an average of 6 cents a pound, as compared with 17 cents for the 1929 crop. In 1932, instead of committing more funds to support the market, it was decided to liquidate. The board lost $300 to $350 million on storage operations, which may be regarded as a measure of its success in supporting prices. But the failure to stabilize prices by storage alone paved the way for new and stronger proposals for production adjustment to be enacted into law.

Foundation of Production Adjustment and Control

With a given level of demand, the control of agricultural production is about the only way of getting higher prices for farm products. The basic idea of controlling production, as we have mentioned, was to withdraw enough farmland from crop production to balance the total farm output with market demand at average prices equivalent to those received before the war. The idea of controlling farm output or marketing had been around for a long time, and the concept of balancing farm output with demand, by controlling the amount of land seeded to crops, was outlined in two stud-

---

[5]See Agricultural Marketing Act of 1929, 46 *Stat.* 11; and Federal Farm Board, *First Annual Report,* 1930, p. 1.

ies in 1926 and 1927.[6] A more complete plan, called "the domestic allotment plan," was presented in 1929 by John D. Black of Harvard University, in the most comprehensive study of agricultural reform and policy published to that time.[7]

The essential principle of the domestic allotment plan was to pay each producer of a commodity that is exported "the free-trade price plus the tariff duty for the part of their crop which is consumed in the United States and this price without the tariff duty for the part of it that is exported, this to be arranged by a system of allotments to individual producers of rights to sell the domestic part of the crop in the domestic market."[8]

This was also called the "transferable-rights plan," because each producer would have the right to sell the allotment to another producer in an open market, or to buy an additional allotment if one were for sale. Using as an example, wheat, which had a tariff duty of 42 cents a bushel, the domestic price would be forced to the level of the world price plus the tariff by requiring all processors of wheat to show the allotment rights for all domestic wheat milled and sold as wheat product in the domestic market. They might import actual wheat, paying the 42-cent duty on it, if not enough allotment rights had been issued. Or, if more allotment rights had been issued than the millers wanted to buy, imports would cease altogether and the allotment rights might sell at a slight discount. It was expected that it would be cheaper to buy domestic wheat than imported wheat in most locations because of the saving in transportation costs. This, it was claimed, would make the tariff effective, by giving the tariff rate a chance to impose itself on the whole of the domestic consumption. It would pass on to consumers the cost of the higher prices that the producers would receive, just exactly as does any effective tariff.[9] It would not raise the price of wheat to those who wanted to use it for feed or seed. Hence, it would not be applicable to most feed crops, such as corn, but would be limited generally to those commodities which largely or almost entirely pass through processing establishments where their purchase could be checked. The principal argument against the domestic allotment plan would be its contribution to raising the cost of living, and the difficulty in administration and revision of the allotments.

The concept of the domestic allotment plan entered importantly into the political campaign that resulted in the Agricultural Adjustment Act of 1933. M. L. Wilson, of Montana State College, who became the recognized leader of the campaign, encouraged farm groups, political leaders, and others to study and refine the plan.[10] With the election of Franklin D. Roosevelt, presidential leadership and support for the campaign were obtained, which was essential to get the bill through Congress.

---

[6]Harry N. Owen, "Getting the Tariff to the Farmer," *Farm Stock and Home,* February 1, 1926; and W. J. Spillman, *Balancing the Farm Output,* Orange Judd Publishing Co., New York, 1927.

[7]See John D. Black, *Agricultural Reform in the United States,* McGraw-Hill Book Company, New York, 1929, Chapter 10.

[8]Black, ibid., p. 271.

[9]Black, ibid., pp. 277–282.

[10]See William A. Rowley, *M. L. Wilson and the Campaign for the Domestic Allotment,* University of Nebraska Press, Lincoln, 1970.

The general goal of the act was "to raise agriculture to a parity with other industry," and "to establish and maintain such balance between the production and consumption of agricultural commodities, and such marketing conditions therefore, as will reestablish prices to farmers at a level that will give agricultural commodities a purchasing power of agricultural commodities in the base period."[11] The act also provided authority to establish the Agricultural Adjustment Administration (AAA) to implement the program.

The secretary of agriculture was granted broad authority to enter into agreements with farmers; to reduce crop acreage or production; and to regulate marketing methods, prices, and margins by means of agreements, licenses, and other provisions. The concept of an individual producer acreage allotment became fundamental, with administration organized by townships and counties, and with committees of farmers elected by program participants having power to review allotments and provide general policy review and advice.

The program was to be financed largely by a processing tax levied on the first sale of designated farm commodities. The participation of individual farmers was voluntary, but program provisions were such that nearly all eligible farmers found it advantageous to comply. A few stayed out for ideological reasons; for example, some believed that controlling farm output was not a proper function of government. Some others did not participate because it was not profitable for them to do so, but most signed up. Acreage allotments were established for their farms. Compliance meant reducing the acreage seeded to the allotment specified for each crop designated as "basic," such as wheat, cotton, field corn, rice, and tobacco.

The allotment generally was determined as a fixed percentage of the average acreage seeded to each crop in the previous five years, and a farmer who signed an agreement and complied with the terms of the contract was paid a certain amount per acre on the base acreage, according to its productivity. Additional basic commodities such as hogs and milk and its products (others were added later) might be controlled through marketing quotas. The Bankhead Cotton Control Act of 1934 and the Kerr-Smith Act for tobacco established provisions for quotas on these commodities. In the case of cotton, if two-thirds of the eligible growers voted for quotas in a referendum called specifically for this purpose, then the secretary would be empowered to levy a tax of 50 percent ad valorem on all cotton sold and each grower who complied with the established quota would receive exemption certificates in the amount of the individual quota. Tobacco required a three-fourths majority to establish quotas. In January 1936, however, the United States Supreme Court declared the processing tax authorized in the 1933 act to be unconstitutional, therefore null and void, and the entire act thereby became unconstitutional. The act was quickly replaced by the Soil Conservation and Domestic Allotment Act of 1936. This, and subsequent acts, have generally withstood legal challenges as being within limits established in the constitution.

The Marketing Agreements Act of 1937 clarified conditions for the secretary to

---

[11] Agricultural Adjustment Act of 1933, 73d Cong., 1st Sess., 48 H.R. 3835, Public Law No. 10.

A uniform high-quality product is the aim of the pork industry. To the extent that this results from a policy of publicly supported research and education, what groups tend to benefit the most? Who bears the real cost of this policy?

enter into agreements with producer organizations and to issue marketing orders to regulate the marketing of specified commodities. It granted authority to the secretary to hold referenda of eligible producers to determine whether or not an order could be issued, or promulgated. Generally, an order, which is binding on all producers, must be approved by a two-thirds majority of those voting in a referendum. Subsequently, orders have been used widely to regulate the pricing and marketing of fluid milk, and the quality and quantity of certain fresh fruits and vegetables coming to market.

The Agricultural Adjustment Act of 1938 was the most comprehensive law among legislation passed in the 1930s, and it has, to great extent, set the terms of price-support policy even to the 1980s. The act authorized soil conservation payments, set specific minimum levels for price supports, provided for acreage allotments on all major crops to be implemented by direct payments to producers, and authorized marketing quotas for commodities approved by producers. It incorporated provisions of the 1937 act for marketing agreements and orders. The Federal Crop Insurance Corporation was established to administer the first federal all-risk crop insurance program. Four new regional laboratories were authorized for scientific research, emphasizing new uses and new outlets for farm products. Finally, the act authorized direct distribution of surplus farm food commodities to the needy, a school-lunch program, a low-cost milk program, and a food-stamp program. But acute problems developed under this act, relating most specifically to the government's effort to raise and stabilize prices.

Production Adjustment: The Principle and the Experience

Production control takes time to be effective in raising prices of farm products and, under given market conditions, a quicker price response can be obtained by setting loans on products at levels higher than going market prices. In October 1934, President Roosevelt—perhaps in recognition of this principle and with an eye on the upcoming midterm elections—established the Commodity Credit Corporation (CCC) to make nonrecourse loans at levels higher than existing market prices for cotton, wheat, corn, and other products. This program worked rather well through 1936, because severe droughts in 1934 and 1936 brought low average yields to most major crop regions, and in some areas there were complete crop failures. In 1937, however, the return of good weather resulted in a large crop, and prices of some commodities fell hard. The price supports set by Congress in the 1938 act soon proved to be well above market-equilibrium levels, and between 1938 and 1940 the index of prices received dropped another 20 percent. By 1941, although acreage allotments were being applied to all the basic crops, and marketing quotas were in effect for wheat, cotton, tobacco, and peanuts, market prices were frequently falling below loan levels and CCC stocks were reaching the capacity of storage facilities. It seemed to be just a matter of time until stronger programs would be needed, or the main part of the price-support program would collapse.

Earlier studies had shown that the AAA had helped to stabilize prices, but that its potential for price support was limited.[12] Now, rapid technological advance was overcoming the efforts to control production. Resources were being wasted, as supports based on parity prevented prices from performing their essential task of directing and regulating economic processes. But farm family incomes were still relatively low. What was to be done?

THE EVOLUTION OF POLICY: THE 1940s TO THE 1970s

Production controls with price-support loans above market-equilibrium levels work rather well when demand is strong and increasing (when, of course, they may not be needed). But when demand is not as strong and it is believed they are needed, they lead to distortions in agricultural incentives and to unnecessarily large surpluses. This was demonstrated in the 30 years from 1940 to 1970.

Demand increased strongly during World War II and remained strong in the early postwar years, as large quantities of food were shipped overseas for the war and for recovery programs. Consequently, World War II may be visualized as an

---

[12]See Edwin G. Nourse, Joseph S. Davis, and John D. Black, *Three Years of the Agricultural Adjustment Administration,* The Brookings Institution, Washington, D.C., 1937.

outlet for policy makers struggling with crop surpluses. Increases in demand pushed prices of farm products well above support levels for most crops, even though Congress, under strong political pressures from farm organizations, raised the minimum levels of price support to 90 percent of parity for the basic commodities and a long list of other products. Congress also created a new degree of certainty or assurance for farm producers by providing that the wartime levels of support should be maintained for two years after the end to hostilities was declared. Supports for cotton were raised to 100 percent of parity for the 1944 and 1945 crops. Provisions for marketing quotas were retained to February 1943 for wheat, to July 1943 for cotton, and to the end of the war for tobacco.

All other constraints on production and marketing were ended, as wartime programs allocating production supplies and labor to agriculture were designed to greatly increase agriculture's output. From 1943 to 1945, a subsidy of 25 cents per bushel for feeding wheat was paid to livestock producers, who increased their use of wheat for feed by about 300 million bushels. Hence, by the summer of 1946, the government-held stocks of grain were nearly used up, and only excess stocks of cotton remained in the inventory of the CCC. From 1946 to 1948, huge demands for food aid in Europe augmented demands for exports. Grain prices rose to new record highs. Farmers seeded more land than ever before, and were exhorted to produce still more. But in 1949, prices of some commodities again began to fall hard from their postwar highs, and a new long period of readjustment began.

Criticisms by Economists Engaged in Policy Analysis

Criticisms by economists of the involvement of government in price-support programs has been directed to the cost of these programs, the distortions of agricultural incentives that occur, and the program's welfare effects, whereby the richest or most productive farmers are helped the most. Although economists designed the first programs as a means of urgent relief to farmers, economists have long recognized the weaknesses in the programs and have been active in efforts of constructive criticism. One of the early criticisms was that price supports based on parity distorted agricultural incentives by preventing prices from performing their essential function of guiding the allocation of resources according to supply and demand. One of the most trenchant arguments in this vein was presented by Theodore W. Schultz, in his book, *Redirecting Farm Policy,* published in 1943. Schultz blasted parity prices as goals for policy, arguing that "prices have a function, and that function is to direct and regulate economic processes."[13]

Schultz concluded that if supplementary income help were to be given to farm families, this aid should be tied to the family, the home, and the needs of the human agent. It should not be allocated according to production criteria, because this is ineffective in supplementing farm family incomes. It tends to increase output based

[13]Theodore W. Schultz, *Redirecting Farm Policy,* The Macmillan Company, New York, 1943, p. 8.

on marginal returns and, because of inelastic demand, prices fall relatively more. Benefit payments of the AAA type, when allotted according to the size of a farm, the productivity of a farm, or the acreage of key crops, enhance the returns of those farm families who already have adequate incomes much more than they do family incomes that, according to social welfare criteria, are too low. Schultz argued that supplementary income is most appropriately granted in kind, in the form of specific public services such as food, houses, medical services, and education. Finally, supplementary income should be made available to all families regardless of their income status, examples being elementary education and rural free delivery of mail.[14]

The actual price supports voted by the Congress would move up with the index of prices received, and as the war began to draw to a close, economists began to warn that it would be necessary to move to lower levels of price support if large surpluses, more stringent production controls, and loss of the export market or more expensive export subsidies were to be avoided. In February 1945, the American Farm Economic Association announced an essay contest on the topic "A Price Policy for Agriculture, Consistent with Economic Progress that Will Promote Adequate and More Stable Income From Farming."[15] The 18 prize-winning papers, selected anonymously by a panel of prominent members of the association, generally argued for price supports in line with market requirements, storage programs limited essentially to price stabilization, and minimum income guarantees by means of direct payments. Few argued for production controls or parity as a guide for price support. More exports of farm products would be encouraged by such a rational price policy, and by further reductions in tariffs around the world. More should be spent on soil conservation. Most argued strongly for more support for education in rural areas to increase career opportunities, which would also increase the opportunity costs for young people to enter farming. Most recognized benefits of community development, which would also increase nonfarm employment opportunities.

These themes tended to dominate in economic literature and journal articles. Individual studies provided the foundation for many committee reports, and in addition developed proposals to help free markets work more efficiently. The first of these to gain wide recognition was written by T. W. Schultz, in a study sponsored by the Committee for Economic Development, outlining a proposed new program for forward prices for agriculture.[16] Schultz proposed that a commission or board would set prices of farm products forward by at least one production period, within a range of prices expected to prevail under conditions of full employment. If the economy achieved full employment, then defined as no more than 4 percent unemployed, no price supports or compensatory payments would be provided. If full employment were not achieved, and market prices fell below the minima of the forward-price ranges, then compensatory payments would be paid to producers to cover the dif-

---

[14]Schultz, ibid., pp. 65–71.

[15]See *Journal of Farm Economics,* vol. 28, no. 4, November 1945, pp. 452, ff.; and William H. Nicholls and D. Gale Johnson, "The Farm Price Policy Awards, 1945: A Topical Digest of the Winning Essays," ibid., vol. 29, no. 1, February 1946, pp. 267–283.

[16]Theodore W. Schultz, *Agriculture in an Unstable Economy,* McGraw-Hill Book Company, New York, 1945.

ference between the minimum forward price and the market price. Such payments would be countercyclical in effect. Production controls would not be used, but there would be special programs to help low-income families to adjust.[17] A broad and more detailed comprehensive program for agricultural development, with only supplementary use of production controls, was presented by John D. Black and Maxine E. Kiefer.[18] In addition, in 1948, Black, in a statement before the Congress House Committee on Agriculture, saw the greatest immediate need as growing out of the postwar food shortage, and recommended a broad program of aid to agriculture aimed at market expansion and food distribution, a program that should eliminate the need for production controls or market quotas.[19]

Four years later, as the threat of surpluses resulting from price supports began to mount again, a committee of 13 prominent agricultural economists, organized under sponsorship of the Farm Foundation, issued a report extolling the benefits of free markets. Storage programs were assigned a rather limited role, to buttress markets in time of depression and to provide for military emergencies. Production controls were largely rejected in favor of programs to aid farm people to adjust to free markets.[20]

Three years later another committee, overlapping somewhat with the Farm Foundation committee, recommended a largely free-market policy for the product markets, but one backed by programs to expand exports and adjust resources.[21] Seven years beyond this, in the early years of the Kennedy administration, another committee of prominent economists again recommended free markets, in a broad program to adapt agriculture to growth in national and world markets.[22] Congress, however, continued to move in a different direction, as it had been doing for so many years. Why?

Programs Adopted by Congress

Throughout these years Congress continued to vote for price supports that were often above market equilibria. The Agricultural Adjustment Act of 1948 renewed acreage allotments, and set price supports at 90 percent of parity for wheat, corn, rice, peanuts, cotton, and tobacco, providing producers did not reject marketing quotas (if a referendum were held to vote on their adoption).

---

[17]The theoretical foundations for forward prices were developed in a Ph.D. dissertation by D. Gale Johnson and published in *Forward Prices for Agriculture,* The University of Chicago Press, Chicago, 1947.

[18]John D. Black and Maxine E. Kiefer, *Future Food and Agricultural Policy, A Program for the Next Ten Years,* McGraw-Hill Book Company, New York, 1948.

[19]James Pierce Cavin (ed.), *Economics for Agriculture, Selected Writings of John D. Black,* with introductory essays by Cavin and others, Harvard University Press, Cambridge, 1959, pp. 594–610.

[20]*Turning the Searchlight on Farm Policy, a Forthright Analysis of Experience, Lessons, Criteria and Recommendations,* The Farm Foundation, Chicago, 1952.

[21]See Murray R. Benedict, *Can We Solve the Farm Problem? An Analysis of Federal Aid to Agriculture,* The Twentieth Century Fund, 1955, in particular, Chapter 12.

[22]See *An Adaptive Program for Agriculture, A Statement on National Policy by the Research and Policy Committee,* Committee for Economic Development, New York, 1962.

The Sliding Scale   Congress provided a new basis for price supports to become effective on January 1, 1950. Under the new provisions price supports would drop from 90 to 60 percent of parity in steps of 2 percent, if the total visible supply of a basic commodity increased from 100 to 130 percent of normal. Before this could go into effect, an amendment introduced by Representative Clifford Hope of Kansas was adopted, setting supports for the basic commodities at 90 percent of parity for the following year. The Agricultural Act of 1949 narrowed the sliding scale from 90 to 75 percent of parity, but this was overridden again by a renewal of the Hope Amendment for another year.

A broader program, making more use of payments to farmers and control of supply, was recommended by Secretary of Agriculture Charles Brannan. It was proposed to shift to a 10-year moving average as a base for price supports and payments. This would generally raise the levels of supports and payments. Price and income supports would be limited to the first 1,800 units of farm production, where a unit was defined as 10 bushels of corn, 8 bushels of wheat, 50 pounds of cotton, or the equivalent. Acreage allotments, marketing quotas, storage programs, marketing agreements, and orders would all be used, if necessary, to bring farm income up to the support level.[23]

The so-called Brannan Plan was strongly opposed by the American Farm Bureau Federation and narrowly defeated in Congress. Then, early in 1952, President Harry Truman asked for repeal of the sliding scale, and Congress extended supports at 90 percent of parity through 1954. Although the Agricultural Act of 1954 provided for the sliding scale at 90 to 82.5 percent of parity for 1955, and 90 to 75 percent thereafter, these provisions never went into effect, as Congress had renewed supports at 90 percent of parity.

New Parity Formula   Congress established a new method for computing parity, to go into effect January 1, 1950, which was designed to help bring price supports in line with recent price trends for a given commodity. Prior to this, a parity price was determined simply by multiplying the average price of each commodity in the base period (August 1909 to July 1914) by the current monthly index of prices paid by farmers (based on 1910–14 = 100). The new parity required two steps: (1) dividing the average price for a commodity in the previous 10 years by the index of prices received in these same years to get a new adjusted base price, and (2) multiplying this base price by the current monthly index of prices paid. The effect of this would be to lower the base price for a commodity that was relatively low in price in the preceding 10 years, and to raise the base price for a commodity that had had a relatively high market price. Hence, over time it would lower parity price-support levels for major grain crops where technological advances were most effective, and raise parity for commodities such as beef, where demand was strong, or where technological advances were less effective. However, because of political pressure for higher supports, new parity was not used in the 1950s in any case where it would have lowered the level of price support.

---

[23]For further discussion, see articles by W. E. Hendrix, Harold G. Halcrow, Roy E. Huffman, and D. Gale Johnson, *Journal of Farm Economics*, vol. 31, no. 3, August 1949, pp. 487–519.

The Soil Bank   In 1956, Congress established the Soil Bank, which included an acreage and a conservation reserve. The object of the acreage reserve was to reduce the amount of land planted to allotment crops: wheat, cotton, corn, tobacco, peanuts, and rice. In 1957, there were 21.4 million acres in the acreage reserve, for which farmers received payments. But, because of its cost and doubts about the effectiveness of the program, it was ended in 1958. The conservation reserve provided for payments to farmers for diverting designated cropland to conservation uses, and in 1960 about 28.6 million acres were under contracts, which ran for a maximum of 10 years.[24]

Mandatory Supports   The Agricultural Act of 1958 made price supports mandatory for most feed grains, wheat, cotton, and tobacco. But corn farmers were given a choice in referendum of (1) ending allotments in 1959 with price supports at 90 percent of the average market price of the preceding three years, or (2) retaining acreage allotments and price supports at 90 to 75 percent of parity as provided in the Agricultural Act of 1954. Farmers voted for the first option, thus lowering the support level and ending allotments for corn.

Although allotments were maintained for the other basic commodities, surplus stocks created by price supports above market-equilibrium levels continued to pile up to record levels. By 1960, the Commodity Credit Corporation (CCC) carryover of wheat was 1.3 billion bushels, about 200 million more than were being produced in an average year. About 1.8 billion bushels of corn were carried over, more than a six-month supply. There were also relatively large inventories of CCC stocks of other feed grains, cotton, and tobacco. In spite of strong support for Public Law 480, extensive use of acreage allotments and nearly 29 million acres in the conservation reserve, and substantial increases in storage stocks, prices were generally too low to satisfy most farmers. Their distress probably was a factor in the 1960 presidential election, in which John F. Kennedy was elected.

Policy of the Kennedy Administration

Kennedy, in campaigning for the presidency, had strongly proposed using the agricultural abundance in the United States to improve living standards in the United States and around the world, and advocated combining this policy with a program to manage agricultural supply and thus improve incomes of farm families. Soon after taking office, one of the first acts the President took was directing the secretary of agriculture to expand distribution of surplus food to needy persons, expand use of food stamps and school-lunch programs, and promote increases in exports through Public Law 480, now called "Food for Peace." This would be combined with stricter control over production and more comprehensive management of supply, much as

---

[24]Wayne D. Rasmussen and Gladys L. Baker, *Price Support and Adjustment Programs from 1933 through 1978: A Short History,* Agricultural Information Bulletin 424, U.S. Department of Agriculture, Washington, D.C., 1979.

proposed in earlier writings of Willard W. Cochrane, who was appointed director of agricultural economics in the Department of Agriculture.[25]

The basic conceptual model underlying the policy of the Kennedy administration was that of very inelastic demand for total farm products in the domestic market and very inelastic short-term supply. Cochrane had visualized supply as tending to jump forward periodically, as a result of increasing productivity, and had claimed it to be a myth that prices could control economic processes in agriculture in a way that would be satisfactory from the standpoint of policy. Instead, the reality was that increases in demand were insufficient to offset the periodic increases in supply. In spite of lower prices, more of the new industrial inputs were being attracted into agriculture. Because of low opportunity cost for cropland, low prices would not shrink the seeded acreage. Although the farm population was declining, this was not happening fast enough to equalize incomes between the farm and the nonfarm population.

The new policy of the Kennedy administration was intended to give more help to farm families, but also to shift the cost of this help from the government to consumers. With inelastic demand for total farm output in the domestic market, management of agricultural supply would raise prices much more than it would reduce total production. Good farm incomes would provide strength to the total economy. The domestic demands for farm products would be supplemented by expanding food-stamp and other consumer programs, as we have noted, and exports would be expanded by increasing support for Public Law 480, and implementing broader foreign economic development programs.

The Issue of More Government Help to Agriculture

The basic policy issue of more help to agriculture by government management of the economy can be expected to receive strong support from some groups, and strong opposition from others. Each side can use economics in support of its position, and each may appeal to some of the beliefs and values that we have discussed. This was evident in the first major agricultural act passed under President Kennedy, the Emergency Feed Grain Act of 1961, which was designed to reduce the acreage of feed grains and grain sorghum, to expand payments to farmers for this purpose, and to raise feed-grain prices. Prior to this, most administrations had preferred a more modest program for feed grains, because feed grains—unlike wheat and cotton—do not go principally into commercial markets. It has always been difficult, and continues to be difficult, to design programs that will fit feed grains in the same fashion as wheat. This explains the separate bill in 1961, and the continuing difficulty with feed grains in government programs. Congress, in spite of its willingness or even eagerness to help agriculture, demonstrates at times a degree of independence or caution that has been frustrating to those favoring stronger government programs.

Late in 1961, the Kennedy administration forwarded a bill to Congress to authorize the secretary to set allotment levels and supports on certain major crops, if Con-

---

[25]See Willard W. Cochrane, *Farm Prices: Myth and Reality,* The University of Minnesota Press, Minneapolis, 1958.

gress did not vote against the proposals within 60 days. But this was too broad a proposal to be acceptable to Congress. Following its rejection, a more specific proposal was sent forward as a bill to establish a general supply-control system for major farm commodities, including feed grains and dairy products. Under the proposed bill, the secretary would be directed to set national quotas for designated commodities, and producers of a commodity for which a quota was proposed would be given an opportunity in a national referendum to vote for or against it. If two-thirds of the eligible producers voted in favor, the quota and the specified price supports would become law. After extensive hearings, this bill passed the Senate, 42 to 38, but was defeated in the House, 205 to 215.

Not all farm organizations, however, favor strong government programs. The American Farm Bureau Federation (AFBF) and many state farm bureaus testified against the bill, arguing that it would bring agriculture under too strict government control and be ineffective in raising farm income. They argued that the use of quotas would be inefficient in allocating resources and would raise the cost of production. Also, to the extent that commodity prices were increased, land prices would rise and other costs would increase so that in the long run, agriculture would not benefit.

Most of the other farm organizations favored the bill. The Farmers Union and some others argued that such a program was necessary to save the family farm and prevent disaster in rural areas. Although Congress did not act to establish a broader supply-control program, the Food and Agricultural Act of 1962 extended the emergency feed-grain program and established procedures for a national wheat referendum.

The 1963 wheat referendum offered a choice of (1) a quota to be set by the secretary to bring wheat production in line with utilization, with price supports at 65 to 90 percent of parity, or (2) continuing with a minimum 55 million–acre allotment, with price supports at 50 percent of parity, then about $1.25 a bushel. Under the first option farmers would be offered marketing certificates to cover their quota, a minimum 15-acre allotment that had been granted to a large number of farmers who did not have a history of growing wheat would be cancelled, and farmers who exceeded their quota or allotment would be penalized. Under the second, there would be no penalty for overplanting, but farmers who did so would be ineligible for non-recourse loans.

The AFBF organized an all-out campaign opposing the first option, characterizing the issue as "freedom to farm," and "who will control agriculture, the bureaucrats or farmers?" The AFBF also promised a better program on which it subsequently was able to deliver. The administration, supported by the Farmers Union and some others, also campaigned vigorously, arguing that a vote for the first option was necessary to save the family farm and avoid economic disaster. About one million wheat growers voted in the referendum, more than five times the farm families voting in any previous referendum. Less than half voted for the first option, which made it necessary to consider new legislation for 1964.[26] Defeat of the 1963 referendum may be regarded as a fundamental turning point in policy.

---

[26]See Don F. Hadwiger and Ross B. Talbot, *Pressures and Protests: The Kennedy Farm Program and the Wheat Referendum of 1963,* Chandler Publishing Company, San Francisco, 1965.

Turkey growers have voted against a marketing-order proposal, apparently preferring a freely competitive market. What would be the advantages and disadvantages of a marketing order for turkeys?

Direct Payments in Lieu of Price Supports   Farm organizations generally have favored price supports over direct payments because price supports are more comfortable politically, and perhaps more reliable. At times, however, the government has turned to direct payments, especially for export commodities, as a way to bring domestic prices more in line with export markets.

The Wheat-Cotton Act of 1964 set a new policy for farm income programs by lowering price supports to levels near those in export markets, and increasing direct payments to participating farmers to bring their total compensation up to designated support levels, at least for that part of their crop sold domestically. By combining direct payments with strong production controls, it was planned that farm incomes would be supported, storage stocks held by the CCC would be reduced, and exports would increase normally with only minimum use of export subsidies. Much of this was achieved, but by the end of the 1960s, the combined costs of the wheat and cotton programs rose to more than $1.5 billion annually.

During the period from 1955 to 1965, there was a continuing struggle between those who advocated more controls over production and marketing in order to hold prices of farm products above their free-market equilibrium levels, and those who wanted to deemphasize or eliminate controls and management programs, and let prices seek their own market-clearing levels. A compromise was reached in the Food and Agricultural Act of 1965, which provided a solution involving (1) voluntary acreage-control programs for the most important crops, where farmers complying with the program were paid to limit their production to allotment levels; (2) price supports at or near world-market levels for farmers participating in programs; (3) supplementary income payments, to make up some of the differences between the price-support levels and prices received in domestic markets; and (4) foreign and domestic disposal of surplus agricultural products.

The compromise of 1965 held together through 1972, as production-control and supply-management techniques were combined to hold down costs of storage and disposal activities, and budgetary constraints limited the total income payments to farmers. But there was considerable discontent in farm areas with continuing declines in real prices of farm products, and in the late 1960s about 20 farm and agribusiness organizations came together to form what was called the "Coalition of Farm Organizations." They wanted higher price supports and more subsidies. This group included all the major farm organizations, with the notable exception of the American Farm Bureau Federation, which publicly favored lower price supports and phasing out production controls and supply-management programs.

The Agricultural Act of 1970 was a compromise between the views of the American Farm Bureau Federation and the Coalition of Farm Organizations. The hearings on the bills were unusually long and protracted and, during the closing days of congressional debate, planeloads of farmers and farm leaders went to Washington to press their views, and the House and Senate came to a virtual impasse over the final bill. Although carryover stocks had been trimmed somewhat, prices were still low. At issue were the means to be used in controlling production, the levels of price supports, the limits on payments to individual producers, and the support to be given to rural development programs. But the real issue was how much help the federal government should give to agriculture and rural communities, an issue which has continued, and is continuing still, in the present day.

CURRENT POLICY ISSUES

When markets boom, the government has more options in setting policy. Since the early 1970s, excess supplies have been only an intermittent problem, a major difference from earlier decades. In 1972 and 1973, and on occasion since then, market prices have soared above price-support levels, and the intermittence of excess supplies and the extent of the price increases largely explain the nature of recent legislation, especially Congress's willingness, if not eagerness, to lift the level of price supports. In the major acts of 1973, 1977, and 1981, Congress largely ignored parity, and set target prices higher in each successive act than they had been before. Loan rates, set somewhat below target prices, have been raised also.

The issue is how much government help should be given to agriculture, and on what terms. Large grain crops in the early 1980s have proved expensive, but markets have been erratic. Unusually large stocks of butter and some other dairy products have been described in the news media as a national scandal. How we might deal with these situations is a major part of policy analysis of the product markets. Congress is under pressure from political groups to stabilize the agricultural economy, but budgetary limits impose strong policy constraints. The specific political pressures on members of Congress coming directly from their constituents tend to put them at odds with the President. So the political pot will continue to boil, and the policy solutions may not be cheap. How to deal with these policy issues in the crops economy will be the subject of our next chapter.

SUMMARY

For more than 60 years, from the early 1920s to the mid-1980s, the federal government has been under political pressure to become involved in the farm product markets. In the 1920s, this pressure was resisted when Congress failed to override the vetoes of the McNary-Haugen bills. The first major involvement with the Federal Farm Board also failed, as the program to support prices by storage alone proved to be inadequate. The Agricultural Adjustment Act of 1933 and other acts in the 1930s set a precedent for production control programs that has continued to our day. The common denominator of all such programs has been land retirement, sometimes accompanied by marketing quotas. Marketing agreements and orders are used for fluid milk, and for some fruits and vegetables. Government-sponsored storage programs are a continuing policy issue.

Agricultural incentives have been distorted by setting prices as goals of policy, but short-term benefits have been realized by farmers, which accounts for the appeal of these programs to farm producers. The long-term benefits to farmers are more difficult to identify, as more stable prices also tend to stimulate output, and the distribution of benefits has not conformed to the generally accepted standards of social equity. What is to be done in the future will be the object of further policy analysis.

IMPORTANT TERMS AND CONCEPTS

Policy improvements in the marketing system

Farm cooperatives as bargaining agents

Concept and theory of export subsidy

How export subsidy aids producers

Export subsidy as price discrimination

Program of the Federal Farm Board

Why the Federal Farm Board failed

Concept of the domestic allotment plan

Concepts and goal of the Agricultural Adjustment Act of 1933

Concepts of acreage allotments and marketing quotas

Function of the Commodity Credit Corporation

Why price supports above free-market levels tend to create surpluses

Major criticisms of parity as a basis for price support

Why benefit payments may fail to improve farm incomes

Major recommendations of economists for policy in the product markets

The sliding scale as a basis for price support

New parity: basis for calculation

Concepts of policy analysis under the Kennedy administration

Direct payments in lieu of price supports: comparative benefits and costs

Provisions of agricultural acts since the beginning of the 1970s

Basic policy differences between Congress and the presidency

LOOKING AHEAD

Now that we have studied some foundations of agricultural policy, the next step will be to analyze policy alternatives by dealing more specifically with the three economies of crops, livestock, and marketing. Since policy analysis of the crops economy is most fundamental, we continue with this topic in the next chapter.

QUESTIONS AND EXERCISES

1 What were the three types of government involvement in the farm product markets proposed by agricultural leaders in the early 1920s? Explain how such involvement might have aided agriculture. What were the necessary conditions that were required to be fulfilled? Use diagrams to illustrate, if appropriate.

2 What were the general results of the policy-making efforts that were undertaken in support of the proposals mentioned in question 1? Explain what was meant by "fair exchange value." In terms of general theory, explain what might have been the general effect of achieving fair exchange value under conditions of the 1920s on agricultural prices, production, and income.

3 What was the policy goal of the Agricultural Marketing Act of 1929? By what means was this goal to be achieved? What were the implementing agencies? What were the major constraints? What conditions would have been necessary for the goals to be achieved?

4 What was the essential principle of the "domestic allotment plan" as proposed by John D. Black in 1929? Why was it also called a "transferable-rights plan"? What would be the necessary conditions for the plan to work as proposed?

5 What was the general policy goal of the Agricultural Adjustment Act of 1933? How were acreage allotments established? How was the policy implemented? What was the purpose of the marketing-quota legislation? How were quotas to be implemented? What is the general advantage of using a quota rather than an acreage allotment as a means of price support?

6 It has been noted that the Agricultural Adjustment Act of 1938 was the most comprehensive of the legislation passed in the 1930s, and it has pretty much set the terms of price-support policy to the 1980s. What were its major features? Which of these are characteristic of current price-support policy? Which are not?

7 What were the main provisions of the Soil Conservation Act of 1935? What was the general policy goal? The policy means, implements, and constraints?

8 What are the major lessons to be learned from the experience of the Agricultural Adjustment Administration with price-support programs in the 1930s?

9 What are the major criticisms made by economists, such as T. W. Schultz, of using parity as a basis for supporting the prices of agricultural products? Summarize the general recommendations of economists in the 1945 essay contest on the topic, "A Price Policy for Agriculture, Consistent with Economic Progress that Will Promote Adequate and More Stable Income From Farming." What was the general theoretical foundation of such recommendations?

10 Summarize the general provisions for forward prices as proposed by T. W. Schultz and D. Gale Johnson. Theoretically speaking, what would be the main advantage of such a program, as compared with price supports based on parity?

11 Summarize the provisions of the so-called sliding scale for farm price supports. What was the experience in Congress with the sliding scale?

12 A so-called new parity formula was passed by Congress to go into effect on January 1, 1950. How did this formula differ from the formula used up to that time? Illustrate, using real or hypothetical prices. Was new parity used in the 1950s? Why?

13 If agriculture is an industry with a long-period decreasing supply price, then what will be the general result of trying to maintain prices at a fixed percentage of parity? Explain what a decreasing supply price is, and illustrate. What could change agriculture from an industry with a decreasing supply price to one with an increasing supply price?

14 How did the price-support policy of the Kennedy administration differ from that of the Eisenhower administration? Explain why there is an inherent tendency to combine price supports with production controls and subsidies to increase both exports and domestic consumption.

15 It has been said that defeat of the 1963 wheat referendum marked a fundamental turning point in agricultural policy. What is the substance of this comment? How did the Wheat-Cotton Act of 1964 differ from previous legislation?

16 The Food and Agriculture Act of 1965 has been regarded as a basic compromise in agricultural policy. What were its main features? In what ways has subsequent legislation of the 1970s and 1980s tended to conform to these features, or differ from them?

17 In the 1970s and 1980s, why has parity largely been dropped as a basis for price-support programs? How have target prices tended to differ from parity? What is the basis for setting target prices and commodity loan rates? How are these prices and rates made effective? In general, why has it not been possible for Congress to meet the goals of some of the more militant farm organizations?

RECOMMENDED READINGS

An Adaptive Program for Agriculture, Committee for Economic Development, New York, 1962.

Black, John D., *Agricultural Reform in the United States,* McGraw-Hill Book Company, New York, 1929, Chapter 10.

Gardner, Bruce L., *The Governing of Agriculture,* The Regents Press of Kansas, Lawrence, 1981, Chapter 2, "Farm-Commodity Policy Today," pp. 17–44.

"Implications of the Agriculture and Food Act of 1981," papers by James Johnson and Kenneth Clayton; Daryll E. Ray, James W. Richardson, and Elton Li; and discussions by William C. Bailey and A. L. Frederick, *American Journal of Agricultural Economics,* vol. 64, no. 5, December 1982, pp. 947–969.

Rowley, William A., *M. L. Wilson and the Campaign for the Domestic Allotment,* University of Nebraska Press, Lincoln, 1970, pp. 107–141.

Schultz, Theodore W., *Agriculture in an Unstable Economy,* McGraw-Hill Book Company, 1945, pp. 225, ff.

CHAPTER 6

POLICY ANALYSIS OF THE CROPS ECONOMY

Policy analysis of the crops economy deals with three major areas of activity: (1) production and trade policy for the major export crops; (2) storage policy affecting feed grains, wheat, cotton, and some other storable crops; and (3) policy for other crops, which includes primarily the sugar and tobacco programs, and marketing agreements for fruits and vegetables.

IN THIS CHAPTER

1 You can learn how to appraise the social benefits and costs of alternatives facing the United States in production and trade policy for the major export crops.

2 You can learn the possible benefits and costs of selected alternatives in grain reserve-storage buffer-stock policy.

3 You can learn how to analyze the benefits and costs of the sugar and tobacco programs, and the use of marketing agreements for fruits and vegetables.

PRODUCTION AND TRADE POLICY FOR THE MAJOR EXPORT CROPS

Since the beginning of the 1980s, the United States has been exporting around $40 billion of crops and crop products annually, the most important of which are wheat and feed grains; soybeans; fruits, nuts, and vegetables; cotton; and tobacco. Exports have used about 60 to 70 percent of the wheat crop, 25 percent or more of the feed grains, about 60 percent of soybeans, at least 50 percent of the rice, 45 to 60 percent of the cotton, and more than 25 percent of the unmanufactured tobacco.[1]

---

[1] *1982 Handbook of Agricultural Charts,* U.S. Department of Agriculture, 1982, p. 59

Policy Alternatives and Options

The United States has several policy options for these crops. One is to follow a policy of crop production at free-market prices, without production controls such as acreage allotments, paid land diversion, or marketing quotas. This was the policy before 1929, and during most of the 1970s. In the latter case, however, this was not by deliberate design, but primarily the result of strong export demand and market prices moving above price-support levels. A second option is to try to support crop prices above free-market equilibrium levels by means of production controls, with subsidies to clear the markets of the commodities that are important in export trade. This was the dominant policy during most of the post–World War II years, up to 1964. A third option is to subsidize producers by means of direct payments, largely to displace price supports, as in the Wheat-Cotton Act of 1964. Or direct payments may be used to supplement price supports, by filling the gap between nonrecourse loan rates and target prices, as has been provided for in the major acts of the 1970s and 1980s. Finally, a fourth option is to control crop production more stringently with the idea of raising domestic prices well above export levels, in which case the United States would give up a large share of the export market, or be forced to heavily subsidize exporters.

In regard to the export market itself, the United States has options of (1) continuing to push for freer world trade, which so far has been most elusive for agricultural products; (2) placing more emphasis on reciprocal trade agreements, such as the grain export agreement with the Soviet Union; or (3) entering into a grain export cartel with other major exporting countries, which would require the United States to be more protectionist in regard to major domestic industries, including agriculture. A fourth, somewhat more farsighted option, is to place more emphasis on economic development programs in other countries, which in the longer term is a way of expanding the demand for agricultural products, including products from the United States.

Policy Values and Goals in Farm Programs

What values to emphasize and what goals to pursue involve arguments which go to the basic roots of agricultural policy. Traditionally, the goal of increasing productivity and expanding output has been fundamental, and the growth of exports is one example of evidence of the success of this policy. Why then should the U.S. government be involved in paying for programs to take land out of crops for the purpose of decreasing output? Why should the government subsidize exporters if this raises domestic food prices and antagonizes other governments? Why should the government distribute direct payments to producers to get them to comply with crop-reducing programs, if these payments are distributed not according to welfare concepts of need, but according to the size and yields of farmers' acreage allotments?

The concepts of farm income support are fundamental. In the past, voluntary acreage reduction has offered as a reward only eligibility for price-support loans and some deficiency payments to bring returns up to the target price-support levels. If markets strengthen, there is no further reward to participants. Hence this kind of program is self-limiting. Then, paid diversion appears somewhat more attractive. In such payment transactions, it makes little real difference whether the payment is in cash, or whether it is a payment in kind (PIK). Under a PIK, it may seem that the government is getting ride of excess stocks and controlling costs. But if the stocks or the warehouse receipts under which the stocks may be claimed are negotiable, then there will be a transfer of wealth, the same as if cash were involved.

The policy goal of helping producers in the short run by reducing their output conflicts with the long-standing goal of government to increase the producers' production. But if the decision has been made to help producers, then there must be a transfer of income to producers from the government or consumers, or both. It is a proper concern of policy to consider how these costs may be allocated, and how the net costs may be minimized for government, for consumers, or for society in general.

Minimizing Costs to Government

With given supply curves, if the government wishes to minimize its cost in reaching a given level of support for producers, then it will follow a supply-reducing program for commodities having the most inelastic demands; and it will follow a demand-increasing program, perhaps with direct payments as a supplement to demand, for commodities sold under more elastic demands. Reducing output when demand is inelastic increases price relatively more than it reduces quantity, and where demand is more elastic, controlling output will have less effect on price. So, if minimizing costs to government is desired (say, for political reasons), when the goal is to increase farm income the government will reduce the domestic supply of wheat, cotton, and other products with inelastic demands in domestic markets. And it may use demand-increasing subsidies in export markets, where demand is thought to be more elastic.

This is the general principle of domestic production-control and export subsidies, which puts the real cost on consumers in the market, while limiting the costs to consumers in their role as taxpayers. A similar application underlies the classified pricing program in the market for dairy products, and in use of marketing agreements for commodities that have no close substitutes, such as some fruits, nuts, and vegetables.

Minimizing Costs to Consumers

If the policy goal is to increase farm incomes without raising costs to consumers, then the government will not use production controls but will simply pay producers directly. The government cannot carry out this policy without involving very large costs, unless increased output is also an important part of the policy goal. Increased output has generally not been a policy goal of most peacetime support programs, so most direct-payment programs also involve control of production.

When direct payments have been used, they most often have been employed to displace price supports, as in the Wheat-Cotton Act of 1964, which authorized payments to producers and control of production in the domestic market, with market prices allowed to drop close to competitive levels in export markets.

We can readily see how to reduce costs to government, or to consumers. But if government support of farm income is an accepted policy, the most important question is how to minimize total cost in terms of the real costs to society. All production-control programs involve a net social cost due to the waste of resources, or the products foregone. Let us discuss how costs may be visualized.

Net Social Cost of Price Support with Production Control

Net social cost of a program is defined as the budgetary cost to government (taxpayer cost), plus the value of production foregone (consumer cost), minus the benefit to producers.

It can be said that all production-control programs involve a net social cost that results from idling resources (mainly land), and loss of the product foregone. We can visualize the net social cost by using diagrams of supply and demand, but we cannot measure it exactly as in an econometric model, because it is almost impossible to estimate what outputs and prices would have been in the absence of programs. In view of the more than 50 years of federal production-control programs, starting with the Agricultural Adjustment Act of 1933, one simply cannot say what the crops economy would be like today if we had not had acreage allotments and land-retirement programs, or how the other economies of agriculture would have been affected.

Difficulty of Analyzing Production Control   Even a short-term analysis of programs, such as the 1983 programs for wheat and corn, raises difficult analytical issues. For one thing, the short-term effects of price enhancement and deficiency payments tend to be output-increasing, under a given supply curve, while acreage reduction and land diversion tend to shift the supply curve backward, or to the left. But, unless the elasticity of substitution between land and nonland resources is zero, idling a certain percentage of the cropland base does not bring a corresponding reduction in output. Farmers tend to idle their poorest land, and to emphasize yield-increasing practices on the land cropped. Given a certain reduction in output, however, the net social cost depends on the elasticity of demand. Let us illustrate.[2]

Effects of Elasticity of Demand   In Figure 6-1, we illustrate how the net social cost of a price-support, production-control program is affected by the elasticity of demand. Diagrams (a) and (b) are assumed to have identical supply curves, while (a) has a very inelastic demand and (b) has a more elastic demand. If P_e is the initial equilibrium price and $\overline{P}$ is the support price, then to establish equilibrium at $\overline{P}$, production must be reduced much more in (b) than in (a). Correspondingly, the net social cost, which, in this case, results primarily from the idling of land, is much larger with the more elastic demand than with the very inelastic demand.

---

[2]For further discussion, see T. D. Wallace, "Measures of Social Costs of Agricultural Programs," *Journal of Farm Economics,* vol. 44, no. 2, May 1962, pp. 580–594; James P. Cavin, "Discussion," ibid., pp. 595–597; and Bruce L. Gardner, *The Governing of Agriculture,* The Regents Press of Kansas, Lawrence, 1981, pp. 131–135.

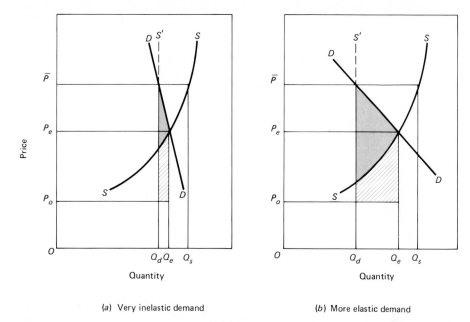

(a) Very inelastic demand (b) More elastic demand

Where: P_e = equilibrium market price

Q_e = quantity produced at market price

$\bar{P}$ = support price

Q_s = quantity supplied at support price without production control

Q_d = quantity demanded at support price $\bar{P}$

SS' = supply curve with supply control

P_o = assumed value of the diverted land in alternative use

Note: This assumes that supply control is completely effective at Q_d. If there were leakage or imperfection in the control, as tends to occur with acreage allotments, then the net social cost will be higher as the incentives for using other resources are distorted. In this case, the portion of $S'S$ above SS would not be vertical.

FIGURE 6-1
Net social cost of supply control with *(a)* very inelastic demand, and *(b)* more elastic demand.

In each diagram in Figure 6-1, the reduction of output from Q_e to Q_d eliminates products, the value of the products to consumers being the area under D between Q_e and Q_d. The resources that are released or idled have value in alternative uses equal to the area under S between Q_e and Q_d. Hence, the net social cost is the solid shaded triangle in (a) and (b) bounded by curve DD, curve SS, and SS'. In most programs, however, even where cross-compliance or offsetting compliance is not required, land may not be used in its best alternative use. If the best permitted uses of diverted resources yield benefits equal to P_o, then the net social costs of the program are increased, as shown in the diagonally shaded area, and the amount of cost added also corresponds to the differences in elasticity of demand.

As an example, the net social cost of production control is low for commodities such as tobacco, where demand is inelastic and trade is stabilized. But the net social costs are higher for feed grains, and for most commodities important in export trade. Let us consider the practical implication of this for conditions expected in the 1980s and 1990s.

Net Social Cost Related to Magnitude and Elasticity of Export Markets

Due to the growth of export markets and the greater elasticity of demand in these markets, the net social cost of production control will be much higher in the 1980s and 1990s than it was in previous decades. During the 1970s, when production controls were dropped, the volume of grain exported annually from the United States increased from around 40 million to about 120 million metric tons (Figure 6-2), and the volume of soybean exports increased from around 10 million to more than 30 million metric tons (Figure 6-3).

If we assume, as discussed in Chapter 4, the following estimate of the elasticity of export demand for corn (-1.31), sorghum (-2.36), and wheat (-1.67), then the

FIGURE 6-2
Total grain exports of major exporting countries, 1961–1982. (*Source: USDA*, Handbook of Agricultural Charts, and Agricultural Statistics, *various years.*)

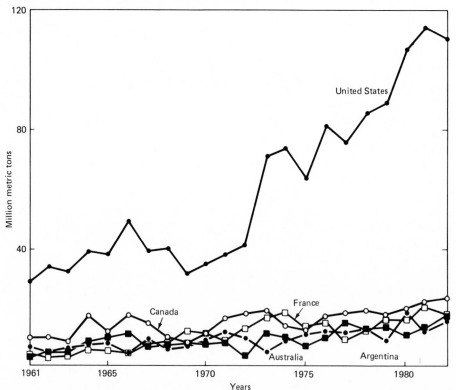

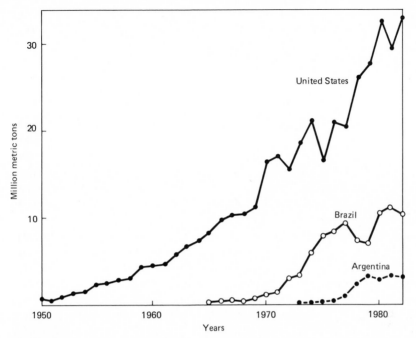

FIGURE 6-3
Total soybean exports of major exporting countries, 1961–1982. (*Source: USDA* Handbook of Agricultural Charts and Agricultural Statistics, *various years.*)

net social cost of a program that does not maintain exports at the free-market level will be very high, indeed. Production control of these commodities without corresponding export subsidies will reduce export earnings and the gross income of producers but raise costs to consumers and government. Furthermore, if price supports for soybeans raise domestic prices above world levels, the net social costs also could be high, due to the loss of export markets and the distortion of incentives in the United States and other countries.

Since 1933, cotton has largely shifted over the years from the free-trade model, where its elasticity of export demand is high, to a more restricted trade model, as far as the United States and other major producing countries are concerned. Since many importing countries do not grow cotton, the elasticity of price transmission is generally high for them, which suggests that the free-trade model has some relevance for exports from the United States. If this is so, then the net social cost of the cotton program is also very high for both producers *and* consumers in the United States.

Comparative Past and Future Net Social Cost of Production Control

Because of the increased volume and relative importance of export trade, the future net social cost of production-control programs for grains and soybeans will be much higher than in the past, while the already relatively high net social cost will be per-petuated by continuing production control on cotton. We cannot measure these social costs directly, for reasons previously mentioned. But we can visualize the compara-tive situations in various decades.

Net social costs of production control tend to be rather low when only the domes-tic market is concerned. In the 1920s and early 1930s, export demands were very weak. With passage of the Agricultural Adjustment Act of 1933, subsequent pro-grams dealt primarily with the domestic market, as agricultural exports dropped to zero by the end of the 1930s. Because of the very inelastic demand for total agricul-tural production in the domestic market, the net social cost was small, as the pro-grams, in essence, transferred income to producers from taxpayers and consumers. In the 1950s, relatively weak production controls under the soil bank program had relatively little effect on total production, and this was largely offset in export mar-kets by use of Public Law 480.

In the 1960s, under the Kennedy policy, more effective production controls trans-ferred more income to producers by means of price supports and government pay-ments. Again, the effects of the program on exports may have been neutralized mainly through more support for Public Law 480 and subsidies for exports in the major commercial markets. Under the Wheat-Cotton Act of 1964, direct payments largely substituted for price supports, and this, combined with Public Law 480, tended to neutralize the effects of the programs in export markets. Similarly, under the Emergency Feed Grain Act of 1961, exports of feed grains were stabilized, with the aid of subsidies, when needed. Soybeans did not require export subsidies because price supports were not involved.

In the future, if production controls are effective in raising prices of grains and soybeans above world market-equilibrium levels, then either (1) there will be a sub-stantial loss of exports, and reduction in gross market receipts by producers, or (2) relatively large appropriations will be required to stabilize exports. There would need to be a very low elasticity of price transmission for these results not to occur. As we have discussed, this would require importing nations to be largely insensitive to sup-port prices in the United States. This, we assume, is generally not the case.

The cost of export subsidy for grains and soybeans could be large. For instance, if grain exports were to be maintained at 120 million tons annually—say, half wheat and half feed grains—this would be the equivalent of about 4.56 billion bushels.[3] Then, for each 10 cents per bushel that domestic prices were held above world prices, an added subsidy of $456 million would be required. A domestic price at 50 cents per bushel above the world price would cost $2.28 billion in export subsidy for grains alone, not counting the costs of acreage allotments and land diversion. Failure to provide this subsidy would cause producers substantial loss in market receipts from production control.

---

[3]See the Glossary for a summary of weights, measures, and conversion factors used by the U.S. Department of Agriculture.

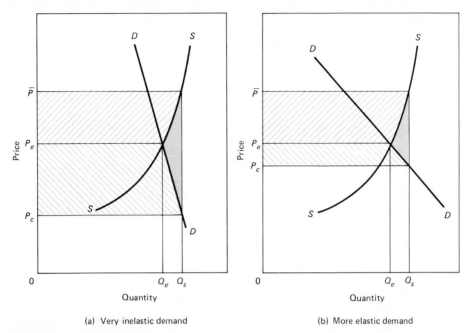

(a) Very inelastic demand   (b) More elastic demand

FIGURE 6-4
Net social cost of payments to producers and no production control with *(a)* very inelastic demand and *(b)* more elastic demand.

Direct Payments and Supplements to Demand

Under given conditions of supply and demand, producers are better off with demand-increasing rather than supply-reducing programs. The net social cost will depend on the elasticity of demand, as in the case of production-control programs, and also on the elasticity of supply above the free-market equilibrium level. These principles are illustrated in Figure 6-4.

The original supply and demand curves in Figure 6-4 are identical to those in Figure 6-1. Also, the level of support at $\overline{P}$ is the same as $\overline{P}$ in Figure 6-1, but this support in Figure 6-4 is realized either (1) by paying producers the differences between $\overline{P}$ and the price at the farm level corresponding to prices paid by consumers or (2) by using a combination of direct payments and supplements to demand. In Figure 6-4, the guarantee of $\overline{P}$ without production control results in the production of Q_s. When the commodity is placed on the market, the equivalent farm price paid by consumers is P_c. Deficiency payments are $(\overline{P} - P_c) \times Q_s$, as producers are subsidized on a basis of total output. With unrestricted production, the support level at $\overline{P}$ creates additional economic rents—returns above those necessary to attract resources into production—equal to the hatched area above P_e and bounded on the right by SS. The availability of the quantity Q_s at the price P_c instead of P_e results in gains to consumers—increase in consumers' surplus—equal to the lower hatched area bounded on the right by DD. The net social loss is equal to the triangle bounded by SS, DD, and Q_s, which is the difference between the large rectangle representing government payments and the sum of the gains to consumers and producers.

Effects of Elasticity of Demand on Net Social Cost

With equal gains to producers in (a) and (b) of Figure 6-4, the net social cost is higher for the commodity in the market with the inelastic demand in (a) than it is for the commodity in the market with a more elastic demand in (b). In contrast, in Figure 6-1 the net social cost was greater for the more elastic demand.

The general inference is that, if the government wishes to minimize the cost of reaching a given level of support for producers, then it will follow a supply-reducing program for commodities having the most inelastic demands, and it will follow a direct-payments program for commodities sold under more elastic demands. This was the principle initially followed by proponents of the McNary-Haugen bills, to control supply in the domestic market where demand was inelastic, and use demand-increasing subsidies in the export market, where demand would be more elastic. A similar application underlies the classified pricing program in the market for dairy products, and in use of marketing agreements for commodities that have no close substitutes, such as some fruits, nuts, and vegetables. This was also the principle of the Wheat-Cotton Act of 1964, which authorized payments to producers and control of production in the domestic market, with market prices being allowed to drop close to competitive levels in export markets.

It is, however, unrealistic to assume that the government will provide direct payments as large as those implied in (a) of Figure 6-4, or allow consumer prices to fall as low as P_c on the same graph. Therefore, direct payments are almost invariably accompanied by production controls, and the incentive for the government to control production is also stronger where demand is inelastic. Where small reductions in consumer prices bring large increases in consumption, as in (b) of Figure 6-4, production controls are not nearly so cost-saving for the government. That is, where a commodity has a close substitute or has a very elastic demand, the most beneficial program for producers will be a system of direct payments without a reduction in production.

Effects of Elasticity of Supply on Net Social Cost

Under either price supports or direct payments, the incentive to control production increases as the elasticity of supply increases, regardless of the elasticity of demand. This is illustrated in Figure 6-5, where in both diagram (a) and (b) the social cost is greater with the more elastic supply S_e (the hatched area plus the shaded area below S_e) than it is with the very inelastic supply S_i (the shaded area below S_i). With price support or payment at $\overline{P}$, the price paid by consumers falls much lower (P_{ce}) when supply is elastic than when supply is inelastic (P_{ci}).

Since the elasticity of supply varies directly with the time allowed for production

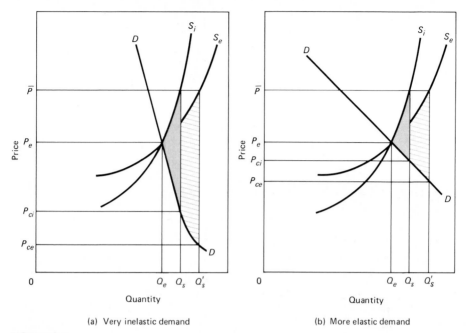

FIGURE 6-5
Joint effects of elasticity of supply and demand on net social cost.

adjustments, the incentive to control production varies directly with the age of the program. Because of this, either price supports or direct payments cannot be maintained for very long, or at significantly high levels, without involving the incentive to control production. Where commodities are important in export trade, export subsidies must be combined with production controls, to maintain the incomes of producers.

More General Inferences for Policy

Since any price support or payment level above a free-market equilibrium creates the same cost of production over a certain period of time, both the supply-reducing and the demand-increasing programs are of only short-term benefit to producers. Although neither program alone can be expected to be supported very long, because one creates a situation requiring the other, the economic interests of agriculture, as well as the general public interest, will be served much more effectively by emphasizing demand-increasing and trade-expanding programs, rather than supply-reducing programs.

Major emphasis on supply-reducing programs, such as in the wheat and feed-grain programs cited above, are undoubtedly a mistake in the strict economic sense, except as short-term emergency measures to regulate the growth of the grain reserve.

These programs will limit the growth of the export market, unless export subsidies are used liberally to fully offset the price-enhancing effects of price supports above world-market prices.

In addition, the emphasis on using land as the sole means of implementing production controls inevitably raises the real cost of production. Restricting the supply of land tends to raise its price, while raising the prices of products increases the demand for all inputs, including land. The joint effect of all this is to distort agricultural incentives and reduce the efficiency of agricultural production while limiting the growth of markets, most especially the export market. How to counteract this with more modest programs, while still maintaining the economic health of agriculture, is the challenge for the future. For this purpose, let us next consider the role of grain-reserve storage policy.

ALTERNATIVES IN GRAIN-RESERVE BUFFER-STOCK POLICY

Stabilizing farm and food prices is generally accepted as the major policy goal of grain reserves held as buffer stocks, the general thesis being that this goal can be approached by increasing stocks in good crop years if prices are low, and reducing stocks in poor crop years if prices are high. If this is done, then storage can operate as an "ever-normal granary," an idea widely popularized by Henry A. Wallace, secretary of agriculture in President Franklin D. Roosevelt's cabinet in the 1930s.

Over the years since the popularization of this concept, the Commodity Credit Corporation (CCC) has implemented a storage program, with the largest stocks amassed and the greatest effects on price stability occurring in the 1950s and 1960s. Although these stocks were accumulated as a consequence of price-support programs, rather than under a specific goal of buffer stocks for price stability, the effect in the 1950s and 1960s was to narrow the range of price fluctuations for both wheat and the feed grains. Greater price stability in the feed-grain economy apparently also contributed to price stability in the livestock economy. In the early 1970s, the CCC stocks were sold during the initial surge of export demand, which began with increased sales to the Soviet Union. For several years thereafter, in the absence of CCC stocks, prices of grain and livestock were more variable. In the early 1980s, rapid accumulation of stocks indicated that price supports were above market-equilibrium levels. To the extent that this accumulation raised prices and restricted exports, it created a more difficult problem for price-support programs in the balance of the 1980s.

The Case for Price-Stabilization Policy in the Crops Economy

A prime area for governmental activity in the public interest in a free-enterprise economy is stabilization policy. The best argument for government use of CCC stocks for this purpose is that this will provide insurance against extreme shortfalls in crop production that might otherwise force expensive adjustments on producers and on consumers as well. The reduction in price variability will help grain producers to reduce risk and produce more efficiently, primarily because they can estimate probable returns from production choices more accurately. More stable grain prices will help stabilize production and prices in the livestock economy, because this helps livestock producers to estimate their costs more accurately. Also, more dependable grain supplies and stable prices in the United States will encourage the long-range development of commercial grain exports that are wanted by both the government and grain producers. Finally, reducing the variability in retail food prices, which may be accomplished in part by use of buffer stocks, is a benefit of particular interest to consumers.

Although it is very difficult to trace the effects of grain reserves on retail food prices, the possible benefits to producers of an effective buffer-stock program can be visualized by looking at prices in the 1970s, when CCC stocks were low or nonexistent (Table 6-1). In this case, the variations in prices were very wide. If these were accurately predicted from one planting season to the next, then producers would be forced to make relatively expensive adjustments. If prices are not predictable as a general rule, then producers will continue without much change in their plans from one year to the next. Producers of corn and soybeans have experienced a rather wide range of prices, such as is summarized in Table 6-1. Producers of wheat and cotton have tended to face even wider price fluctuations from year to year, as shown in Table 6-2.

Prior to planting, producers may use the commodity futures market to establish a definite price at harvest by selling a contract for future delivery. But since cash prices will rise or fall between the time the contract price is set and the product is delivered, there is generally no assurance that it will be advantageous to a producer to sell a contract. Consequently, only a small minority of grain producers use the futures market for this purpose. In the absence of a buffer-stock program, prices of the major crops will continue to fluctuate within relatively wide ranges, and the effects this has on producers are only partially offset by the types of price-support

TABLE 6-1

LOW, HIGH, AND AVERAGE MONTHLY PRICES OF CORN AND SOYBEANS PER BUSHEL

(Figures for East Central Illinois, for Crop Years 1973 to 1981)

Year*	Corn (dollars/bushel)			Soybeans (dollars/bushel)		
	Low	High	Average	Low	High	Average
1973	$2.25	$3.50	$2.82	$5.48	$7.79	$6.11
1974	2.72	3.70	3.02	5.15	7.54	6.12
1975	2.40	2.88	2.64	4.38	6.64	5.33
1976	1.66	2.44	2.20	5.36	9.66	7.23
1977	1.74	2.50	2.18	5.02	7.04	6.25
1978	2.08	2.94	2.46	6.69	7.71	7.16
1979	2.42	3.28	2.66	5.73	8.15	6.58
1980	2.55	3.46	3.25	6.24	8.87	7.48
1981	2.31	2.78	2.60	5.45	6.58	6.21

*Year beginning October 1 for corn and September 1 for soybeans.
Source: Agricultural Economics Reference Room, University of Illinois, Urbana-Champaign.

TABLE 6-2
LOW, HIGH, AND AVERAGE MONTHLY PRICES OF WHEAT PER BUSHEL AND
COTTON PER POUND
(Figures for the United States, Calendar Years 1973 to 1981)

Year	All wheat dollars/bushel			Cotton lint, upland cents/lb.		
	Low	High	Average*	Low	High	Average*
1973	$1.97	$4.78	$3.95	22.4c	47.6c	44.4c
1974	3.52	5.52	4.09	43.8	54.9	42.7
1975	2.92	4.11	3.56	32.6	49.9	51.1
1976	2.39	3.66	2.73	50.5	68.8	63.8
1977	2.03	2.47	2.33	48.7	70.1	52.1
1978	2.53	3.04	2.97	49.1	61.1	58.1
1979	2.97	3.98	3.78	53.5	61.9	63.1
1980	3.58	4.32	3.91	60.9	80.9	74.4
1981	3.62	4.21	3.65	51.2	72.7	54.5

*Refers to crop or designated year, and includes an allowance for unredeemed govenment
loans and purchases.

Source: For 1973–75, Agricultural Prices Annual Summary 1978, wheat, p. 27; cotton, p. 35.
For 1976–81, Agricultural Prices Annual Summary 1981, wheat, pp. 34 and 42: cotton, pp. 29
and 45.

and payment programs we have discussed. Since 1977, agricultural acts have provided for relatively modest buffer stocks for some of the major commodities. It is
important therefore to consider the general concepts and rules that may be applied.

Concepts of Buffer-Stock Programs

Buffer-stock programs are generally conceived as a means of stabilizing agricultural
supply in the face of fluctuating crop production, and therefore also a means of stabilizing prices of major crops at the farm level, and, consequently, retail food prices
as well. The implication is that such programs can provide gains for both producers
and consumers. In the case of producers, over several years' time total revenue
derived from a given total production will be larger if the quantity supplied is stabilized, providing demand is more elastic at high prices than at low prices. That is,
two crops of average size will sell for more than one large and one small one, ceteris
paribus. Although not all agricultural demand curves fulfill this condition, it is
believed that a number of them do, and this may be especially important in respect
to the export market. Stabilizing the export supply curve under conditions of
fluctuating crop harvests will not only increase aggregate market receipts, given a
demand that is more elastic at high prices than at low prices, but also will tend to
increase importing countries' demand for these exports over several years, because
they are assured of a stable export supply from the United States.

In the case of domestic consumers, the utility of a given total quantity supplied
over several years should be higher under stable prices. Although consumers may
gain from food-price instability from season to season over the course of a year, it

may be practically impossible for them to gain from price instability from one year to the next. Even though food prices might average somewhat higher if the export demand were enhanced by price stability, consumers would gain from increased foreign-exchange earnings by the United States. On balance, therefore, both consumers and producers stand to gain from a buffer-stock program.

If the buffer-stock program is financed out of federal tax revenue, then it will constitute a general tax cost, and the marginal benefits of price stability as compared with the marginal cost of such a program will determine the optimum buffer-stock program. What general principles determine the optimum size of the buffer stock? Theoretically speaking, storage can increase the general welfare only if the discounted value of the storage stocks in some future year, minus the real costs of storage facilities, is higher in that year than it is at present. Using this principle to determine the optimal stockpiling of grain in a closed economy, R. L. Gustafson demonstrated several years ago that the optimal carryover beyond normal "pipeline" stocks is zero when the available supply of grain is below a certain critical level, and increases to between zero and +1.0, the latter being the maximum storage possible, when the quantity supplied rises to that critical level.[4] Since then, the reserves required to achieve a given level of supply or price stability have been estimated for the United States, with the maximum storage required generally falling within the levels of stocks carried by the CCC in the 1950s and 1960s.[5] A systems analysis of grain reserves by David J. Eaton has shown that a significant degree of food stability and security can be achieved by world stocks on the order of, for instance, 20 to 40 million metric tons (mmt), and with free trade, almost complete supply stability could be achieved by stocks reaching a maximum of 100 mmt.[6]

Management Rules for Buffer Stocks

A buffer-stock management rule may be based either on quantity or on price; each has a practical or intuitive appeal. One of the first operational rules based on quantity was suggested by William H. Nicholls, whose paper was awarded first prize in an essay contest sponsored by the American Farm Economics Association.[7] The proposed storage policy for cotton, corn, wheat, and oats was:

[4]R. L. Gustafson, *Carryover Levels for Grains,* U.S. Department of Agriculture, Technical Bulletin no. 1178, October 1958.

[5]See, for example, *Analysis of Grain Reserves, A Proceedings,* compiled by David J. Eaton and W. Scott Steele, Economic Research Service, U.S. Department of Agriculture, in cooperation with the National Science Foundation. Economic Research Service Report no. 634, August 1976. See also Bruce L. Gardner, *Optimal Stockpiling of Grain,* D. C. Heath Co., Lexington, Massachusetts, 1979.

[6]David J. Eaton, *A Systems Analysis of Grain Reserves,* U.S. Department of Agriculture, Economics and Statistics Service, Technical Bulletin no. 1611, January 1980. For further theoretical analysis, see Keith C. Knapp, "Optimal Grain Carryovers in Open Economies: A Graphical Analysis," *American Journal of Agricultural Economics,* vol. 64, no. 2, May 1982, pp. 197–204; and Peter G. Helmberger, Robert D. Weaver, and Kathleen T. Haygood, "Rational Expectations and Competitive Pricing and Storage," ibid., pp. 266–270.

[7]William H. Nicholls, "A Price Policy for Agriculture, Consistent with Economic Progress, That Will Promote Adequate and More Stable Income from Farming," *Journal of Farm Ecomomics,* vol. 27, November 1945, pp. 737–756.

that, for each storable commodity, Congress should designate (1) an operating range in terms of specific minimum and maximum carryovers; (2) five-year moving averages of production as the criteria of storage policy within this range; and (3) specific percentages of the excess of actual production above (or the deficit below) this average by which year-end total stocks, private and public, would be increased (or diminished) by CCC operations.[8]

When, in any year, the actual production of (say) cotton exceeds the five-year moving average ending with that year, the corporation should purchase sufficient cotton so that the aggregate increase in stocks, public and private (including stocks under loan), equals (say) 60 percent of the excess of actual production over the average. Conversely, when actual production falls short of the moving average, the corporation should sell that amount necessary to decrease total stocks by (say) 60 percent of the production deficit.[9]

Under this rule, over a period of years when cotton production was gradually rising, stocks would rise too, but not to the extent of the amount of increase in production, and supply would be somewhat stabilized. For corn, the proposed change in carryover equaled 75 percent of the difference between the actual production and the moving average, when the latter was larger; thus, unless the carryover were already at the minimum, the change would provide a heavy counterweight to a single bad-crop year in the corn belt. If actual production were larger than the five-year average, only 50 percent of the difference would go into storage, thus minimizing the increase in stocks that would otherwise occur during several years of strong upward trends in production. For wheat, and oats, the proposed rule for change in carryover was 75 percent of the difference between actual production and the five-year moving average production. Suggested operating ranges were set at 150 to 850 million bushels for corn, 100 to 400 million for wheat, and 100 to 350 million for oats. In a bad-crop year, stocks would not be drawn down below the minimum by government action nor would they be raised above the maximum in a good crop year.

If we were to adapt the proposal of Nicholls to the production levels foreseen for 1985 to 2000, then the physical limits would need to be approximately doubled. This is well within the available storage capacity in the United States, and hence such a program could be carried out. Although the United States could use such a quantity rule, or could adopt a price rule, with the CCC taking over all free stocks if prices fell to certain minimum levels and the CCC selling when prices reached a designated ceiling, neither rule would be very successful without something being done to help stabilize exports. The United States may use export subsidies to stabilize exports, or to negotiate with other countries in the interests of reaching an export goal, but the rule to follow in storage is critical.

The government has used a price rule rather than a quantity rule in carrying out a buffer-stock storage policy. That is, increases and decreases in storage stocks are determined by the relationship between price-support loan rates and market prices, rather than by the size of the crop, be it large or small. Under certain conditions, the price rule will help as well as a quantity rule to stabilize the grain supply available for domestic use and export. From 1975 to 1979, for instance, increases in year-

[8] *Ibid.*, p. 752.
[9] *Ibid.*, p. 747.

TABLE 6-3
TOTAL U.S. GRAIN PRODUCTION, 1975–1982

Year*	Production†	Domestic use	Exports	Ending stocks	Food grains	Feed grains and hay
	Million metric tons (mmt)				Index of prices received 1967 = 100	
1975	249.1	155.6	84.5	37.1	242	230
1976	258.1	153.9	79.4	62.1	202	218
1977	265.8	163.2	90.2	74.8	156	181
1978	276.5	182.4	96.1	72.9	191	184
1979	302.9	184.9	112.5	78.5	229	207
1980	267.9	170.5	113.7	62.1	257	239
1981	331.1	179.7	109.5	104.5	259	255
1982	337.0	183.5	103.2	155.2	227	217

*Year beginning October 1 for corn and sorghum; June 1 for oats, barley, wheat, and rye; and August 1 for rice.
†Imports are omitted because they are negligible, averaging less than 0.5 mmt per year.
Source: Agricultural Statistics 1981, U.S. Department of Agriculture, Washington, D.C., 1981, pp. 1 and 450; *World Agricultural Supply and Demand Estimates,* WASDE-195, February 14, 1983, U.S. Department of Agriculture; *Agricultural Prices,* U.S. Department of Agriculture, various issues, 1982.

ending stocks, which were based on significant declines in the index of prices received by farmers for food grains and feed grains, helped to offset increases in production above the long-term trend. In 1980, a decrease in stocks helped to offset about half of the deficit in production of a poor-crop year (Table 6-3).

During the period from 1975 to 1980, had there been a stricter rule based on quantity produced, and account taken of exports and the crop outlook during the growing season, supply would also have stabilized, and allowed prices to clear the market, after decisions concerning storage had been made. In 1981 and 1982, increases in loan rates, based on the 1981 act, brought a rapid accumulation of stocks. These loan rates restricted exports, just when an increase in exports was required to absorb the large crops. This in turn created a basis for the payment-in-kind (PIK) programs begun in 1983.

The storage program based on the price rule tends to be destabilizing. In years of good crops, the accumulation of stocks tends to be excessively large, as in 1976, 1981, and 1982. A program based on the price rule prevents prices from moving soon enough to allow expansion of exports in years of good crops. Between 1975 and 1976, exports decreased by 5.1 million metric tons (mmt). Year-ending stocks increased by 25.0 mmt, even though production was only 9.0 mmt more than in 1975. Based on a quantity rule, stocks would have increased only 6 or 7 mmt and prices would have moved more quickly to clear the market. In 1980, the decrease in stocks was perhaps 10 mmt smaller than would have been programmed under an appropriate quantity rule. As a result, grain prices rose rapidly, while domestic use declined, and exports did not increase as they might have with a smaller price increase. These conditions continued in 1981 and 1982, with the effect of price supports compounded by the embargo on grain shipments to the Soviet Union.

The acceptance of an appropriate quantity rule for storage is, of course, contrary to the long-standing political experience with farm organizations and the subsequent rules followed by Congress. In the future, perhaps more can be done to help stabilize export demand, as well as supply. Unless a quantity rule is adopted, at least to modify, if not displace, the price rules that have been followed, it is not likely that the government will be any more successful in stabilizing grain prices in the future than it has been in the past. With growth of the export market, the benefits to be gained by such a rule have increased. Hence, it may be politically expedient to have a more rational storage policy in the future, and policy for the major export commodities may be coordinated with that for other crops.

POLICY ALTERNATIVES FOR OTHER CROPS

Government programs for tobacco, sugar, and certain fruits and vegetables are important in policy analysis. Although consumer protection and abundant supplies are frequently mentioned as policy goals, most programs are designed primarily to aid producers by managing supply, the policy goal being to stabilize prices somewhat above the equilibrium prices that would prevail in freely competitive markets. The concept of an inelastic demand is a common rationale for most programs, which tends to make the control of supply beneficial to producers in the short run. Also, since short-run supply is inelastic, changes in supply or demand will bring wide fluctuations in price.

Tobacco Policy Alternatives

Since 1934, acreage allotments and price supports have been used continuously for tobacco, sometimes combined with marketing quotas, to raise prices to growers, perhaps as much as one-third (and sometimes more) over what they would be otherwise. Since the early 1950s (when per capita consumption of tobacco was at its peak), the total acreage harvested has been reduced by more than one-half. Total production has been cut by only about one-fourth, however, as yields have risen. Per capita consumption has declined by about one-third. About three-fourths of the crop is used domestically, and the rest is exported.

Since the domestic demand for tobacco is very inelastic, the program increases returns to growers, as income is transferred from consumers to the growers. Because of inelastic demand and effective control over production at relatively low government cost, the net social cost of the program tends to be very low. But the program is often criticized as providing an unnecessary subsidy to the tobacco industry, as conflicting with public health efforts to reduce tobacco consumption, and as failing to solve the problems of low incomes among the small-scale tobacco producers. The benefits of the program are reflected as an economic rent to owners of allotments, with the larger owners getting the most benefit, while long-term average costs of production rise to reach equilibrium with the higher prices. Although manufacturers must pay higher prices for tobacco than they would in a free market, these costs are passed on to consumers through oligopoly pricing of the final products, which are differentiated by brand name and advertising.

It also may be said that if reduced consumption is a valid social objective, then the higher prices passed on to consumers are a social benefit of the program. Greater stability of income among growers and the reduction of acreage used for tobacco is a further benefit. Although the program may not "solve the problems of low incomes" of smaller farmers, it does give them considerable protection. In fact, smaller producers are probably more sheltered in growing tobacco than in any other product. The smooth functioning of the program at small cost to government may be regarded as the reason why the program has been continued for such a long time, and why it may continue without much change in the future. How does this compare with some of the other programs?

Sugar Policy Alternatives

The United States sugar policy—like the program for tobacco—has been designed primarily to help domestic industry, and in so doing it imposes higher costs on consumers. In contrast to tobacco, however, the continental United States has never enjoyed a comparative advantage in production of sugar, the cheapest natural source of sugar being sugarcane grown in tropical areas. Under free trade perhaps as little as one-fifth of the sugar consumed would be produced in the continental United States, but in recent years, more than 60 percent of the total supply has been grown here. Also, because of restrictions obtained by sugar refiners on importing refined sugar, practically all of the sugar consumed in the continental United States has been refined here.

The domestic sugar industry is a product of a long-continuing policy of protection. Prior to 1934 there was a tariff of $2\frac{1}{2}$ cents per pound on imported raw sugar. But in 1934, industry representatives were successful in getting more protection under the Jones-Costigan Act. From 1934 to 1974, a system of quotas was used to govern the supply of sugar from all sources, foreign and domestic, according to a formula established by Congress. The secretary of agriculture was mandated to determine the overall size of the quota prior to each year, and to allocate quotas according to this formula. Prices received by domestic producers were supplemented by direct payments financed from a tariff of 0.625 cents per pound on imported raw sugar. This assured that domestic producers would fulfill their quotas, and holding domestic prices above world prices assured that foreign countries would fulfill their quotas. Domestic refiners, as we said, were protected by restrictions on imports of refined sugar.

Estimates of the cost to domestic consumers of sugar under this program have varied from about $800 million to over $1.0 billion annually, more than what the cost of the same amount of sugar would have been under free trade. But the benefits to producers have been largely eroded because average costs of production have risen to equal the average price plus government payments.[10] During the 40 years from 1934 to 1974, industry representatives argued that the program provided an assured

---

[10]For further discussion, see D. Gale Johnson, *The United States Sugar Program: Large Costs and Small Benefits,* The American Enterprise Institute, Washington, D.C., 1974.

supply of sugar to domestic consumers and protected them from occasionally higher prices that might occur under a policy of free trade. But in 1974, when world sugar prices exploded as a result of a few poor crops, the domestic prices went right up with the world price. The program of quotas and subsidies proved worthless as an assurance of a stable supply. Subsequently, Congress let the program lapse, and efforts to reinstate it were defeated in 1977 and in 1981. But in 1976, the tariff on sugar imports had been tripled; and in 1982, partial reimposition of quotas made sugar the most highly protected of all crops.

The Agriculture and Food Act of 1981 provided for price supports on raw cane sugar initially at 16.75 cents per pound, increasing annually to reach 18 cents per pound for the 1985–86 crop year. This provided not only a support for cane and beet sugar, but also a price umbrella for high-fructose corn syrup (HFCS), which in 1980 had about 15 percent of the total caloric sweetener market. Based on projected demand for HFCS, the use of corn for this purpose would rise from about 127 million bushels in 1980 to about 245 million bushels in 1990 (the latter equivalent to 3.7 percent of the 1980 corn crop).[11]

Our general policy conclusion is that the tariff on imported raw sugar and restricting imports of refined sugar imposes additional costs on consumers that are not offset by corresponding benefits to producers. The costs of producing sugarcane and sugar beets in the continental United States tend to rise to the support levels plus payments, as farmers integrate these crops into their farming systems. Although a sugar contract with a refiner tends to be a good enterprise for most growers, it is generally not excessively profitable, and any profits above those necessary to attract growers are mainly of short-term benefit to only a few thousand producers. Protection of the sugar industry is a factor in development of the high-fructose corn-syrup industry, but the limits to development of this industry seem to be defined rather clearly. The net effect is the establishment of a domestic sugar industry at relatively high cost which is sustained politically by a demonstrably effective sugar lobby. Limits to the program and subsidy are probably not defined so much by economic criteria, however, as they are by the political interaction of producer and refiner groups and their PACs on the one side, and the growing consumer interests and their PACs on the other. An inelastic demand for sugar creates great political pressure from both growers and refiners for restriction of imports, and a specific price support, as we mentioned above, almost assures that the government will be involved in storage of surplus sugar, the value of which to consumers is most difficult to substantiate.

Marketing Agreements and Orders in Markets for Fruits and Vegetables

Agreements and orders have been used extensively to regulate the marketing of fruits and vegetables, as a supplement to competitive markets rather than as a substitute

---

[11]See Hoy F. Carman, "A Trend Projection of High Fructose Corn Syrup Substitution for Sugar," *American Journal of Agricultural Economics,* vol. 64, no. 4, November 1982, pp. 625–633.

for them. An *agreement* is a voluntary statement of understanding between the secretary of agriculture and the handlers of a commodity that covers certain marketing rules and regulations. An *order* is a binding commitment covering all those operating in a specified market.

To establish an order, a proposal is generally developed at the request of industry representatives, discussed in various industry groups, and reviewed in the Department of Agriculture. Public hearings are held to hear evidence and arguments for or against the proposal. If the results appear to be favorable and consistent with the purposes of the Marketing Agreement Act and have substantial industry support, a proposed order may be submitted to a vote by producers.

Each order establishes an administrative organization and specifies the controls to be used and other regulations to be followed, including the mechanics of operation. For each order a control board, appointed by the secretary of agriculture from nominees chosen by the industry, acts as an intermediary between the secretary and the industry, works up regulations, and recommends them to the secretary for issuance as an order. For some programs a second committee, composed largely of handlers, serves in an advisory capacity and furnishes information on marketing conditions. The control board selects a program manager and staff to collect information and report alleged violations for possible enforcement action, collects assessments, and disburses monies to pay expenses of the program.

General Provisions of Orders for Fruits, Nuts, and Vegetables

An order for a fruit, nut, or vegetable may permit or provide for any one or all of the following:

1 Specifying grades, size, quality, or maturity of the commodity that handlers may ship to market
2 Allotting the amount which each handler may purchase or handle on behalf of any and all producers
3 Establishing the quantity of the commodity that may be shipped to market during any specified period
4 Establishing methods for determining the extent of any surplus, for control and disposition of the surplus, and for equalizing the burden of surplus elimination among producers and handlers
5 Establishing a reserve pool of the product
6 Inspecting the commodity
7 Fixing of the size, capacity, weight, dimensions, or pack, of the container used in handling of the commodity.

In addition, a major component of many orders provides for funding of research and promotion, primarily the latter, by means of a check-off, which is equivalent to a small sales tax on the commodity covered by the order. The major policy goal of this is to expand the market for the commodity, or increase its demand. Research may be directed toward finding new markets or improving the quality of the commodity.

Some orders give considerable emphasis to "orderly marketing" to avoid waste through shipping uniform products. Standardizing grades, containers, etc., is an acceptable protection for consumers, providing such standardization does not become overly restrictive, as has occurred in a few orders. In some orders, provisions may authorize actions to prohibit certain unfair trade practices in interstate commerce, or to coordinate federal orders with those of individual states. Although controls over marketing vary among the states, in general the states with enabling legislation do not attempt to control the volume of supplies going to market, but limit their activity to quality, size, or pack regulation, to control of advertising and sales promotion, and to support of research and investigation. The federal legislation, however, is very comprehensive in terms of the commodities to which it applies, and the marketing rules and regulations it covers. Fruits and vegetables for processing are only two of many exclusions made at the request of industry groups. Enforcement of sanitary and other standards for consumer protection is not, of course, dependent on the existence of an agreement or order.

Marketing agreements and orders were first authorized in the Agricultural Adjustment Act of 1933, at which time many producers and marketing firms looked upon them as temporary devices to boost farm prices and incomes in the great depression. Later they were regarded more as aids in dealing with marketing problems through good as well as bad times. The Marketing Agreements Act of 1937 put them on a more regular basis and served as the parent legislation for succeeding amendments. In the early years, control over volume was stressed, but in later years, less than one-third of the orders employed volume control or provided for diversions to secondary markets. A number of agreements have done little more than keep products of inferior quality off the market. A few California and Arizona citrus agreements simply allocate shipments by weeks throughout the shipping season, thus avoiding waste and spoilage and excessive bulges in market flows.

General Evaluation of Orders for Fruits, Nuts, and Vegetables

Most orders involve a net social cost because the volume of a particular commodity is reduced below what would be sold in freely competitive markets. An order deliberately grants monopoly power to a private sector of the economy with strict limitations on its use, including government and industry approval for each action that is taken. Generally, it is believed that incomes of producers are improved to some degree in the short run, depending most importantly on the elasticity of demand for the commodity. Usually, orders are most applicable and most popular among growers for whom the quantity or quality of a perishable crop varies from season to season; where production is highly localized; where demand is relatively inelastic; where production is not dominated by a few large firms who may combine as oligopolists or vertically integrate through the marketing chain; or where a strong cooperative has much influence on the marketing of the product and growers want the protection of an order. Where surplus diversion is to be undertaken, an order is sometimes helpful for attaining market order and stability.

A general study of two decades of experience with orders for fruits and vegetables was published in 1956,[12] and since then literally hundreds of studies of individual programs have been made. Some orders have brought increased returns to growers where demand is inelastic, or there are no close substitutes for the commodity that is being controlled. But most orders are limited by the facts that there generally is more than one producing area, nearly every fruit or vegetable has one or more close substitutes, and improvements in processing have made the processed product a closer substitute for the fresh commodity. Accurate quantitative evaluation is difficult because most orders do not stay in continuous operation for more than a few years. More important, there is no dependable basis for judging what prices and marketing conditions would be if no program were undertaken. Market conditions, demand, production, and timing vary greatly from year to year and even from season to season. Hence, any attempt to relate prices and other factors to conditions that might have prevailed in the absence of an order is beset with great difficulties. A frequent contention has been that because order programs engender greater certainty, they tend to induce larger plantings than would otherwise occur. But the proof of this has not been developed with any consistency. To the extent that it is true, of course, consumers would gain. Producers might not be hurt; in fact, they also could gain over time through wider acceptance of their product and a larger market.

In addition, the future role of marketing agreements and orders must be related to questions of producer organization and market structure. An evaluation of whether an order is good or bad may depend on its effect on the structure of the market. At issue is not only whether an order favors marketing cooperatives—often it will. Also of concern is whether it helps smaller independent firms to survive and whether it helps the family farm in competition with large-scale producers, some of whom are highly integrated in producing and marketing, and for whom an order may be of little or no benefit.[13]

SUMMARY

Policy analysis of the crops economy has concentrated on the effects of government involvement in the markets for crops. Generally, this involvement affects the levels of income and the distribution of income to producers and other groups. This also results in a net social cost that is borne by consumers and taxpayers. The magnitude of the net social cost depends on the type of program, the conditions and elasticity of supply and demand, and the elasticity of substitution among land and other

---

[12]Murray R. Benedict and Oscar C. Stine, *The Agricultural Commodity Programs, Two Decades of Experience,* The Twentieth Century Fund, New York, 1956, pp. 380–415.

[13]For further discussion, see Harold F. Breimyer, *Individual Freedom and the Economic Organization of Agriculture,* The University of Illinois Press, Urbana, 1965, pp. 166–169 and 293–295.

resources in production. The net social cost of production control will be highest for commodities that have relatively elastic demands and high elasticities of substitution among land and other resources. The net social cost of demand-creating or demand-supplementing programs will be highest for commodites having inelastic demands and inelastic supply above the equilibrium level of prices in free markets. Any price-support program tends to involve the government in supply control and subsidies to demand, and this tendency will be strongest for the major crops that are most important in export trade.

The concept of a grain-reserve buffer-stock program will continue to be important in policy. Although buffer stocks can be used to general advantage in the United States to offset fluctuations in crop production, the general tendency has been to set a price standard for operation of a program. This may fail to move sufficient quantities into export trade when crops are large, which may in the end damage export markets for the United States and create larger policy problems for government. Modifying the price rules with quantity rules and increasing the competitiveness of export supply could reduce the cost of storage programs and increase the benefits to be gained from them.

Programs for tobacco and sugar bear some resemblance to each other, but, for reasons stated, the net social cost of the sugar program must be much higher than the tobacco program. Marketing orders for fruits, nuts, and vegetables have been viewed as supplements to free markets, rather than substitutes for them. Orders generally are designed to help producers, but they may also have other desired effects on price stability and economic structure of production and markets. The net social cost of order programs is limited by the fact that most orders are rather temporary in effect, and price-raising efforts are limited by the existence of many substitute commodities.

IMPORTANT TERMS AND CONCEPTS

Alternatives in crop production policy

Net social cost of price support with production control

Net social cost related to magnitude and elasticity of export demand

Comparative past and future net social cost of production control

Advantages and disadvantages of direct payments and supplements to demand

Effects of elasticity of supply on net social costs of direct payments and other supplements to demand

Alternatives in grain-reserve buffer-stock policy

The case for price stabilization through use of grain reserves

Concepts of buffer-stock programs

Alternative management rules for buffer stocks

Limitations of a domestic grain reserve to stabilize supply

Reasons for low social cost of the tobacco program

Concepts of large costs and small benefits in the sugar program

General provisions of marketing agreements and orders for fruits, nuts, and vegetables

Concepts of net social costs and benefits of agreement and order programs

LOOKING AHEAD

Policy analysis of the livestock economy in the next chapter complements our study of policy in the crops economy. We will study the reasons that various policy alternatives are followed in the livestock markets, and the possible consequences of choosing one alternative or another in the future.

QUESTIONS AND EXERCISES

1 What are the three or four major alternatives for policy in the markets for the major export crops: wheat, feed grains, cotton, and tobacco? What are the general advantages and disadvantages of each?

2 Recent wheat and feed-grain programs have generally ignored parity prices and substituted target prices and specifically designated loan rates for commodities placed under CCC loan or included in the farmer-owned reserve. Explain why parity has been dropped. What are the market factors or critieria for setting target prices and loan rates?

3 What are the political advantages (if any) of the payment-in-kind program as compared with the more traditional price-support and production-control programs? The political disadvantages (if any)? What are the economic advantages and disadvantages? Explain.

4 It has been said that all production-control programs involve a net social cost, which results from idling resources (mainly land), and loss of the product foregone. Illustrate and explain how this net social cost can be identified (at least theoretically). Explain why it is generally difficult, if not impossible, to measure the net social cost empirically.

5 Illustrate and explain how the net social cost of a price-support program is influenced by the elasticity of demand and the elasticity of supply.

6 It has been said that the budgetary cost to government of a price-support program is much higher for the major export commodities than for commodities that are not exported. Explain why. Does this mean that the net social cost of a price-support program is also correspondingly higher for the exported commodities? Explain why.

7 What are the political and economic advantages or disadvantages of using direct payments in lieu of price supports or a means of supplementing farm income?

8 It has been suggested that price supports and direct payments are of only limited short-term benefit to farm producers. Is this correct? Explain your answer.

9 It has been stated that using land as the sole means of implementing farm production controls inevitably raises the real cost of production. Is this correct? Explain your answer.

10 It has been said that a prime area for governmental activity in the public interest is stabilization policy. If this is true for agricultural policy, what are the criteria for operating grain storage in order to maximize the benefits of a program? Will such a program be of equal benefit to producers and to consumers? Explain.

11 Under what conditions of demand will two crops of average size sell for more than one large and one small crop? Under what conditions will the two crops of average size sell for less?

12 Theoretically speaking, publicly financed storage of grain beyond the level of stocks normally held by producers and marketing firms can increase the general welfare only if the discounted value of the publicly held stocks in some future year, minus the real costs of storage, is higher in that year than at present. By application of this concept, if the United States is assumed to be always a net exporter of grain, is it possible to justify a publicly supported grain storage program in the United States: (a) In terms of producers in the United States? (b) In terms of consumers in the United States? (c) In terms of consumers in other countries? If not, why not? If so, what will be the appropriate constraint to put on the program?

13 A buffer-stock management rule may be based either on quantity or on price. Economists have often suggested a rule based on quantity, while Congress has generally followed a price-support goal or a rule based on price. Economically speaking, what are the advantages and disadvantages of each rule? What are the political advantages and disadvantages of each rule?

14 There has been considerable discussion and analysis of alternatives for buffer stocks of grain to be held in importing as well as exporting countries. But governments of importing countries have shown relatively little interest in these proposals. Speaking theoretically, and without going into details, can you explain why?

15 Generally speaking, the magnitude of world stocks of grain required to provide a high level of food security is well within the limits of storage capacity in the United States. Does this mean that the rest of the world can rely on the United States to provide its food security? Why?

16 In terms of the basic elements of policy, how does the price-support problem for tobacco, sugar, and most fruits and vegetables differ from that for grains, oilseeds, and cotton?

17 It has been stated that, because of inelastic demand and effective control over production at relatively low government cost, the net social cost of the tobacco price-support program tends to be very low. Do you agree? Why?

18 In comparison with that of some other programs, the net social cost of the price-support program for domestic sugar producers has been identified as very large. In addition, the benefits are claimed to be small. In general economic terms, explain why you do or do not agree with this assessment.

19 What are the general provisions for marketing orders for fruits, nuts, and vegetables?

20 Most marketing orders for fruits and vegetables are believed to involve a net social cost. If so, what is the source of this cost? What are some of the benefits of orders that tend to reduce the net social cost? Is it possible that some of these benefits are large enough to result in a net social benefit? Explain why or why not, specifying your criteria for evaluation.

RECOMMENDED READINGS

Analysis of Grain Reserves, A Proceedings. Compiled by David J. Eaton and W. Scott Steele, Economic Research Service, U.S. Department of Agriculture, in cooperation with the National Science Foundation. Economic Research Report no. 634, August 1976.

Bigman, David, and Shlomo Reutlinger, "Food Price and Supply Stabilization: National Buffer Stocks and Trade Policies," *American Journal of Agricultural Economics,* vol. 61, no. 4, November 1979, pp. 657–667.

Chambers, Robert G., and Richard E. Just, "Effects of Exchange Rate Changes on U.S. Agriculture: A Dynamic Analysis," *American Journal of Agricultural Economics,* vol. 64, no. 5, December 1982, pp. 916–923; and Ronald W. Ward, "Discussion," ibid., pp. 926–927.

Gardner, Bruce L., *The Governing of Agriculture,* The Regents Press of Kansas, Lawrence 1981, pp. 63–84 and 131–135.

Offutt, Susan E., *The Impact of Instability on the U.S. Corn and Livestock Markets: An Econometric Analysis,* Cornell University, Ithaca, New York, A.E. Res. 82-45, December 1982, especially pp. 83–89.

CHAPTER 7

POLICY ANALYSIS OF THE LIVESTOCK ECONOMY

The livestock economy is viewed in policy analysis as an intermediate industry transforming feedstuffs and related commodities into other commodities that are more suitable for processing, marketing, and consumption. The general goal of policy in the livestock economy is to see that this process of transformation is carried out efficiently and equitably, under conditions favorable to increasing productivity and economic stability.

IN THIS CHAPTER

1 You can learn how to visualize the system of marketing orders in the dairy economy, how to appraise some of the consequences of this policy, and about various alternatives for the future.

2 You can learn how to identify the major policy issues in the other subsectors of the livestock economy, and you will learn how to appraise the effects of government involvement in livestock markets.

3 You can learn how to appraise some of the political forces influencing policy in the livestock economy.

POLICY ANALYSIS OF MARKETS FOR DAIRY PRODUCTS

The dairy industry may be viewed as a distinct sector of the livestock economy, with a market having a unique set of problems for policy. Dairy production competes for most of the same resources that are used to produce other livestock products. But the market is separated into two distinct types of products, fluid milk and manufactured dairy products, which are quite different in their economic characteristics. Demand for fluid milk is very inelastic, and the product is seasonal and comes to market in a rush. Consequently, prices are, or would be, very seasonal and unstable in uncontrolled markets. Individual demands for manufactured products—butter, cheese, yogurt, ice cream, and others—are more elastic, as almost every product has one or more close substitutes.

Goals of Dairy Programs

Before the federal government set up programs in 1933, large cooperatives and some state governments had tried to perform stabilization functions, but they met with only partial success. So, when the Agricultural Adjustment Act was passed in 1933, cooperatives and dairy producers asked for a program of federal marketing orders to regulate the flow of fluid milk to market. The policy goals that have developed are to assure a reliable supply of fluid at all times and places, and to stabilize both farm and retail prices so as to provide stable incomes to farmers and a smoothly functioning market. Complete stabilization of prices is not the objective, however, because this would create seasonal and locational shortages and surpluses of fluid milk.

Milk Marketing Orders[1]

In the United States, each major milk market, which draws supplies from an adjacent area called a "milkshed," is covered by either a federal or a state milk-marketing order. The principal objective and function of an order is to convert the entire milk supply of the market area into a pool within which milk is allocated to alternative uses, yet the price to producers is a uniform poolwide average. About two-thirds of all milk is delivered to processing plants under federal orders, and most of the balance is under state orders, which are coordinated with federal programs.

These orders are therefore a means for bringing distribution by all milk handlers in a market under uniform control, placing all handlers under uniform competitive positions in regard to the minimum price for milk, providing for uniform participation by producers, and overcoming much of the variability of fluid milk markets.

Terms of Orders   The terms of each order are developed through public hearings, and the role of the government is to hear arguments and proposals, to evaluate and resolve differences, and to enforce orders as promulgated under the authority of the secretary of agriculture, in the case of a federal order; or under authority of the government of a state, in the case of a state order. In regard to prices, order programs establish two things. One is the minimum price that regulated handlers in each market must pay for milk, and the other is the price that producers are entitled to receive for their milk. The first is based on a classified pricing system which regulates the price of milk according to the end use or "class" of the milk. The second is based on an average price or "blend," where all producers in each specifically designated area

---

[1]This section draws in part on Ronald E. Deiter, "U.S. Dairy Cooperative Service Behavior: An Overview of the North Central Region and a Case Study of the Chicago Market," unpublished Ph.D. dissertation, University of Illinois, October 1979.

Milk marketing orders and federal price supports have tended to raise and stabilize the incomes of dairy farmers. This probably has helped to increase the rate of innovation in dairy production, and accelerate the trend toward large-scale dairy farms. The federal outlay may be as much or more than a billion dollars a year, however. If so, who benefits? And, who bears the real cost? On what grounds can you attack or defend the program?

or zone who meet the sanitary requirements for fluid grade milk receive the same price for their milk, regardless of the end use of that milk.

Classes of Milk   The federal order classified pricing system establishes different prices for milk depending on how the handlers use the milk. Three different classes of milk are identified in most federal order markets, although a few have only two classes. Class I usually includes all fluid milk products, which comprise whole milk, skim milk, lowfat milk, milk drinks, buttermilk, filled milk, milkshakes, and ice-milk mixes. Class II usually includes cream, sour cream, eggnog, yogurt, cottage cheese, frozen desserts, custards, puddings, pancake mixes, and some feeding formulas. Class III typically consists of cheese other than cottage cheese, butter, powdered milk, evaporated or condensed milk, and milk products disposed of in animal feed.

Grades of Milk   Both producers and handlers of milk are subject to government inspection, and milk is graded according to the sanitary standards that are maintained. Grade A or "fluid-grade" milk is that which meets all of the necessary sanitation requirements of the area for milk that is to be used for fluid consumption. Federal order regulations apply only to Grade A milk, and only Grade A milk is permitted to be sold for Class I use. Grade B or "manufactured-grade" milk is that which does not meet the sanitation requirements for Grade A milk, and is used solely for manufactured products and never for fluid products.

Class I Prices   The minimum price for Class I milk is established in most markets according to a formula based on what is called the "Minnesota-Wisconsin price," or the "MW price," plus a "fluid or Class I differential." The MW price for a given month is the amount paid for Grade B milk by a number of manufacturing plants in Minnesota and Wisconsin in the second month preceding the given month. About 100 of these plants are surveyed each month by the United States Department of Agriculture and an audit is made of the prices they reportedly pay for milk of manufacturing grade. The MW price is supposedly a good indication of the value of milk used for the minimum price for milk used in Class III. The Class II price in most order markets is the Class III price plus 10 cents per hundredweight.

The minimum price for Class I milk is established in each order as the MW price for the second preceding month plus a "fluid differential" specified as a fixed amount in dollars and cents. This differential varies from market to market, generally increasing with the distance of the market center from the Minnesota-Wisconsin marketing area, or milkshed. In the late 1970s, for example, the differential varied from a low of a little more than $1 per hundredweight in the Minneapolis–St. Paul and southeastern Minnesota–Northern Iowa orders to more than $3 in the southeastern Florida order.[2] In addition, in markets that cover a wide area, concentric zones radiating out from the market center are established. Then processing plants are authorized to reduce their Class I price by a few cents per hundredweight from one zone to the next, out from the market center. This is to offset costs of transporting fluid milk, and such zoning is required for reasons of market efficiency, with the result that the percentage of milk going into Class I use decreases as the concentric zones radiate out from the market center. This also makes it necessary to have a specific formula for determining the blend price to be paid to producers in each zone.

Determining the Blend Price   The blend price to be paid to a producer, or to a producers' cooperative handling the milk of several producers, is a weighted average of all the milk sold in the order-marketing area, adjusted by zones as discussed above.

---

[2]*Federal Milk Order Market Statistics,* Annual Summary for 1978, U.S. Department of Agriculture, 1979, pp. 65–75.

All of the milk covered by the order is said to be "pooled," and the market administrator calculates the amount and value of pooled milk going into each class, from which is derived the weighted average value per hundredweight. Each handler is required to pay each producer or each cooperative from which milk is purchased the average or blend price, adjusted for location or zone.

In addition, all regulated handlers in a given order pay money into, or draw money out of, "the pool," or "the producers' settlement fund," depending on the distribution or sale of their milk, according to use. Most markets operate with a marketwide pool, although a few have been authorized to establish individual-handler pools, in which case the blend price to be paid to producers is calculated for each handler separately. Producers shipping to different handlers receive different blend prices if these handlers have different utilization percentages, regardless of location. Each handler pays the producer the full amount of the obligation only.

Implementing Price Supports   The federal government buys all the milk not sold at or above the support level. In some years, the government has removed as much as 5 percent or more of the total milk brought to market, while in other years supports have not been operative and the blend price mechanism has worked quite well. The secretary of agriculture is mandated to use the Commodity Credit Corporation (CCC) to buy sufficient quantities of dairy products to keep milk prices at support levels and to dispose of them outside of regular market channels. This mandate may involve exporting dairy products at world market prices and under Public Law 480, diverting dairy products to school-lunch and welfare programs at prices below price-support levels, and distributing to the United States military forces, veterans' hospitals, and as emergency relief.

The price supports set by Congress serve as a lever to raise and stabilize prices for all dairy products, and there are at least two concepts of costs that apply. One is the government cost of storage and disposal of products at less than support levels, which in some years has been more than $2 billion. The other is the added cost to consumers of prices that are higher than necessary to produce the quantity of milk that would satisfy the consumers' demands. Just how large this cost may be is difficult to determine. An analytical study has concluded that, in spite of increasing surpluses in the late 1970s and early 1980s, the producers' advantage from classified pricing of milk has tended to decline over several years.[3] This may mean that the program has encouraged a high rate of technological advance in the dairy industry and that the benefits to consumers are more real than apparent. Also, the furnishing of surplus products to welfare programs is a benefit that should not be overlooked.

Illustration of Classified Milk Pricing

Figure 7-1 illustrates the general theory of classified milk pricing. The market is in general equilibrium when the blend price is P_b, the Class I price is P_f, and the gov-

---

[3]See D. Hee Song and M. C. Hallberg, "Measuring Producers' Advantage from Classified Pricing of Milk," *American Journal of Agricultural Economics,* vol. 64, no. 1, February 1982, pp. 1–7.

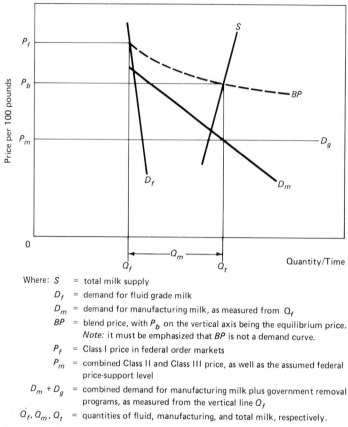

Where:
- S = total milk supply
- D_f = demand for fluid grade milk
- D_m = demand for manufacturing milk, as measured from Q_f
- BP = blend price, with P_b on the vertical axis being the equilibrium price. *Note:* it must be emphasized that BP is not a demand curve.
- P_f = Class I price in federal order markets
- P_m = combined Class II and Class III price, as well as the assumed federal price-support level
- $D_m + D_g$ = combined demand for manufacturing milk plus government removal programs, as measured from the vertical line Q_f
- Q_f, Q_m, Q_t = quantities of fluid, manufacturing, and total milk, respectively.

FIGURE 7-1
Hypothetical diagram of classified milk pricing.

ernment's price-support level for the milk that is used for manufactured products is P_m. As long as the supply fluctuates around the given supply and demand curves, or supply and demand move in the same direction and amount over time, prices can be maintained at these levels. But if technological advance increases supply and there is not an equivalent increase in demand, the government will accumulate surpluses, or price supports must be lowered.

In Figure 7-1, if the price for fluid milk is raised above P_f, other things remaining equal, then the widening of the Class I differential will create an unnecessary surplus of fluid milk. An unncessary surplus is defined as the amount of milk left after deducting from total milk receipts the Class I sales, a necessary reserve of 20 percent, and the seasonal surplus. Typically, in federal order markets, only a little more than half of the producer deliveries of milk are used in Class I. If the differential is wider than is necessary this will increase the amount of Grade A milk that must be diverted to manufactured products.

Under such conditions, if the level of price support is above P_m in Figure 7-1, then this will be reflected in increases in government stocks. Eventually, these may spoil, be sold in domestic or export markets at a loss, or be given away in aid programs.

Political Forces and Pressures in the Dairy Market

In most sessions, Congress is under pressure to raise the mandated support level, and this has been a major source of the difficulty associated with classified milk pricing. Generally, the National Milk Producers Federation, which is the registered congressional lobbyist for dairy cooperatives and producers, has called for supports at higher levels of parity. It has then tried to balance the market by calling for more support for federal nutritional assistance programs designed to supplement the diets of low-income families and children. At times, it has urged that the government not sell nonfat dry milk at less than 115 percent of its purchase price, that it limit imports of milk products to avoid putting pressure on domestic prices or government support programs, and that dairy product donations through CARE, Catholic Relief Services, Church World Service, and other agencies, be increased.

In addition, the major dairy cooperatives have established political action committees (PACs), which generally are very large contributors to the election campaigns of candidates for Congress. Prominent supporters of these PACs are the Associated Milk Producers, Inc., headquartered in San Antonio; Mid-America Dairymen of Springfield, Missouri; and Dairymen, Inc., at Louisville, Kentucky. Increased political activity of these PACs has brought protests from consumer groups; regional cooperatives have brought reactions of protest from consumer groups such as the Consumer Federation of America, National Consumers Congress (which merged in 1977 with the National Consumers League), Congress Watch, and the general citizen organization, Common Cause. In addition, there have been objections to the growth of labor union activity in dairy marketing, which has tended to raise costs through higher negotiated delivery charges and "make-work" restrictive work rules. Finally, Congress has been under continuing pressure to limit imports of dairy products with tariffs and quotas, and total imports consisting largely of cheese and specialty products have generally amounted to less than 1 or 2 percent of domestic production. Imports are largely Danish cheese and other specialty products, from the European Community (EC), which—perhaps more often than not—are subsidized; and this is a basis for continuing policy complaint by U.S. dairy producers.

Implications for Future Policy

There is nothing basically wrong with the concept of classified pricing for dairy products, unless one wishes to object to the concept of price discrimination per se. There may be a net social cost of substantial proportions, however, if the price of Class I milk is raised higher and higher above the equilibrium price for manufactured dairy products, or above the government's price-support level. This would be particularly true if the protected price for Class I were high enough to assure a stable supply in all seasons. The cost could not be offset by raising the price-support level because this will encourage more production and restrict consumption. If the government were to try to get around this by placing individual-producer quotas on milk production, then this would create another type of distortion in agricultural incentives, and perhaps a higher net social cost.

An optimum solution for classified pricing may be some modification of the government's price-support levels toward equilibrium market levels, with restrictions on the Class I price differential. As recent experience has shown, failure to do this will result in excessively large surpluses, distortions of incentives to produce, restriction of unsubsidized consumption, and large federal costs. The dairy policy is manageable, but it will take very strong political leadership to achieve a solution that reduces the net social cost, provides stability in the industry, and makes dairy products more price-competitive with other domestically produced foods. Imports of dairy products, which might under new circumstances be admitted duty free, may be restricted as the EC subsidizes its exports.

Under any circumstances it appears that the dairy industry will continue to become more and more concentrated in both its producing and marketing economy. In the last two or three decades especially, the size of dairy herd that minimizes total average cost has grown substantially. In some areas of the United States, dairy herds of 100 to 200 cows, which used to be considered an efficient size, have practically disappeared, and some operations have grown to 1,000 cows, or more, which formerly would have been considered an enormous size. This trend is not going to be reversed in the foreseeable future.

Dairy policy must adapt to the fact of increasing concentration in dairy production, as well as to the fact that there are a small number of very large processing and marketing cooperatives. Pricing of products cannot revert to the free-market model that at times existed, prior to 1933, without handing over oligopsony-oligopoly power to the large marketing firms. This does not appear to be a viable alternative for either producers or consumers. Hence, the problem will be to find suitable policy, compatible with the level of concentration that is almost certain to exist. Class I price differentials must be held in appropriate check, and government price supports must be set at a level that is consistent with the federal government's budgetary goals.

Dairy policy will continue to be unique, very different from that of most of the other livestock sectors. So let us consider policy alternatives in the other livestock markets.

POLICY ANALYSIS OF MARKETS FOR MEAT ANIMALS AND POULTRY PRODUCTS

The foundations of policy in the markets for meat animals and poultry products are quite different from foundations of policy in the markets for dairy products. There is no such system of classified pricing. The markets conform more closely to models of free competition in auction markets, although large numbers of producers face a small number of buyers who may have a degree of oligopsony power in local markets, and cattle producers, especially, have achieved a degree of protection from imports with a modest tariff of 3 cents a pound on dressed beef, and a quota on total imports.

Accurate reporting of prices has been a policy issue, because producers sometimes think that they are getting less than what they deem a fair market price. New systems of electronic price reporting are developing and futures markets have been established for some products. But the most important problem of the future may relate to market instability, so we begin by considering this.

Basic Economics of Markets for Meat Animals

Demand for total meat output is highly inelastic and demands for most individual kinds of meat—beef, pork, veal, and lamb—are less inelastic (Table 4-1). Both cattle and hog markets and, to a lesser extent, lamb markets, exhibit strong cyclical characteristics of production and prices. Because of inelastic demands and inelastic short-run supply, the fluctuations in prices are much wider than those in production. Characteristically, because of the biology of production and the unprofitability of storing the finished product for long periods, markets also exhibit rather uniform cycles.

Hog production responds to changes in market prices, with a typical lag of one to three years. Hog producers seemingly cannot predict future prices with a high degree of accuracy. The general theory is that, when hog prices are high, some producers hold back brood sows from market and increase their farrowings. But it takes several

The beef cattle industry has been one of the faster-growing sectors of American agriculture. Is this growth more dependent on increase in demand, or increase in supply? How could you determine this? What are the major implications for international trade policy exports and imports?

months from the time decisions are made until the increased volume can come to market. When it does, hog prices are depressed. More brood sows are sent to market. Farrowings are reduced, and eventually the reduced output brings higher prices; then the cycle repeats.

The cattle cycle is longer and typically less regular than the hog cycle, tending to reach a peak or a trough at approximately 10-year intervals. Typically, cattle numbers build up during periods of relatively high prices, and herds are reduced by heavy culling of breeding stock during periods of low prices. Increases in production lag two or three years or more behind increases in numbers, and decreases in production at least a year or two behind decreases in cattle numbers.

In addition to the 10-year production cycle, there is a cattle feeding-marketing cycle to consider. The typical cattle feeding-marketing period is about one year. In a cattle-feeding operation that is about six months long, the feeder stock can be contracted (purchase of feeders and feed, and pricing of fat cattle) as much as six months before the physical start of the operation. Trading in fed-cattle futures extends about 13 months forward so as to cover this operation, and feeder-cattle futures extend seven to nine months forward. This provides time for decisions on purchases and sales to be made.

In appraising market trends and deciding what to do from one season to another, both the cattle producer and cattle feeder must deal with a considerable amount of uncertainty, however. Cattle feeding is a notoriously risky business and, in a real sense, no policy has been found that can counteract swings in either cattle production or the cattle-feeding cycle. Due to inelastic demand, prices of cattle typically fluctuate more widely than cattle numbers, and cattle prices may be depressed for a year, or even two or three years in a row.

Policy Positions of Hog and Cattle Producers Compared

Although producers of both hogs and cattle have favored a freely competitive auction-type market for their products, only cattle producers have wanted some protection from foreign competition. This is because only a small amount of speciality-type pork, Danish ham, for example, is imported, and some pork products are exported. But the United States regularly imports some beef products, especially lean beef from Australia, used mainly in hamburgers and in production of processed meat products. In addition, when beef cattle prices are high, the volume of beef imports typically increases. Later, volume may become a factor, or cattle producers and feeders may think it is a factor, in depressing cattle prices.

Import Protection Policy for Beef and Mutton

Protection for producers of beef and mutton has taken the form of a tariff and an import quota. Prior to 1964, there was only a tariff of 3 cents per pound, or comparable ad valorem duties, on imports of fresh, chilled, or frozen beef. Starting in 1956, imports of beef increased from 200 million pounds (carcass weight), reaching 1.7 billion pounds in 1963. Over the same period, consumption of beef rose from 15.7

Advances in science and technology in breeding, housing, feeding, and sanitation have greatly increased the advantages of large-scale hog farms, and disadvantaged the traditional smaller-scale farm. This being so, what is the case for and against government intervention to protect or support the small-scale hog farm? Pork-producer organizations generally have not asked for government price supports, or other direct income aids. Why?

billion to 18.6 billion pounds, so that beef imports accounted for one-half of the total increase in domestic consumption of beef over the eight-year period. This growth in imports was regarded by cattle raisers and their representative organizations, which have been combined in the National Cattlemens Association, as a major factor in depressing cattle prices. Whether this was true or not, they wanted more protection from imports, and carried out a political campaign to get it.

In 1964, Congress adopted an act (Public Law 88-482) providing for quarterly quotas of no more than 4 percent of the quarterly average of domestic production in the previous three years on imports of fresh, chilled, or frozen cattle meat, or meat of goats and sheep (except lambs).[4] The secretary of agriculture was directed to impose quotas whenever imports were projected to exceed this amount. Quotas might be suspended, if the President found that it was in the overriding interest of the United States to do so, taking account of economic and national security interests, domestic prices, and other possible superseding trade agreements. Following enactment of the 1964 law, imports seldom reached the quota level and, in two instances when they did, the quota was suspended because beef prices were near a cyclical peak.

[4]*U.S. Code Congressional and Administrative News,* 88th Cong., 2d Sess., 1964, pp. 680–682 and 3070–3080.

The Meat Import Act of 1979, which replaced the 1964 law, had the so-called countercyclical objective of preventing imports from increasing when beef production was projected to increase, reflecting a desire on the part of producers to stabilize the numbers and prices of cattle inventories according to the following formula:

$$\frac{\text{Annual}}{\text{quota}} = \frac{\text{Average annual imports}}{(1968\text{--}77)} \times \frac{\text{3-yr. moving average of domestic production}}{\text{10-yr. average of domestic production }(1968\text{--}77)} \times \frac{\text{5-yr. moving average of domestic cow beef production}}{\text{2-yr. moving average of domestic cow beef production}}$$

Under the 1979 law, the quota would increase proportionately as the 3-year moving average of domestic beef production went above the 10-year average of 1968–77, and it would decrease as the 2-year moving average of domestic cow production (numbers) moved ahead of the 5-year moving average. For example, according to the last factor in the equation, an increase in cow numbers, which would signal a future increase in beef production, would decrease the quota, thus apparently stabilizing supply. However, according to the second factor on the right-hand side, the quota would be allowed to increase proportionately with the growth in domestic beef production.

As has been pointed out,[5] whether the quota indicated by this formula would be countercyclical, as intended, or destabilizing, would depend on the interaction of beef cow numbers with beef production. If a cycle similar to that of the 1970s were projected for the 1980s, then the result could be countercyclical. But the law would not operate in the fashion intended if growth in beef cattle production was slower, but continuous, after 1985. In other words, the 1979 law is another example of legislation enacted as the result of an identified need, but which may operate in a way quite different from that intended.[6]

In most years, the tariff of 3 cents per pound apparently has had a modest influence in holding imports to less than quota levels. In instances where imports have been higher as a result of high domestic prices, the imports may have been a factor in limiting increases in meat prices. In the future, however, much broader policy issues will involve export trade in livestock and poultry products. Let us consider these.

Broader Policy Issues Related to Export Trade in Livestock and Poultry Products

It may be said that, until the early 1970s, the question of exports of livestock and poultry products was a relatively unimportant policy issue. But beginning in the early

---

[5]See James R. Simpson, "The Countercyclical Aspects of the U.S. Meat Import Act of 1979," *American Journal of Agricultural Economics,* vol. 64, no. 2, May 1982, pp. 243–248.
[6]Ibid., p. 248.

1970s, and most importantly, since 1975, the policy issue concerning exports has become increasingly significant. Since 1975, exports of livestock products have more than doubled in value, and exports of broilers and eggs have increased severalfold. These trends suggest that either there have been important increases in export demand for livestock and poultry products, or that the United States has an increasing comparative advantage in producing these products. Viewed against these trends, imports of beef and pork have not grown in volume.

If the United States has an increasing comparative advantage in beef and pork production, then the question of protection for the domestic cattle industry may be largely a policy issue of the past, and more important, in the future the major policy issue will involve export trade in livestock and poultry products. According to general theory concerning the location of agricultural production, there is a comparative advantage in producing most livestock and some poultry products near the major sources of feed, and in shipping finished products to points of consumption. This principle applies uniformly within the United States, with respect to beef and pork production especially. With some modifications for other factors, it applies to broiler and egg production as well. If certain tariff and nontariff barriers to trade (NTBs), chiefly involving protection of producers in other countries, can be overcome, then livestock and poultry products could constitute a much larger percentage of total agricultural exports.

Political Consideration in Meat Exports

Meat exports would give real gains to all trading countries, and perhaps particularly to Japan. All of the feed grains and soybeans that are shipped to Japan (about one-third of the U.S. corn exports and one-fourth of the soybeans) go through the Panama Canal, and, when combined with other costs, result in relatively expensive total transportation costs. For exports to Japan, as well as to most other countries, it would be consistent with comparative advantage to encourage expansion of exports of livestock and poultry products rather than to follow the policy of protecting the domestic livestock and poultry industry in Japan from imports, as has been emphasized in the past.

Whether this can be done or not depends on the mutual agreement of the governments involved. Japan and most other countries would have to overcome some of the objections of their own livestock producers. The United States would have to negotiate from a broad base, involving agriculture and other industries. Selling finished livestock and some poultry products rather than feed grains and soybeans would be of great benefit to the United States. It would permit a more balanced use of land and other resources, help to conserve soils, and result in a higher-value product. A country with relatively fixed resources that spends to import food products might not increase the value of its imports proportionately, but there should still be a saving to both the importing and the exporting country.

The answer to greater exports of livestock and poultry products lies in the reduction or elimination of tariffs and nontariff barriers to trade. This may, in time, come about through further trade negotiations and agreements cutting across agriculture

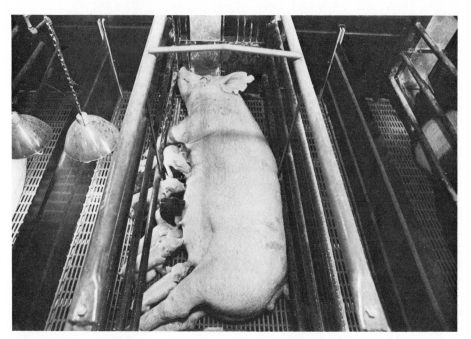

Modern automation in pork production has not completely eliminated the need for the personal touch. Who gains from increasing efficiency in pork production? Who tends to lose? Is there a gain in net social income?

and other industries. As a first step, the United States may have to repeal the legislation that sets the quota on imports of beef and veal. This quota law apparently achieves little or nothing, and causes harm by serving as a psychological barrier to trade negotiations.

The 3-cent tariff on imports is shifted either back to foreign producers or forward to American consumers, depending on the comparative elasticities of supply and demand. If the domestic demand for meat is less elastic than the supply of meat exported to the United States, which we may assume is the case, then more of the tariff will be shifted to consumers. But this will be felt primarily in the price of hamburger and prepared meats, where the effect may be insignificant to consumers of these products, and will have little or no effect on prices of other meat and poultry products. If it has any effect on domestic prices of beef and mutton, this will tend to increase production. Hence, beyond the short run, the tariff will be of little benefit to the cattle or the sheep industry.

In summary, producers of meat and poultry products gain little, if anything, from the protectionist policy that has been followed. The industry would gain much more through a free-trade policy in meat and poultry. This would help to reduce the distortions in agricultural incentives, from which both agriculture and the general public would benefit.

Wool policy may also be linked to that for meat and poultry products. Let us next consider this.

ANALYSIS OF UNITED STATES WOOL POLICY

The basic foundation for current wool policy was set in the National Wool Act of 1954, which set a goal of 300 million pounds of shorn wool (grease basis) and mohair "at prices fair to both producers and consumers in a manner which will have the least adverse effects on foreign trade."[7] The secretary of agriculture was directed to support the prices of wool and mohair by means of loans, purchases, payments, or other operations, using the Commodity Credit Corporation as the implementing agency. The act also continued the tariff on wool imports, which in recent years has been 35 cents per pound (grease basis), and equivalent ad valorem duties on wool thread and cloth of textile grade (a small amount of wool of carpet grade is admitted duty free). In addition, direct payments are made to wool producers to bring their returns up to price-support levels, which have been around $1.80 per pound (grease basis).

Reasons for the Current Wool Policy

After the close of World War II, wool production in the United States declined, and the goal of the Congress in the 1954 act was to maintain domestic sheep and wool production at a stable level without increasing the tariff or increasing costs to consumers. In 1947, President Truman had vetoed a bill which would have increased the tariff on wool by 50 percent. Perhaps largely to forestall another attempt to increase the tariff, the Eisenhower administration supported a more modest policy, placing the emphasis on direct payments to wool producers, which were intended to be and have been offset by customs receipts. The resulting wool policy is largely a product of the wool industry, which is represented by the National Wool Growers Association and congressional members from the major wool-growing states.

Impact of Wool Policy on Producers and Consumers

Since the early 1960s, in spite of the efforts to aid wool growers, domestic wool production has declined by about two-thirds, or to scarcely more than one-fifth of the goal set in the 1954 act. Domestic consumption of wool—based on imports and domestic production—has declined to less than half of what it was in the early 1960s, and domestic production is less than one-third of consumption. In the early 1980s, receipts of sheep producers from the sale of wool averaged about $50 to $60 million annually (as compared with total farm receipts from marketing of nearly $150 billion), which makes wool a very minor commodity, indeed.

---

[7]Public Law 690, 83rd Cong., 2d Sess., 1954.

Domestic consumption of apparel wool has dropped to less than 1 pound per capita, as compared with more than 50 pounds per capita for cotton and manufactured fibers. Prices in the United States have averaged slightly lower than in other major importing countries due to a better quality of wool in the other countries and correspondingly stronger demand.

Implications for National Policy

Wool policy based on the 1954 act has not only fallen far short of the stated policy goals for production, but the effect of the tariff on imports of fine wools has also apparently reduced the demand for wool. Consequently, the price objectives of the wool industry have not been met, and the industry has declined to a degree that is unique in American agriculture. Current domestic production of some 50 to 60 million pounds is less than 1.5 percent of total world production. What is to be done?

First, it will do little or no good for wool growers to ask for further tariff protection for the domestic wool industry. Wool imports have fallen so low that their further reduction would not increase demand for domestically produced wool, or, at the best, would increase demand very little.

Second, the real costs of the current policy in loss of the consumer market for wool, especially the finer grades of wool, imposes a considerable cost on consumers in terms of the value of the product foregone, or the distortion of consumption patterns. Although it may be impossible to measure this cost precisely, one may judge that the real cost is many times greater than the benefits to wool producers. If the United States were to eliminate the tariff, then this would provide a large benefit for consumers. In addition, if it were assumed that maintaining the industry near its current level would be in the national interest, then this could be done with direct payments to wool growers.

Wool Policy Alternatives

In respect to future wool policy, it may be in the national interest to eliminate the tariff, either with or without compensating payments to wool producers. Let us visualize a basic model for this policy as it might appear in a diagram (Figure 7-2).

In Figure 7-2, under the tariff, the total domestic supply of wool (S_t) is made up of the domestic supply (S_d) and the foreign supply (S_{ft}), which is imported over the tariff. The domestic supply is visualized as very inelastic because (1) wool is a joint product with mutton and lamb and (2) some of the resources used in sheep production, such as high-altitude summer range, have no good alternative use, and hence have a low opportunity cost. The foreign supply is much more elastic because the United States imports are only a small fraction of total international trade in wool. The equilibrium price in the domestic market (P_t) is determined by the intersection of the total supply (S_t) and the domestic demand (D).

When the tariff is removed, the domestic supply is not affected, providing every-

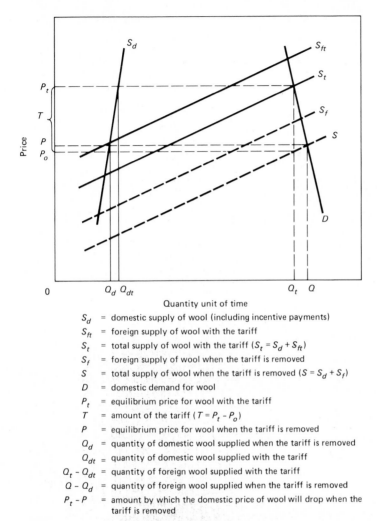

S_d = domestic supply of wool (including incentive payments)
S_{ft} = foreign supply of wool with the tariff
S_t = total supply of wool with the tariff $(S_t = S_d + S_{ft})$
S_f = foreign supply of wool when the tariff is removed
S = total supply of wool when the tariff is removed $(S = S_d + S_f)$
D = domestic demand for wool
P_t = equilibrium price for wool with the tariff
T = amount of the tariff $(T = P_t - P_o)$
P = equilibrium price for wool when the tariff is removed
Q_d = quantity of domestic wool supplied when the tariff is removed
Q_{dt} = quantity of domestic wool supplied with the tariff
$Q_t - Q_{dt}$ = quantity of foreign wool supplied with the tariff
$Q - Q_d$ = quantity of foreign wool supplied when the tariff is removed
$P_t - P$ = amount by which the domestic price of wool will drop when the tariff is removed

FIGURE 7-2
Visualizing the effects on equilibrium prices and quantities resulting from removing the tariff on wool.

thing else remains the same. But the foreign supply increases (from S_{ft} to S_f), because the removal of the tariff constitutes a decrease in cost. The new equilibrium price in the domestic market *(P)* is determined by the intersection of the total supply without the tariff *(S)* and the domestic demand *(D)*. The major direct benefit of tariff removal accrues to consumers, while foreign producers have the advantage of a slightly higher price and increase in quantity demanded, other things remaining equal.

Because of the inelastic supply for domestic wool production and a presumably inelastic demand in the short run, Figure 7-2 may be regarded as a rather short-run solution of perhaps only a year or two in duration. Over several years the domestic supply would become more elastic. Domestic demand would also become more elastic and increase as consumers' fashions or styles changed and the clothing industry began to use more wool. If demand were to increase, then wool prices would recover some of the decline experienced when the tariff was removed.

Perhaps the most important policy question for the future concerns the possible link between wool policy and general agricultural trade policy. At a time when the United States is seeking freer trade for agricultural exports, does the wool tariff tend to inhibit development of this policy? If so, then the real cost of protecting the wool industry would be much greater than has been implied in this discussion. If the tariff and all incentives to continue production were removed, current sheep producers could be compensated—that is, either bought out, or helped to convert to other enterprises—at a small fraction of the cost of the policy followed since 1954. Then those who continued could compete in a freer market with producers of other farm products.

SUMMARY

Policy analysis of the livestock economy and the markets for its products has revealed important differences in policy among these markets. The dairy program is by far the most expensive to government and to consumers. These results do not come from flaws in the original concepts of federal or state order programs, but from political responses to pressures from the dairy industry in setting Class I prices in federal order markets, and from the pressures on Congress for setting price supports too high for the milk that goes into manufactured products. The dairy industry, however, has maintained a high rate of technological advance, and the programs have stabilized prices.

Government intervention in the markets for meat animals and poultry products has been much less extensive, as organizations representing the beef, hog, sheep, and poultry industries have generally supported a policy of open-market competition. But cattle producers and feeders have succeeded in getting and in maintaining a tariff on imports of beef and mutton, and in getting an import-quota law passed in 1964. Our analysis of the quota suggests that this law is generally ineffective, while the tariff on imports may be inhibiting in getting freer trade for exports of beef and other livestock products. The potential for expanding these exports is large, indeed. But realization of this potential will depend on generally freer trade in agricultural products around the world.

The national wool policy—like policy for beef and mutton—has been protectionist, which our analysis suggests involves large costs and small benefits. Removing the tariff could result in significantly large benefits to consumers and increasing demand for wool. Domestic wool growers could be compensated directly, at a small fraction of the real cost of the wool policy that has been followed since 1954.

IMPORTANT TERMS AND CONCEPTS

Inelastic demand for fluid milk

Goals of federal and state marketing orders for milk

Provisions of milk marketing orders: fluid milk and manufactured milk

Two milk prices established by orders: minimum prices paid by handlers prices that milk producers are entitled to receive

Classes of milk: I, II, and III

Grades of milk: A and B

Fluid milk price differential

Pricing zones in milk-order markets

How blend prices for milk are determined

Basis for federal price supports for manufacturing milk

Reasons for surpluses of milk and milk products

Reasons for increasing concentration in milk production and marketing

Inelastic demand for total meat output

Biological reasons for lags in livestock production

Reasons for cycles in cattle and hog production

Relationships between cattle numbers and production

Comparative positions of hog and cattle producers in respect to import trade

Import protection policy for beef and mutton

Reasons for failure of the import-quota law

Mutual advantages in exporting frozen or processed meat

Policy changes needed in order to export meat

Provisions and effects of the National Wool Act of 1954

Three policy alternatives for the national wool market

Effects of the tariff on wool prices and quantity

LOOKING AHEAD

Policy analysis of the marketing economy in the next chapter largely completes our study of policy in the product markets. The main questions for policy analysis will involve the marketing margin, which is the difference between prices received by producers and those paid by consumers. Policy analysis is concerned with the width of the margin, and the organization and efficiency of the marketing economy.

QUESTIONS AND EXERCISES

1 There are three generally stated policy goals for federal and state milk marketing-order programs. What are they? Given these goals, what is an order generally designed to regulate?

2 As a general rule, what two types of prices are established by milk-order programs? What is the basis for establishing each price?

3 Three different classes of milk are identified in most federal milk-order programs. What is included in each class? What is the difference between Grade A and Grade B milk?

4 What is the general basis or formula for establishing the minimum price for Class I milk? How are pricing zones established in the larger milksheds? Why are they used?

5 How are blend prices established in federal order milk markets? Why are federal price

supports necessary for Class II and Class III milk as a means of making the classified milk pricing system operational?

6 In what ways do price supports set by Congress serve as a lever to raise and stabilize prices for all dairy products?

7 What are the two ways in which the dairy price-support program increases costs? It has been suggested that some of this increased cost may be offset by stimulating technological advance in dairy production and marketing. If so, will this tend to increase or decrease the total cost of the program? Explain how, or why.

8 How can the net social cost of the federal dairy price-support policy be minimized? What prevents the federal government from doing this? Can it be less costly to do this than to adopt a policy of free competitive market prices? Why?

9 Typically, the percentage change in hog prices from the same quarter a year earlier is much greater than the percentage change in production per capita. What does this tell us about the elasticity of demand for pork?

10 The cattle cycle is longer and typically less regular than the hog cycle. Explain why. Why is it necessary to distinguish between cattle numbers and cattle production?

11 The beef quota has been described as ineffective in protecting the beef cattle industry. Do you agree? Why?

12 Although it would be more economical to export meat than feed grains, very little meat is exported from the United States. Why? What changes in policy would be required to substitute meat exports for feed grains?

13 It has been stated that the real cost of the national wool policy to consumers greatly exceeds the real benefits to producers. Do you agree? Why?

14 What are the major alternatives for wool policy that might reduce the real costs relative to the real benefits?

RECOMMENDED READINGS

Ball, V. Eldon, and Robert G. Chambers, "An Economic Analysis of Technology in the Products Industry," *American Journal of Agricultural Economics,* vol. 64, no. 4, November 1982, pp. 699–709.

Freebairn, J. W., and Gordon C. Rausser, "Effects of Changes in the Level of U.S. Beef Imports," *American Journal of Agricultural Economics,* vol. 57, no. 4, November 1975, pp. 676–688.

Hee Song, D., and M. C. Hallberg, "Measuring Producers' Advantage from Classified Pricing of Milk," *American Journal of Agricultural Economics,* vol. 64, no. 1, February 1982, pp. 1–7.

Manchester, Alden C., *Market Structure, Institutions, and Performances in the Fluid Milk Industry,* Economic Research Service, U.S. Department of Agriculture, Agricultural Economic report no. 248, Washington, D.C., 1974.

Simpson, James R., "The Countercyclical Aspects of the U.S. Meat Import Act of 1979," *American Journal of Agricultural Economics,* vol. 64, no. 2, May 1982, pp. 243–248.

CHAPTER 8

POLICY ANALYSIS OF THE MARKETING ECONOMY

Policy in the marketing economy involves the important goals of efficiency and equity, and a wide array of means, implements, and constraints. Publicly supported programs include price reports and market news; commodity grading; marketing orders; assistance to farmers' cooperatives, including antitrust exemption; action by the Federal Trade Commission to permit and sometimes limit mergers of food firms; regulation of spot and futures markets; food safety rules and regulations; and public programs to improve nutrition. These programs are the public contribution to the economic setting and the trading rules under which agricultural markets operate.

IN THIS CHAPTER

1 You can learn the purpose of the trading rules that regulate agricultural markets, and learn the major policy concerns associated with growth of the marketing economy.

2 You can learn how supply and demand interact to determine the marketing margin (the difference between prices at retail and farm levels), what the major components of marketing costs are, and why marketing margins and costs tend to change in the way they do. The marketing system currently receives more than $200 billion annually for food services alone, more than double the value of domestically consumed farm foods as marketed from the farm.

3 You can learn to identify the major policy alternatives in the marketing economy, including the role of farmer cooperatives, options for controlling economic concentration, and the options for nutrition policy.

TRADING RULES AND POLICY CONCERNS

Policy analysis of the marketing economy may best begin with a study of the codes, customs, and regulations, or "trading rules," that govern this economy. Such rules are derived from tradition, public law, and administrative decision. Hence, they may be either customary or contractual, and they may be accepted willingly or require government enforcement, involving threat of penalty.

Public and Private Rules

An important distinction is made between public and private rules. Public rules are codified into laws, which are implemented through programs, rules, and regulations, these being the essence of public marketing policy. Private rules encompass the customary practices and ethics of those in marketing, including rules adopted by managers of marketing firms, brokers, and others. Public rules are frequently established to mold or modify private rules.

Public rules that are compatible with private rules are designed to assure the competitive and financial integrity of the widely dispersed agricultural marketing system. One of the simplest rules is that for testing scales at public markets, a procedure usually done by a state agency. Other rules apply to a wide variety of public services, such as price reports and market news, standards and grades, and publicly supported marketing programs. Some rules are permissive, such as those granting authority for farmers to organize cooperatives. Some grant more specific types of authority and assign responsibility, such as those defining the power and responsibility of the secretary of agriculture to administer marketing orders, food stamps, and grain storage programs. A relatively new law establishes a trading rule under which producers may collect funds for the purpose of advertising, promotion, and research, the primary purpose of which is to increase the demand for their products.

The idea of trading rules applies particularly well to the kind of agricultural marketing system that traditionally has been preferred in the United States. The long-standing policy preference is for a system that is relatively atomistic and decentralized, yet orderly. The image of many buyers and sellers interacting in purely competitive markets under well-defined public trading rules has traditionally been idealized. In reality, the modern marketing system to which policy must be applied reflects this image only partially. In some raw-product markets, competition is relatively pure, or perfect. But in later stages, imperfect competition is the norm. Some rules must be adapted to only a few buyers and sellers, and to a few giant firms with a high degree of concentration operating under oligopsonistic and oligopolistic competition.

The five stages of agricultural marketing include local assembly, central assembly, processing, wholesaling, and retailing. The traditional image of decentralized competition among firms that buy and sell in open trading, almost entirely on the basis of price, fits part of the economy, especially in the first stage of two. But, under modern technology, as agricultural commodities move through processing, wholesaling, and retailing stages, economies of large scale tend to become more pronounced. Products become differentiated in terms of quality and brand, and in form of processing and variety of services. Various kinds of contract services are employed. The structure of purely competitive, decentralized markets gives way to a more complex large-scale, highly automated, imperfectly competitive marketing system. It is with this mixed system of marketing, and its related concerns, that we must deal. What are the major policy concerns?

Policy Concerns with Marketing Progress

In large part, the agricultural marketing system works rather well, and its rate of growth generally has been more than adequate to accommodate the relatively rapid increases in farm output. As the science and technology of processing and marketing foods and nonfood products have advanced, the marketing system has responded to various demands by creating new products, and new methods for processing, packaging, and delivery. Improvements can be measured in terms of more variety and higher quality, as well as growth of volume. But in spite of this progress, serious policy concerns are being expressed relative to the performance of the agricultural marketing economy.

A 1983 study by the congressional Office of Technology Assessment concluded that little progress has been made since 1972 in improving the efficiency of food storage, assembly, processing, packaging, warehousing, transportation, and distribution.[1] Failure to improve the handling of food after it leaves the farm has been a major factor in rising food costs. Increases in costs of postharvest technology and marketing have contributed significantly to the inflationary spiral in the United States since 1972. Food technology research has resulted in improved diets through food enrichment, such as the addition of vitamins B_1, B_2, and niacin to cereal products, vitamin D to milk, and iodine to salt.

The congressional study linked the high costs of marketing to slow growth in federal appropriations for marketing research, enforcement, and other programs over the last two or three decades. It noted that states in major farming areas had increased their support for marketing research. But for more than two decades, federal funds for research have been declining in real terms. The major policy conclusion of the study was that additional commitments of federal funds would result in increased labor productivity, improved food processing and preservation, and more efficient marketing and distribution. This would mean even greater savings for low-income Americans, for whom food is a major budget item.

This emphasis on marketing research, important as it is, may be compared with broader conclusions of other national studies. For instance, in a study by the National Commission on Food Marketing published in 1966, the agricultural marketing system was evaluated as being one of the outstanding achievements of the American economy.[2] The system was cited for its growth and dynamism, its vitality,

---

[1] *Agricultural Postharvest Technology and Marketing Economics Research: A Technical Memorandum*, Office of Technology Assessment, Congress of the United States, Washington, D.C., April 1983.

[2] National Commission on Food Marketing, *Food from Farmer to Consumer*, June 1966, and Technical Studies no. 1 to 10, U.S. Government Printing Office, Washington, D.C., 1966.

and its wide-ranging market services. Nevertheless, a majority of the members on the commission were concerned about the quality of competition within the system.

Although a minority of members disagreed, the commission's majority proposal was that to improve competition, there should be more stringent antitrust enforcement, product-line reporting of income by large food firms, and a new autonomous agency to regulate market activities. More specifically, the majority concluded that enforcement of the Packers and Stockyards Act should be transferred from the Department of Agriculture to the Judiciary. The Perishable Agricultural Commodities Act should be strengthened. There should be expanded standards of identity for food, a new central consumer agency, expanded federal administration of marketing orders, and a new marketing-board authority.

There was more general agreement within the commission that there should be new laws to strengthen bargaining rights for farmers, establish mandatory price reporting for all publicly regulated markets, establish more uniform state rules and regulations, and provide more support for various areas of marketing research. Many of these conclusions were supported or expanded by a new presidential commission, called the National Advisory Commission on Food and Fiber, although this group largely avoided the more controversial issues of economic structure.[3]

Some of the suggested actions have been taken, but most have not. So many of the concerns are still with us and, as the marketing systems have continued to grow and become more concentrated, some of the most important concerns have tended to intensify. Specifically, the most intensive concerns center on the consequences of vertical integration, imperfect competition among firms, and the pricing practices of oligopsony and oligopoly.

Concerns Related to Vertical Integration

With vertical integration of agricultural commodity markets, commodities move from stage to stage in the marketing sequence from producer to consumer, under owner or contract integration, rather than through competitive buying and selling by individual firms. With owner integration, commodities are simply transferred from division to division of an owner-integrated firm. For instance, large corporate retail food chains own most of their own wholesaling facilities, and wholesalers may also own farm firms, or integrate with growers through contracts.

Under contractual integration, the terms of contracts that govern market delivery are bilaterally negotiated on a periodic or annual basis. This practice is now commonplace in broiler and other poultry operations. It is the usual practice in fruits and vegetables used for canning or freezing, some of which is done by farmer cooperatives. In addition, an increasing share of the sales of grain and livestock products is based on agreements or contracts between buyers and sellers. The most pervasive trends appear to be in hogs and beef, and sales of grain and cotton under some form of contract are becoming increasingly prevalent.

---

[3]See Report of the National Advisory Commission on Food and Fiber, *Food and Fiber for the Future*, U.S. Government Printing Office, Washington, D.C., July 1967.

Both owner and contract integration may offer important advantages to large-scale firms. Both prices and delivery dates can be specified, which leads to certainty and efficiency in operation. This is consistent with some goals of policy generally accepted as important. But this changes the competitive relationships among firms, generally with relative disadvantages accruing to small independent farms and marketing firms. Hence, integration leads to concentrations or conglomerations of large firms within the marketing system. In addition, this tends to promote large-scale farm firms in production. This raises concerns about economic structure and income distribution within the system; other major concerns relate to the effectiveness of competition among firms.

Effectiveness of Competition among Firms

If large integrated firms have competitive advantages over small independent firms, and price making among large firms is characterized by oligopsonistic and oligopolistic competition, then this type of competition will be dominant throughout most of the agricultural marketing economy. The large integrated firms may enjoy comfortable and relatively stable marketing margins, while competition is characterized by product differentiation, with emphasis on quality and variety of products, rather than by competitive pricing of undifferentiated products. This type of competition is most typical of large sectors of the processing-wholesaling and the retail-consumer stages of the marketing economy.

With modern technology, as we have noted, economies of scale are important in processing and wholesaling, so firms tend to integrate horizontally as well as vertically. The giant grain firms provide a good example. Where grades are standardized and commodities are not otherwise differentiated, as in the auction grain markets, a firm's size may be of little or no advantage in buying, and competition is largely on the basis of price. But the large firms may have a significant advantage in processing, wholesaling, and selling its product. This may involve both internal and external economies, as a large firm may also establish an advantage by differentiating its product in the minds of the consumer. The quality of competition may decline as firms enjoy the benefits of oligopsony and oligopoly.

The quality of competition among firms weighs heavily in choosing among alternatives in marketing policy. In large measure, many public trading rules and regulations exist to improve integrity and equity and maintain a degree of open competition among firms of uneven size and power. But in recent years, mere size has not been taken as a basis for antitrust action, and there is no groundswell of demand for public policy to support the Federal Trade Commission in reversing the trend toward fewer and larger firms. The general emphasis in policy over the years and today has been (1) to offset private market power with countervailing power, such as by use of farm price supports, marketing orders, cooperatives, and farmer bargaining associations; and (2) to provide market services such as those mentioned above to keep concentrated markets operating more competitively than might be the case otherwise.

Concern over Pricing

Marketing policy is dominated by concerns over the effectiveness of the pricing system to allocate resources efficiently, yet still provide an equitable distribution of income. Trends toward vertical integration and market concentration bring into question the traditional concepts of equity, and the equitableness of the relationship of prices at the farm level to those at retail. Where direct marketing on the basis of contracts or vertical integration replaces the more open auction market, the development of adequate price information becomes more difficult. Frequently, what is being priced is not a product, but a combination of labor and management services provided by the grower. As the independent farmer (grower) is usually at a disadvantage in negotiating, farmers have turned increasingly to collective bargaining, just as organized industrial workers have done for years.

But the effectiveness of farmer bargaining is suspect; the spread or margin between prices at the farm and retail levels has tended to widen, or at least not narrow, as one might assume with advancing technology; and policy questions about the marketing economy cannot be laid to rest. Is the marketing economy performing its function? How wide should the marketing margin be?

THE MARKETING MARGIN AND COSTS

With increasing specialization in production and advances in food technology, there is both an increasing demand for marketing services, and a reduction in the real cost of most services, which is equivalent to an increase in supply. With economic growth, the marketing economy increases in magnitude, both absolutely and relative to the crops and the livestock economies. Although this is a characteristic of economic growth and progress, when viewed as a cost the increasing share of the consumer's dollar that goes to marketing is a matter of some concern.

If there truly is an equivalent growing demand for market services, there is no reason to object to the change in distribution of the consumer's dollar. But if this change occurs because the services are too elaborate and competitive relationships are not good and efficient, then this is a cause for concern among both producers and consumers in formulating policy.

The issue is not the size of the marketing economy per se, but its productivity or output relative to input, its economic structure and competitive relationships, and the prices that result. The problem is to discern what policy can do to improve the marketing economy, if this is an agreed goal, or to increase its competitiveness in the ways that are desired. It is important to develop our vision in respect to the concepts involved.

Consumer Expenditures: Farm Value and Marketing Bill

Consumer expenditures on food may be visualized as covering the farm value of food and the marketing bill for food (Figure 8-1). The marketing bill is an estimate, prepared by professionals in the U.S. Department of Agriculture, of all receipts of the marketing sector for assembling, transporting, processing, and distributing foods

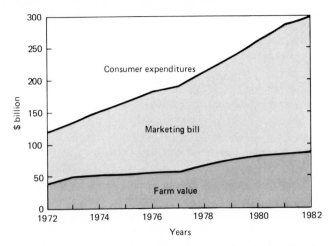

1981 preliminary, 1982 projected. For domestic farm foods purchased by civilian consumers for consumption both at home and away from home.

FIGURE 8-1
Consumer expenditures, marketing bill, and farm value for farm food products in the United States. *(Source: USDA, 1982 Handbook of Agricultural Charts, p. 34.)*

originating on American farms. Since it omits fibers such as cotton and wool, it is not a complete estimate of all costs or receipts of the agricultural marketing sector. Also, since it omits some of the costs of marketing other foods, such as fish and game, and some food inputs, it is not a complete estimate of all food marketing costs. It is, however, a helpful concept for policy analysis, and we may use it for this purpose.

Distribution of Consumer Expenditures for Farm Foods

In any year, the distribution of consumer expenditures for farm foods may be divided into the farm value of the foods, and the marketing costs of labor, packaging, transportation, and other components. This distribution is shown in Figure 8-2, which illustrates the major categories of the total consumer cost. The annual increases in consumer expenditures are more a reflection of increasing prices for services than of increasing volume of farm food marketed (Figure 8-2).

The Farm-Retail Price Spread

The difference between farm and retail prices for farm foods is sometimes known as the "farm-retail price spread." It is calculated by deducting the farm value of a raw farm food product (adjusted for the value of by-products, if any) from the retail price of the corresponding unit, such as a pound of beef, a one-pound loaf of bread, or a dozen eggs. The value of the designated raw product in the unit of consumer product is estimated as a joint cost in the final product. Then the farm share of the retail

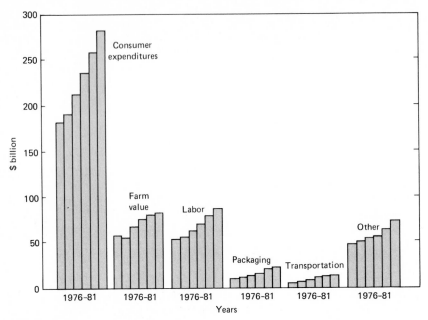

FIGURE 8-2
Components of consumer expenditures for farm foods in the United States. (*Source: USDA, 1982 Handbook of Agricultural Charts, p. 35.*)

food value can be expressed as a percentage of the retail food price for selected commodities (Figure 8-3).

Concepts of Marketing Margins

The difference between the farm and retail price is also known as a *marketing margin.* It may be defined either (a) as a difference between the price paid by consumers

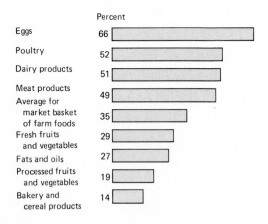

FIGURE 8-3
Farm share of retail food prices, expressed as a percentage of the retail price, in the United States. (*Source: USDA* 1982 Handbook of Agricultural Charts, *p. 39.*)

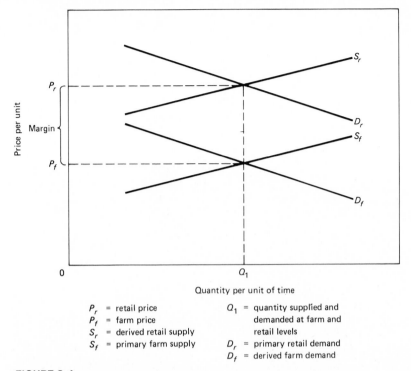

P_r = retail price
P_f = farm price
S_r = derived retail supply
S_f = primary farm supply

Q_1 = quantity supplied and
      demanded at farm and
      retail levels
D_r = primary retail demand
D_f = derived farm demand

FIGURE 8-4
Concept of the marketing margin for farm food products related to supply and demand at the farm and the retail levels. Both the supply and the demand for total farm food products are very inelastic in the short run at both the farm and retail levels. But each curve is more inelastic at the farm than at the retail level.

and that obtained by producers, or (b) as the price or cost of a collection of marketing services that is the outcome of the demand and the supply of such services.

Under the first definition, which is generally more useful in policy analysis, a marketing margin for a farm food commodity is the difference between the retail price—determined by the intersection of supply and demand in retail markets—and the price received by primary producers (farmers)—determined by the intersection of supply and demand at the farm level. The margin may be visualized hypothetically, as in Figure 8-4.

The retail demand is a primary demand, and also a joint demand for all the inputs in the final product. Conceptually, as a joint demand it may be divided into demands for two types of inputs: the farm-based components and the processing-marketing components. Then, the demand for each input is a derived demand, based on the primary demand at retail. Demand is based on the determinants we have discussed, and can change in either market as a result of change in one or more of the determinants.

The farm supply is a primary supply, and the retail supply is a joint product of

Cattle feeding is a year-around operation in which price changes can greatly influence profits. Federal policy enforces trading rules for futures contracts which permits forward-contracting by feeders as a means of shifting the risk of price changes. Who benefits from such a policy? Who may bear the cost? Is it possible for there to be a gain in net social income from the policy?

the farm and marketing economies. Again, the supply can change in either market as a result of changes in one or more of the determinants.

The width of the marketing margin or price spread depends on the location of supply and demand in the farm and retail markets. Given the elasticities of supply and demand, the margin will change as one or more of the curves changes. Prices at the farm and the retail level move in their respective ways; they depend on whether the events causing the movement arise from a shift in the primary retail demand or primary farm supply, or from a shift in the supply or the demand for marketing inputs. Consistency with market equilibrium in the marketing economy puts constraints on the pricing practices of marketing firms. Hence, no simple mark-up rule—such as a fixed percentage margin, a fixed absolute margin, or a combination

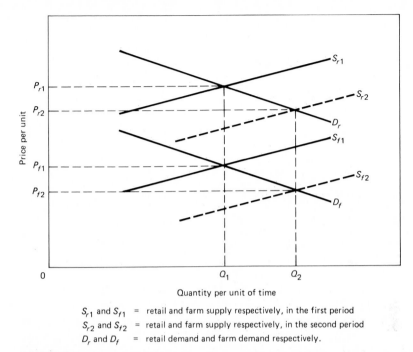

S_{r1} and S_{f1} = retail and farm supply respectively, in the first period
S_{r2} and S_{f2} = retail and farm supply respectively, in the second period
D_r and D_f = retail demand and farm demand respectively.

FIGURE 8-5
When the farm and retail demand curves are parallel and the supply changes, the change in the price at the farm level will be *relatively* greater than the change at the retail level, ceteris paribus.

of the two—can establish the marketing margin, the relationship between the farm and the retail price. Changes in equilibrium prices depend on changes in one or more of the four curves, and on the respective elasticities of the curves.[4]

Policy Implications of Elasticity

Both supply and demand are more inelastic at the farm level than at retail; the width of the marketing margin, or the breadth of the farm-retail price spread, does not necessarily change when prices rise or fall. With parallel demand curves (as in Figure 8-4), an increase in supply at the farm level, which is passed through to the retail market, will bring the same absolute change in both the farm and the retail price (Figure 8-5). But because of the more inelastic demand at the farm level, the price at the farm level will change *relatively* more than at the retail level. When there are changes in supply, therefore, with no change in demand, prices fluctuate relatively more at the farm than at the retail level.

Similarly, supply at the farm level is more inelastic than at the retail level. When

[4]For more formal discussion and econometric modeling, see Bruce L. Gardner, "The Farm-Retail Price Spread in a Competitive Food Industry," *American Journal of Agricultural Economics,* vol. 57, no. 3, August 1975, pp. 399–409.

there are changes in demand with no change in supply, prices fluctuate relatively more at the farm than at the retail level.

Changes in the Marketing Margin

The marketing margin and the retail price spread can change absolutely, however, when a change in supply or demand at one level is not reflected in a similar change at the other level. For instance, a large crop that increases supply at the farm level is not immediately passed through to the domestic retail market, or to export. In this case, the marketing margin and the farm-retail price spread will widen, as farm prices fall both absolutely and relative to retail prices. This compounds the effects of the more inelastic farm-level demand on prices at the farm level.

As another example, an increase in demand for grain exports tends to be passed through as an increase in demand at the farm level, while the demand for domestic marketing services does not change. Other things being equal, the farm-retail price spread does not necessarily have to change, but often will, because the increase in demand at the farm level is largely independent of the demand for marketing services, and it takes time for the higher farm prices to be passed on to retail markets. Thus, the marketing margin may narrow as farmers enjoy the higher prices brought by an increase in export demand. But, typically, this narrowing of the margin will be only temporary, lasting until the normal competitive relationships are reestablished in the marketing economy. Similarly, a large crop may widen the marketing margin, as the increase in supply at the farm level is not immediately reflected in an increase in supply at the retail level.

Because it takes time for commodities to be processed and passed through the marketing economy, changes in prices at the farm level generally are not reflected immediately at the retail level. Although we say that the margin does not necessarily change as prices rise and fall, the margin often does decrease when farm prices rise, and increase when they fall. Increases in the primary farm supply, ceteris paribus, will increase the ratio of retail prices to farm prices, whether the margin, or the price spread, increases or stays the same. Farm prices may fall both absolutely and relative to retail prices. Unless there are corresponding increases in demand, the depressed farm prices will tend to spur policy steps to reduce farm output by control of production and reduce marketing costs, or to reduce the farm-retail price spread by increasing the efficiency and competitiveness of marketing. Why is the last a policy issue, and what may be done about it?

POLICY ALTERNATIVES IN THE MARKETING ECONOMY

As we have said, the agricultural marketing economy, over the years, has become more and more concentrated, both at the food-processing and manufacturing level, and at the retail-marketing level. This is believed to hurt farmers and consumers by allowing marketing firms to take advantage of the gains from imperfect competition, oligopsony-oligopoly, especially. Therefore, there have been many policy movements aimed at making marketing more purely competitive. Let us consider these.

Cooperatives and Bargaining Associations in Food Processing

One of the major thrusts in modern food processing and marketing has been to build strong cooperatives and farmer-bargaining associations as a means of grappling with oligopoly-type processing firms. These new firms have met with some success, but where the cooperatives have been most successful, as in fluid milk marketing, they in turn have become highly concentrated oligopolies, practically necessitating government control of pricing.

In other cases, where the restructuring of the existing processing-marketing industry might improve competition, or where the political will to improve competition can be organized, the economic arguments often seem weak; and, where the economic arguments seem strong, the political opposition to restructuring usually is formidable. Where one or two major firms gain a dominant position in a market, it usually is the result of their superior performance over a period of time sufficient to drive out their competitors. Once a technically efficient concentration is established, attempts to break it up, or to limit its further expansion, may in fact simply reduce the supply of marketing services and increase marketing margins, at least for a time, until new firms are attracted to the market. Often, where the economic arguments are strong for breaking up a concentrated oligopoly, there may be little political support for doing so.

Controlling Concentration of Dominant Firms

Dominant firms in some of the most highly concentrated industries on an area basis have achieved their position as a result of superior performance. In beef packing, for example, one or two firms have reached a dominant position in regional markets because their greater efficiency has permitted them to undercut other sellers of carcass beef while offering more attractive deals to cattle producers and feeders than other packers were able to offer. This is how most large meat-packing firms have originated and grown. The question of whether the government should become involved in controlling dominant firms cannot be answered in terms of a general rule, but must be approached on a case-by-case basis. Similar conclusions may apply to performance of the major dairy cooperatives in federal-order milk markets, major fruit and vegetable marketing firms, and even to the major international grain firms.

This fact has created great uncertainty in political movements aimed at restructuring or improving the competitiveness of the marketing economy. In the mid 1960s, as we noted, two high-level national commissions, the National Commission on Food Marketing established by Congress, and the National Advisory Commission on Food and Fiber established by President Johnson, each failed to agree on any major policy concerning restructuring, or reducing concentration in food manufacturing, wholesaling, and retailing. Although data from individual large-city markets show that marketing margins and profits of retail firms are higher where concentration is high, a consistent policy for dealing with concentration still has not been devised.

In a number of cases in retail markets, the Federal Trade Commission has issued consent orders to permit and limit mergers of food firms, and in 1967 the FTC issued a set of guidelines to limit mergers of major food chains. The guidelines stated that

Modern fast-food restaurants are a rapidly growing part of the marketing economy. How do they tend to change the competitive structure of the marketing system? On the whole, is this good or bad for the farmer? For the consumer?

any but very small acquisitions by large chains (defined as chains with annual sales exceeding $500 million) would be very carefully scrutinized. The guidelines applied to horizontal mergers between direct competitors, and to market-extension mergers between firms operating in different metropolitan markets. For almost a decade, these guidelines were apparently successful in controlling mergers. But in the mid 1970s, five substantial mergers occurred, and went unchallenged by the FTC. From that time until to the end of the 1970s, the FTC did not enforce the 1967 merger policy, which had been pursued with apparent success for a number of years.

Although some economic analysts have concluded that entry into highly concentrated wholesale and retail markets having one or more dominant firms may have a beneficial effect on competition, in relatively unconcentrated markets the competitive impacts of a new firm are less clear. In the latter case, if entry of the new firm triggers a competitive battle or price war, concentration may eventually increase. But if restrictive leasing arrangements are eliminated, selective price cutting is prohibited, and saturation advertising is restricted, entry of a new firm can reduce concentration and encourage more effective competition in food processing, and in wholesale or retail markets.

A number of writers have cautioned, however, that a general extension of antimonopoly policy to food-processing and the food-manufacturing industry must be approached with extreme caution. Most of the firms in food manufacturing have demonstrated important economies of large scale. Any serious attempt by antitrust agencies to restructure this industry in order to reduce concentration might deprive society of important welfare gains made possible by the economies of large scale that some of the large manufacturing firms enjoy. It has been argued, for instance, that increased concentration in the food-manufacturing industries in the United States is associated with increased input productivity, which tends to offset the "deadweight" welfare losses due to oligopoly pricing on the part of these firms.[5]

Under a given level of productivity, the welfare loss depends on the elasticity of demand for the manufactured product. That is, the welfare loss to society tends to vary inversely with the elasticity of demand. With an elasticity of -1.0 the deadweight loss to society of oligopoly pricing is very small. Theoretically, the oligopolist cannot increase gross revenue by increasing the price of the product, and net revenue gains from raising prices will be small. If the elasticity of demand is -0.5 or less, gross revenue can be increased by restricting sales, and the resulting deadweight loss to society of oligopoly pricing would be much higher. But it has been concluded that once the shift in the production function of the leading firms is incorporated into the model of the food-manufacturing industry, the increase in total factor productivity that is linked to concentration roughly offsets the entire loss to consumers.[6] This reinforces the policy conclusion mentioned above, that attempts to regulate the food-manufacturing industry must be approached on a case-by-case basis, rather than on the basis of an all-inclusive regulatory rule.

Other Policy Alternatives

There are a number of other policy alternatives, on which there appears to be a more general concensus among students of the marketing economy. These include lowering barriers to entry, improving consumer information, and encouraging consumer cooperatives.[7]

Lowering Barriers to Entry In food retailing, concentration can be reduced if new firms enter the market, or if smaller firms already in the market expand at the expense of the larger firms. One barrier can be reduced if new firms are helped to gain access to preferred store sites, or at least not disadvantaged by local agencies' favoring firms which already have preferred locations in major urban market areas.

Sometimes existing firms have discouraged new entrants by selectively cutting their prices to prevent the new firm from succeeding, or they may threaten to cut

---

[5]See Micha Gisser, "Welfare Implications of Oligopoly in U.S. Food Manufacturing," *American Journal of Agricultural Economics,* vol. 64, no. 4, November 1982, pp. 616–624.

[6]Ibid., pp. 623 and 624.

[7]For results of several studies and further discussion, see Bruce W. Marion, Willard F. Mueller, Ronald W. Cotterill, Federick E. Geithman, and John R. Schmelzer, *The Food Retailing Industry: Market Structure, Profits, and Prices,* Praeger Publishers, Praeger Special Studies, New York, 1979. Further details of the policy foundation and alternatives can be found in Harold G. Halcrow, *Food Policy for America,* McGraw-Hill Book Company, New York, 1977, pp. 176–187, 280–283, and 530–544.

prices to prevent a new firm from attempting to enter a market. An existing firm may spend an excessive amount on advertising and offer inducements to customers to prevent a new firm from succeeding. Although price cutting and excessive advertising that discourage entry probably violate the Robinson-Patman Act, the Federal Trade Commission Act, or the Sherman Act, federal antitrust agencies have been slow to challenge these practices. If antitrust agencies do not have the necessary resources to mount such a challenge, Congress could strengthen provisions of the relevant act or acts.

Improving Consumer Information   More consumer information will generally make pricing and trade practices more competitive, to the benefit of both producers and consumers. Individual consumers can seldom afford the time and energy required to become adequately informed about a full array of supermarket stock of some 8,000 items, however. This is especially true if prices change often and a variety of day-to-day or weekly specials are offered to customers. Although some may argue that publicly financed consumer information is an invasion of business privacy, and should be limited, it is clearly established that information on prices, qualities, and grades of consumer items is in the public interest; and is therefore a legitimate function of appropriate government agencies. Recent advances in consumer education,

Soybean milk is a new product resulting from research undertaken as a result of decisions in agricultural policy. What beliefs and values underlie this work?

food labeling, and nutrition education must be supported if major advances are to be made in making retail food markets more competitive.

Encouraging Consumer Cooperatives Although consumer cooperatives have played a small role in the United States, as compared with many other countries, several policy steps could be taken to promote the creation of consumer cooperatives. The environment for cooperatives can be encouraged by two of the steps just mentioned: lowering barriers to entry and improving consumer education. Consumer organizations, which apparently have grown much stronger in recent years, could give more positive help to new cooperatives in highly concentrated markets, where both the greatest savings may be realized and the strongest opposition may be encountered. The legislation establishing a bank for consumer cooperatives may help to finance cooperatives so they can become more efficient competitors. But aggressive efforts will be required for this potential to be realized in the most concentrated food markets.

Politics of Policy to Improve Competition

Further trends toward conglomeration in the food industry could be slowed by strengthening the existing antimerger law. Specifically, the law could be strengthened by requiring large corporations in the food industry to receive their corporate charters from the federal government rather than from state governments. A law could place an absolute prohibition on large mergers unless it could be shown that the merger would help to improve competition. A law could spell out the corporations' responsibilities to the public, as well as their rights under the law. Provisions requiring large corporations to disclose all of their various lines of business would be an important step in obtaining more corporate accountability in the interests of more effective competition.[8]

It must be recognized that the food industry may continue to exert strong political opposition to such policy, however. Going back to the Nixon administration in the late 1960s and early 1970s, the federal government has not effectively opposed a number of important large-scale mergers. Some results of this failure are as follows: The Greyhound Corporation took over Armour Foods. The Ling-Temco-Vought conglomerate bought a controlling interest in Wilson and Company. The ITT Corporation expanded into such diverse areas as Wonder Bread, Morton pies and dinners, Gwaltney Smithfield ham and bacon, Pearson candies, and Hostess products. In 1970, a bill to establish a consumer-protection agency failed in a tie vote in the House Rules Committee, the defeat apparently the result of opposition tactics by the Grocery Manufacturers of America (GMA). In 1971, when the bill was again moving toward passage, the GMA evidently defeated it again by adding so many compromising amendments that consumer organizations withdrew their support. By 1974,

---

[8]For further discussion, see Willard F. Mueller, "The Food Conglomerates," *Food Policy and Farm Programs,* Don F. Hadwiger and Ross B. Talbot (eds.), Proceedings of the Academy of Political Science, vol. 34, no. 3, New York, 1982, pp. 54–67.

the public support for consumer protection had grown so strong that, even under threat of a presidential veto, the House passed a bill by a 3-to-1 margin. Although Montgomery Ward, Zenith, Polaroid, Motorola, and several other large firms switched their positions to come out in favor of the bill, the GMA and the National Association of Food Chains (NAFC) were able to maintain a united opposition front in the food industry. On September 19, 1974, the Senate, by a vote of 64 to 34, failed by 2 votes to end a filibuster being conducted in opposition to the bill.

For several years after the big jump in food prices in 1973, the large food firms also were able to prevent government action from monitoring food-price margins or counteracting the growth of oligopsony-oligopoly. During this time the economic structure of the food industry tended to stabilize, but it was a stability involving considerable concentration of market power. In 1973, although nationally only 41 percent of total grocery sales were made by the 20 largest firms, and only 20 percent by the largest four,[9] out of 120 positions of market control in 30 large cities, the large supermarket chains held 101.[10] In 1973 and 1974 there were four major congressional hearings dealing with issues of imperfect competition or monopoly power in the food industry, but the committees were unable to get the leading firms to testify under oath as to the effects of their pricing and market-supply policies on food prices in local food-market areas.[11] Since then, although congressional committees have continued to hold hearings and gather information, the political stance of successive national administrations has not favored strong antitrust action.

Political efforts to improve the competitive structure of the marketing economy will continue to encounter strong opposition from the food industry. The rising power of consumer groups may serve as a countervailing power to further conglomeration. But it will be necessary to strengthen certain laws, such as those requiring firms in excess of a certain size to get their charters from the federal government, rather than from the individual states. It will be necessary to have more consistent support for the antitrust activities of the Federal Trade Commission. The FTC's power was used rather effectively in the 1950s and early 1960s. But in the 1970s and 1980s, as we have mentioned, a number of mergers which could have been challenged under existing law were not, and, in general, mergers took place without challenge by the FTC.[12]

More aggressive action by the FTC might slow the trend toward further concentration over the next several years. Whether this action is taken or not, the public's interest will depend on some of the other programs in public policy, such as public price reporting, commodity grading, trade practice regulation, farm food commodity

[9]*Supermarket News,* July 1, 1974, p. 1.

[10]Metropolitan Market Studies, Inc., *1973 Grocery Distribution Guide,* 1973, Table II-3.

[11]These hearings were "Food Price Investigation," June and July 1973, House Subcommittees on Monopolies and Commercial Law, Serial No. 15; "Corporate Giantism and Food Prices," Dec. 10, 11, and 12, 1973, Senate Select Committee on Small Business; "Federal Trade Commission Oversight," Senate Commerce Committee, March and May 1974, Serial No. 93–78; and "Hearings on the Farm-Retail Price Spread," Joint Economic Committee, Consumer Economics Subcommittee, May 1974.

[12]For further discussion of antitrust law and specific antitrust actions, see Harold G. Halcrow, *Food Policy for America,* McGraw-Hill Book Company, New York, 1977, pp. 181, ff.

Examination of agricultural produce in retail markets helps to protect the interests of consumers of agricultural products.

programs, and marketing research.[13] In addition, there is a case for more emphasis to be placed on nutrition policy.

The Setting for Nutrition Policy[14]

As we have noted, the growth of agriculture has freed the American people from the age-old threat of food shortages while greatly expanding U.S. capacity to export. A large majority of Americans have an adequate, if not luxurious, food supply, with good opportunities for well-balanced and nutritious diets. Only a relative few in the lower income brackets have real limitations in purchasing power necessary to achieve adequate diets, and much of their deficiency has been filled in recent years by growth in the federal food-stamp program, subsidized school lunches, and a special program for women, infants, and children (WIC). The great expansion in the public's knowledge of diet and nutrition, and the increasing emphasis on health-related exercise and medical care, has continued to improve the health of people of all ages. The American public is probably healthier now than in any previous time. In comparison with the populations of other countries, it is near the top (although not at the top) in measures of general health and longevity.

Yet this relatively favorable assessment must be tempered by the fact that more than one-fourth of all Americans are more than 10 percent overweight, some 15 to 20 percent of adolescents are obese as a result of overeating and too little exercise, and a higher percentage of older people are overweight. Studies of a few years ago found that in various regions one-quarter to one-half of all women were 10 percent or more overweight and more than half of these were more than 20 percent overweight. In a 10-state survey, the percentage of men who were 10 percent or more overweight varied from 24 percent in California and Colorado to 39 percent in New Jersey, and more than half in these groups were more than 20 percent overweight.[15] Many overweight people and a still larger percentage of the poor have too high a percentage of sugar and fat in their diets. The intake of salt is generally excessive, or significantly more than is required for good health. Dental care is deficient in about a fourth of the population. The poor, especially, suffer from inadequate dental care, and from dietary deficiencies of calcium, iron, and vitamins A and C. It is stated in a leading textbook that appropriate nutrition intervention activities could reduce morbidity and mortality from heart disease by 25 percent, respiratory and infectious diseases by 20 percent, cancer by 20 percent, and diabetes by 50 percent.[16]

---

[13]For further discussion, see *Federal Marketing Programs in Agriculture: Issues and Options*, Walter J. Armbruster, Dennis R. Henderson, and Ronald D. Knutson (eds.), The Interstate Printers and Publishers, Danville, Illinois, 1983.

[14]For a more detailed discussion of nutrition policy, see Harold G. Halcrow, *Food Policy for America*, McGraw-Hill Book Company, New York, 1977, pp. 492–545.

[15]Comparative data are from *Nutritional Status, USA*, Agnes Fay Morgan (ed.), University of California at Berkeley, California Agricultural Experiment Station Bulletin 769, 1959; *Dietary Levels of Households in the United States, Spring 1965: A Preliminary Report*, U.S. Department of Agriculture, Economic Research Service, no. 67-17, January 1968; and *Ten-State Nutrition Survey, 1968–1970*, DHEW Publication no. (HSM) 72-8120, 5 vols., Washington, D.C., 1972.

[16]Helen Andrews Guthrie, *Introductory Nutrition*, The C. V. Mosby Company, St. Louis, 1975, 3d ed., p. 8.

This highly nutritious meal is made largely out of soybeans with some other vegetable products. Such products were not available just a few years ago. The increasing productivity of agriculture to which this importantly contributes is the result of public-policy support for agricultural and food-science research.

The Elements of Nutrition Policy

Generally, it is accepted that the goals of nutrition policy involve an emphasis on healthy diets and high-level nutrition, correcting some of the weaknesses in diets and nutrition just mentioned. A variety of means have been proposed to accomplish this. These include continuing public support for research in food science and technology, more nutrition education in the schools and public media, more effective regulation of food advertising, and more emphasis on public regulation and support programs affecting the elderly.

Education In regard to education, studies by nutritionists have shown that schoolchildren without nutrition education are generally not capable of selecting a good and nutritious diet from among an array of food items. Nutrition education is required to combat the deleterious effects of some food advertising on television, radio, and in the press, and to correct some misinformation on diet and nutrition. The general thesis of nutritionists is that good nutrition must be learned, and the earlier this learning occurs, the better.

Advertising In regard to advertising, both the Food and Drug Administration and the Federal Trade Commission are responsible for issuing and enforcing regulations on food; the FDA in the areas of food purity and sanitation, and the FTC in

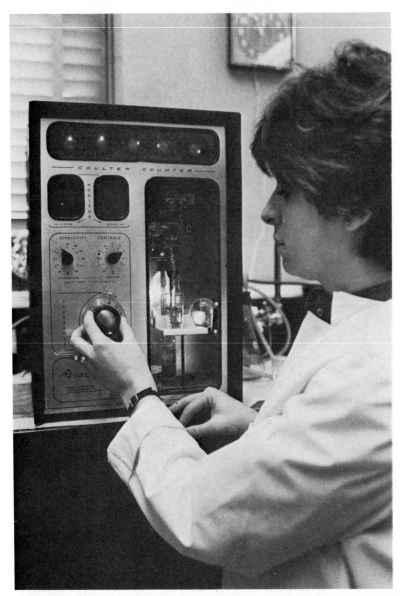

A "Coulter Counter" is used to count red-blood corpuscles in analyses of diets and nutrition.

the areas of information, advertising, and certain trade practices. Specifically, the FTC is charged with promulgating and enforcing trade regulation rules (TRRs) concerning advertising claims for food. Typically, a TRR not only prohibits making untrue claims, but specific levels of nutrient content may be required before certain nutrition information can be included in advertisements. Additionally, certain limited nutrient information may be required in virtually all food advertisements.

The FTC Improvement Act, signed by President Ford on January 5, 1975, set specific limits to FTC authority in writing and enforcing a TRR. This act more specifically authorized the FTC to define unfair acts or practices and required it to issue TRRs to prevent them. It strengthened the FTC requirements for informal hearings on a proposed TRR, for establishment of procedural rules for the public input and hearings, and for appropriate time for comments and criticism from the public, nutritionists, and industry representatives.

The FTC has authority to appoint a presiding officer for a hearing, who is given broad and extensive powers. This officer must designate the issues of fact to be covered at hearings and publish them together with notices of proposed rule making. The presiding officer may or may not choose to allow any petitioner's appeal, add or modify any designated issue of specific fact, or consider petitions from other persons to add or modify any issues. The officer has power to identify the disputed issues of fact, to control the conduct of hearings, and to rule on the disputed issues of law or policy. At the termination of a set of hearings on a proposed TRR, the presiding officer is required to prepare a summary of the record, which the FTC staff uses to develop final recommendations for action by the full FTC.

On completion of this process, which takes five to six months and sometimes longer, the FTC may issue the TRR, ask for more information, table the entire effort, or substantially modify the original proposal and begin the entire procedure again. If the proceeding is reopened, it will be limited to those issues not already covered. Throughout the process, the public has an opportunity to submit (1) comments on the entire proposal, (2) issues of specific fact, which should be included in the public hearing, (3) petitions for additions, deletions, or modifications to the published issues of fact, (4) statements of interest on specific issues, and (5) comments and/or requests for review.[17]

Consumer Information   For several years, studies of consumer preferences showed that consumers wanted to know more about the food they were eating. In 1975, the Comptroller General issued a study by the Government Accounting Office (GAO), which recommended improvements in trading rules to inform consumers about what they were buying. Specifically, the GAO recommended:[18]

1 *Full disclosure* of all ingredients on packaged food products, to displace the provisions of the then active Food, Drug and Cosmetic Act, which exempted some food products and required only a general ingredient listing.

2 *Percentage labeling,* to show the amounts of various ingredients that make up a product, because various manufacturers use different formulas for the same product.

3 *Nutrition labeling,* to overcome the lack of nutritional and educational information on food labels, because Americans suffer dietary and health problems due in part to lack of good nutrition.

4 *Quality grading* on a mandatory basis, in lieu of the voluntary USDA quality grad-

[17]Mahlon A. Burnette III, "The Food Advertising TRR Proceedings: A Scenario," *Food Product Development,* vol. 9, September 1975.

[18]U.S. General Accounting Office, *Food Labeling: Goals, Shortcomings, and Proposed Changes,* Report of the Comptroller General of the United States, Washington, D.C., 1975.

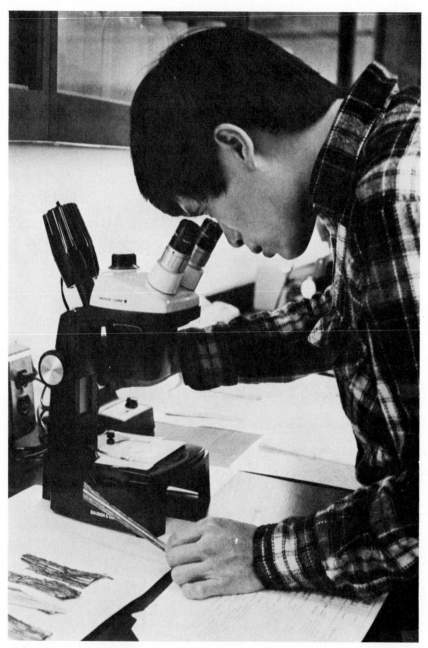

High-powered microscopes are used in agricultural research for analysis of animal tissues in studies of diet and nutrition.

ing system, to provide more complete information for consumers to judge the comparative quality and value of alternative products.

5 *A uniform dating system* for perishable and semiperishable goods, because the variety and types of dates then in use were generally not well understood, which resulted in limited consumer use.

6 *A federal unit pricing program* to help consumers compare prices because, although unit pricing was available on about 50 percent of the items in chain-operated grocery stores, use of the system often required complicated mathematical calculations.

Following the GAO report, several bills were introduced in Congress to implement these recommendations and others. A main policy goal of the Congress was to disclose basic facts about food in terms that consumers could understand. It was thought that disclosure of more factual information could have a salutary effect on the food industry. Especially, if combined with new and improved programs on nutrition education, such disclosure could provide the basis for more healthful diets and eating habits.

Drawing attention to nutritional factors has been found to have educational benefits for consumers. It acts as a stimulant for the industry to improve the quality of some manufactured foods, and it serves as a disciplinary factor for food advertising. Benefits from nutrition labeling tend to increase with program duration, as consumer

Through use of recently established trading rules, producer groups have been able to raise small amounts of money for advertising and research. Is it possible to have a gain in net social income from such a policy?

food habits change to make more use of the information. Most consumers see nutrition labeling as having a positive or desirable effect on food advertising and on the nutritional accountability of food manufacturers. Labels tend to inspire consumer confidence in the food industry, encourage the production and manufacture of more nutritious foods, stimulate consumer education concerning nutrition, and satisfy the consumer's right and desire to know. Although evidence that consumers' purchasing decisions may be altered by nutrition labeling is extremely scarce and superficial, there is general agreement among nutritionists that benefits are substantial.

Consumer Advocacy   The development of consumer-oriented groups has become an important force in nutrition policy. This is demonstrated in a large number of state and national conferences, including a number of White House conferences, which have been held, at irregular intervals, since 1930. Generally, the national conferences have had broad agendas dealing with general issues such as the needs of children, nutrition education and research, public health, national defense, and health and care of the elderly. In nearly all conferences, food and nutrition policy has played a prominent role. For instance, the 1981 White House Conference on Aging passed the following:[19]

Issue 1: The role of nutrition, exercise, stress, and activity in the promotion and maintenance of wellness

Be it resolved that:

• Government agencies and private agencies be urged to disseminate information to the elderly stressing: (1) the importance of good nutrition, exercise, and an active lifestyle to their physical well-being; and (2) specific guidelines for doing so.
• To promote and maintain a sense of well-being among seniors, mental, spiritual, and physical health should be included in all concerns.
• We should develop a national health care policy that includes programs at all levels of community structure in order to provide nutritional assessments, exercise programs, and health care management for all citizens.
• Nutrition programs for older Americans shall include provisions for nutrition education, transportation services, and recognition of special populations. This shall be done in partnership between public, private and nonprofit sectors.
• Registered dieticians should be reimbursed by Medicare, Medicaid and private insurance for counseling services on physician-prescribed therapeutic diets.

The Technical Committee on Health Maintenance and Health Promotion for the 1981 White House Conference concluded that adequate nutrition is the most important factor in improving the health and status of the elderly. There is a need for well-conducted nutrition education programs. There is limited research on nutrient requirements for older people. Educational activities have been conducted only sporadically, although specific provision is made for them in the Older Americans Act. Nutrition education has competed unfavorably with other social services. Therefore,

---

[19]See *Final Report of the 1981 White House Conference on Aging* (in three volumes), vol. 2, p. 77. Distributed by the U.S. Department of Health and Human Services.

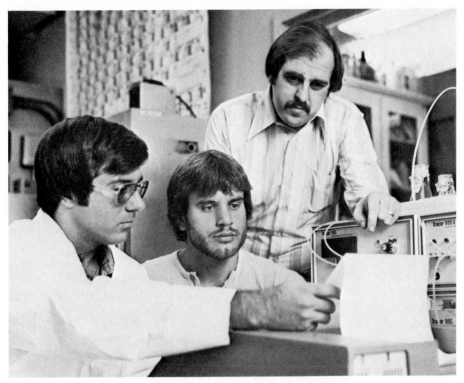

Food scientists study the results of an experiment in nutrition. Modern laboratories and computers have greatly increased the speed and accuracy of such research. Who benefits? Should such research be supported with public funds?

it is important to involve older Americans in nutrition education programs, to expand research on their nutritional needs, and to give financial assistance to those who are in need.[20]

A Policy Conclusion   An acceptable national policy for good nutrition will require a number of approaches. Agreement on food standards is important as a basis for most government programs, including food regulation by the FDA and the FTC. To meet some of the criticisms that have been made, food stamps, subsidized school-lunch programs, and the special programs for women, infants, and children (WIC), must be combined more effectively with Social Security, unemployment insurance, and other programs of aid to the poor. Finally, a strong continuing commitment to research and education is essential, offering hope for further dietary improvements in the years ahead.

[20] *The 1981 White House Conference on Aging, Executive Summary of Technical Committee on Health Maintenance and Health Promotion,* p. 6.

SUMMARY

The main questions for policy analysis of the marketing economy involve the improvement of public trading rules, analysis of the marketing margin, and appraisal of alternatives in policy to improve competition and the quality of the food supply. Most agricultural markets are imperfectly competitive, with degrees of perfection or imperfection varying from one market to another. Oligopolistic competition helps to account for some of the rigidity in retail food prices relative to farm prices, and for substitution of advertising and sales promotion for aggressive price competition in retail food markets.

The policy-making efforts affecting the marketing economy have been very extensive over the years. But various commissions and study groups have not agreed on what kind of government involvement there should be in the marketing economy, or how strenuously various policy alternatives should be pursued. There is a conflict of interest among farm producers, marketing firms, and consumer groups. A number of policy alternatives that presumably would be in the public interest have been identified. Apparently, major restructuring of the marketing economy will not be supported politically, but there is an important continuing role for government in surveillance and regulation, price reporting, commodity grading, regulation of spot and futures markets, enforcement of food safety rules, and development of public programs to improve nutrition.

IMPORTANT TERMS AND CONCEPTS

Public and private trading rules
Five stages of agricultural marketing
Policy concerns with marketing progress
Quality of competition in agricultural marketing
Concerns related to vertical integration
Effectiveness of competition among firms
Concern over pricing
The marketing margin: concept and definition
Reasons for growth of the marketing economy
The farm food marketing bill
Components of consumer expenditures for farm foods
Composition of the farm food marketing bill
The farm-retail price spread: how it is calculated

The marketing margin: two definitions
How supply and demand determine the marketing margin
Policy implications of elasticity of supply and demand
Role of cooperatives and bargaining associations
Policy controls over concentration in food marketing
Politics of policy to improve competition
Status of nutrition in the United States
Elements of a national nutrition policy
Role of the FDA and the FTC in food and nutrition policy
Consumer information and consumer advocacy in nutrition policy
Policy alternatives for dealing with the marketing economy

LOOKING AHEAD

Policy analysis of the input markets, covered in the next four chapters, is a topic which, in the long view, may be just as important for agriculture, if not more so, than the areas of policy we have just discussed. Although there is no natural hierarchical order for policy study of the various topics, there is a certain convenience and logic in dealing first with the financial input markets. Financial policy can be studied independently, and it provides a foundation for studying the other topics. We turn next, therefore, to policy analysis of financial input markets.

QUESTIONS AND EXERCISES

1 What are trading rules? What is the difference between public and private rules? Give three examples of each. What is the purpose of each rule in your example?

2 What are the five stages of agricultural marketing? How do these stages compare in terms of type and presumed quality of competition?

3 What are the major policy concerns with the performance and progress of the agricultural marketing economy? What were the majority recommendations of the National Commission on Food Marketing? Why are some of these concerns still with us?

4 What is the difference between owner and contract integrations? Why has vertical integration tended to increase rather than diminish in the marketing economy? What are the major policy conerns with vertical integration? What are some of the more important ways in which such concerns could be alleviated?

5 How does the type and quality of competition tend to change as vertical and horizontal integration become more prevalent? Given a certain level of integration, how might the quality of competition be improved?

6 As the level of concentration in agricultural markets increases, why are there concerns about pricing?

7 What are the two ways in which to define the marketing margin? Which is used more often in agricultural policy analysis? Why?

8 What is the marketing bill? What are its major conponents?

9 When there are changes in primary demand at the retail level, prices tend to fluctuate relatively more at the farm level than at the retail level. Why? Illustrate with use of supply and demand curves.

10 In a competitive market economy, are there any conditions under which changes in domestic or export demand could bring a relatively smaller change in prices at the farm level than at retail? Explain your answer.

11 We have observed that when there are changes in primary supply at the farm level, prices tend to fluctuate relatively more at the farm level than at retail. What conditions must be fulfilled for this situation to occur? What types of policy actions might be successful in stabilizing farm prices and farm incomes without increasing retail prices?

12 It has been suggested that the farm supply curve is less elastic than the supply curve of food marketing services. If this is so, will the farmers' share of the retail price of farm food products tend to increase or to decrease (ceteris paribus) when there are increases in retail demand for food? Increases in farm supply? Decreases in retail demand? Decreases in farm supply?

13 Although the major food firms do not exhibit a high degree of market concentration on a national basis, many local markets are much more highly concentrated. How does the degree of market concentration tend to affect the market performance of food firms in respect to their price policy, advertising, and product promotion? Why?

14 Theoretically speaking, why do the major supermarket chains oppose most of the political efforts to improve competition in wholesale and retail food markets?

15 What are the general goals in nutrition policy? In what ways does the status of nutrition in the United States fall short of these goals? Be as specific as you can.

16 What are the major elements of a national nutrition policy, such as advocated by nutritionists? What are the general constraints placed on this policy?

17 What were the six items proposed in the 1975 study of the GAO for improvement of consumer information in food and nutrition?

18 Comment on the nutritional goals of the 1981 White House Conference on Aging. Summarize the case for and against the conference resolutions.

RECOMMENDED READINGS

Armbruster, Walter J., Dennis R. Henderson, and Ronald D. Knutson (eds.), *Federal Marketing Programs in Agriculture: Issues and Options,* The Interstate Printers and Publishers, Danville, Illinois, 1983.

Gardner, Bruce L., "The Farm-Retail Price Spread in a Competitive Food Industry," *American Journal of Agricultural Economics,* vol. 57, no. 3, August 1975, pp. 399–409.

Gisser, Micha, "Welfare Implications of Oligopoly in U.S. Food Manufacturing," *American Journal of Agricultural Economics,* vol. 64, no. 4, November 1982, pp. 616–624.

Hadwiger, Don F., and Ross B. Talbot (eds.), *Food Policy and Farm Programs,* The American Academy of Political Science, vol. 34, no. 3, New York, 1982, pp. 12–24 and 40–88.

Ladd, George W., and Dennis R. Lifferth, "An Analysis of Alternative Grain Distribution Systems," *American Journal of Agricultural Economics,* vol. 57, no. 3, August 1975, pp. 420–430.

Marion, Bruce W., et al., *The Food Retailing Industry: Market Structure, Profits, and Prices,* Praeger Publishers, Praeger Special Studies, New York, 1979, pp. 142–160.

Parker, Russell C., and John M. Connor, "Estimates of Consumer Loss Due to Monopoly in the U.S. Food-Manufacturing Industries,"*American Journal of Agricultural Economics,* vol. 61, no. 4, November 1979, pp. 626–639.

PART THREE

POLICY ANALYSIS OF THE INPUT MARKETS

POLICY ANALYSIS OF FINANCIAL INPUT MARKETS

Policy in the money market, farm credit, and public finance influence agriculture's resource use, economic structure, and income distribution. There is first the federal government's monetary policy, or money market policy, which is controlled directly by the Board of Governors of the Federal Reserve System, Congress, and the President. Second, there is a federal credit policy, directed more specifically toward agriculture, and providing agriculture with the most complete system of publicly directed credit services offered to any industry. Finally, there is the fiscal policy of federal, state, and local governments, involving taxing and public spending, which relates importantly to agricultural policy.

IN THIS CHAPTER

1 You can learn to visualize how monetary policy influences agriculture, why farm leaders and their organizations react as they do to various alternatives, and how one alternative or another will affect agriculture in the future.

2 You can learn how agriculture is served by the most complete system of federally sponsored credit and federal direct-lending programs provided for any industry. You can learn why this system has been created, and what the effects will be of following one policy alternative or another in the future.

3 You can learn how agriculture is influenced by the complex of federal, state, and local fiscal policy, and why tax reform and control of public expenditures are of great interest to agriculture.

HOW MONETARY POLICY INFLUENCES AGRICULTURE

Industrial capitalism is subject to progress in fits and starts, which is reflected in wide swings in the general price level, employment, and income, and, in recent decades, in a persistent tendency toward inflation. Whether agriculture benefits from inflation or not, it is especially vulnerable in such a system because (1) it maintains production in the face of unfavorable prices, (2) the prices of raw farm products are subject to some of the greatest amplitudes of change, and (3) changes in farm income expectations are strongly reflected in land values. The great land boom of the 1970s, which was triggered by a combination of inflation, increasing export demand, tax concessions favoring agriculture, more flexible monetary policy, and great expansion in farm credit, resulted in the most explosive and long-sustained increases in land prices in the history of the United States. The repercussions of this boom will be felt for decades to come. Such long-term structural changes tend to overshadow the shorter-term trends and fluctuations of the business cycle.

The financing of inputs such as this has been facilitated by policy applied to the financial input markets. Who tends to benefit from this policy?

Effects of Business Cycles on Agriculture

Agriculture is uniquely affected by business cycles because it does not increase or decrease output during the course of the cycle, as do most other industries. It tends to stay in full production. This is good for consumers because it assures them of a stable food supply. Also, this is good for the agricultural marketing economy, because the economy is geared to handle a steady volume of farm food products, and there is a relatively stable farm food marketing bill, determined, as we have seen, by the interaction of supply and demand at the farm and the retail levels. Finally, this is good for the nation's international trade, because if markets are allowed to run their course, then the steady volume of farm output will help to stabilize the volume of agricultural exports and trade.

Sustained high-level output under conditions of variable demand is generally bad for farmers, however, because they bear the brunt of the wide price fluctuations and the downward-trending price spirals arising out of inelastic supply and demand. The results are often vicarious and not predictable. As was experienced in the 1970s, for example, increases in export demand tended to cause soaring prices for some commodities, while hurting others. The prices of industrial farm inputs might shoot up, not because of farm-related changes in demand, but because of the effects of inflation on farm supply firms. The low elasticity of substitution for inputs such as fuel and fertilizer imposes a rigid cost structure on farming, while higher elasticity of substitution in production, of one farm commodity for another, generally assures that eventually both the crops and the livestock economy will share in the gains from increasing demand and the losses from increasing costs of inputs.

So, although farmers enjoy the gains from soaring product prices, they also fear the effects of inflation on the costs of their inputs, and they normally support a type of monetary policy which they associate with a stable dollar and moderation in the business cycle. The control of inflation has required direct constraints on the volume of money, high discount rates by the Federal Reserve, and high interest rates for borrowers. This has increased the credit costs paid by farmers. To be more effective, this policy must be supplemented by only moderate federal budget deficits, or even surpluses. Farm organizations, the American Farm Bureau Federation especially, have passed resolutions regularly each year, which call on the federal government to balance its budget. But all farm organizations are aware of the effects of high interest rates, and they have often opposed this part of inflation-control policy. Even though this policy may be in the interest of farmers, they tend to fight it.

Why Farmers Fight Deflation

A policy of monetary restraint, or "hard-money" policy, necessary as it may be in the public interest to control inflation, can bring great hardship to people in the farm sector. It works its hardship on farmers by increasing the costs of capital and farm credit, and by tending to restrict exports. The latter occurs as a result of strengthening the American dollar versus the currencies of major importing countries, and other major farm-commodity exporting countries. The effect on agricultural exports depends not just on the value of the dollar, however, but on the elasticity of price transmission as well. Where trade is relatively free, an increase in the value of the dollar will tend to restrict exports from the United States because it increases the prices that importing countries must pay in terms of their own currency. But when the elasticity of price transmission is low, an increase in the value of the dollar may have relatively little effect.

Over time, however, it may be assumed that a strong dollar will make farm products less competitive in export markets. When this result is combined with the effects of inflation controls in the domestic economy, the combined effect is to increase the costs of farm inputs relative to the prices of products. Consequently, the political influence of agriculture tends to be in opposition to a strongly deflationary policy, even though there is uncertainty about the long-term effects of inflation.

Direct and Indirect Effects of a Strong Dollar

A strong dollar may affect agriculture more indirectly than directly, however. Between 1978 and the summer of 1981, for instance, the dollar soared by some 50 percent against the German mark and most other European currencies, by about 40 percent against the Japanese yen, and by roughly 25 percent on a general trade-weighted basis. The general effects would be to dampen the upward trend in total exports from the United States, stimulate imports, widen the trade deficit of the United States, and drag down the rate of growth in the gross national product (GNP). But the effects on total agricultural exports were unclear at this stage. Agricultural exports continued to increase in value through 1981 and into 1982.

The increase in the value of the dollar tends to affect agriculture more indirectly, and perhaps with some lag. The overall effects on the domestic market are not apparent for some time, and, when apparent, they show up more among the general indicators of economic growth than in the statistics of agricultural exports. Still, there is a feeling that a strong dollar, based on a policy of monetary restraint and high interest rates, is disadvantageous to agriculture. Farm organizations and agrarian interests have frequently opposed this policy.

How Agriculture Relates to Monetary Policy

Farmers have fought deflationary policies even while fighting against high prices of goods used in agricultural production. The history of how farmers and affiliated groups have related to monetary policy is an important part of the foundation for understanding agricultural policy.

The details of this fight or struggle cover the 200 years since the founding of the United States as a free and independent nation. In 1791, Alexander Hamilton, then secretary of the treasury, established the National Bank of the United States. During its first 20-year charter, it had a restraining influence on note issues of state banks and a vitally important and stabilizing effect on the monetary system. The charter was not renewed in 1811, and until the second bank was chartered in 1816, state banks engaged in reckless expansion. The second National Bank did not follow the conservative policies of its predecessor, but it had to correct the badly expanded situation by a period of contraction. Even a modest contraction was unpopular in rural areas, however, and in 1836 President Andrew Jackson vetoed the act to renew the bank's charter because he feared that such concentration of monetary power would dictate the monetary policy for the country. From that time until passage of the National Banking Act of 1863, state banks were in their heyday. Bank notes were issued sometimes without any idea of redemption and, particularly in the western and southern states, many banks violated all canons of sound banking practice. Sporadic panics—the most severe one, in 1837—occurred when banks were unable to meet the demands of their depositors.

Passage of the National Banking Act in 1863 ushered in a new era, a 30-year period of marked deflation culminating about the mid-1890s. Amendments to the act in 1865 drove state bank notes out of circulation by taxing them prohibitively, which centered monetary control again in the federal government. The early plans to redeem the paper currency that had been printed to help finance the Civil War tended to shrink the supply of money, and that tended to have deflationary results. Farm organizations, led by the newly formed National Grange of the Patrons of Husbandry (or the National Grange), tried to get the government to force down railroad rates, on the assumption that this would narrow the marketing margin and raise farm prices. When they failed to get the desired results they turned to monetary policy, and this became the center of interest for the next 30 years.

The Populist Revolt   From the mid-1860s to the presidential campaign of 1896, farm people and those who sympathized with them were involved in a struggle against a "hard-money" monetary policy, which severely limited the volume of money and credit. During this era wholesale prices dropped to one-third their previous level. The purchasing power of the dollar tripled. Evidence suggests that farm income rose in the 1860s, fell sharply in the 1870s, rose somewhat in the 1880s, and fell sharply again in the early 1890s, although it was highly constant for the decade.[1]

As the tide of land settlement moved westward, increased demand for farm products was met by surges of settlement into new, rich lands of greater fertility, resulting in low prices for farm products, and in productivity gains that were passed on to consumers in the form of lower food prices.[2] The productivity gains that ultimately brought hardship to agriculture because lower prices were collected also contributed importantly to industrial development through their effect on food prices and trade.

For a time, the political leadership of the Populist Revolt concentrated on the so-called greenback movement, which had as its basic objective the expansion of the

---

[1]John D. Hicks, *The Populist Revolt, A History of the Farmers' Alliance and the People's Party,* University of Nebraska Press, Lincoln, 1968 (first published by The University of Minnesota Press, 1931).

[2]From John Bowman, "Trends in Midwestern Farm Values, 1860–1914," unpublished doctoral dissertation, Yale University, 1964; and Allan G. Bogue, *From Prairie to Corn Belt,* The University of Chicago Press, Chicago, 1963, as discussed by Douglass C. North, *Growth and Welfare in the American Past, A New Economic History,* Prentice-Hall, Inc., Englewood Cliffs, N.J., 1966, pp. 145–148.

monetary system of the country, the creation of money by printing, or by bank notes. It was hoped this policy would bring about a rise in the general level of prices, thus reducing the burden of agricultural debts and moving agriculture into a more favorable income position relative to the rest of society. The movement received wide support from farm groups, but the "greenbackers" were defeated at the polls by the Republicans in 1868 and 1872. The majority voted for "sound" currency and for little expansion in money or credit. The greenbackers formed a third party in 1876 and nominated their own presidential candidate. The party lost, but it polled a large number of votes, particularly in the midwest, and it attained sufficient influence to force the federal government to abandon plans to retire the printed greenbacks that were in circulation in the monetary system. The greenbackers ran candidates in the presidential elections of 1880 and 1884, but lost again.

The Silver Coinage Campaigns   Defeat of the populists in the elections of 1880 and 1884 signaled the beginning of the campaign to expand the currency by free coinage of silver. Historically, silver had been underpriced in the Coinage Act of 1834. That is, the price offered for use of silver in coins was less than it continued to sell for in the commercial market. Accordingly, in the following years, little silver was purchased or coined by the government because it could command a higher price in other uses. By 1850 the silver dollar had virtually ceased to be used in commercial trade, and in the Coinage Act of 1873, silver was dropped from the coinage lists. This act received little opposition at the time it was passed because the government was not coining silver anyway. But, as luck would have it, silver was soon discovered in several western states. The fabulous Comstock Lode was developed in Nevada. Huge silver and copper deposits were found in Montana. The price of silver declined.

Since silver was not being coined, those who wanted to see prices raised from the existing low levels combined in a political campaign to get more coinage of silver. They were quickly joined, or led, by the silver-mine owners and others in the west who also wanted higher prices for silver. An act, known as the Bland-Allison Act, was passed in 1878. It directed the secretary of the treasury to purchase a certain quantity of silver at the ratio of 16 to 1; that is, one ounce of gold for sixteen ounces of silver. Provision also was made for issuance of silver certificates. Silver purchase operations, however, did not bring about the expansion in currency and the rise in prices that had been expected by the backers of the act. The silver coins and silver certificates that went into circulation generally were used in place of money that would have circulated had silver not been coined.

The result was that popular support increased for free or unlimited coinage of silver. In 1890 an act was passed, with the provision that the treasury must buy a certain amount of silver, estimated to be equal to the total annual output of the silver mines of the United States, to be paid for in treasury notes redeemable in gold or silver. This imposed a heavy drain on the gold reserves of the treasury. By 1893 gold stocks had been reduced to such a low level that President Cleveland called Congress into special session to repeal the Silver Purhcase Act and to "save the gold standard." This was done, but the action was contrary to the wishes of those who wanted the currency system expanded as a means of raising prices and improving the income position of agriculture.

Repeal of the Silver Purchase Act set the stage for the presidential campaign of 1896, in which a major campaign issue was whether further action should be taken to expand the currency system of the country. William Jennings Bryan, who became widely known for his "cross-of-gold" speech, stampeded the presidential convention of the Democratic party with the call for free coinage of silver and became the party's candidate for the presidency. Free coinage, however, was not to be. The Republican party, supporting "sound" money and only limited issuance of paper money, won the election and continued the policy of careful regulation of the quantity of money in circulation.

"The Golden Age of Agriculture"   The 20 years from the mid-1890s to the outbreak of World War I have sometimes been called the golden age of American agriculture because a combination of events turned the terms of trade strongly in favor of farmers. Over these two decades, the prices received by farmers increased by at least 50 percent relative to the prices farmers paid. As a result, the strong agitation for sweeping populist reform died out. Farm organizations that took root during this period, such as the American Society of Equity and the Farmers Union, concentrated on rather mild reforms. They fought for cheaper and more adequate sources of credit for farmers. Some of their objectives were realized when the Federal Farm Loan Act of 1916 was passed. They supported farm cooperatives and railroad regulation, which had been made possible by the establishment of the Interstate Commerce Commission. They generally dropped the idea of the managed dollar. Currency reform did not become a major issue again until the dark days of the great depression.

The Great Depression   As was shown in Figure 1-1, the indexes of prices paid and received by farmers were higher in the 1920s than in prewar years. As far as the overall level of prices was concerned, farmers generally got what they had lobbied for in the greenback and silver-coinage campaigns. But the trouble was that farm prices, compared with their pre–World War I levels, were relatively low. Compared with prices before the war, those now paid by farmers were much higher than the prices they were receiving. As a result, farm groups did not base their political campaigns on monetary reform. Instead they turned to direct action to improve the price of farm products through an export subsidy program. The ensuing battle over export subsidy, as we have discussed, dominated the field of agricultural policy during most of the 1920s.

In the 1930s, however, the situation was different. Now farmers were, if anything, more desperate. In 1932 the Republican strongholds in the midwest and other agricultural areas were overrun by Democratic candidates. Again farmers were ready for monetary action that would expand the money supply and raise prices, while reducing the cost of credit. The former was achieved when the gold content of the dollar was reduced, by increasing the price of gold from $22.67 to $35.00 an ounce, and a broad program of deficit financing was begun by President Roosevelt and the Democratic majorities in Congress.

The administration also adopted a program for expanding the credit system by establishing new credit agencies, such as the Reconstruction Finance Corporation and the Home Owners Loan Corporation, and by greatly expanding the leading powers of the federally sponsored farm credit agencies. Emergency acts in 1933 and 1934 provided policy direction for widespread refinancing of farm mortages by the federal land banks at lower rates of interest and with longer terms for repayment.

The political position of farm organizations in the great depression was consistent with the long tradition of agriculture. The American Farm Bureau Federation waged a relentless campaign in favor of an inflationary program. The Farmers Union favored inflation. What we need, said the national president of the Farmers Union, is "a straight-out price fixing measure on the basis of cost of production ... the remonetization of silver, a good supply of paper money, and a sprinkling of counterfeit to take care of the situation."[3] Farm people, as their thoughts on the subject can best be determined, were solidly behind the proposals for inflation—and they were not alone. Although the administration did not favor many of the more radical proposals for printing money and coining silver, it followed in essence a program that was counter-deflationary on the one hand, and especially favorable to agriculture in terms of credit and debt refinancing on the other.

Monetary Policy during World War II and in the Years Since

The monetary policy generally favored by agriculture has been more conservative than in the long years of the Populist Revolt and the great depression, but not consistently so. Generally, farm groups have favored balanced budgets, thus resisting the monetary expansion spurred by federal deficits. But they have not always supported the program of the Federal Reserve, which in the 1980s, especially, has been aimed at control of the nation's total money supply through regulating (increasing) the discount rate that the Federal Reserve charges member banks. This policy has resulted in high and volatile interest rates, and it has had a significant impact on agriculture, an industry that is very dependent on credit to meet its current and long-term capital requirements. The great increase in farm debt since the early 1970s makes this policy of monetary restraint especially burdensome. An important question for policy is whether the farm sector can remain solvent under the impact of high interest rates and heavy debt charges. To deal with this question, let us turn next to a more specific analysis of federal credit policy relating to agriculture.

POLICY ANALYSIS OF FEDERAL FARM CREDIT PROGRAMS

Federal farm credit programs have been established and have grown as a result of farmers' efforts to get cheaper and more adequate sources of credit. As a result of a variety of requests and needs, two distinct types of programs have been developed. The largest of these is the government-sponsored Farm Credit System (FCS), and its affiliated operating banks—the federal land bank system for long-term farm mortgage loans, the intermediate credit bank system for shorter-term farm production credit, and the system of banks for cooperatives to provide both short- and long-term credit for farm cooperatives. The other program involves direct lending of more

[3]*United States Daily News,* April 8, 1933.

emergency-type loans under the Farmers Home Administration (FHA or FmHA). It makes loans to farmers who cannot get adequate credit from other lenders, and extends an array of credit services to agribusiness firms and other rural entities that are qualified for these services.

The Federally Sponsored Farm Credit System

The general policy of the farm credit system is coordinated by the federal Farm Credit Board, which has 12 members appointed by the President, one from each of the 12 farm credit districts, who serve six-year staggered terms. One additional member is appointed by the secretary of agriculture, to convey the secretary's views. The governor of the system is chief executive officer, elected by the board to carry out its wishes.

Each of the farm credit districts has a federal land bank, an intermediate credit bank, and a bank for cooperatives. There is also a Central Bank for Cooperatives in Denver to service the other 12 cooperative banks and make some of the larger loans required by large farm cooperatives. Each federal land bank implements its local credit program through a number of federal land bank associations (FLBAs), there being about 500 of these in total, with the FLBAs in each district serving as agents of a land bank. Each intermediate credit bank works with a number of production credit associations (PCAs), of which there are more than 400 in total. PCAs, in contrast to the FLBAs, operate as actual loaning agencies.

In each district, a board of seven members directs the loan policy for that district, within the general policy of the Farm Credit Board. One of these members is appointed by the governor of the Farm Credit System with advice and consent of the board. The other six are elected by borrowers in each district, two by borrowers from the land banks, two by borrowers from PCAs, and two by borrowers from the bank for cooperatives.

Federally Sponsored Farm Mortgage Credit

The foundation for this program was established in the Farm Loan Act of 1916, the policy goal of which was "to provide capital for agricultural development, to create standard forms of investment based on farm mortgages and to equalize rates of interest on farm mortgages." This meant to equalize rates of interest among loans of different sizes and maturities, and among various regions of the country. The act also authorized an appropriation to provide capital stock for the banks, which was used for many years and subsequently repaid out of earnings. Emergency acts in 1933 and 1934 greatly expanded the loaning powers of the banks, permitting them to carry out a nationwide program of refinancing farm mortgages. This helped to prevent an avalanche of foreclosures and bankruptcies that otherwise might have occurred before the end of the great depression. From then until 1971 the banks grew at a steady but rather conservative pace. At the beginning of 1971, they held $7.1 billion in farm mortgage debt, not quite one-quarter of the $29.5 billion then outstanding.

The Farm Credit Act of 1971, which was passed with the strong support of almost all farm groups, greatly expanded the lending power of the federal land banks. The act authorized the banks to raise their lending limits from 65 to 85 percent of the appraised long-term market value of a farm property. Variable interest rates were authorized for new loans, which enabled the bank's income to increase as competitive interest rates subsequently rose. The maximum mortgage that could be set without prior approval of the Farm Credit Board was increased from $100,000 to $400,000. The act authorized a land bank to participate in loans with another bank and to enter into loss-sharing agreements with their own FLBAs. Open-end mortgages were authorized, which meant that a mortgage could be increased if this was justified, based on increasing assets and net worth of the borrower. The act deleted mandatory personal liability for loans to family corporations, and permitted a bank to own and lease property to an individual borrower.

The lending power of individual banks was increased when they were authorized to require investment in stock by a land-bank borrower of up to $10 per each $100 of money loaned, up from $5 per $100 of loan as required before this. The act provided for the issue of a unified security covering all banks in the system, which could be purchased by investors to provide additional capital for the system's expansion. This replaced a generally less attractive security that had been issued by individual banks. Finally, the act broadened the potential clientele of the system by authorizing loans on single-family, nonfarm rural residences, not to exceed 15 percent of the total loans of a bank; permitting financing of service firms relating to farming, such as custom spraying, harvesting, and other contract services; and permitting the issuance of nonvoting stock and participation certificates to nonfarm borrowers. Supported by these measures, the farm real estate debt increased by about three times in the 10 years from the beginning of 1972 to 1982, as the increased supply of credit was made

FIGURE 9-1
Farmland in the United States change in real current value per acre from the previous year.
(*Source: USDA*, 1982 Handbook of Agricultural Charts, *p. 9.*)

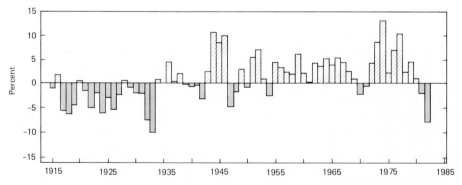

Reported as of March 1, 1913–75, February 1, 1976–81, and April 1, 1982. Excludes Alaska and Hawaii. The indexes of real farmland value computed by dividing the nominal land value indexes by the Consumer Price Index.

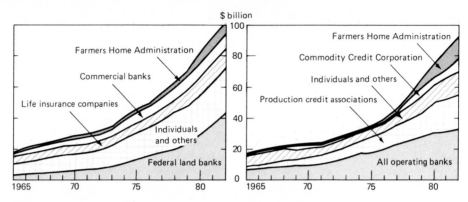

1982 preliminary. Production Credit Association includes Federal Intermediate
Credit Bank loans to other financial institutions.

(a) Real estate debt   (b) Non-real estate debt

FIGURE 9-2
Who holds the farm real estate and non-real estate farm debt. *(Source: USDA,* 1982 Handbook
of Agricultural Charts, *p. 7.)*

available at interest rates attractive to borrowers. During most years in the 1970s,
with land prices increasing as they did (Figure 9-1), the capital gain would often
equal or exceed the interest charged on individual mortgages. So, in effect, many
farm-mortgage borrowers were making an investment, which for a time might
appear to be costless. The policy direction given to the land banks by the act of 1971
may be regarded as the leading catalyst in these events (Figures 9-1, 9-2, and 9-3).

FIGURE 9-3
Interest rates on *(a)* farm real estate loans, and *(b)* farm non-real estate loans. *(Source:*
USDA, 1982 Handbook of Agricultural Charts, *p. 8.)*

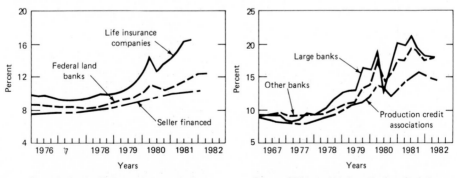

Quarterly data for life insurance companies (new
commitments) and Federal land banks (new loans).
Semiannual data for seller financed, annual beginning
in 1980. Federal land bank rates do not include
charge for the stock borrowers are required to buy.

(a) Real estate interest rates

Rates on PCA loans include service fees. Bank data
starting in 1977 are from surveys made by the Federal
Reserve System; data from prior years relate to different
groupings of banks, collected by the Federal Reserve
System and the Federal Reserve Bank of Minneapolis.

(b) Non-real estate interest rates

Farm real estate loans provided by the Farmers Home Administration (FHA) have also been an important additional source of farm-mortgage credit. The FHA was formed in 1946 to take over a number of emergency farm credit programs, and to coordinate the federal government's direct lending to farmers, by providing credits and other services to borrowers who could not get adequate credit from other sources. Since then the FHA has been broadened and expanded a number of times, both to enlarge its programs for farmers, and to provide credit funds for a variety of rural development programs, such as low-income rural housing and essential community services. The FHA also supplements direct lending with loan insurance and loan guarantee programs.

As in the case of the federal land banks, the most significant increases in FHA farm real estate loans have occurred since 1971. In fact, until 1975 the total farm real estate debt held by the FHA was less than $3.0 billion. By 1981, it had risen to about $8.5 billion, and the net debt was rising by more than $1.0 billion annually in the 1980s.

The crucial policy question for both the land banks and the FHA is what to do in the remaining years of the 1980s, in the 1990s, and beyond. Most of the farm real estate debt is set for a long term of 20 years or more. Nearly all of it is amortized, and the costs must be paid at least annually out of the gross marketing receipts. In many farm situations, it may be assumed that the debt charge is high enough to wipe out most if not all of the economic rent usually associated with owning farmland. Perhaps an increasing percentage of all farmers will not be able to pay the heavy debt charge that is implied. The alternatives will be either to refinance, to sell out voluntarily or under threat of foreclosure, or to increase current income sufficiently to remain solvent. If the farmland market experiences a long-term decline, or only modest capital gains, as indeed it has in some times past (Figure 9-1), then the federal land bank system and the FHA may need to prepare for large-scale refinancing, to avoid a farm crisis of major proportions.

To see the broader implications of this, we must also consider policy developments in the markets for non–real estate farm credit. This involves the system of intermediate credit banks and the production credit associations (PCAs), and the non–real estate farm loans of the FHA.

Non–Real Estate Farm-Lending Programs: Federally Sponsored and Direct

Major trends in non–real estate farm credit have been closely correlated with trends in real estate credit (Figure 9-2b), which suggests that supply and demand tend to change in similar ways in the two markets. Interest rates are somewhat more variable in the non–real estate loan market (Figure 9-3b), which tends to reflect a demand for credit that is more sensitive to farm income prospects, and a supply that is more sensitive to changes in national monetary policy, involving changes in the prime discount rate set by the Federal Reserve and variations in the supply and demand for loanable funds. Perhaps one of the most important inferences to make for policy is to recognize that the costs of short-term production credit can be changed more easily by changes in national monetary policy than can the costs of farm real estate credit.

The system of federally sponsored farm production credit has been developed with strong political support of almost all farm groups, and over the objections of competing commercial banks as this makes added competition for them. The general policy goal of the various federal acts has been to develop a reliable supply of credit to be offered at rather uniform interest rates throughout the United States, based on the same credit principals, and types of security usually accepted by other lenders. The system was founded under the Agricultural Credits Act of 1923, which authorized $60 million to provide capital stock for 12 intermediate credit banks. Initially these were intended to serve as banks of discount for short-term agricultural loans held by commercial banks. They languished in this capacity, however, and the Farm Credit Act of 1933 provided for 12 production credit corporations to be associated with the intermediate credit banks, and authorized another $120 million for purchasing stock in local production credit associations (PCAs), which would serve as local lending agencies. An additional $40 million was provided in the Federal Farm Mortgage Act of 1934 to increase the capital stock of PCAs. From then until 1953 the PCAs operated without additional appropriations, and, in the Farm Credit Act of 1953, Congress directed the Farm Credit Board to develop a plan to retire all the capital invested by the government. This was accomplished by 1968.

The Farm Credit Act of 1971 authorized changes in policy that expanded the supply of credit that could be made available through PCAs. For instance, intermediate credit banks were authorized to purchase stock in PCAs, to participate in loans with PCAs, to own and lease farm equipment to eligible borrowers, and to offer loan services to agribusinesses serving farmers. PCAs were authorized to participate in loans with national banks, the object being to enable local lenders to meet the full credit demand of the larger farm operators.

These authorizations helped PCAs and other lenders to increase the supply of loanable funds, with results as shown in Figure 9-2b. This was undoubtedly an important contributing factor to the growth in agricultural output that has occurred since 1971. The 1971 act also granted additional authority to the banks for cooperatives to issue stock and increase their lending, which undoubtedly contributed to a remarkable increase in the business volume of farmers' cooperatives since 1971 (Figure 9-4).

Some General Inferences for Policy

Much, although not all, of the remarkable increase in agricultural credit since 1971, for farmers and many agribusinesses as well, can be attributed, directly or indirectly, to national policy. National policy increased the supply of credit, which in the case of real estate credit especially influenced the land market. Although the increase in real estate credit may have had only a small effect on total farm output, it may be presumed that the increase in production credit increased the aggregate supply of agricultural products. This would tend to depress farm food prices, ceteris paribus, and increase the volume of farm products available for export. The residual legacy

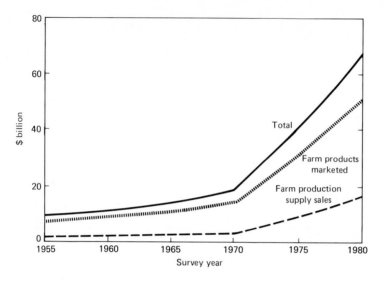

For survey purposes, a cooperative is defined as an association that meets the following requirements.

1 Farmers or agricultural producers hold the controlling interest in the cooperative;
2 No member of the cooperative is allowed more than one vote because of the amount of stock or membership capital owned or the cooperative does not pay dividends on stock or membership capital in excess of 8 percent a year, or the legal rate in the State, whichever is higher; and
3 The cooperative does not deal in products of nonmembers in an amount greater in value than it handles for its members.

FIGURE 9-4
Business volume of farmer cooperatives. *(Source: USDA,* 1982 Handbook of Agricultural Charts, *p. 17.)*

is a substantial increase in the aggregate costs of farm and ranch financing projected for the rest of the 1980s. Although declines in interest rates may help to reduce this cost, one may suggest that the financial situation projected for the next several years is more than just another downturn in a normal cycle. In the late 1970s, farmers and ranchers were caught in a cash-flow cost-price squeeze, with inflated costs and falling net incomes; rising land prices provided equity for more borrowing to keep most farmers and ranchers in production. But this situation can scarcely be repeated in the 1980s or 1990s, and difficult periods for debt management and financial policy may lie ahead.

In the future, although the farm sector as a whole may enjoy a favorable asset/debt ratio, there seems no escaping the fact that many farm families will face a cash-flow cost-price squeeze, and an equity crisis that may threaten their survival in agriculture. What is to be done? If Congress continues to increase target prices as it has in recent agricultural acts, then this will call for higher payments to farmers to supplement market prices and price-support loans; or, if market prices are supported above export-equilibrium levels, then larger export subsidies will be required to move the major export crops. If none of this is done, then the effective level of price supports must drop, or the dollar must be devalued relative to the currencies of other countries.

If higher price supports encourage more farm borrowing based on capital gain, then farmers will continue to experience low rates of current cash returns. Hence, it may be suggested that the Congress must back away from further commitments to raise target prices of commodities, both because of the adverse impacts of this action on markets, especially export markets, and because of its eventual adverse effect on current rates of return. But in the interest of maintaining a certain economic structure in farming, it may be desirable to help farmers who are experiencing short-term cash-flow problems by refinancing and extending their debts, as was done on a wide scale in the 1930s. The financial structures of the land banks and the FHA are well suited to this purpose, providing there is appropriate support from the federal government. But it seems evident that constraints must be placed on further increases in the aggregate debt burden of agriculture if the situation is eventually to be stabilized. Furthermore, this policy must be coordinated with tax policy.

ANALYSIS OF TAX POLICY AFFECTING AGRICULTURE

Tax policies of both federal and state governments have important effects on agricultural production and income distribution. The federal tax policy tends to give an advantage to all investors in agriculture who are in the higher income brackets, and especially to those who can exploit capital gains concessions, which apply to both farmers and nonfarmers who invest. The tax policies of the individual states, which apply most importantly to the tax on farm real estate, also have important effects on agriculture. Farmers often complain that the real estate or farm property tax is inequitable and unfair because it heavily affects their incomes. Farming is a capital-intensive industry in which large assets of land and other real estate are involved, relative to net income. But if the tax is accurately related to the genuine earning power of the land, it is hard to characterize it as an unfair tax.

Problems arise from two sources. One is that, unlike income taxation, the real estate tax is a fixed tax which does not reflect or adjust to the highly volatile incomes of farmers. The second, of course, is that where land is subject to overpricing in relation to its current earning power, tax assessments can get out of line with incomes, and hardship may ensue. The irony of this is that tax assessments of farmland have failed to keep pace with increases in land values, and this amounts to a concession to agriculture that may be capitalized into even higher property values. Attempts to control taxes by differential assessments can aggravate this situation. What is to be done about taxes?

Regressiveness of Federal Tax Policy Affecting Farming

Federal tax policy favors investments in farm property by high-income taxpayers especially in a period of asset appreciation, such as the 1970s, and this effect continues to be emphasized by changes such as contained in the Economic Recovery Tax Act of 1981. This act tended to accentuate trends already underway.

Although it is a basic tenet of federal tax policy that taxpayers having equal ability to pay should be treated equally, there are three primary sources of preferential treatment for farm income. First, on the basis of a 1915 administrative decision, farmers are allowed a choice of either cash or accrual accounting in reporting income for tax purposes. Most use the cash method, which permits them to "average" their year-to-year income, so that in high-income years taxes are reduced, or at least postponed. Second, a regulation adopted in 1919 has permitted farmers to claim capital expenditures as current expense in developing some types of orchards and ranches, instead of amortizing over the useful life of the investment, as most other businesses must do. Recent tax acts have broadened this privilege, and the 1981 act set up a new Accelerated Cost Recovery System (ACRS), which shortens the write-off period for investments in farm machinery, livestock, and farm buildings to substantially less than the useful life of the investment. The purpose of this is to reduce the net cost of current investments by permitting the farmer to retain a larger percentage of current income. Third, and often of greatest importance, 1951 legislation validated the farmer's right to report receipts from sales of certain livestock used for draft, dairy, or breeding purposes as capital gain rather than cash income. Certain livestock used for sporting purposes were added in 1969. Tax reduction scheduled in the 1981 act would tend to increase the advantage of reporting income as capital gain.

In addition, taxpayers in high brackets may use the capital-gains provisions to create losses for income-tax purposes. Suppose, for example, that a taxpayer in the 50 percent bracket has $100,000 of cash receipts from sale of livestock that qualifies as capital gains. Only $40,000 will be taxable. Certain cash outlays may be reported as expenses to offset this. Suppose that $80,000 of expenses are reportable. Set against the $40,000 of capital gain, there is the expense of $80,000, which results in a loss of $40,000 for income-tax purposes, even though there is a net gain in cash flow of $20,000. The loss of $40,000 may be set against $40,000 of other income to reduce the net tax to zero, even though the net cash flow in favor of the farmer is $60,000.

Although the tax law limits the amount of loss that can be taken in a given year, by use of judicious management taxes can be substantially reduced over a period of time. Since farmers are permitted to use the cash receipts and disbursements method of accounting, year-end inventories of raised products such as crops and livestock can be ignored for income-tax purposes. Operating losses can occur often, especially in cattle operations, because only one-half of the calf crop need be sold in a year if the heifer calves are converted into breeding stock, and after that the long-term build-up can be taxed as capital gain. Either too large a loss in a given year or no loss at all are the conditions to be avoided for most profitable income-tax management.

Farm and Nonfarm Tax Effects

As a result of capital gains and other federal income-tax provisions, high-income families with most of their income from farming have a substantially lower tax bur-

Farm income-tax schools have been sponsored by the Cooperative Extension Service and the Internal Revenue Service as a means of improving the accuracy and promptness of federal and state farm income tax payments.

den than families in most nonfarm occupations, and most of this advantage is due to the difference in the federal income-tax burden. In fact, in spite of the progressive rates of the federal income tax, the total tax burden of farm families, as a percent of net income before taxes, increases very little beyond $100,000 net income.[4] More specifically, individuals with more than half their income from farm sources would have paid nearly $1.1 billion more in taxes if their tax burdens had been commensurate with tax burdens of the general population.[5]

Because such tax advantages attract investment funds to agriculture that would not otherwise be invested in that area, and this tends to result in higher total agricultural production, the tax savings do not necessarily result in higher aggregate net farm and ranch income. In fact, depending on the effect of tax savings on total output and the elasticity of aggregate demand for agricultural output, aggregate net farm income may be reduced. This will be the case in the short run, for example, if demand is very inelastic, and the output response is positive, other things being equal. The increased incentives to invest will raise the equilibrium prices or costs of the affected inputs, and the increased total output will reduce the equilibrium prices for some products. In the long run, with more elastic demand assumed and new equilibrium in the input and product markets, profits will return to normal at a generally higher level of output.

But the costs and benefits are not spread evenly over the farm and ranch economy. Large farms and ranches will gain at the expense of small ones. High-income farm and ranch investors, who have substantial nonfarm income, which they may offset with income-tax losses based on capital-gain reporting, will gain relatively more than large farmers who derive all, or nearly all, their income from farming. The overall effect will be to accelerate the trend toward fewer and larger operating units, which is a progressive and continuous trend with no natural limits. To the extent that units become larger than is most economical within the existing set-up of internal on-farm technology, and the external advantages of large-scale operations, the overall efficiency of agriculture is reduced, and income distribution shifts farther away from the original ideal of family-sized farms.

What is to be done? Since the provisions accelerate investments and increase output, some of the general welfare loss will be offset by growth of output and further evolution of agriculture into the export market. But the effects on economic structure of agriculture are perverse, and, especially in a time when programs setting aside land and reducing acreage are being supported, the reduction of taxes on capital gains and the Accelerated Cost Recovery System in the 1981 act give misleading signals to farm and ranch investors. In this situation, higher target prices will tend

---

[4]Charles A. Sisson, "An Intersectoral Examination of Tax Equity: Farm and Nonfarm Burdens," *Public Finance Quarterly,* vol. 7, no. 4, October 1979, pp. 455–478.

[5]Ibid., p. 467. These estimates are based on the MERGE data file of the Brookings Institution, Washington, D.C., which combines the Internal Revenue Service tax file on nearly 87,000 individual income tax returns from 1966, and the 1967 Survey of Economic Opportunity data file, based on a random sample of 30,000 households in 1966. Joseph Peckman, the cocreator of the MERGE file, remarked at a meeting in 1975 that the MERGE file still showed the gist of income and tax distributions. See Sisson, ibid., p. 476.

to become more and more expensive, while current returns to farming and ranching will tend to fall. One may judge that the government has gone too far in its efforts to aid agriculture, and that the effects are not consistent with the general norms of tax equity.

The tax law applying to farm corporations is also involved. Let us next consider this.

Federal Income-Tax Policy Affecting Farm Corporations

Federal law does not place direct restrictions on corporations in farming, although a few states have attempted to do so, and tax laws are generally not intended to discriminate between incorporated and unincorporated enterprises. But farm corporations have grown at a rather steady pace where economies of scale have favored large units, and where incorporation has been advantageous for managing resources and investments. About 8 to 9 percent of total farm output is produced by corporations; corporations are relatively more important in livestock and poultry operations, and in large-scale fruit and vegetable enterprises. What are the tax advantages and disadvantages, and the alternatives for tax policy?

As a separate legal entity, the corporation is also a separate taxpayer for most tax purposes, but two methods of taxing the income of farm corporations are available. The standard method taxes corporate income to the corporation. An alternate method permits shareholders of a closely held corporation to choose to have corporate income taxed to them.[6] If such a choice is made, the corporation may be described as a "corporation taxed like a partnership," a "pseudo-corporation," a "tax-option corporation," or a "Subchapter S corporation." Shareholders of a Subchapter S corporation pay taxes on their share of corporate income at their own individual tax rates, whether the money is distributed to them or left in the corporation. If the corporation loses money, shareholders report the appropriate share as a loss on their own return. Likewise, each shareholder reports the appropriate share of capital gains (or losses) as required. To qualify for the special status as such a corporation, the corporation must have only one class of outstanding stock, there must be no more than 10 stockholders, all shareholders must be individuals or estates, and all shareholders must consent to the election by the corporation.

Such a corporation presents few new problems that we need to consider, so let us turn our attention to the standard method of taxing the corporation, which is done in much the same way as taxing an individual, with one exception: A corporation has no personal or nonbusiness deductions. Salaries paid to shareholder-employees, rent paid to shareholder-landlords, and interest paid to shareholder-creditors are allowable corporate deductions. Fertilizer and lime expenditures, up to a certain maximum of gross income, are deductible, and land-clearing expenditures for making land suit-

---

[6]Cooperative Extension Service, *The Corporate Farm,* North Central Regional Extension Publication no. 11, pamphlet 273, Iowa State University, Ames, 1960, pp. 10–11.

able for utilization in the farm business are deductible. Both individuals and corporations are eligible for these operating-expense deductions.

Income of corporations can be taxed twice—as dividends distributed to shareholders, and as taxable income to the shareholder. To get around this a certain small amount of income distributed to shareholders is exempt from taxation and, to pressure corporations not to retain earnings in excess of certain business needs to avoid paying taxes on dividends, an accumulated earnings provision has been adopted. But corporations may carry back and carry forward excess capital losses against capital gains. In addition, partly to balance the reductions in taxes to individuals in the 1981 tax act, tax rates on small farm corporations have been reduced modestly.

Family-sized corporations will retain their advantages of limited liability, easy transfer of ownership, and continuity of operations. Tax advantages of permitting corporate income to be reinvested in the farm business are somewhat lessened, however, by the provisions of the act that apply to individuals. Corporations are expected to survive in agriculture, so the great policy debate is not over their survival. Rather, it is over the effects of credit regulations and tax laws on the economic structure of agriculture, as we have discussed, and on the effects of state and local tax policy, to which we now turn.

STATE AND LOCAL TAX POLICY RELATED TO AGRICULTURE

As may be seen from a comparison of trends in farm real estate taxes, the average tax per acre on agricultural land has more than doubled since the beginning of the 1970s, and quadrupled since the beginning of the 1960s. But the farm real estate tax per $100 of market value declined sharply from the early 1970s to the early 1980s, which was primarily the result of delinquency on the part of assessors in keeping assessments in line with increases in property values (Figure 9-5).

State laws generally provide that real estate shall be assessed at some percentage

FIGURE 9-5
Trends in farm real estate taxes in the United States, 1920–1981. *(Source: USDA,* 1982 Handbook of Agricultural Charts, *p. 8.)*

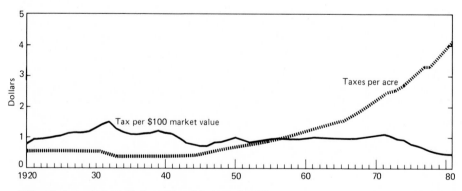

1981 preliminary. Includes Alaska and Hawaii beginning in 1960.

of its full and true value, but, partly to forestall a more drastic increase in farm real estate taxes, special legislation has been passed in nearly all states to provide three general types of tax relief for farmland and open-space land: (1) use-value assessment, (2) deferred taxation, and (3) restrictive agreements.[7] Types 2 and 3, however, are for keeping land in farm use as well as tax relief. What is each of these measures intended to accomplish, and how effective are they?

Use-Value Assessment[8]

There are two general methods for calculating agricultural use value as a basis for assessing farmland for real estate taxation: (1) the comparable sales approach for land used for farming, and (2) the residual income-capitalization approach. The first requires that the behavior and intentions of local farmland market participants be known and that land be assessed on its value in farming only, rather than on the basis of its highest and best use. This has tended to discount some of the effects of inflation on land values, and to ignore the increases in market value based on the land's potential for urban and industrial development. The second approach, based on income capitalization, takes account of past and present income as a guide to future income. Both methods require knowledge about soils, topography, access, microclimate, and location. Variation in soil productivity must be taken into account, so that all farmland with a similar soil rating and other comparable features will have the same value. Income capitalization can be expressed symbolically, as follows:

$$V = \frac{I}{R}$$

where V = value (agricultural use value in this case)
  I = future income projected into perpetuity
  R = the capitalization rate

Forty-five states currently mandate agricultural use-value assessments for farm real estate taxes. However, 33 of these 45 either provide no specific guidelines for determining use values, or simply mention one or more factors that are to be considered, while the other 12 states mandate an income-capitalization approach. Three of these 12 states leave the entire process of estimating income-capitalization values to the counties. The other nine require the state to develop values based on capitalized farm income, or the state officials are required to advise counties and develop guidelines for the local assessors and other officials.

Although there have been many efforts to obtain uniformity in assessments of

---

[7]U.S. General Accounting Office (GAO), *Effects of Tax Policies on Land Use,* CED 78-97, 1978, pp. 9–13.
  [8]This section is based in part on David L. Chicoine and John T. Scott, Jr., "Farmland Use-Value Assessment: Illinois Approach," *Journal of the American Society of Farm Managers and Rural Appraisers,* vol. 46, no. 2, October 1982, pp. 16–22; and Chicoine and Scott, "Agricultural Use-Valuation Using Farm Level Data," *Property Tax Journal,* vol. 2, no. 1, March 1983, pp. 1–12.

farmland, considerable arbitrariness exists within individual states, as well as among the various states. So the equity of taxes varies considerably both within and among states. Furthermore, during the evolution of use-value assessments for farmland, questions of tax equity among classes of real-property owners have tended to be ignored. For farmland assessments, all of the informational problems associated with the need for detailed soil surveys have not been overcome, and in most states competent and diligent state review of the process has not been achieved. The general policy of use-value assessment of farmland appears to be firmly established, however, which is in contrast to deferred taxation programs and restrictive agreements applying to agricultural land.

Deferred Taxation Programs

These laws also provide for assessment based on value in current use but impose a sanction on owners who convert land to a noneligible use.[9] Under certain circumstances owners of agricultural land may apply for deferment of the additional tax that might apply to their land if it were valued for urban or industrial development. In return for this they agree to refrain from selling or converting the land to another use. This provision is most applicable to agricultural land in the rural-urban fringe. But a general conclusion, based on experience in several states, is that such laws have had only limited effect on land use, the main reason being the landowners' reluctance to make a commitment not to sell even if a profitable opportunity to do so should arise.[10] Landowners must apply to receive the benefits of tax deferral, and their reluctance to become involved in the process is another factor contributing to the lack of participation in this program.[11]

Restrictive Agreements

In addition to the tax deferral programs, some states permit local governments to make agreements with landowners under which the owners agree to restrict the use of their land to a specified use in return for more permanent tax concessions. Generally, the restriction on use is in effect for 10 years, and penalties are provided for changing the use contrary to the agreement. The agreements are made at the option of the state or local government and are generally limited to specified areas where open space is to be preserved. Provisions of state laws vary widely and in some cases there is no clear distinction between a restrictive agreement and a tax deferral program.

---

[9] For further discussion see Thomas I. Hady and Ann Gordon Sibold, *State Programs for the Differential Assessment of Farm and Open-Space Land,* U.S. Department of Agriculture, Economic Research Service, Agricultural Economic report 256, 1974; and David E. Hansen and S. J. Schwartz, "Landowners' Behavior at the Rural-Urban Fringe in Response to Preferential Property Taxation," *Land Economics,* vol. 4, November 1975, pp. 341–354.

[10] Ibid., p. 253.

[11] See also Franklin J. Reiss, "Taxation–Land Use Relationships," *Illinois Agricultural Economics,* University of Illinois at Urbana-Champaign, vol. 15, no. 1, January 1975, pp. 1–7.

The restrictive agreement based on a 10-year term and tied to a local government's land-use plan has been expected to be more effective than a 3-year tax deferral. But its use has been limited by the fact that, if opportunity exists for converting agricultural land to other uses, the potential gains from selling or developing the land generally far outweigh any tax savings available to the owner from signing a restrictive agreement. Hence, programs based on such agreements have had limited success in reducing taxes or in preserving agricultural land and open space in their current uses.

Inferences for Agricultural Policy

As a general rule, if farm real estate taxes are correctly anticipated by the purchasers of farmland, then the real estate tax is a burdenless tax because it will be discounted in bids or offers to buy. But when values of farmland fluctuate as they have done, then the real estate tax becomes something of a capricious cost that cannot be controlled by the farmer, and increases in taxes cannot be discounted accurately. Also, tax increases cannot be passed on to others, at least in the short run. Because of the capital intensiveness of modern agriculture, increases in real estate taxes influence the farm sector in a more restrictive way than they do most other industries. All farm owners are affected, not only those who have recently bought land.

This is the general rationale behind the efforts of individual states to establish a system of use-value assessment for farmland. But, although the rationale can be understood, much remains to be done to make the system efficient and equitable. Even then, questions may be raised about the beneficial effects for agriculture over a number of years. In essence, the proponents of use-value assessment are suggesting that market prices overvalue the earning power of land. Although this can be the case in a period of inflation, such as the 1970s, it probably is not the case over the longer term.

Use-value assessment is a useful policy technique for avoiding excessive tax increases on farmland in a period of inflation, especially on farmland that is located in the rural-urban fringe, and it can help pull agriculture through a period of adversity, until more fundamental or far-reaching reforms can be made. Let us consider some of these other reforms.

State and Federal Alternatives to Increases in Real Estate Taxes

Taxes on real estate in general, as well as on farmland, have been criticized as an inequitable system, especially in terms of their contribution to the support of primary and secondary education. In many states, to significantly reduce or even contain the tax burden on agriculture, while still achieving an adequate level of funding for local government and elementary and secondary education, it will be necessary to shift a larger portion of the total cost to state and federal tax sources. The issue for agricultural policy analysis has been highlighted not only by the alarming trends in farm real estate taxes, but also by court decisions based on constitutional arguments of equal protection and equal opportunity. Tax burdens often vary widely among school districts; because of unequal funding, the quality of education also varies from district to district and state to state.

The first comprehensive court review of the issue was presented over a span of 18 months. On August 30, 1971, the California Supreme Court ruled that the local property tax school-funding scheme "invidiously discriminates against the poor because it makes the quality of a child's education a function of the wealth of his parents and neighbors." Although uniform education expenditures were not mandated by the California constitution, the court concluded "that the right to an education in our public schools is a fundamental interest which cannot be conditioned on wealth, . . . that such a system cannot withstand constitutional challenge and must fall before the equal protection clause (of the Fourteenth Amendment, hence is unconstitutional)."[12]

The California decision was followed by similar rulings by United States district courts in Minnesota[13] and Texas,[14] and by the Michigan Supreme Court.[15] Finally, the United States Supreme Court, in a 5 to 4 ruling on March 21, 1973, reversed the Texas decision, holding that education "is not among the rights afforded explicit protection under our federal Constitution."[16] But Justice Lewis F. Powell, Jr., writing for the majority, noted: "The need is apparent for reform in tax systems which may well have relied too long and too heavily on the local property tax. . . ." A minority dissenting opinion, written by Justice Thurgood Marshall, regarded the majority view "as a retreat from our historic commitment to equality of educational opportunity and as unsupportable acquiescence in a system which deprives children in their earliest years of the chance to reach their full potential as citizens."

The policy issue of equal funding of school systems can be related to school tax options affecting agriculture. In Illinois it has been found that the portion of real estate tax revenue used for schools, which is about 65 percent of the total tax revenue from real estate outside of Cook County, could be displaced by increased revenues from either state or federal income taxes with a substantial net gain to agriculture. The greatest relative gains would accrue to small and medium-sized family farms, primarily because the amount of net income from farm property is very low. School funding would be made uniform over the state, as well as more equal between farm and nonfarm taxpayers in similar income situations. In Illinois greater reliance on the personal income tax would result in a more uniform tax burden over the state and help to equalize funding among school districts.[17]

---

[12]*Serrano v. Priest,* cited in *The United States Law Week,* vol. 40, Sept. 14, 1971, p. 2128.

[13]*Van Dusartz v. Hatfield,* cited in *The United States Law Week,* vol. 40, Oct. 26, 1971, p. 2228.

[14]*Rodriguez v. San Antonio Independent School District,* 337 F. Supp. 280 (D.C. Tex. 1971).

[15]*Milliken v. Green,* Michigan Supreme Court, *The United States Law Week,* vol. 41, Jan. 9, 1973, p. 2348.

[16]*San Antonio Independent School District* v. *Rodriguez, cited in The United States Law Week,* vol. 41, March 20, 1973, p. 4407.

[17]H. G. Halcrow, Folke Dovring, Arthur Eith, F. J. Reiss, J. T. Scott, Jr., W. D. Seitz, and R. G. F. Spitze, *School Tax Options Affecting Illinois Agriculture,* University of Illinois at Urbana-Champaign, College of Agriculture Agricultural Experiment Station, bulletin 744, April 1973, especially pp. 8–10.

Although the tax situation differs from state to state, the principles of tax reform of special interest in agricultural policy analysis will involve the two major alternatives that we have discussed: (1) a trend toward use-value assessment of farmland, and (2) a gradual shifting of some of the tax burden from real estate to income and other sources. For the most part, these changes can result in a more efficient and equitable tax system. The most critical policy issue for the future will be whether or not owners of agricultural land will be able to retain the tax concessions gained under use-value assessment programs. Unless there is a shifting of tax burden from property to income and other sources, heavier property taxes may be levied on farm real estate. Higher farm property taxes are not inevitable, but tax relief will be limited both by the economics of the situation and by the political interests and forces at work.

SUMMARY

Monetary policy has a crucial effect on agriculture. There is a long history of agricultural involvement in making monetary policy, with farm groups generally favoring an inflationary rather than a deflationary policy. But, since agriculture may also be hurt by inflation, which increases prices of inputs, farm groups in recent years have tended to favor a generally conservative policy.

Federal credit programs have been used to accelerate the growth of the agricultural economy. Not only has agriculture been served by the most complete programs of government credit services available to any sector of the economy, but these services have also been used in the greatest variety of ways to bring relief to agriculture; to facilitate investment and growth; and, since the beginning of the 1970s especially, to create capital gains in agriculture far exceeding anything previously experienced. These policies have contributed importantly to the great structural transformation that has occurred in agriculture and to the evolution of agriculture into export markets. The recent federal tax acts have tended to accentuate these trends rather than constrain them. Recent trends in farm property taxes will tend to offset the tax relief offered by the 1981 act. The combined effect of the credit and financial policy that has been followed, while contributing importantly to growth and structural change, will magnify policy problems in this area in the years ahead.

IMPORTANT TERMS AND CONCEPTS

Influence of monetary policy on agriculture

Effects of business cycles on agriculture

Policy position of agriculture in respect to inflation and deflation

History of monetary policy affecting agriculture

Cooperative Farm Credit System

Organization of the FCS

Federal Farm Credit Act of 1916

Agricultural Credits Act of 1923

Agricultural Marketing Act of 1929

Provisions of Farm Credit Act of 1971

The Farmers Home Administration (FHA, or FmHA)

Rural Development Act of 1972

Federally sponsored credit services

Comparative roles of federal land bank associations (FLBAs) and production credit associations (PCAs)

Effects of farm debt increases on land prices and farm income

Solutions to current farm debt problems

Farm capital formation vs. farm debt

Relationships between capital gain and current farm income

Sources of preferential tax treatment of farm income

Provisions of the Economic Recovery Tax Act of 1981

Effects of progressive income tax rates on farm investment

Effects of capital-gains treatment on investments of taxpayers

Effects of federal tax policy on productivity and welfare

Federal income tax policy affecting farm corporations

Trends in farm property taxes

Preferential assessment laws applied to farmland

Deferred taxation programs applied to farmland

Restrictive agreement laws applied to farmland

State and federal alternatives to increasing taxes on farmland

LOOKING AHEAD

It is important to understand how the other major input markets relate to one another and to the credit and financial policy that we have just discussed. The question for policy in each case concerns the public action that should or should not be taken to influence the economic structure of the market and its performance. The next chapter continues with policy analysis of the natural resource markets. This involves the land market; and policy analysis of the alternatives for land use, for soil and water conservation, and for crop insurance using the concept of weather as a natural resource. The last two chapters will deal with the agribusiness input markets and with human capital as the ultimate resource in agricultural input markets.

QUESTIONS AND EXERCISES

1 It has been said that credit and financial policy generated by the Farm Credit Act of 1971 has been one of the most influential of all policies in bringing about the great structural transformation in agriculture that has occurred since the beginning of the 1970s. Do you agree? Explain your answer.

2 It may be argued that expansion in federal land bank loans and in those of the production credit associations was needed to finance agricultural development and growth. Commercial banks and other lenders followed along as a means of protecting their share of the farm credit market. Since this helped to support agriculture's movement into the international market, all major sectors tended to gain. Do you agree? Explain.

3 It has been said that the political movements supported by agricultural groups have been weighted in favor of credit and monetary expansion. Cite at least three instances in which this was true. In each case, why did farm and rural people take the position they did? Do you expect them to react the same way in the future? Why? Is there any instance in which they have been generally deflationary in their outlook?

4 The two decades from 1895 to 1914 are sometimes referred to as the "golden age of American agriculture." What were the essential economic factors tending to create this situation? Can somewhat similar conditions develop in the next decade or two? That is, what part of the general picture is in place? What would have to change? Why?

5 We have said that, under the current financial structure of the farm sector, a current growth rate of 4 to 5 percent in the constant dollar returns to current assets will require the sector to take a relatively low rate of return on the market value of assets that existed in the early 1980s. Why? Given the current farm financial situation, is it possible to raise the current rate of return on farm assets by policy action? If not, why not? If so, then how?

6 What will be the general effect of the Economic Recovery Tax Act of 1981 on investments in the farm sector? More specifically, what types of investors will tend to benefit most from the Accelerated Cost Recovery System (ACRS)? Will individuals reporting large capital gains be favored by use of ACRS? Why?

7 It has been suggested that the federal income-tax structure tends to favor high-income investors in agriculture. Do you agree? Explain your answer, giving an example to illustrate.

8 We have said that tax provisions that attract investment funds into the farm sector, which would not otherwise be made, do not necessarily result in higher aggregate net farm income. Do you agree? If you disagree, explain why. If you agree, explain how this result can occur.

9 What are the essential differences in the federal income-tax code between treatment of farmers and treatment of farm corporations? What are the advantages accruing to corporations? To individuals?

10 Since the property tax on income-earning real estate is in general theory a burdenless tax, why is the farm property tax such a sensitive policy issue in most states? What are the policy alternatives for tax relief for farmers? Which of these alternatives holds the most promise for the 1980s? Why?

More Advanced Assignments

1 It has been suggested that foreign exchange traders will respond to a widening trade deficit of the United States by generating an even sharper dollar devaluation.
   a Why might this tend to occur?
   b What would be its general effect on exports and imports of the United States?
   c How would dollar devaluation tend to affect exports of farm commodities from the United States? Why?

2 Emanuel Melichar makes the case, in his article "Capital Gain versus Current Income in the Farming Sector," *American Journal of Agriculture Economics,* vol. 61, no. 5, December 1979, pp. 1085–1092, that the success or failure of policy actions which are designed to increase the rate of current return to farming—such as higher price supports—depends on the degree to which profit takes the form of capital gains rather than current income. That is, the more that increased farm income is reflected in capital gain, the lower will be the return on current assets.

   In a later article, Haim Shalit and Andrew Schmitz, "Farmland Accumulation Prices," ibid., vol. 64, no. 4, November 1982, pp. 710–719, show that savings (the difference between farm income and consumption) and accumulated real estate debt are the main determinants of high farmland prices. Given these two conclusions, what combination of credit, price, and market or trade policy will be most successful in increasing the current rate of return to farm assets over the next decade? Explain.

RECOMMENDED READINGS

Boehlje, Michael, and Hoy F. Carman, "Tax Policy: Implications for Producers and the Agricultural Sector," *American Journal of Agricultural Economics,* vol. 64, no. 5, December 1982, pp. 1030–1038; and George L. Casler, "Discussion," ibid., pp. 1047–1049.

Chicoine, David L., and John T. Scott, Jr., "Agricultural Use-Valuation Using Farm Level Data," *Property Tax Journal,* vol. 2, no. 1, March 1983, pp. 1–12.

Melichar, Emanuel, "Capital Gains versus Current Income in the Farming Sector," *American Journal of Agricultural Economics,* vol. 61, no. 5, December 1979, pp. 1085–1092.

CHAPTER 10

POLICY ANALYSIS OF NATURAL RESOURCE MARKETS

Policy applied to the natural resource markets that supply land, water, and minerals is crucial in determining how agriculture will be organized and how it will function. Because of concerns about the adequacy of these resources and the directions of policy applying to them, renewed uncertainty has arisen over the last several years about the ability of American agriculture to sustain continued increase in productivity.[1] There is a perception that agricultural land resources are rapidly being lost to nonagricultural uses, that land use practices of modern agriculture are leading to excessive erosion of soil resources, and that energy resources are not sufficient to sustain the type and rate of growth to which we have become accustomed over the last half century of so. Although many of these concerns are well founded, some oft-stated ones are not, and the purpose of this chapter is to sort out some of the issues and consider the options for policy.

IN THIS CHAPTER

1 You can learn how to appraise the major issues in land use, including protection of agricultural land and the organization of policy for control of land use.

2 You can learn how to appraise the problem of soil erosion and the alternatives in conservation policy that aim to deal with it.

3 You can learn how to appraise alternatives in crop insurance as a means of dealing with an important natural resource problem, the variability of weather. The issue of fuel-energy resources and other industrial inputs will be discussed in Chapter 11.

---

[1] *Disappearing Farmlands: A Citizen's Guide to Agricultural Land Preservation,* National Association of Counties Research Foundation, Washington, D.C., 1979.

215

There are about 127 million acres of land in the United States not currently in crops which have some potential for crops. What are the implications for future land-use policy?

ISSUES IN LAND USE

Although land is of declining relative importance in agricultural production, future food supplies will depend on its continued productivity, and the economic structure of agriculture will depend on how it is organized and used. Choices in land-use policy will determine who will own and control agricultural land, and how land will be allocated to farming (and ranching) and other uses. Let us consider the basic concepts for land-use policy.

The Cropland Base

Primary interest in policy is centered on the cropland base, which is fixed in the Department of Agriculture's *Natural Agricultural Lands Study* at 540 million acres (Figure 10-1). Some 413 million acres are readily available cropland, and the remaining 127 million acres have some potential for crops. In the late 1970s, when production-control programs were not restricting the use of land for crops, about 370 million acres were used for crops.[2] For comparison, in the early 1920s there were about 365 million acres in crops.[3]

[2] *Agricultural Statistics,* 1981, U.S. Department of Agriculture, Washington, D.C., p. 417.
[3] *Yearbook of Agriculture,* 1923, Ibid., pp. 415–506.

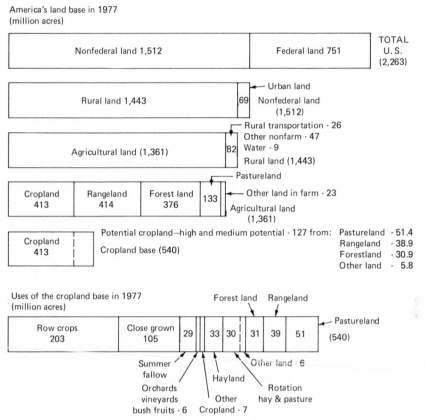

FIGURE 10-1
America's land base and uses of the cropland base in 1977. *(Source: National Agricultural Lands Study, Final Report, 1981, p. 28.)*

Supply and Demand in the Short Run

The supply of land for crops is very inelastic in the short run, as increases in the crop price index of 50 percent or more have brought increases in planted acreage of only about 5 percent. Similarly, decreases in crop prices have brought relatively small decreases in total land seeded to crops, even though there have been much larger shifts from one crop to another.

It may be assumed that the opportunity cost of keeping cropland in use for crops is very low in the short run of two or three years, and that the cost of preparing land that has not been cropped previously to be used for crops is relatively high. Hence, the supply is very inelastic in the short run, for both rising and falling crop prices.

The supply of land used for grazing is also very inelastic, and the supply in semi-arid regions is uniquely affected by rainfall. That is, the supply curve shifts to the right in years of good rainfall, and to the left in dry years. This tends to affect the cycles in production of range cattle, as has been previously discussed. Much of the land used for grazing is controlled by the federal Bureau of Land Management and other public agencies, which limit the number of cattle and other livestock that can be grazed, so the supply is largely determined by public policy. The available grazing lands tend to be utilized up to the capacity determined by weather and agency policy, so the supply is very inelastic. The demand for feeder livestock off the range is derived from the demand for finished livestock—beef cattle and lambs. So, while the demand will fluctuate according to market conditions, it does tend to be rather inelastic.

Supply and Demand for Land in the Long Run

Over the long run, a continuing strong demand for agricultural commodities for export presumably would bring tens of millions of acres of the 127 million acres of potential cropland not now in crops into use for crops, while a more modest increase in demand would tend to stabilize the total acreage used for crops at historic levels. Since the domestic demand is more stable and can be projected within narrow limits, one of the important facts with which to contend in land-use and conservation policy is that a continuing strong export demand will tend to intensify competition for land and exacerbate soil erosion problems.

In the long run, the demand for cropland for crops will be influenced far more by the demand for exports than by any other factor. Recently, for example, a little more than one-third of the crop output has been exported, and various studies have projected that the demand for exports could double or even triple by the year 2000. If so, this could mean the export of the crop from another 50 to 75 million acres. As a basis for comparison, studies have projected that the land devoted to urban and transportation uses will rise from 2.6 percent of the total land base in the late 1970s to 3.2 percent in the year 2000, an increase of some 13.6 million acres, about one-third of which, or 4.5 million acres, would be cropland.[4] This would take a little less than 1 percent of the total cropland base, an amount that can be offset in crop production by converting some of the potential cropland base to crops, or by increased use of other inputs.

Even so, such a projection of converting agricultural land to other uses may be too high. The net demand for more land for urban and transportation use may be considerably smaller in the future than in the past. There are five reasons for this:[5]

1 The conversion of land to highway use, which occurred at an unprecedented pace during the building of the interstate superhighway system, has largely come to a close. Indeed, it is possible that some land that has been used for highways and railroads will be converted back to agricultural use.

[4]Earl O. Heady, "The Adequacy of Agricultural Land: A Demand-Supply Perspective,"*The Cropland Crisis: Myth or Reality?,* Pierre R. Crosson (ed.), published for Resources for the Future by the Johns Hopkins University Press, Baltimore and London, 1982, pp. 23–56.

[5]Philip M. Raup, "Competition for Land and the Future of American Agriculture," *The Future of American Agriculture as a Strategic Resource,* Sandra S. Batie and Robert G. Healy (eds.), The Conservation Foundation, Washington, D.C., 1980.

Homes built in the country often use two or three times as much land as is used for homes in the city, or in more built-up areas. If it is in the national interest to conserve good farmland, should the use of land for home building be limited by zoning? Farmers generally oppose this policy. What beliefs and values are involved? What are the pros and cons of more restrictive zoning laws?

2 The loss of agricultural land from the building of large dams and reservoirs has largely come to an end.

3 Although the trend toward country living may continue to use more land, a countertrend induced by high transportation costs may cause most large cities to cease to grow in total area, and cause an overall slowing of the conversion of agricultural land to urban use.

4 If increasing travel costs increase the demand for recreational land close to large centers of population, this could result in conversion of a relatively small amount of additional agricultural land.

5 A continuing demand for coal and strip-mining will use up small acreages of

Strip-mining of coal often uses good farmland. Should the strip-miner be required to restore the land for crop use even though the expense is much more than the land is worth? What are the policy arguments?

land from year to year, which is not very significant in a decade or two, but can be very important in the longer run. Most of the cropland cannot be restored to use for crops, except at exorbitant cost, and the political obstacles to restoration are formidable.

Effects of Gasohol on Demand for Land

In the long run, it is possible that the effects of all of the above could be swamped by increasing the subsidy for producing ethanol from corn and other grains. The subsidy has arisen from exempting gasohol, which is about 10 percent ethanol and 90 percent gasoline, from the sales taxes levied on gasoline. If these taxes were to be increased over the years by either the states or the federal government, while gasohol continued to be exempt, this would increase the subsidy and increase the demand for land for crop production. It must be understood that this would constitute an increasing distortion of agricultural incentives, therefore, an increasing waste of resources. If the tax on a gallon of gasoline is 5 cents and gasohol is exempt, this is equivalent to a subsidy of 50 cents per gallon on the production of ethanol. A tax of 10 cents would be a subsidy of $1.00 a gallon, and so on.

If political considerations favor gasohol as a way of subsidizing grain producers, then the impact of this on demand for land could be great, indeed. But, if economic considerations dominate over the political incentives to subsidize grain producers, then the impact of gasohol on land use will be relatively insignificant. Policy decisions will determine how much pressure is put on agricultural land resources by the production of gasohol.

Local, State, and Federal Land-Use Policy

Policy decisions will also determine how much of the conversion of agricultural land to other uses will be controlled by planning and zoning, and how much by market forces of supply and demand. Nearly all states have land-use planning and zoning laws, but considerable variation exists throughout the country as to their effectiveness in regulating the conversion of agricultural land to other uses. Implementation is generally a local matter, with interests of the local community uppermost in the minds of local planning and zoning agencies. Concern over the loss of good farmland is high in some states and communities, while others are less concerned.

One of the issues that has arisen in recent years and which may become more important in the future concerns the participation of the federal government to support the efforts of states and communities, and ensure more uniform application of planning and zoning laws. A bill to involve federal support was introduced in the United States Senate in January 1970, and after extensive hearings was reported to the floor, but no action was taken. It was introduced again early in 1971, as the proposed Land Use Policy and Planning Assistance Act. After 10 days of hearings, numerous committee executive sessions, and consultations with the National Governors' Conference, the National League of Cities, the United States Conference of Mayors, representatives of industry groups, and environmental citizens' groups, the bill was again reported to the Senate. On September 19, 1972, after accepting several amendments, the Senate passed the bill (S. 632) by a vote of 60 to 18, but the House failed to act.

The bill was introduced again early in 1973 (as S. 268), and another series of hearings was held.[6] The bill, virtually the same one that had passed the year before, again passed the Senate by a wide margin, but its companion bill (H.R. 10294) was defeated in the House in June 1974 by a few votes. It had appeared headed for

---

[6]See *Land Use Policy and Planning Assistance Act,* Hearings before the Committee on Interior and Insular Affairs, U.S. Senate, 93d Cong., 1st Sess., Feb. 6, 7, 26, 27, and April 2, 3, 1973, parts 1 and 2.

passage in the House until President Nixon announced his opposition. The bill failed in spite of the fact that it had received the strong and often vocal support of such diverse groups as the National Governors' Conference (and nearly 30 individual governors), the National Association of Counties, the League of Cities, the United States Conference of Mayors, all the major environmental organizations, various water resources associations, the National Association of Manufacturers, and the Federation of Rocky Mountain States, Inc.

The bill was also supported by such prestigious publications as *Business Week, The New York Times, The Wall Street Journal,* both the *Washington Post* and the *Star,* the *Boston Globe,* the *St. Louis Post-Dispatch,* the *Christian Science Monitor,* and the *Minneapolis Star.* The need for national land-use legislation also was recognized by the Advisory Commission on Intergovernmental Relations, as it had been earlier by the National Commission on Food Marketing, and the National Advisory Commission on Food and Fiber.

The main policy proposal in the bill was to provide federal assistance to the states rather than have direct federal involvement in directing land use. It was proposed that a new Office of Land Use Policy Administration would be established in the Department of the Interior to help coordinate a wide range of studies on land use, to administer a grant-in-aid program to the states and local governments, and to coordinate a range of assistance activities. There would be a new National Advisory Board on Land Use Policy drawn from federal departments and agencies, state and local governments, and other public entities having land-use planning and management responsibilities. To comply with eligibility requirements for grants, both the Senate and the House bills would require each state to establish a land-use planning agency, and a state intergovernmental advisory council would be composed of elected officials of local governments.

Since the 1973 bill did not pass, a new effort was begun in 1975, when a new bill was introduced as the proposed Land Use and Resource Conservation Act of 1975. It would have authorized $500 million to states over six years, to provide financial incentives and policy direction for developing state land-use programs, and to coordinate federal agencies with states. This bill, with some provisions similar to the National Coastal Zone Management Act of 1972, would have authorized grants for developing state land-use programs within three years, and grants for three more years for implementation, once a program was approved by the secretary of the interior. It would have provided for assessing and regulating developments of regional impact, large-scale subdivisions, and key facilities tending to induce growth. It specified procedures to identify, designate, and regulate areas of critical environmental concern. It offered support for developing state policies to encourage energy conservation through efficient land-use plans, to formulate policies for commercial needs, housing, transportation, recreation, and open space. One section, apparently designed to get agriculture's political support, offered assistance for formulating state policies for food and fiber production, but distinguished lands used for this purpose from other critical lands. But the major farm organizations actively opposed the bill, and they were joined in opposition by some nonagricultural groups.

The Issue of Federal Involvement in Land-Use Policy

The broad variety of organizations and interests supporting the action to establish federal participation in land-use planning are probably united in feeling that land-use development has not been well planned and has been unnecessarily wasteful of land resources. Their major concerns have been directed at planning to reduce the wastefulness of land-use patterns that have developed around most major centers of population in developing urban, industrial, and transportation facilities. The patterns tend to add unnecessarily to costs of public services relating to transportation, gas and electrical power, water systems, public security, fire protection, and other services. It is thought that a more coordinated public input in the developmental process will result in lower costs and more attractive and functional urban communities and countryside.

The basic theoretical foundation for this rests in large part on the concept of externalities. That is, whenever there are substantial external costs in any firm or industry, then that firm or industry will use more resources than are socially desirable, and thus impose additional costs on society. The concept is illustrated in Figure 10-2, where it may be noted that when external costs are not included the firm uses more resources than when they are. If a developer is not required to economize in terms of external costs, then it will not view as necessary economizing on use of land or other natural resources. More land will be used and the resulting costs to the rest of society will be higher. Incorporation of external costs into the plans of the developer

FIGURE 10-2
Equilibrium of the firm in the short run is Q_0 when external costs are included and Q_1 when they are not.

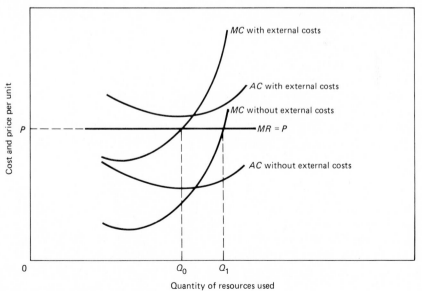

results in use of less resources. This is the basic concept of planning and zoning to conserve resources, or to achieve other results desired by society.

Role of the States as an Issue in Land-Use Policy

All state governments have the power, granted in their constitutions, to promote the general welfare, including the right to establish land-use plans and controls, and to pass laws to regulate the process of land-use planning and approval of zoning ordinances and regulations. The constitutional requirement is that (1) the objectives of the regulation must promote the general welfare, (2) the methods used must have a substantial relation to the ends or objectives to be sought, and (3) the regulation must not be arbitrary, unreasonable, or oppressive.[7]

Zoning ordinances adopted by local governments under state law generally describe the areas or districts to be zoned, the regulations applied to each, and the means of enforcing them. The districts are normally defined on maps available in local government offices. Certain land uses listed as nonconforming are either regulated and controlled or forbidden entirely, under the theory that, by guiding or controlling economic development on private lands, the government will help to prevent the wastefulness of urban sprawl, pollution of the environment, and unnecessary or undesirable conflicts in land use.

Although zoning ordinances have long been used to control development of towns and cities, the zoning of rural lands has lagged far behind. Zoning was first tried in rural areas in Wisconsin in 1929 to prevent and control settlement of rural lands in the northern cut-over regions of the state. The success of zoning in these submarginal lands led to more general adoption of zoning laws, and, in recent years, almost all states have enacted legislation permitting local government units to zone rural lands. These ordinances are designed to prevent construction of undesirable buildings, mobile-home parks, and undesirable suburban developments, especially near lakes, streams, and other scenic areas.

In respect to agriculture, the trend has not been to use zoning to regulate the use of land for crops, but to adopt more broadly based laws for regulating and controlling livestock enterprises, and for preventing pollution through regulations concerning livestock waste and effluent, and the use of farm chemicals. In some areas, the major thrust of policy has been to protect the municipal water supplies. Farmers, of course, are not opposed to this; they, too, want their water protected from contamination.

Summary of Issues Affecting Agriculture

According to our view of the relationship of land and other natural resources to agricultural development and growth in the United States, any expansion of the acreage in crop production will come very slowly; the land used for grazing has reached its peak and will decline as the acreage in crops increases; and urban-industrial devel-

---

[7]*State Legislation for Better Land Use,* Interbureau Committee Report, U.S. Department of Agriculture, Washington, D.C., April 1941, pp. xii–xv.

opment will take very small amounts of farmland out of production. Further increases in agricultural output will come mainly from further intensification of land use and more technological advance.

Agricultural groups have resisted more federal and state involvement in land-use planning and control because they want to be free to respond to market forces. Federal involvement could lead to further restrictions, although not necessarily so. If done correctly, federal involvement could lend support to the activities of states and municipalities so that they are more consistent in planning and zoning in accordance with national goals. The sale of agricultural land for urban-industrial development might be slowed somewhat. This could have an effect on the agricultural land market in the rural-urban fringe, but this would be a relatively minor influence. If such planning results in a more efficient use of land, then farmers would stand to gain from the reduction in costs of public services. If more restrictions were placed on agriculture's use of land, this has the potential to either increase or decrease net farm income.

In perspective, both the transfer of agricultural land to other uses and the transfer of new land to crop production will be more modest in the future than in the past. The image of agriculture "running out of land" because of urban-industrial development will be less meaningful than it has been historically. But, because of induced innovation and the advance of technology, preventing erosion of agricultural lands will continue to be important in terms of the national economy. Soil and water conservation will be a policy issue in the future, so let us consider this.

POLICY ANALYSIS OF SOIL AND WATER CONSERVATION

Soil erosion is of policy concern because the major costs are external to the farm firm in terms of sedimentation and water pollution, and the costs continue over the years. Hence, it is expedient for the farmer to use more soil resources than is optimum for society. As crop production intensifies, the incentive for the farmer to use more soil resources increases and, as the process continues, the damage to the environment in the form of sedimentation and water pollution tends to be cumulative.

The problem for conservation policy is greatly complicated by the fact that increased exposure of the soil by modern cropping and grazing systems and practices has greatly accelerated the process of erosion, to surpass the more natural geological and biological processes by which most of the productive soils have been formed. The rate of erosion differs widely by types of farming and grazing areas, and by major regions in the United States; the damage that is caused by a given rate also differs widely, depending on a number of factors. Where topsoils are deep and fertile, as in most river valleys and the plains of the midwest, a relatively high rate of soil erosion may do little damage in terms of the on-farm internal costs. But unless drainage is well developed, the external off-farm costs are high, as a result of siltation in streams and reservoirs and other damage to the environment. Where the topsoil is thin, or more fragile, the internal cost of erosion is higher for a given rate of soil loss, but the external cost is generally no higher than for deep or more fertile soils. The real damage done externally by a given soil loss also depends on the environment. Sediment

If land that is cultivated like this blows badly in the spring and creates hazardous dust storms, who should bear the cost of the damage that is external to the farm firm?

from erosion is part of the soil-building process in some environments, while in most cases sediment has a negative value.

In spite of these complications, it is possible to generalize about the process of erosion, and the demonstrated need for conservation.

Generalizing about Soil Erosion and Conservation

In 1977, the United States Soil Conservation Service conducted the first National Resource Inventory (NRI).[8] This provided statistically reliable estimates concerning the dimensions of erosion, and identified the key physical parameters underlying erosion. The NRI did not establish how much soil loss would be acceptable in a long-time planning horizon, nor did it define a specific recommended policy goal to be followed in the future. For the nation as a whole, it was found that about two-thirds of the total soil loss was due to water and about one-third due to wind, with water erosion being most serious in the north central states and in other humid areas such as the southeast, and wind erosion being more damaging in the great plains and drier regions.

[8]*National Resource Inventory,* U.S. Department of Agriculture, Soil Conservation Service, 1978.

Excessive runoff from tilled fields can cause flooding of bottom land along creeks and rivers, the major costs of which may be external to the farm. The crux of the policy issue is how much public money to invest, or what public penalties to impose, to get the farming systems that will maximize net social income.

The NRI used a standard rule of thumb of 5 tons of soil loss per acre annually as a generally acceptable rate of loss for cropped land. On this basis, it found that on 60 percent of the land used for small grains and row crops in 1977, the loss from erosion did not exceed the generally accepted level of 5 tons per acre. On another 20 percent of the land, losses were between 5 and 9.9 tons per acre. The remaining 20 percent of the land accounted for 91.5 percent of the excess erosion, with a little more than half of this land having soil losses of 10 to 24.9 tons per acre, and 30 percent of the excess erosion; and the remaining half having soil losses ranging up to 200 tons and more per acre, and almost 60 percent of the total excess erosion.

Soil loss tolerance (T) levels, the tolerance level at which soil formation would offset soil loss in maintaining productivity, were defined for both crop and grazing lands. These T levels ranged from the 5 tons mentioned above for most cropped land down to about 2 tons for grazing lands in the western great plains and mountain regions. Such standards are useful in visualizing some of the changes in land use that would be required to reach T levels, but they do not necessarily define general goals for policy. For instance, although at least 60 percent of the land in crops is currently eroding at an annual rate of 5 tons per acre or less, it may still be in the interest of society to achieve lower rates of soil erosion to further reduce external costs of soil loss. On the other hand, on some deep and fertile soils, such as the Paloose area in eastern Washington, the Highwood Bench area north of the Missouri River in north central Montana, and parts of the cornbelt, soil losses above the 5-ton T level may be sustained for centuries without measureable loss of soil productivity or severe external off-farm damage. In some other major crop areas, soil losses up to 10, 15, or even 20 tons may be sustained for 50 years or more without much loss in productivity, and in some localities without much external environmental damage. Still, an important inference for policy may be drawn from the NRI and its establishment of T levels.

The inference for policy from the NRI is that the excess erosion from agricultural production is highly concentrated, even though some conservation practices may be required on all land to keep the total soil loss within acceptable limits. But what is generally acceptable for the farmer is not what is acceptable for society, and this is the essence of the policy problem. On the large majority of erosive soils, the internal on-site costs from soil loss are only a small fraction of the external off-site damage costs. On most deep and fertile soils, an annual soil loss of 5 tons or less can be sustained indefinitely, without any appreciable loss of crop yield or productivity. A loss of 5 to 10 tons may or may not be significant in lowering yields, depending on soil depth and the extent of rilling or gullying accompanying the erosion. A loss of 10 tons or more will result in significant lowering of crop yields on some soil after several years of cropping. But this loss may be masked by using other yield-increasing technologies. Even so, in almost all, if not all, instances, the external damage cost from a ton of sediment will greatly exceed the value of the crop lost from erosion.

This may be taken as a suggestion that neither the internal on-site costs of a ton of soil loss nor the external damages of a ton of sediment can be viewed as a constant in a given soil or cropping situation. The internal cost of lowered yields from loss of a ton of soil will tend to increase at an increasing rate, until the land becomes unprofitable for crop production. The external off-site damage cost will also increase at an increasing rate up to some point, after which it increases at a decreasing rate until the environment is saturated, and no further damage can be done. The problem is not how to reduce soil loss to zero, but how to contain erosion to acceptable levels. Theoretically, the general problem for soil conservation policy, on land that is profitable for crop use, is to develop conservation programs that will encourage farmers to establish crop rotations, tillage systems, and conservation practices that will maximize net social income. *Net social income* is defined as the net value of crop production after all costs have been deducted, including the internal on-site damage costs of soil loss and the external off-site damage costs. Since it is not practical to actually measure these costs, a generalized method has been developed to estimate them.

Measuring Soil Losses Using the Universal Soil Loss Equation

What is called the "universal soil loss equation" (USLE) has been developed to provide a theoretical estimate of soil loss from an acre of land by making use of a rainfall factor for a type of farming area or crop region; a soil erodibility factor; a slope and a length factor; a cropping management factor, including crop rotations and tillage systems; and an erosion control practice factor. The equation is usually written as follows:

$$A = RKLSCP$$

where A is computed soil loss per acre per year
$\quad R$ is the rainfall factor for the region
$\quad K$ is the soil erodibility factor
$\quad LS$ is the slope and slope length factor
$\quad C$ is the cropping management factor
$\quad P$ is the erosion control practice factor

Values for the factors in the universal soil loss equation may be developed for any situation where there are adequate data on rainfall, soils and slope, cropping systems, and conservation practices.

The next step is to place values on the damage that sediment causes as it is delivered off-site by the drainage system. Another equation, as follows, is required to express aggregate sediment damage in dollars per year:

$$D_S = A_N D_r E P_r$$

where D_S is sediment damage (dollars per year)
$\quad A_N$ is the net drainage area
$\quad D_r$ is the sediment delivery ratio
$\quad E$ is soil loss (tons per acre)
$\quad P_r$ is the cost of sediment damage per ton of sediment

TABLE 10-1

NET INCOME AND SEDIMENT DAMAGE PER ACRE PER YEAR
(Polecat Creek Subwatershed Cropland in Illinois)

Crop rotation[a]	Tillage system[b] (1)	Conservation practice[c] (2)	Net farm income[d] (3)	Sediment damage[e] (4)	Net social income[f] (5)	Sediment damage percent of net income (6)
Continuous corn	Con	UD	$82.55	$10.20	$72.35	12.4
		CT	81.80	4.96	76.84	6.1
		CT/T	81.51	4.50	77.01	5.5
	PP	UD	81.50	3.84	77.66	4.7
		CT	80.75	2.31	78.44	2.9
		CT/T	80.46	1.88	78.58	2.3
	CP	UD	68.99	0.77	68.22	1.1
		CT	68.24	0.30	67.94	0.4
		CT/T	67.94	0.29	67.65	0.4
C-Sb	Con	UD	78.40	12.68	65.72	16.1
		CT	77.65	6.28	71.37	8.1
		CT/T	77.36	5.70	71.66	7.3
	PP	UD	77.35	5.94	71.41	7.7
		CT	76.60	2.76	73.84	3.6
		CT/T	76.31	2.56	73.75	3.4
	CP	UD	66.57	1.28	65.29	1.9
		CT	65.82	0.56	65.26	0.9
		CT/T	65.53	0.31	65.22	0.5
C-Sb-C-Wx	Con	UD	67.87	8.55	59.32	12.6
		CT	67.12	4.08	63.04	6.1
		CT/T	66.83	3.63	63.20	5.4
	PP	UD	66.82	3.88	62.94	5.8
		CT	66.07	1.77	64.30	2.7
		CT/T	65.78	1.44	64.34	2.2
	CP	UD	57.14	0.65	56.49	1.1
		CT	56.39	0.31	56.08	0.5
		CT/T	56.11	0.28	55.83	0.5
W-M-M-M	Con	UD	47.58	0.13	47.45	0.3
		CT	47.39	0.06	47.33	0.1
		CT/T	47.32	0.05	47.27	0.1
	PP	UD	47.32	0.12	47.20	0.3
		CT	47.13	0.05	47.08	0.1
		CT/T	47.06	0.04	47.02	0.1
	CP	UD	46.16	0.08	46.08	0.2
		CT	45.98	0.04	45.94	0.1
		CT/T	45.91	0.03	45.88	0.1

[a]Where C is corn, Sb is soybeans, Wx is wheat with a catch crop, W is wheat, and M is meadow.
[b]Con is conventional tillage, PP is plow-plant tillage, and CP is chisel-plow tillage.
[c]UD is up-and-down cultivation, CT is contouring, and CT/T is contouring and terracing.
[d]Net of nonland costs, weighted average for the cropland.
[e]As discussed in *Economic Analysis of Erosion and Sedimentation*, University of Illinois at Urbana-Champaign, Department of Agricultural Economics, in cooperation with State of Illinois, Institute for Environmental Quality, AERR 135.
[f]Column 3 minus column 4.

Source: M. T. Lee, A. S. Narayanan, and E. R. Swanson, *Economic Analysis of Erosion and Sedimentation: Upper Embarras River Basin*, University of Illinois at Urbana-Champaign in cooperation with State of Illinois, Institute for Environmental Quality, IIEQ document no, 74-41, AERR 135, April 1975, pp. 24–25.

In this equation, the net drainage area is defined to include a watershed or sub-watershed. The sediment delivery ratio is expressed as the percentage of total sediment that is actually delivered to the place where it causes damage, as in filling a reservoir or clogging a drainage system. The soil loss (tons per acre) is taken from the previously used universal soil loss equation. The cost of sediment damage per ton is estimated from costs of dredging to remove a ton of sediment from a reservoir, the average cost of building a new reservoir, or dredging a new drainage system. Alternatively, if a new system is not to be built, the off-site damage cost of sediment may be estimated in terms of ecological damage, including crop losses downstream, pollution and losses of lakes and reservoirs, and possible flood-loss damages.[9]

An example is given in Table 10-1, based on real production data, with the external damage costs of sediment set at $4 per ton. Net farm income is maximized with a cropping plan of continuous corn; conventional tillage; and cultivation straight across the field, identified as "up-and-down cultivation." But, with this program, the net social income is more than $6 per acre lower than could be achieved with plow-plant tillage, contouring, and terracing. If the farmer were to shift to this system, however, net farm income would be reduced by more than $2 per acre. Actually, the farmer could be equally well off with a payment of this amount for using plow-plant tillage, contouring, and terracing, and the net gain to society would be $4 per acre.

In situations such as this, where net farm income is nearly as high under the optimum plan for conservation as it would be under more erosive farming systems, the farmer may be persuaded to adopt the more soil-conserving system. An educational program might be all that is required to encourage such adoption. One of the first steps is to help farmers develop a procedure for estimating the soil losses under alternative crop rotations, tillage systems, and conservation practices.[10] Then, the farmer may estimate the costs of machinery and pesticides with different tillage systems, the fuel cost, the total energy used for field operations, and the crop yields.[11] If the farmer finds that the most profitable farm plan is also the most satisfactory from the standpoint of conservation, then the most widely acceptable result may be achieved by education, with adoption of recommended crop rotations, low tillage or no tillage crop systems, and other conservation practices. But if the acceptable plan from the standpoint of conservation is too costly or too low in yield for the farmer to adopt it, then conservation goals may require a soil-conservation payment to get the desired result. An alternative that would be more economical for the government, but which has not been used for political reasons, would be to levy a special tax on soil-eroding practices to get the desired conservation results.

[9]See U.S. Department of Agriculture, Soil Conservation Service, *Universal Soil Loss Equation,* Agronomy Technical note 1, Champaign, Illinois, 1970. For a more detailed description, see W. H. Wischmeier and D. D. Smith, *Predicting Rainfall Erosion Losses from Cropland East of Rocky Mountains,* U.S. Department of Agriculture Agricultural Handbook 282, 1962.

[10]See Robert D. Walker and Robert A. Pope, *Estimating Your Soil Erosion Losses with the Universal Soil Loss Equation (USLE),* Cooperative Extension Service, College of Agriculture, University of Illinois at Urbana-Champaign, September 1979, revised May 1980.

[11]For an example, see J. C. Siemens et al., *Tillage Systems for Illinois,* Cooperative Extension Service, College of Agriculture, University of Illinois at Urbana-Champaign, Circular 1172, revised August 1980.

Much of the forage for beef cattle comes from land that is not well suited for crop production. But, land such as this might be used for either crops or livestock. What might be the net social gain from keeping this land in beef production? From shifting it to crops?

In recent years, the Cooperative Extension Service, the Soil Conservation Service, and the departments of agriculture in a number of states have combined their resources to expand their programs of education, farm planning, and programming for conservation. In addition, research efforts have been expanded in the Natural Resources Economics Division, Economic Research Service, U.S. Department of Agriculture, and in a number of other agencies, institutes, and foundations. New farm equipment has been designed which will make it less costly for the farmer to follow recommended soil-conserving plans. Improvement in pesticide use has become crucial for minimum tillage systems. So progress in soil conservation is being made.

Soil erosion is not uniformly damaging to farmland, however, and the benefits to be derived from more conservation efforts vary widely according to soil conditions and farming systems. More accurate methods are required for developing procedures that will determine what is best to do, or what will be socially optimal.

Using Linear Programming Models for Conservation Planning

Modern computers are making it possible to develop linear programming models that will be useful for conservation planning, beginning with what is optimum for the farmer in respect to crop rotations, tillage systems, and conservation practices. A linear programming model maximizes (or minimizes) a linear objective function subject to a simultaneous system of linear constraints. Given information (constraints) such as included in the USLE, and a system of prices for inputs and outputs, farm plans can be specified that will maximize net farm income, or minimize the cost of a given level of output. In fact, an optimum plan can then be specified with any given system of resource constraints and prices, including all soil classes, slopes, rainfall conditions, and any other relevant factors. A model can reveal what is optimum for the farmer and what the level of soil erosion will be under the given constraint. What have some of the recently developed models revealed?

A Soil Conservation Economic Model (SOILEC) has been developed and applied to crop systems in Illinois.[12] This model provides for detailed specification of physical parameters (arbitrary values) associated with location, soil characteristics, topography, and weather. This information is used together with management parameters associated with choices of cropping systems, mechanical erosion-control practices, and technology, to achieve specific results concerning crop yields and soil data. Physical output from the model includes tabulations and plots of annual soil losses, crop yields, and depth of soil horizons. Financial output is generated for each management system, in comparison with a base-management system, showing net present values over time, the remaining annual soil loss, the reduction in annual soil loss, and the cost of reducing erosion.

Both short-run (one year) and long-run (fifty years with extension to perpetuity) analyses can be performed with use of a model such as SOILEC. Short-run results depend on one-year costs and yields, while the long-run results depend, in addition, on the cumulative effects and the discount rate applied to future costs and yields. The model requires technical data that are specific to the soils and fields being analyzed, and specific economic information on costs of production and product prices.

A study by the Center for Agricultural and Rural Development (CARD) at Iowa State University shows that under a number of conditions Iowa farmers can reduce soil loss considerably by using no-till planting, while actually increasing their net farm incomes.[13] Linear programming models were used to maximize net returns before taxes for 18 representative farms, five tillage systems, and 15 crop rotations. Sixteen scenarios were run, using various assumptions about use of conservation practices, roughages, soil-loss subsidies and constraints, terrace subsidies, and livestock operations. Terracing, which has been a practice recommended for a long time for many fields, was found to be economical on only the most highly erosive, high-productivity soils.

The CARD study also examined the potential impacts of using a policy that taxes farmers for each ton of soil eroding from their cropland. Although this is a policy

[12]Robert G. Dumsday and Wesley D. Seitz, *A System for Improving the Efficiency of Soil Conservation Incentive Programs,* University of Illinois at Urbana-Champaign, Department of Agricultural Economics, AE-4533, June 1982. Continuing work on this model and development of additional new models is currently led by Bartelt Eleveld and Gary Johnson at the University of Illinois.

[13]For an outline of the study (which is published in five bulletins), see *The Economics of Soil and Water Conservation Practices in Iowa: Model and Data Documentation,* by C. Arden Pope III, Shashanda Bhide, and Earl O. Heady, CARD Report 108, SWCP Series I, The Center for Agricultural and Rural Development, Iowa State University, Ames, Iowa, August 1982.

that generally has been thought to be politically unacceptable, it may be required to achieve conservation goals in some of the most highly erosive farmland. Using taxes of 50 cents, $1, and $3 per ton, it was found that farmers were often better off paying the taxes of 50 cents and $1 per ton, rather than taking the corrective actions to halt erosion. The impact of the tax depends directly on the erosiveness of the land and the tax level. The inference is that higher taxes, or larger payments for instituting new conservation practices, will be required to reach the general conservation goals on the most highly erosive farmland. Specifically, it will be necessary to estimate the value of the erosion damage function, or the cost of erosion, both internally for the farmer, and externally for society.

Estimating the Soil-Erosion Damage Function for Conservation Policy

An erosion damage function, which measures the on-site damage from agricultural soil loss, can be developed to compare soil loss using conventional farming with soil loss using conservation practices. The incremental damage from erosion, or the mar-

One of the best practices for controlling erosion is to leave the crop stubble on the land over winter and cultivate in the spring, rather than plow in the fall. Although the farmer knows this, most do not follow the practice. Why? What arguments are there for using taxes to get the result desired by the public? For using payments? For using a combination of taxes and payments?

ginal cost to the soil user, can be evaluated annually, and includes any cost to remedy the soil loss plus lost future revenue from reduced yield. Apparently, under many soil conditions in the United States, many, if not most, farmers continue to "mine" their soil by employing erosive-farming systems which maximize current net income, but which diminish the soil's future productivity while also imposing higher external costs on society from soil run-off and sediment damage.

The reason that more progress has not been made in soil conservation is that many conservation practices seem to be more costly than conventional ones, at least in the short run. Typically, the farmer's damage function will assume a higher positive value, encouraging the farmer to mine the soil, as (a) the yield of the erosive practice increases relative to the yield of the conservation practice, (b) the cost of the conservation practice increases relative to the cost of the erosive practice, (c) the price of the crop increases, (d) the rate of discount applied to future farm income increases (that is, as future income decreases in value relative to current income) and, as (3) the decline in yields from soil erosion decreases.

Using these concepts, the damage function has shown that as long as the private economic value of choosing the erosive practice over the conservation practice is positive, the farmer will tend to choose the erosive practice, and conservation will be delayed.[14] For instance, suppose a farmer has been using conventional tillage, and currently evaluates the option of switching to a conservation practice beginning in a decision year t. The erosion damage function can compare the profitability to the farmer of choosing the erosive conventional practice over the conservation practice in the current year, as:

$$\delta_t = \pi_e - \pi_c$$

where δ_t is the value of the damage function in year t—the private economic value of choosing the erosive practice over the conservation practice in decision year t

π_c is the private profitability of choosing the conservation practice in the current year

π_e is the private profitability of choosing the conventional erosive practice currently and delaying conservation adoption another year

The farmer's choice of cropping practice affects immediate profit in the current crop year as well as long-term profit as soil productivity is reduced.[15]

As long as δ_t is greater than zero, the farmer will gain from choosing the erosive practice for another season. The private economic incentives would encourage "mining" the soil. The conservation practice becomes profitable for the farmer only when the value of δ_t becomes less than zero. In the meantime, until this year is reached, heavy external costs may have been imposed on society.

---

[14]See David J. Walker, "A Damage Function to Evaluate Erosion Control Economics," *American Journal of Agricultural Economics*, vol. 64, no. 4, November 1982, pp. 690–698 and especially pp. 691–692.
[15]Walker, ibid., p. 691.

If we assume that educational programs have done their job in helping the farmer to learn how to make rational choices in terms of the farm firm, then the essence of the remaining conservation policy is concerned with reducing the external costs of soil erosion to the point where the net value of total farm output is maximized, counting all internal (private) and external (social) costs. Let us consider the policy problem more broadly in terms of the National Resource Inventory (NRI), previously mentioned.

Using the NRI as a Guide to Conservation Policy

Under the NRI, the 406.3 million acres of readily available cropland were classified according to their inherent erosion potential, as estimated using the universal soil loss equation, with the crop management practice (C), and the price (P), set equal to 1.0. This provides estimates of the erosion that would occur, based on the product of $RKLS$,[16] if the land were left in continuous fallow, or tilled straight up and down, with no soil-conserving practices being applied. As shown in Table 10-2, column 2, only 109.0 million acres would have soil losses of less than 5.0 tons per acre, and the inherent erosion potentials range upward to 100 tons and over. The average inherent potential soil loss was estimated to be 24.8 tons per acre on the 406.3 million acres of readily available cropland.

The question for conservation policy is: What conservation practices did farmers use on this cropland, and how effective were these practices in reducing erosion? The first part of this question is answered in Table 10-2, and the second part in Table 10-3. Answers to the question will help us visualize future policy alternatives.

Use of Conservation Practices

As shown in Table 10-2, column 3, terraces were used on 27.5 million of the 406.3 million acres, or on 6.8 percent (column 4) of the available cropland; and the frequency with which terraces were used generally increased as the inherent erosion potential increased. But, even on the most inherently erosive soils with potentials for erosion of 20 tons or more, the use of terraces was rather infrequent, which suggests that terracing is a costly and unprofitable practice for most farmers.

In comparison, the practices of crop residue use, minimum tillage, or contouring were used on 175.3 million acres (column 5), or on 43.1 percent of the available cropland (column 6); but the frequency of use of these practices was generally inversely correlated with the inherent erosion potential. This may suggest that the effectiveness of these practices, or the profitability of using them, generally tends to decrease as the inherent erosion potential increases, even though it may be expected that the tons of soil saved per acre will be positively correlated with the inherent erosion potential. This brings us to the second part of the question above: How effective were these practices in reducing erosion?

---

[16] $RKLS$ refers to the factors of rainfall, soil erodibility, slope, and slope length.

TABLE 10-2
INHERENT POTENTIAL FOR EROSION
(Readily Available Cropland Compared with Acreage Terraced; and with Acreage under Crop Residue Use, Minimum Tillage, or Contouring, 1977)

Inherent potential for erosion* (tons per acre)	Readily available cropland† (million acres)	Acreage terraced		Acreage under crop residue use, minimum tillage, or contouring	
		Total‡ (million acres)	%	Total (million acres)	%
(1)	(2)	(3)	(4)	(5)	(6)
0–4.99	109.0	0.5	4.6	51.7	47.4
5–9.99	92.6	3.0	3.2	44.7	48.3
10–14.99	58.7	4.0	6.8	27.2	46.3
15–19.99	33.4	2.1	6.3	13.7	41.0
20–24.99	20.6	2.4	11.6	7.7	37.4
25–29.99	14.8	2.1	14.2	5.2	35.1
30–39.99	17.9	3.8	21.2	6.5	36.3
40–49.99	12.0	1.6	13.3	4.0	33.3
50–99.99	26.6	5.4	20.3	8.4	31.6
100 and over	20.7	2.6	12.6	6.2	30.0
Total acres	406.3	27.5	6.8	175.3	43.1

* *RKLS* product; assumes $C = 1.0$ and $P = 1.0$, where C is the cropping practice and P is price of product.
†Excludes 6.9 million acres of wild hay and mountain meadows.
‡Measured by using slope length without terraces.
Source: National Resource Inventory, 1978. From data presented by Clayton Ogg and Arnold Miller, "Minimizing Erosion on Cultivated Land: Concentration of Erosion Problems and the Effectiveness of Conservation Practices," *Policy Research Notes,* July 1980–January 1981, U.S. Department of Agriculture, Economic Research Service, August 1981.

Effectiveness of Conservation Practices

Table 10-3 compares average erosion rates observed in the NRI (column 2), with an arbitrary standard (where $C = 0.32$, and $P = 1.0$, column 3) which does not include any of the listed conservation practices, and the average erosion rates achieved on the lands on which the designated practices were used (columns 4 through 10). The effectiveness of these practices in reducing erosion can be measured against values achieved in column 3, while the actual NRI in column 2 tends to show how much erosion has been reduced on the average, by use of the actual conservation practices listed. The critical question for policy is: How much would soil erosion be reduced below the levels in column 3 if certain conservation practices were used on the lands of varying erosion potentials?

In Table 10-3, the results, with individual conservation practices shown in columns 4 through 6, and combinations of practices in columns 7 through 10, may be compared with the erosion levels in column 3. In general, substantial reductions in erosion can be made, up to 50 percent or more of the values shown in column 3. On

TABLE 10-3
POTENTIAL AND ACTUAL SHEET AND RILL EROSION CROPLAND TREATED WITH SELECTED PRACTICES IN 1977

Inherent potential for erosion* (tons per acre)	All land in row crops and small grains		Crop residue use alone (Actual NRI)	Minimum tillage alone (Actual NRI)	Contour farming alone (assumes C = .32, P is actual NRI)	Minimum tillage and crop residue use (Actual NRI)	Contour farming and crop residue use (Actual NRI)	Contour farming, minimum tillage, and crop residue use (Actual NRI)	Terraces and supporting practices (Actual NRI)
	Actual NRI	Assumes C = .32, P = 1.0							
(1)	(2)	(3)	(4)	(5)	(6)	(7)	(8)	(9)	(10)
					Average erosion rate in tons per acre per year				
0–24.99	6.0	7.1	6.4	5.5	3.8	5.3	4.1	3.6	4.2
25–29.99	7.1	8.7	7.3	7.3	5.1	6.5	4.8	4.6	4.8
30–34.99	8.3	10.4	9.3	8.3	6.0	7.1	5.6	4.0	5.4
35–39.99	9.5	12.0	11.0	7.4	7.0	9.2	6.9	5.7	6.3
40–44.99	10.9	13.6	13.2	9.3	7.4	9.4	7.7	5.8	6.8
45–79.99	11.6	15.2	12.3	11.2	9.3	8.6	7.8	5.8	7.0
80–84.99	14.4	19.5	15.7	16.7	11.2	13.0	10.3	3.4	9.4
85–99.99	19.8	27.7	20.2	17.6	16.7	16.6	11.3	16.2	14.4
100–149.99	27.8	38.3	32.4	26.4	25.4	25.6	16.2	17.5	18.9
150–199.99	38.8	54.4	39.5	26.6	35.3	26.3	32.5	24.0	33.2
200 and over	68.7	96.0	72.0	30.0	73.4	45.0	52.1	38.3	54.6†
					Millions of acres				
Acres	85.9	85.9	18.3	2.1	6.2	4.9	3.0	0.9	17.9

*Product of the R, K, L, and S factors in the soil loss equation as reported for NRI sample points. Assumes C and P are both equal to 1.
†Average erosion rates on land with RKLS products of 200 or more without terrace condition.
Source: National Resource Inventory, 1978. From data presented by Clayton Ogg and Arnold Miller, "Minimizing Erosion on Cultivated Land: Concentration of Erosion Problems and the Effectiveness of Conservation Practices," Policy Research Notes, July 1980–January 1981, U.S. Department of Agriculture, Economic Research Service, August 1981.

some of the most inherently erosive land, such as that having a potential of 30 to 85 tons per acre soil loss, the actual soil loss can be reduced to one-third or less of the levels in column 3. Terracing in combination with these practices appears to add little if any to these results (columns 9 and 10), however, which is a result somewhat similar to that in the CARD study reviewed above. What are some of the general inferences for policy?

General Inferences for National Conservation Policy

If we accept the results of the NRI as a base for conservation policy, it appears evident that farmers do not find it profitable to increase the percentage of land under minimum tillage, residue use, or contouring as the inherent potential for erosion increases above T levels. The apparent reason is that benefits to farmers of using conservation practices are not positively correlated with the inherent rates of erosion. If farmers use the rational concept of equating marginal cost and return, then they will attempt to maximize their net incomes over a planning period which may encompass only a few years.[17] By using conservation practices, farmers on the more erosive soils may reduce their net incomes as much or more than farmers on the less erosive soils. This may occur even though conservation practices can save more soil on the highly erosive lands.

Society has a more substantial interest in controlling erosion on the more highly erosive lands; however, a given conservation practice will tend to save more soil, and have a correspondingly greater impact on reducing the important off-site damages. Hence, it will be more beneficial for society, or the nation as a whole, to correlate levels of conservation payments with the estimated yields of conservation practices on erosive lands. Additionally, farmers could be taxed for the external damage they cause, as suggested in the CARD study above. Use of conservation practices could be required as a basis for receiving benefits of other farm programs (sometimes called "cross-compliance"). Zoning could be used to keep the most highly erosive lands out of crop production. Or, the government could buy the most erosive land and retire it from crop production. But important political constraints to some of these suggestions must be recognized.

Political Constraints in Conservation Policy

Since publication of the NRI, conservation programs have shifted somewhat, from giving rather uniform attention to all cropland, to concentrating more on the more erosive soils. But this shift has been constrained considerably by the political interests of all concerned to share in the federal appropriations for conservation. Apart from

---

[17]For further discussion of basic concepts see Harold G. Halcrow, *Economics of Agriculture,* McGraw-Hill Book Company, New York, 1980, pp. 166–177. For a more advanced analytical discussion, see Bartelt Eleveld and Harold G. Halcrow, "How Much Conservation is Optimum for Society?", *Soil Conservation Policies, Institutions, and Incentives,* Harold G. Halcrow, Earl O. Heady, and Melvin L. Cotner (eds.), published for North Central Research Committee 111: Natural Resource Use and Environmental Policy, by the Soil Conservation Society of America, Ankeny, Iowa, 1982, pp. 233–250.

the teaching of profitable conservation practices to the farmer—such as reduced tillage, rotations, contouring, and terracing, the real issue in conservation policy is political. Can the Congress and an administration actually tax, as indicated above, a measure which may prove necessary to offset the worst conditions? And can government allocate public money in soil conservation payments according to the principles of marginal cost and return?

In 1977, Congress passed the Soil and Water Resources Conservation Act (RCA) to establish a system for more thorough review of conservation programs and to develop a broader political base for building new ones. [18] The extensive public review process revealed important political dilemmas in evaluating and budgeting programs.[19] But conservation needs have been more accurately identified. Some of the political obstacles that must be overcome have been recognized; and there is hope that conservation can be made more efficient as programs are more specifically targeted.

Soil conservation programs and expenditures have not been well targeted. On-farm planning and technical assistance by the Soil Conservation Service (SCS) has been provided on request of farmers, on a first-come-first-serve basis, which generally does not emphasize priority needs for conservation. SCS plans have often been too expensive for farmers to carry out, especially for farmers in the more erosive soils. A major portion of the soil conservation payments under the Agricultural Conservation Program (ACP) of the Agricultural Stabilization and Conservation Service (ASCS) has not been well targeted on conservation problems. A 1977 study by the General Accounting Office (GAO), for instance, revealed that in 1975 some 55 percent of cost-sharing funds under the ACP actually went to increase production, rather than to conserve soil or water.[20] A 1980 study by the ASCS found that more than half of the ACP's cost-share funds were being applied on land with annual soil loss from erosion of less than 5 tons per acre, and only 21 percent of the funds were spent on land with an annual soil loss of 14 tons per acre, or more.[21]

Such results, we may assume, arise out of the political pressure from farm producers to share in funds distributed through the ACP and the failure of Congress and administrative agencies to give more specific directions to the programs. These issues are not easy to resolve politically. But with appropriate economic research and policy direction, we may be able to base conservation policy more on targeted areas in the future. What types of research are needed?

---

[18]See Wayne D. Rasmussen, "History of Soil Conservation, Institutions and Incentives," *Soil Conservaion Policies, Institutions, and Incentives,* Harold G. Halcrow, Earl O. Heady, and Melvin L. Cotner (eds.), published for North Central Research Committee: Natural Resource Use and Environmental Policy, by the Soil Conservation Society of America, Ankeny, Iowa, 1982, pp. 3–18.

[19]See Christopher Leman, "Political Dilemmas in Evaluating and Budgeting Soil Conservation Programs," ibid., pp. 47–89.

[20]U.S. General Accounting Office, *To Protect Tomorrow's Food Supply, Soil Conservation Needs Priority Attention,* Report to the Congress by the Comptroller General of the United States, CED-77-30, February 14, 1977.

[21]U.S. Department of Agriculture, Agricultural Stabilization and Conservation Service, *National Summary Evaluation of the Agricultural Conservation Program,* U.S. Government Printing Office, Washington, D.C., Phase I, 1981.

Conservation Policy Based on Research[22]

As a basis for targeting conservation programs, it is necessary to (1) identify the net loss of farm productivity and the net external costs of erosion under various conditions, (2) determine the relative efficiencies of alternative strategies in reducing erosion, and (3) compare some of the alternative incentives that can be used to implement programs, such as education, new technology, payments or taxes, zoning, or land purchase.

Soil erosion must be calculated as a cost of production, with both internal and external costs taken into account. It must be established what soil-conserving practices can be followed without declines in productivity, what these practices will cost, and what the benefits will be to the landowner and to society in both the short and the long term. It will be necessary to develop more accurate measures of the effectiveness of alternative programs in reducing erosion and the social impacts of the programs. Social costs of soil erosion include pollution and loss of soil productivity. As we have said, public funds have not been concentrated in the geographic areas of greatest need, and the research need is to identify what the costs and returns will be for more program emphasis in these areas.

The data requirements for an effective conservation policy are both specific and extensive but manageable with modern computer technology. It is necessary to have more precise definitions of various soil characteristics to recommend best land uses and to predict the costs of erosion and the benefits of selected conservation strategies. Data analysis can be reduced by establishing a well-distributed network of sampling and study areas in each state, with a uniform format for compiling and extrapolating the properties and behavioral characteristics of soils in a computerized data bank. Agreement must be reached on the data required to maintain the needed information system.

Distinctions need to be made between the conservation requirements of humid areas and those of arid and semiarid regions. The farmers require knowledge on conservation-tillage technologies for sustaining soil productivity, on impacts of alternative management systems on water quality, and on the most cost-effective systems for soil and water management. New technologies, which can be the product of research, must be a priority goal of research for economical reclamation of severely eroded lands, and for economical conversion of land such as from forest to pasture or cropland. Research to sustain land and water resources in the arid and semiarid regions of the United States should emphasize water conservation, efficient use of the diminishing water supplies that may be available for irrigation in future years, methods that managers can use for profitable crop and livestock production, and new technology for arid and semiarid regions. All this is possible, with perhaps only modest increases in cost over what has been done before, providing there is a national commitment to develop a more efficient conservation policy.

If sustained high-level agricultural output is an overriding policy goal in the

---

[22]This section draws on a study by Harold G. Halcrow and Wesley D. Seitz, presented to congressional staff and administrators in the U.S. Department of Agriculture, Washington, D.C., November 1, 1983; and on the book, *Soil Conservation Policies, Institutions, and Incentives,* previously cited.

future, then there is some hope for more economically rational and efficient conservation programs. Furthermore, if more of the uncertainty in growing crops can be eliminated, then this may be a positive force in land use and conservation. Let us consider crop insurance in this role.

CROP INSURANCE AS A NATURAL RESOURCE POLICY[23]

Crop insurance may be used to protect farmers and ranchers against yield losses due to adverse weather and weather-related variables. Weather itself may be viewed as a natural resource to which risk and uncertainty is attached. The basic concept is that crop insurance can be offered as a contract between seller and buyer to protect the farmer against the risks and uncertainties of weather, not against low yields as caused by action of the farmer. The former are insurable, the latter are not.

Crop Insurance Experience

After a number of failures by states and insurance companies to establish all-risk crop insurance, in 1938 the Federal Crop Insurance Act established the Federal Crop Insurance Corporation (FCIC) to offer farmers all-risk crop insurance on some of the major crops. The FCIC was authorized to fix premiums on a countywide basis, at so much per acre, to cover claims on insured crops, the insured levels being a certain percentage (such as 50 percent or 75 percent) of a farm's normal verified yield experience. Initially, the FCIC was authorized to fix premiums at rates sufficient to cover claims for crop losses and to establish a reserve against unforeseen losses, but not to cover operating and administrative expenses and the direct cost of loss adjustment. The general policy goal was to assure a given level of crop return and to provide for greater stability in land tenure and farming operations.

Over the years, however, the FCIC program has added only a very modest amount of income stability to the crops economy. Although the FCIC has experienced a modest net loss of capital, which has been covered by federal appropriations, and costs of administration have also been covered by the federal government, generally only a very small percentage of all the cropland for which insurance is available has been covered by an insurance contract. In most years, at least until recently, less than 5 percent of the total crop acreage eligible for insurance coverage has been insured. But the program has been of considerable importance in some areas, such as the higher risk areas of the great plains, where in some years more than 25 percent of the wheat, and lesser amounts of other crops, have been insured. In such areas,

---

[23]This section draws on a series of studies by Harold G. Halcrow, "The Theory of Crop Insurance," unpublished dissertation, The University of Chicago, 1948; "Actuarial Structures for Crop Insurance," *Journal of Farm Economics,* vol. 31, August 1949; ("Outstanding Journal Article," award 1949); *Agricultural Policy of the United States,* Prentice-Hall, Englewood Cliffs, N.J., 1953, pp. 407–420; *Food Policy for America,* McGraw-Hill Book Company, New York, 1977, pp. 425–429; and "A New Proposal for Federal Crop Insurance," *Illinois Agricultural Economics,* vol. 18, no. 2, July 1978, pp. 20–29. (The last study was done at the request of the United States Senate Committee on Agriculture, Nutrition and Foresty.)

losses have been experienced by the FCIC in years of poor crops, and these have been partially offset by gains in more favorable crop years.

Farmers have indicated a strong interest in crop insurance. But the majority have felt that the levels of coverage have been too low, relative to the premiums charged. Over the years, most farmers have indicated by their actions that they believe they are better off without crop insurance. Sample studies have revealed that as many as half of the farmers who buy insurance do so in lieu of greater diversification of crops and livestock. Insurance is considered to be important, therefore, and it is of interest in policy analysis because of its potential, and the possibilities that exist for expanding the program. Let us consider these topics.

Federal Crop Insurance in the 1980s

Because of the high cost of disaster payment programs in the 1970s, and the perceived demand and potential for crop insurance, the federal crop insurance program was expanded in the early 1980s, with the goal of making it the nation's primary means of disaster protection for farmers. The Federal Crop Insurance Act of 1980 authorized up to 30 percent of the crop insurance premium to be paid by the federal government. It also provided for higher yield guarantees and larger indemnities for each bushel or pound of crop loss, and established the basis for expanding the program to cover several more crops and many more counties than had been served previously. Private insurance companies were authorized to serve as agents for the FCIC.

By 1983, a new liberalized Individual Yield Coverage plan (IYC) had been developed that would enable top producers to qualify for higher production guarantees without increasing their per-acre insurance cost. Farmers could choose to insure their crop for 50 percent, 65 percent, or 75 percent of average yield, with the federal government paying 30 percent of the premium up to the 65 percent coverage level. With the federal subsidy, the FCIC's goal was a 90 percent loss pay-out, with 10 percent added to a reserve for catastrophic losses.

Indemnity for losses has been determined on a unit basis, with payment being made when production was less than the guarantee, units of production being converted to dollars at preselected prices, and premiums varying directly with the price selected. In 1983, for instance, corn producers could choose a price per bushel of $2.00, $2.40 or $2.70, with the premium varying according to the percentage of yield insured and the price selected. For example, if a farmer had an average yield of 122 bushels of corn certified by the FCIC and selected an insured level of 65 percent, or 79 bushels, at a price of $2.70 per bushel, then a return of up to $213.30 per acre would be assured.[24] The premium would vary according to the record of crop variability for the area, between $6.00 to $12.00 per acre, as determined by the FCIC.

The 1980 act provided that indemnities would not be paid if yield losses were due to the farmer's neglect, poor farming, or crop theft. This might mean that the average yields of other representative farms in a community could be taken into account

---

[24]From information pamphlets distributed by the FCIC.

to determine whether a farmer's low yield was due to poor crop conditions, such as bad weather; or due to poor farming, neglect, or theft. If a crop was planted after the FCIC's final planting date, yield coverage would be reduced by 10 percent for each five-day period that the farmer went past the planting deadline. In addition, premium rates were to be continuously updated for each area to reflect its changing yield and loss experience. Specified discounts were provided for individual policy holders who had a history of minimal loss.

Policy Problems Related to Actuarial Questions

The evolution of the FCIC program presents a number of continuing problems for policy:

1 Although the premium subsidies authorized in the 1980 act can make insurance contracts generally more attractive to farmers, they will constitute a subsidy for crop insurance in general, and they may result in extending crop production into more high-risk marginal areas. This may not only distort agricultural incentives, but it may put the federal government in the ironic position of paying farmers to grow more crops while it simultaneously pays them, under acreage adjustment programs, to produce less. About the only realistic way out of this dilemma is to practice a considerable degree of constraint in both the insurance and the production-control programs.

2 The effort to make crop insurance more attractive to high-level producers, which is necessary for the program to reach policy goals, exposes the FCIC to possible adverse selectivity. That is, a farmer's Individual Yield Coverage (IYC) may be set too high, and a high percentage of farmers in this position may buy insurance, while those with a lower IYC stay out of the program.

3 If recent yield trends are overemphasized in setting the IYC, then after a few years of good crops a farmer will be insured at too high a level, and the FCIC's losses might be chronic. On the other hand, after a few poor crops the insured levels will be too low, and the program might be of little use to such farmers.

4 If the standard deviation in yields is not the same for all farms in a county, those farmers with large yield variations will receive greater total indemnities over a number of years than those with small yield variations. Although an individual actuarial schedule might be constructed for each farm to offset this tendency, the FCIC has found that it is impractical to do this. Furthermore, the desirability of doing so is questionable, because a series of wide or narrow yield variations would cause the actuarial probabilities to be at variance with the actual yield probabilities.

5 If a farmer grows more than a single crop, or is allowed to vary the insured area from year to year, an additional factor involving adverse selection appears. In years when the yield prospects are relatively poor, an insured crop may have a potentially higher expected value than an uninsured crop. The opposite is true in years when yield prospects are good. In some high-risk farming areas, such as parts of the great plains, where crop yields are highly correlated with conditions at planting time, the tendency for an adverse selection is especially strong. The FCIC can decrease adverse selection by providing only a long-term contract and by writing insurance

Too much wind and rain may damage a corn crop in one field while leaving a neighboring corn field in good condition. What kind of a problem does this create for crop insurance? What are the major solutions to this problem? How has the Federal Crop Insurance Corporation handled this problem?

for approximately the same number of acres each year. Since seedbed preparation is not uniform, however, adverse selection cannot be prevented if the farmer is allowed to insure part but not all of the fields in the insurance unit. Farmers will tend to insure those fields for which the probability of indemnity is relatively high. If all farmers have an equal opportunity to select fields in this manner, no adverse selection need result among farmers, but, to the extent that yield expectations are not uniformly similar, the conditions for an adverse selection remain.

Policy Solutions to Actuarial Problems

The general policy solution to most of the above actuarial problems is for the FCIC to adhere to a rigorous standard in determining indemnities for low yields, and to assure that low yields are not due to poor farming, neglect, or theft. This would bring the FCIC close to what has been called, in previous studies, "area-yield crop insurance" and "weather crop insurance."[25]

The idea in area-yield crop insurance is to base both premiums and indemnities on an area basis, such as a township or a type of farming area. Indemnities would be paid whenever the actual yield of the area falls below the insured yield selected by a farmer. The area should be small enough so that crop conditions are generally similar throughout the area, yet large enough for efficient administration. As few as

[25]For further dicussion of these concepts, see the references cited in footnote 23.

25 farms or as many as 300 to 400 farms might be included in an area. As a practical matter, enough farmers are needed in an area so that an individual farm has only a small effect on the overall yield. It is sufficient to have only enough insured farms for a workable sample and an efficient level of operation for insurance purposes.

Within an area, a statistical sample of farms can be used to establish the area yield; since all farmers who are insured at the same percentage of area yield pay the same premium and receive the same indemnity, adverse selection could not occur. The only possible source of adverse selection might be in differences among areas, and those can be offset by developing accurate data on area yields.

For weather crop insurance, the area can also be used to define an insurance unit. The insurance can be based on selected meteorological data from one or more weather stations, including factors such as rainfall and temperature during, and possibly before, the growing season. Trend yields for an area adjusted by the selected meteorological data can be used for setting premiums and paying indemnities. Again, no adverse selection within an area can occur; if the actuarial data are correct, then there will be no adverse selection among areas. Advances in meteorology and measurement of weather factors could make the proposal for weather crop insurance more widely applicable in the years ahead.

By recognizing the necessity of checking the farmer's performance in farming before paying an indemnity, the FCIC has tended to move toward the concepts of area-yield crop insurance and weather crop insurance, while still retaining the concept of an individual insured yield. Establishing an appropriate and accurate individual base yield will continue to be a problem for the reasons discussed. But federal coverage of part of the insurance premium will make crop insurance more popular. If it is used in the way Congress has intended, crop insurance will help to bring more stability to agriculture, while continuing high-level output.

SUMMARY

Policy analysis of natural-resource markets that provide inputs for agricultural production covers the topics of land-use alternatives among agriculture and other uses, soil-conservation policy alternatives, and crop insurance as natural-resource policy.

The shift of agricultural land to other uses has proceeded rather steadily over the last few decades, but the area in crops has nevertheless expanded slowly, as new land has been developed for crops at a slightly faster rate than land has been shifted to other uses. Both the supply and demand for cropland are very inelastic in the short run, but considerable increases in supply may be achieved over the longer run. The shift of agricultural land to other uses will not be as great in the future as it has been in the past, and this will have a relatively minor effect on aggregate agricultural production over the next generation. Economical use of land for urban and transportation development is required, however, if the costs associated with land transfer and development are to be minimized. Federal assistance in land-use planning by the states has been discussed as a policy alternative in the future.

An appraisal of soil-conservation policy reveals that excess erosion is concentrated on a small percentage of the total cropped land, but policy has not been designed to concentrate publicly supported conservation efforts on these lands. The need to do so has been discussed. Some of the limits of soil-conserving practices have been identified as a basis for redirection of policy in the future.

The experience with crop insurance and an appraisal of actuarial problems with all-risk crop insurance suggest that certain policy constraints must be placed on this program for satisfactory results. For instance, it will be necessary to take account of crop conditions in an area before an indemnity is authorized. Modifications in Individual Yield Coverage (IYC) must be accurately programmed, taking account of long-term trends.

IMPORTANT TERMS AND CONCEPTS

Nation's land base

Cropland base

Supply and demand for agricultural land: short run and long run

Policy-making experience in national land-use planning

Reasons for supporting federal participation in land-use planning

Role of the states in land-use planning and control

Concepts of external costs in land use and development

Agriculture's interest in land-use alternatives

Concepts of internal and external costs in soil erosion

Concentration of excess erosion on a small percentage of cropland

Measuring soil losses using the universal soil loss equation (USLE)

Concepts of net social income applied to conservation programs

Foundation and evolution of national soil conservation policy

Soil Conservation Districts

Agricultural Conservation Program (ACP)

The Soil Bank

Water conservation and pollution control

Regional conservation programs

Soil and Water Resources Conservation Act (RCA)

Principle of equal marginal returns applied to conservation

Inherent potential for erosion and use of conservation practices

Effectiveness of soil-conserving practices

Relation of tax policy to soil erosion

Changes required in conservation policy to meet conservation goals

Basic concept of crop insurance

Crop insurance experience

Appraisal of actuarial concepts in crop insurance

QUESTIONS AND EXERCISES

1 Conceptually, what is the difference between the cropland base, the readily available cropland, and the land in crops?

2 What evidence is there for asserting that the supply of land for crops is inelastic in the short run? Why might the supply not be so inelastic in the long run?

3 How can the subsidy of gasohol affect the demand for land for crops? Why does a subsidy for production of gasohol tend to distort agricultural incentives? What policy reasons are there for supporting such a subsidy?

4 What are the respective roles in land-use policy of local, state, and federal governments? Why might agricultural groups oppose the involvement of the federal government in land-use planning and in controlling land use? Why do some other groups support it?

5 What is the general constitutional requirement for zoning ordinances and land-use controls? Which level of government—local, state, or federal—has the constitutional power to control land use? May this power be delegated? Why?

6 It has been suggested that the transfer of agricultural land to other uses will occur more slowly in the future than in the past. In your opinion, are these reasons logical? Explain your answer.

7 What were the general findings in regard to soil erosion of the *National Resources Inventory* (NRI) published by the U.S. Department of Agriculture in 1978?

8 What factors are included in the universal soil loss equation (USLE)? In respect to soil erosion, which is generally greater, the internal or the external cost? Why?

9 What is an erosion-damage function? How has it been estimated in recent studies? In general, what do these studies show?

10 In general terms, how much of the inherent erosion of soils can be controlled by using recommended crop rotations, tillage systems, and conservation practices? Supposing a farmer has perfect knowledge concerning this, why might the recommendations not be used? What policy options are there for getting use of the recommendations?

11 How will federal expenditures on conservation be allocated to get the maximum return in terms of conservation? Illustrate.

12 What are the major provisions of the Federal Crop Insurance Act of 1980? What are the provisions of the Individual Yield Coverage plan (IYC)? What actuarial problems or questions are present in the program of the Federal Crop Insurance Corporation (FCIC)? In what ways may some of these be overcome?

RECOMMENDED READINGS

Eleveld, Bartelt, and Harold G. Halcrow, "How Much Conservation Is Optimum for Society?", *Soil Conservation Policies, Institutions, and Incentives,* Harold G. Halcrow, Earl O. Heady, and Melvin L. Cotner (eds.), Soil Conservation Society of America, Ankeny, Iowa, 1982, pp. 233–250.

Halcrow, Harold G., "Actuarial Structures for Crop Insurance, *Journal of Farm Economics,* vol. 31, August 1949, and "A New Proposal for Federal Crop Insurance," *Illinois Agricultural Economics,* vol. 18, no. 2, July 1978, pp. 20–29.

Heady, Earl O., "The Adequacy of Agricultural Land: A Demand-Supply Perspective," *The Cropland Crisis: Myth or Reality?,* Pierre R. Crosson (ed.), published for Resources for the Future by the Johns Hopkins University Press, Baltimore and London, 1982, pp. 23–56.

Leman, Christopher, "Political Dilemmas in Evaluating and Budgeting Soil Conservation Programs: The RCA Process," *Soil Conservation Policies, Institutions, and Incentives,* op. cit., pp. 47–88.

Rasmussen, Wayne D., "History of Soil Conservation, Institutions, and Incentives," *Soil Conservation Policies, Institutions, and Incentives,* ibid., pp. 3–18.

Raup, Philip M., "Competition for Land and the Future of American Agriculture," *The Future of American Agriculture as a Strategic Resource,* Sandra S. Batie and Robert G. Healy (eds.), The Conservation Foundation, Washington, D.C., 1980.

CHAPTER 11

POLICY ANALYSIS OF AGRIBUSINESS INPUT MARKETS

Policy analysis of the agribusiness input markets deals with policy issues of production, pricing, and competition among the firms in the markets that supply the major industrial inputs used in farming. These inputs include farm machinery, seeds, fuels, fertilizers, and pesticides. Development and growth of these industries is necessary for agricultural progress; in the United States, these industries have played a strong leadership role in transforming agriculture from what it was in the past into the modern industrial system existing today. But these firms and industries generally compete in markets that are imperfectly competitive, and their production and pricing practices have long been of concern to farmers and agricultural policy makers. The policy issues in the input markets are: (1) market concentration, the effects of industry concentration on output, prices, and performance, and (2) externalities, the external costs of the input industries to other sectors of agriculture and to society in general.

IN THIS CHAPTER

1 You can broaden your vision of the major policy issues inherent in the concentrated competitive structure of the agribusiness industrial-input markets.

2 You can learn how to evaluate some of the external costs involved in the agribusiness inputs, by looking at the policy issue of safety in pesticide use.

3 You can learn about some of the experience in developing pesticide policy.

POLICY ISSUES IN THE AGRIBUSINESS INPUT MARKETS[1]

Imperfect competition characterizes the competitive structure of the agribusiness input markets, as well as the competitive relationships among firms that supply the industrial inputs for farm production: farm machinery and equipment, commercial seeds, fuels, fertilizers, and pesticides. Annual costs of these inputs have accounted for more than 40 percent of the more than $125 billion of farm production expenses in the early 1980s. Imperfect competition is common in all of the markets, with firms generally facing downward-sloping demand curves, and with some apparently facing the kinked demand curve characteristic of oligopoly.

The firms generally purchase raw materials identified only by quality and grade, and they market products that are differentiated according to brand name and firm, or company. Advertising of final products is generally used for purposes of product differentiation. Pricing follows the model of imperfect competition, rather than pure or perfect competition. So purely competitive farm producers are generally competing for inputs in imperfectly competitive markets of farm service and supply.

One of the major policy issues concerns the organization and structure of these markets, and the effect of this structure on production, prices, and services to farmers. Farm organizations have organized cooperatives to deal in farm services and supplies, and many of these have become major competitive forces in the input industries. Still, the issues of concentration and externalities survive, and are important in agricultural policy. Let us consider these issues.

Issues in the Farm Machinery and Equipment Input Market

Farm machinery and equipment is the largest single expense in farmers' total outlay for industrial inputs, amounting to some $13 to $15 billion annually in the early 1980s. Modern machinery and equipment are critical in increasing farm productivity, and their prices have increased rapidly since the early 1970s, with machinery and equipment prices in 1981 soaring to 369 percent of the 1967 base, as compared with 257 percent for fertilizer, and 173 percent for farm chemicals.

Concentration among firms in the farm machinery and equipment market is substantially higher than among firms in most other input markets. For many years, before World War II, the great expense of establishing a new company served as an effective barrier to entry of new firms, except in the so-called short-line of small and specialized machinery and equipment. While profits in the industry have been sufficient for rather steady growth, concentration at the four-firm level has reached as much as 80 percent for some of the major machines, making this industry one of the most concentrated in the United States.

The reasons for this high level of concentration can be found in long-continuing substantial economies of large scale in both manufacturing and marketing. A 1969

[1]This section draws on about 200 individual studies, most of which are cited in Robert F. Leibenluft, *Competition in Farm Inputs: An Examination of Four Industries,* Policy Issues Planning Paper, Office of Policy Planning, Federal Trade Commission, February 1981; and in Harold G. Halcrow, *Food Policy for America,* McGraw-Hill Book Company, New York, 1977, Chapter 4.

Advances in agribusiness inputs such as this are responsible for the evolution of agriculture into a highly capital-intensive industry. What are the major policy issues created by this development?

study, for instance, showed that in 1968 the cost of a certain average-sized tractor declined by 12 percent, as production increased from 20,000 to 60,000 units; and an additional 9 percent when production increased to 90,000 units.[2] As a result, rates of return on investment typically have risen as the size of plant has increased, with economies of scale being attributed almost equally to savings in costs of materials, capital, and facilities; and to increased fabrication (as opposed to purchase) of components. In addition, there can be substantial non-plant economies of scale in administration, distribution costs, interest expenses, and research and development. The total non-plant costs per unit of a large firm, with annual 1968 sales of $450 million or more, were estimated at roughly 80 percent of those of a small firm with $100 million annual sales or less.[3] Advertising, marketing, and servicing of farm machinery also constitute important advantages for large-scale full-line firms, as most farm machinery is distributed through a network of independent franchised dealers and service firms. The major manufacturers generally use a system of

[2]Royal Commission on Farm Machinery, *Special Report on Prices of Tractors and Combines in Canada and Other Countries,* Ottawa, Ontario, Canada, 1966, and *Report of the Royal Commission on Farm Machinery, 1971;* and Canadian Council on Wage and Price Stability, *Report on Prices for Agricultural Machinery and Equipment, 1976.*
[3]Leibenluft, op. cit., pp. 140–149.

"branch houses," which operate as regional sales offices for administrative and sales personnel and serve as regional warehouses for parts and service supplies. They also provide assistance and close supervision for retail dealers. In addition, the manufacturers are involved through their financial subsidiaries, which provide financing for both dealers and farmers as a supplement to other sources of credit available to them.

Most successful dealers cultivate reputations for having top-quality service departments, often open 24 hours a day in peak seasons, and for offering machines on loan when a farmer's equipment is down for repair. The larger dealers have an advantage in providing such service because they enjoy some economy of scale in investing in buildings and repair equipment. They also have an advantage in more efficient utilization of skilled labor, including more opportunity for workers to specialize. In addition, since a large dealership generally services a wider range of machinery and equipment, it is less affected than a smaller dealer by seasonal changes in the demand for service.

The influence of all this is to push the industry toward large-scale firms, under oligopolistic market competition. During the 1950s and 1960s, manufacturers in the United States concentrated on producing the larger, more powerful tractors and large-scale equipment. Demand for this was increasing as the great structural transformation of farms increased the advantages of operating large-scale machines. Gradually, these firms ceased their production of small tractors below 40 horsepower in size, creating an opening for European and Japanese firms. By the late 1970s, eight Japanese firms were exporting tractors to the United States, with the largest of these, the Kubota Tractor Corporation, accounting for about half of these exports.[4] At the same time, the domestic producers, apparently led by John Deere, were moving back into the small-tractor market, with a more versatile line of attachments and equipment than ever before.[5] Competition within the market, although imperfect and oligopolistic in structure, was continuing to push the industry toward product innovation and development.

More general inferences for policy tend to rise out of the continuing trend toward greater concentration. A tight oligopoly model of producer control of output will enable the industry to maintain prices at a high level, even in years when the demand for new farm machinery and equipment is weak. But when production is cut back, there will be few bargains for farmers. If farm income remains low, eventually the oligopolist's price must be paid. Although anti-trust action to prevent further acquisitions and mergers by the larger companies may be seen as in the public interest, a concerted effort to break up the few largest firms to get more effective competition might be counterproductive. The options for government regulation of output or price do not appear to be attractive, even if there is more concentration, and government-directed anti-trust action may or may not be beneficial to the farm and ranch economy.

---

[4]"Tractors from Japan," *Implement and Tractor*, vol. 94, April 21, 1979, pp. 8–26.
[5]"Back Home for Farm Equipment," *Business Week*, May 7, 1979, pp. 74, 78, and 82.

Issues in the Commercial Seed Input Markets

The commercial seed industry, whose importance for increasing productivity and agricultural output far exceeds the $3 billion farmers annually spend on seeds, has been transformed since passage of the Plant Variety Protection Act of 1970. This act made it possible for the developer of a new plant variety to receive a 17-year patent covering sale of the seed. In 1980, Congress adopted a number of amendments. One extended the patent-protection period to 18 years, and another added six major vegetables that had been exempted in 1970, at the request of the H. J. Heinz Company and the Campbell Soup Company.

Prior to the passage of the 1970 act, practically all basic research on new varieties was carried out through publicly funded agricultural experiment stations. Private seed companies had become prominent in developing and marketing new varieties, being most successful with hybrid seeds, because such seeds could not be reproduced without control of the parent stock used to create the hybrid. This included corn and sorghum hybrids, and some hybrids of onions, tomatoes, broccoli, cabbage, melons, and spinach. But most other crops resisted hybridization, so any firm could collect the seed of a new variety and market it as its own. This tended to discourage most seed companies from investing in basic research.

The 1970 act provided commercial plant breeders with some of the protection they required so that they could benefit from their research efforts in non-hybrids. It permitted them to apply for a patent on a new seed variety, which would prevent other seed companies from selling the seed as their own. A farmer, whose primary occupation was growing crops commercially for family use, feed, or sale, still could save seed for farm use, and seed companies could use some varieties to develop other varieties. But enforcement of the act made it profitable for plant breeders to apply for patents and, by October 1, 1980, of the applications received by the Plant Variety Protection Office, 92 had come from foreign countries, 140 from experiment stations, and 946 from private breeders.[6] The rationale for granting patents depends on the success of new varieties.

The new legislation made it profitable for existing seed companies to invest more in research and development, and it also attracted a large number of firms not previously in the seed business, most of which were capable of research and development. The seed companies tended to concentrate their work in states where the crops in which they invested had a comparative advantage. But they also spread out to new states. In Minnesota, for example, which had not been a large soybean-producing state, 65 different varieties of soybeans developed by 23 different companies were available and compared in yield tests from 1977 to 1979. In addition, seven publicly developed varieties were being tested.[7] Only time will tell whether this activity is

---

[6]Leibenluft, op. cit., p. 96, based on a telephone conversation with Kenneth Evans, Chief Examiner, Plant Variety Protection Office, October 15, 1980.
    [7]*Varietal Trials of Farm Crops,* University of Minnesota Agricultural Experiment Station Bulletin 24-5, 1980.

truly productive. Experience of several decades suggests that it will be highly effective in increasing agricultural productivity and growth.

There are substantial economies of scale in advertising and marketing a new plant variety, and there are advantages for large companies in developing seed varieties. Hence, while many new companies have started to research and develop new varieties, not a large number are expected to survive, and more concentration should be expected. In hybrid corn, for example, which is the largest and most mature of the markets. a few large-scale firms tend to dominate. The two leading producers of hybrid seed corn each market more than 100 different corn hybrids, with relatively large expenditures in advertising and sales.[8] In 1978, for example, advertising by major seed companies in agricultural publications included $1,121,000 by Pioneer Hi-bred, $1,271,000 by DeKalb Ag Research, $1,454,000 by Northrup-King, and $881,000 by Jacques (a subsidiary of Rorer-Amchem, in turn a subsidiary of Union Carbide).[9] In 1977, Pioneer had a sales force of about 3,500, including part-time dealers and commissioned sales agents.[10] Since then the larger firms have generally grown, so concentration has continued to increase.

Large integrated firms in oligopolistic competition are capable of maintaining higher prices than are likely to exist in more dispersed industries, and prices and profit margins in the seed industry tend to confirm this. But, while concentration may reach higher levels, and rigid oligopoly prices may be maintained in hybrid varieties, two factors tend to limit the market power of firms in the self-pollinating seed sector. One is that farmers have the option of growing their own seed after initial seed stock has been obtained. The other is that agricultural experiment stations, with support from the public, will continue to research and develop new varieties, thus tending to lessen the impact of concentrated market power among a few large firms.

Issues in the Fuel-Energy Input Market

Of the industrial fuels and energy used in the production, processing, and marketing of farm products, only about 25 percent of the total is used in farming and the manufacture and delivery of farm inputs. About 40 percent is used in processing, storing, transporting, and marketing food and nonfood products, and in manufacturing machinery and equipment for these purposes. The remainder of about 35 percent is used in home and restaurant refrigerating and cooking, and in manufacturing equipment for these purposes. In aggregate, the entire system uses about 15 to 16 percent of the total fuel-energy used in the United States.

The total farm-fuel use reached a peak in 1975, and has been gradually declining (Figure 11-1), as energy-saving technologies have come increasingly into use. Among these are the increasing use of fertilizer and pesticides as a way of increasing productivity and, at the same time, minimizing tillage. As may be noted in Figure 11-

---

[8]"Seed corn's long, hot, bruising Summer," *Business Week,* August 25, 1980, p. 52, 54, and 56.

[9]"Agrimarketing is more than a man in Oshkosh B' Goshes," *Advertising Age,* vol. 50, December 5, 1979, pp. 5–15.

[10]"A Sustained Harvest," *Forbes,* vol. 124, no. 8, October 15, 1979, pp. 121 and 122.

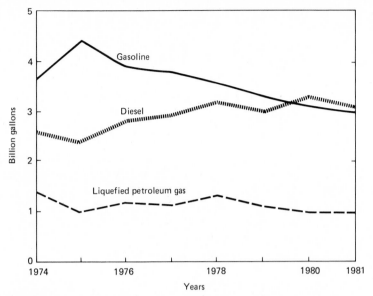

FIGURE 11-1
Farm fuel use. (*Source: USDA,* 1982 Handbook of Agricultural Charts, *p. 13.*)

2, more than 40 percent of the total energy used in agricultural or farm production is petrochemicals (pesticides and fertilizers). Advancing technology in this area, as well as in others, has tended to increase productivity. The net result is that increasing farm output is achieved with stable or declining total use of fuels and energy.

Since there is not a unique fuels and energy policy to apply to agriculture, it may be observed that the supply of fuels is largely dependent on exogenous factors, with the exception of gasohol made from corn or other farm products. The production of gasohol has had to be heavily subsidized for it to compete in the fuels market, and it is apparent that continued heavy subsidy will be required, if it is to be a significant

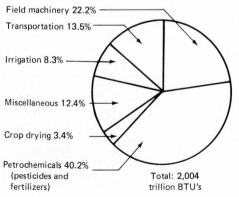

Field machinery 22.2%

Transportation 13.5%

Irrigation 8.3%

Miscellaneous 12.4%

Crop drying 3.4%

Petrochemicals 40.2%
 (pesticides and
 fertilizers)

Total: 2,004
trillion BTU's

FIGURE 11-2
Energy used in agricultural production.
(*Source: USDA,* 1982 Handbook of Agricultural Charts, *p. 13.*)

source of energy in the United States. This means that the supply of fuel-energy for agricultural use will be rather elastic, because agriculture uses such a small percentage of the total fuel-energy consumed in the United States. But, apparently the agricultural demand is very stable, and also very inelastic. That is, the total quantities demanded have not changed, or have changed very little, as a result of changing real prices. Farmers, as well as most entrepreneurs in the marketing economy, have tended to absorb the increased costs of price hikes, and enjoy some of the windfall gains of price decreases. But sharp increases and decreases in prices are unsettling in farming, as in most other fuel-using industries, and this suggests that agriculture could benefit from a stabilization of the nation's fuel supply. A national policy that increases the total fuel supply would tend, therefore, to be beneficial to agriculture.

Increases in crop yields are a result of improvements in agribusiness inputs such as fertilizer and other farm chemicals. Who benefits from this?

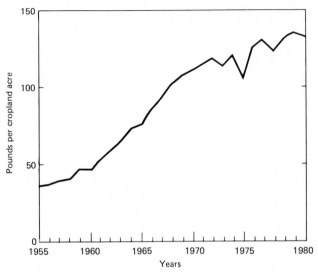

FIGURE 11-3
Fertilizer nutrients used per acre. *(Source: USDA,* 1982 Handbook of Agricultural Charts, *p. 13.)*

Issues in the Fertilizer Input Market

In the early 1980s, farmers were spending about $10 billion a year on fertilizer, by far the largest part of which was on commercially integrated materials supplying nitrogen, potassium, and phosphorus, the three major nutrients of the sixteen nutrients essential for plant growth. From 1955 to 1980, the total fertilizer nutrients used increased from about 40 to almost 140 pounds per crop acre, with about a 20 percent increase during the decade of the 1970s alone (Figure 11-3). Use of all three major nutrients increased, with the greatest relative increases in nitrogen and potash (Figure 11-4).

The supply of fertilizer has grown rapidly based on development of new sources of raw materials, adoption of technological innovations in manufacturing, and integration of firms. Fertilizer manufacturers have tended to integrate vertically both to gain control over their own sources of raw material and to promote their own brand names in the finished product. They also tend to integrate horizontally because of the economies of large scale in managing raw materials, manufacturing, advertising, and marketing.

Growth in the fertilizer industry is not necessarily well correlated with growth in demand, with the result that prices have tended to decline over several years, and then to shoot up as demand apparently increased faster than supply. Throughout the 1950s and 1960s, the real prices of fertilizer tended to decline, as new discoveries of phosphate rock and potash were developed, and as important technological advances were adopted in manufacturing. In the late 1960s and early 1970s, the industry apparently reached a stage of substantial excess capacity. The real prices of fertilizer

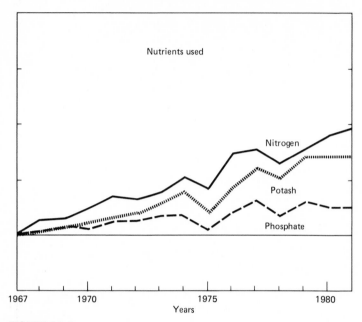

FIGURE 11-4
Trends in use of nitrogen, potash, and phosphate. (*Source: USDA,* 1982 Handbook of Agricultural Charts, *p. 11.*)

declined to record lows as domestic use increased rapidly and exports also increased. Then, from 1973 to 1975, domestic prices more than doubled, as growth in demand apparently caught up with production. Prices declined and rose again to enter the 1980s at more than two and a half times the 1967 prices (Figure 11-5).

Both demand and supply appear to be very inelatic in the short run, and price fluctuations typical of the last decade may be projected into the future. The best determination of policy alternatives that will achieve more stability can be made by looking at the individual sectors of the economy, which involve nitrogen, phosphate, and potash.

The Nitrogenous Fertilizer Industry   There are more than 60 individual firms producing nitrogenous fertilizers. The industry has only a modest degree of concentration, with four-firm and eight-firm concentration ratios of 35 and 45 percent, respectively, and these producers also face competition from Canadian and Mexican firms. Although there are substantial economies in large-scale production, and a significant amount of vertical integration backward into sources of raw materials and forward into distribution, entry into the industry has been relatively easy. Many firms are also integrated horizontally in production of other plant nutrients. So, because of its low concentration ratios and weak barriers to entry, production has tended to expand rapidly when prices are favorable, and an oligopoly-type of supply control by the competing firms has not been evident.

The stability of the industry might be increased by a government-sponsored pro-

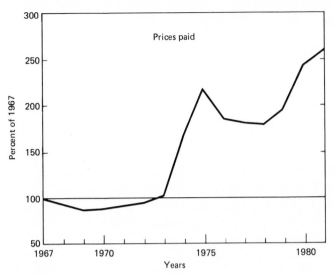

FIGURE 11-5
Prices paid for fertilizer. (*Source: USDA*, 1982, Handbook of Agricultural Charts, *p. 11.*)

gram of reserve stocks, but there is little evidence to suggest that this would be cost-effective, or that it would be beneficial in terms of competition. The industry, in other words, does not conform to an oligopoly model of restrictive anticompetitive practices, and it is responsive to market forces.

The Phosphatic Fertilizer Industry   This industry is built around some 40 firms, with four-firm and eight-firm concentration ratios of 40 and 60 percent. Although there is a high degree of vertical integration, with many firms having large operations at both the raw-material and end-product stages, barriers to entry appear to be low and an oligopoly-type model of pricing does not appear to apply.

The Potash Fertilizer Industry   "Potash" is the term used to describe the minerals and chemicals that are valued for their potassium content. Because potash is obtained solely from a mining operation, and needs only to be washed and processed to increase its concentration, it has been the least expensive of the primary nutrients. Although the domestic industry is highly concentrated, with four firms producing more than 75 percent of the domestic output, the industry is subject to foreign competition, especially from huge deposits of potash ore found in the province of Saskatchewan in western Canada. Apparently, a significant measure of production control has been exerted by the Saskatchewan Potash Conservation Board, a government corporation, as prices of potash almost tripled in the 1970s. A law passed in 1976 enabled the Saskatchewan government to purchase 50 percent or more of the industry in that province, and to budget some $2.5 billion for capital expenditures over the next 10 years. Measured by consumption in the United States in the early 1980s, potash fertilizers at the user level have been approximately a billion-dollar industry. Whether to let the industry develop as it has under the current economic stucture, or to seek new international agreements on output and prices, appears to be the main policy issue for the future.

Issues in the Pesticide Input Market

The $4 billion pesticide industry, which has experienced more than a six fold increase in its market since 1950, resembles the pharmaceutical industry in organization and structure, with many firms involved in both industries. Market shares for particular products change quickly, as new chemical compounds are developed, and most firms place much emphasis on research in order to develop new products, because very high profits may be earned while patent protection is enjoyed.

The market is widely dispersed at the distributor and retailer level, but highly concentrated in synthesizing and formulating products. Although there are many firms in these activities, the appropriate market definition in most cases is no larger than a specific pesticide class used for a particular crop, such as corn herbicides or soybean insecticides, because it is only at this level that the product of one firm can be substituted for another. The actual concentration in individual markets is much higher, therefore, than general statistics of the industry would indicate, with oligopoly being the dominant economic structure of the market.

Classes of Pesticides   The major pesticides are broadly classified, according to the target species of pests to which they are applied, as: insecticides, herbicides, fungicides, rodenticides, acaricides (ticks), and miticides. In addition, there are nematicides, molluscicides, and bactericides. There are attractants to lure pests and repellents to force them away. And there are growth regulators, defoliants, and desiccants, which will draw moisture from a plant, causing it to wither and die.

Within each class, individual products are often specifically targeted to control a specific disease or pest. Therefore substitution of one specifically targeted pesticide for another is usually quite limited. Although within each class there are hundreds of formulations that have been developed, commercial use generally settles on a small number of preparations, each of which is dominated by a few active ingredients.

Concentration Ratios in Manufacturing   Because almost all of the active ingredients are manufactured by only three or fewer firms, the concentration ratios for basic pesticide producers are extremely high. For instance, at least 90 percent of the corn herbicide market has been supplied by no more than four firms, at least 67 percent of the cotton herbicides have been supplied by two firms, some 66 percent of the herbicides used on sorghum have been supplied by just one firm, and more than 75 percent of soybean herbicides have been produced by only four firms. Insecticide markets for materials used on crops and livestock are regarded as being somewhat less concentrated, but the ratios are still very high.[11]

---

[11]The data cited above are from *Economic Profile of the Pesticide Industry*, published by the U.S. Environmental Protection Agency, Office of Pesticide Programs, Washington, D.C., August 1980.

Although economies of large scale are not very significant in either pesticide synthesizing or formulating, the cost of bringing a new chemical to market has risen substantially, which encourages integration and consolidation of firms. Differentiation of products by brand name also encourages individual firms to specialize in fewer and more profitable products. Hence, there is a constant tendency for the industry to move toward more consolidation and concentration based on brand-name consciousness, with much advertising effort directed at differentiating the product of one firm from that of another.

Inelastic Demand for Individual Products   Since the pesticide market is actually fragmented into several submarkets within which only a very few firms compete, each of these firms tends to face a highly inelastic demand for its own brand-name product. The products of competing firms that are targeted for similar pests are generally very close substitutes, but the high concentration in individual markets practically assures that each firm faces the kinked demand curve characteristic of oligopoly. That is, when supply is large, individual firms will advertise to market their product, and generally will not find it profitable to reduce their prices, because then competing firms will tend to reduce theirs, and all will be worse off. When demand increases, firms may raise their prices, depending on how successful they have been in identifying and differentiating their product.

Profitability Based on Little Excess Capacity   Since the pesticide industry has had little excess capacity, overt collusion is not necessary to establish oligopoly pricing as the mere fact of mutual interdependence tends to stabilize prices.[12] Flexibility on the part of manufacturers in use of their plant and equipment permits them to idle part of a plant when stocks accumulate, or modify product lines to offset surpluses or shortages at the existing market price. Where a pesticide has established a stable share of the total market, the kinked demand curve faced by the oligopolist tends to result in careful management of supply and nonprice competition. As a result, the industry has a record of extraordinary profitability. A study in the mid 1970s, for instance, estimated pretax profit margins at about 35 percent of gross sales, while a 1980 estimate of pretax profits as a percentage of sales ranged from 20 percent to more than 40 percent.[13]

Policy Alternatives   The record of pricing and profits does not necessarily provide a case for the government to act under the anti-trust laws. A company can shift from one product to another, or change the level of its output so rapidly that a particular anti-trust case may be moot before it can come to trial. Nevertheless, there is an argument on the part of the Federal Trade Commission for constant surveillance to determine the status of competition, and for taking action at times to assure

---

[12]F. Scherer, *Industrial Market Structure and Economic Performance,* Rand McNally and Co., Chicago, 2d ed., 1980, p. 303.

[13]William Blair and Co., *The Pesticide Industry—An Overview,* July 1975, and *Chemical Engineering News,* April 28, 1980.

that concentration does not restrict an essential product excessively, and result in unusually high prices.

Although the rate of change in the price index of an industry's product is not a very reliable guide to its quality of market performance, the fact is that the general index of pesticide prices has moved up less rapidly than the prices of almost all of the other major farm production inputs. This is especially so if the improvements in quality of product are taken into account. But, given the incentives for concentration and the record of very high profits from restrictive control of certain pesticides, there is a strong case for a government agency that would be specifically charged with monitoring the industry, and with recommending action if appropriate for the public interest.

The policy issues of concentration and pricing must be kept separate from those relating to externalities, or to the problems of safety in use of the industrial inputs. Although this is a problem for almost all of these inputs, it is most acute for pesticides. So let us treat the policy issue of safety in use of pesticides as the primary case.

POLICY ISSUE OF SAFETY IN PESTICIDE USE

The policy issue of safety in pesticide use arises out of the facts that (1) modern industrial agriculture is highly dependent on pesticides for its productivity, and (2) pesticides by nature are poisons. This is a hazard for those who use pesticides. But much of the possible adverse effect of these poisons appears as an external cost in crop and livestock production. Generally, the newest and most effective pesticides are the most toxic to human beings and animals. Also, many of them are persistent in the environment—that is, nonbiodegradable—and, if they enter the food chain either directly, or from plant to animal and to human consumption, their use can be especially hazardous, indeed.

Use and Productivity of Pesticides

For several years the use of pesticides has increased more than that of any other major class of industrial inputs. This implies a high marginal rate of return from use of pesticides, and also a substitution of pesticides for other inputs. In fact, as noted in the last chapter, pesticides are necessary for certain recommended soil conservation practices, such as reduced cultivation, or minimum tillage, and for crop systems that maximize total output by getting high yields under continuous cropping. Pesticides have resulted in savings of labor, machinery, and fuel, of as much as 50 percent or more, in producing crops such as wheat, rice, and potatoes.[14] The fact that most of the crops economy is dependent on pesticides is revealed by estimates of the return from one pound of pesticides, or the value of the crop saved by one pound of pesticides, such as in the following:[15]

---

[14]W. C. Shaw and L. L. Jansen, "Chemical Weed Control Strategies for the Future," *Pest Control Strategies for the Future,* National Academy of Sciences, Washington, D.C., 1972.

[15]Gerald A. Carlson and Emery N. Castle, "Economics of Pest Control," *Pest Control Strategies for the Future,* p. 91.

Commodity	Insecticides	Herbicides	Fungicides
Cotton	$ 19.25	$ 688.55	$896.98
Apples	23.16	*	19.00
Peanuts	49.14	93.72	16.44
Potatoes	208.54	274.12	175.52
Corn	215.19	103.19	†
Alfalfa	502.84	1,397.19‡	†
Soybeans	683.27	245.31	†
Wheat	2,322.13	259.54	†

*Mostly petroleum.
†Fungicide totals not available.
‡Includes herbicides used on all hay.

Concept of Optimum Use of Pesticides

As has been noted, in almost all pesticides, but especially among insecticides, the evolution of more powerful chemicals seems to favor the use of compounds that are both highly toxic and hazardous to humans. The benefits of use accrue to the individual farmer or firm as an increase in net return. Theoretically, the farmer will maximize net return when the marginal resource cost of the last unit of a pesticide that is used is equal to the marginal revenue product (the $MRC = MRP$ rule). But one of the real costs of using some pesticides is the danger done to the environment and the food supply, which is an externality, or a cost that is external to the firm.

The general theoretical concept of optimum pesticide use may be visualized as in Figure 11-6. The total positive benefits less the total cost of pesticides at market

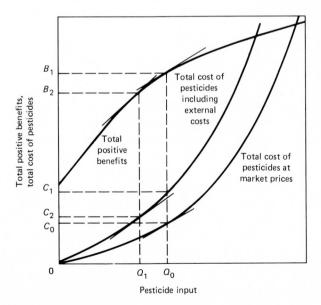

FIGURE 11-6
Optimum use of pesticides at Q_1, including external costs, and at Q_0 at market prices, not including external costs.
(*Source: Adapted from J. C. Headley and J. N. Lewis,* The Pesticide Problem, *Resources for the Future, 1967.*)

prices is maximized at that point where lines drawn tangent to these curves are parallel, which is at the level of pesticide input equal to Q_0. The positive benefit ignoring external costs is equal to $B_1 - C_0$. At this level of pesticide input, however, the external costs are $C_1 - C_0$, and net benefits (equal to $B_1 - C_1$) are not at the maximum. The net benefits are maximized at a lower level of pesticide input at Q_1, where tangents to the curve of total positive benefits and the curve of total cost of pesticides, including external costs are parallel.

The concept of pesticide cost and benefit in Figure 11-6 implies that there is an optimum level of input for any pesticide. In the case that is illustrated, it will not be optimum to ban the pesticide because the total positive benefits when no pesticide is used are less than can be attained with some use of pesticides. In some other cases, where a pesticide is very hazardous or persistent, or both, its use should be banned, as has been the case in the United States with a number of pesticides that are no longer available. In most cases, however, where pesticides are not banned, the more difficult policy problem involves the determination of how best to control the use of the pesticide, taking account of external as well as internal costs. Let us consider how this problem can be formulated and approached, as in a policy solution.

Toxicity and Persistence of Pesticides

The toxicity of a pesticide, and its persistence in the environment or the food chain, together provide a measure of the hazard in using a pesticide. To measure toxicity, a rating scale, called the mammalian selectivity ratio (MSR), has been developed with the hazard related inversely and geometrically to the magnitude of the number.[16] Malathion, for example, which has a high MSR number of 37.7, is one of the least toxic of the common pesticides. It is widely used as a garden and household insecticide. Parathion, in comparison, has a much lower MSR rating of 4.0. It is extremely toxic, and not recommended for garden or household use. But it is widely used in commercial agriculture. It is relatively safe, if used with appropriate precautions, because it is not overly persistent in the environment and normally does not enter the food chain. Methyl parathion, another widely used insecticide, has an MSR of 20.

Although people may be sickened or even killed by inhaling a pesticide vapor or from a severe skin exposure, nearly all pesticide deaths in both humans and animals are caused by eating or drinking the product or its residue. Nearly half the accidental deaths in the United States from pesticide poisoning are those of children under 12 years of age. In the cases of occupational poisoning and death, the organic phosphorus compounds, called organophosphates, are most commonly involved. These are insecticides, such as the highly toxic parathion and methyl parathions, and the somewhat less toxic malathion. The carbamates, including carbaryl (Sevin), and carbofuran (Furadan), the newest class of insecticides to be developed, may cause the

---

[16]MSR ratings are from Robert L. Metcalf,"Development of Selective and Biodegradable Pesticides,"*Pest Control Strategies for the Future,* 1972, pp. 137–156.

same symptoms as the organophosphates, but they are generally less enduring in effect and are generally considered safer.

The hazard to humanity is not fully defined by the MSR, but lies in the persistence of the insecticide. DDT, which has been widely used worldwide for control of malaria, without immediate adverse effects on human life, has an MSR of 59. But it has been banned in the United States because of its persistence in a variety of ecological niches—soil, water, plant surface, animal bodies—and its slow degradation in biological systems, to form DDE and DDD. These are highly soluble in lipids (fats) and extremely insoluble in water. Hence, they may accumulate over wide limits in the food chain, as from plant to fish, bird, or mammal, and finally to humans.

This progression in the food chain may establish a concentration that is highly injurious, or even lethal. DDE, which has a high safety factor, is responsible for a major portion of the adverse environmental effects of concentration and storage in animal tissues occurring after the use of DDT. The other three DDT analogues, methoxychlor, methiochlor, and methylchlor, are each substantially biodegradable through oxidation; that is, the substance breaks down and disappears. When they are absorbed into living organisms, they have weak points for attack by multifunction oxidases (enzymes that promote oxidation), thus promoting rapid detoxication and elimination as water-soluble products of the metabolism. They have advantages, therefore, as safe, relatively stable, and potentially inexpensive residual insecticides. But, although they are highly preferable to the original DDT, they are still dangerous during their active lives. The policy problem is how best to impose proper limits on their sale and use.

Lessons Derived from the Poisoning of the Food Chain[17]

The food chain can be poisoned by use of pesticides when plants absorb the poison in the pesticide, are then eaten by livestock, and the livestock products eaten by people or other animals. Any agricultural crop that absorbs a pesticide may constitute a hazard. Consequently, pesticides must be continually studied and evaluated before permission can be given for their manufacture and sale. Even with a supposedly safe pesticide, however, poisoning of the food chain can occur as a result of concentration. Let us consider such a case.

A classic example of food-chain poisoning occurred at Clear Lake, California, a shallow, warm body of water of about 72 square miles, located 90 to 100 miles north of San Francisco, when attempts were made to eradicate a small, highly annoying gnat with a carefully designed program using DDD. Although this gnat resembles the common mosquito, it is not a bloodsucker, and the many fishing parties who used the lake found it annoying mainly because of its large numbers. Efforts to control the gnat were fruitless until a program was begun in 1949 to apply DDD in 1 part

---

[17]For discussion of large-scale control programs somewhat beyond the scope of agricultural policy, see Harold G. Halcrow, *Food Policy for America,* McGraw-Hill Book Company, New York, 1977, pp. 116–126.

to 70 million parts (1 to 70 ppm) of water. In 1954 the dosage was repeated at 1 to 50 ppm, and in 1957 was applied again.

Then ecological disaster struck, with overtones for all types of food. Prior to the first spraying in 1949, about 1,000 pairs of grebes, which are swanlike diving birds that live on fish, had made their summer homes around the lake. After the spraying, they migrated elsewhere for summer breeding and rearing of their young. But they returned in the winter for feeding, and after the 1954 spraying more than 100 were found dead. After the 1957 spraying many more were killed. Studies revealed that some of their fatty tissues contained as much as 1,600 ppm of DDD—a concentration 80,000 times as great as that of the 0.02 ppm found in the lake.[18] Microscopic plants and animal organisms had stored DDD at about 5 ppm. Fish that ate this food had overall DDD concentrations at 40 to 2,500 ppm in their livers, kidneys, and fatty tissues, and the birds that ate this fish absorbed a lethal dose. What loss there was to other life, such as herons, was not determined. As far as the hazard to fish-eating humans was concerned, the levels of concentration of DDD in flesh of the fish, although lower than in the vital organs, were often well above the 7 ppm set by the Food and Drug Administration as the maximum tolerance for DDD residues in marketed foodstuffs. Upon recommendations of the Lake County Mosquito Abatement District, no further applications of DDD were made to the lake. But it is clear, as has been observed, that this experience "still stands as a fascinating example of the complexities of chemical transferal in living systems, and as a pointed warning to professional workers not to oversimplify their solutions to pest control problems."[19]

Policy for control of pesticides must take account of the conditions under which a pesticide is to be used, as well as the way in which it is used. An example of the need for this occurred in the Klamath Basin refuges in Northern California, which are administered by the United States Fish and Wildlife Service.[20] In the summer of 1960, the refuge staff began to pick up dead and dying birds, and soon 307 birds were identified, all of which were fish eaters. The birds were found to contain lethal doses of taxaphene, DDD, and DDE, concentrated in their liver, kidneys, and subcutaneous fat, ranging from as little as 2.2 ppm of taxaphene to over 6001 ppm of DDT and DDD.This condition was traced to spraying, some two years before, of crops that were irrigated from the Upper Klamath Lake, just over the border in Oregon. The runoff from these sprayed fields, which spread out over the swampy refuge, carried the lethal concentration.

Resolving Policy Conflicts

In some instances, society must be prepared to deal with almost irreconcilable conflicts, as in the classic case regarding the western sheep-range country. This concerns the banning of poison bait on this land by the United States Environmental Protec-

---

[18]Robert J. Rudd, *Pesticides and the Living Landscape,* The University of Wisconsin Press, Madison, 1964, pp. 138 and 250–254.
[19]Robert J. Rudd, ibid., p. 254.
[20]Ibid. pp. 255–259.

tion Agency (EPA). Until 1972, sheep ranchers were permitted to use poison bait to control predators, especially coyotes, which are natural and deadly enemies of sheep. But the poison bait also killed other wildlife, including scavengers that fed on poisoned carcasses. Some scavenger birds, such as the bald eagle, were threatened with extinction. In 1972, after several years of wildlife losses, and swelling protests from various individuals and groups about the damage to wildlife from the bait, the EPA banned use of the poison bait on federal lands and soon thereafter also prohibited bait shipment in interstate traffic, thus making it practically unavailable for use on private lands as well.

Soon a howl of protest against the ban arose from sheep ranchers, who claimed that they were suffering large losses from predators, and their influence was quickly reflected in political pressures. Twenty-one senators from western states signed a letter accusing the Department of the Interior, which administered the EPA, of failing to protect livestock from predators. The 1974 Western Governors' Conference passed a resolution to urge the EPA to reinstate predator poisons and also to transfer responsibility for predator control from the Department of the Interior to Agriculture. In November 1974, more than 100 biologists met for four days in Denver to concentrate on possible policy solutions. But there was no ideal solution that would contain the coyote population without having other adverse consequences. Although each antagonist could make a telling point, responsible administration required decisions that were decidedly unpopular with one group or another. The external cost of using the bait was evaluated by the EPA as greatly in excess of the benefit to the sheep industry and to consumers from a continuation of its use.

Quite clearly there will continue to be important conflicts around any policy that attempts to reduce the external costs of pesticides, when reducing their cost imposes internal costs on producers. How these conflicts have been handled and will be handled in the future can best be understood by studying the history of pesticide policy. So let us conclude this chapter with a brief review of this policy-making experience.

EXPERIENCE IN MAKING PESTICIDE POLICY

The experience in the United States in making pesticide policy stretches over several decades, beginning with the rather simple regulations first set by the Federal Insecticide Act of 1910, and by numerous state laws, some passed prior to 1910. Since then, because of the need to standardize regulations and to control pesticide use uniformly within states as well as in interstate commerce, the federal government has assumed a progressively larger role. The 1910 act merely prevented the manufacture, sale, or transportation of adulterated or misbranded insecticides and fungicides and authorized state regulation of sales of insecticides and fungicides. In 1946, the Council of State Governments developed a uniform insecticide, fungicide, and rodenticide act for consideration and adoption by individual states.

In 1947, the Federal Insecticide, Fungicide, and Rodenticide Act replaced the 1910 act to conform with numerous state acts, and required the following: (1) the registration of chemical pesticides before their sale or shipment in interstate or foreign commerce; (2) prominent display of poison warnings on labels of highly toxic materials; (3) coloring of insecticides to prevent their being mistaken for foodstuffs; (4) inclusion of instructions for use to provide protection to the public; and (5) furnishing of information to the administrator of the act with respect to the delivery, movement, or holding of pesticides.

In 1954, an amendment to the Food and Drug Act authorized the administrator of the Federal Insecticide, Fungicide, and Rodenticide Act to set tolerance limits for the residues of pesticides in foods, required the pretesting of a chemical pesticide before it could be used on food crops, and required the manufacturer to provide both detailed data demonstrating the usefulness of the chemical to agriculture and scientific data on the toxicity of the chemical to warm-blooded animals. In 1959, the 1947 act was amended again to include several new types of chemicals. In 1964, further amendments eliminated provisions allowing use of a pesticide while it was under protest, authorized each pesticide to carry a license number identification, and expedited procedures for suspending the marketing of previously registered pesticides which were found to be unsafe. Finally, in 1970, under a presidential reorganization plan, the pesticide and pure food regulatory staffs located throughout the Departments of Agriculture; Interior; and Health, Education and Welfare were transferred to the new Environmental Protection Agency.

The Federal Environmental Pesticide Control Act of 1972 completely revised and replaced the 1947 act and its amendments under the general policy goal of regulating the use of pesticides to protect humans and the environment by extending federal regulations to cover all pesticide manufacture, sale, and use within states, as well as among states. Major provisions prohibit—that is, make unlawful—sale or use of any pesticide in a manner inconsistent with its labeling, and require all pesticides to be classified for general or restricted use. Those pesticides in the restricted category can be used only by or under the supervision of certified applicators, or are subject to such other restrictions as the administrator may determine. General or seasonal licenses, permits, or other forms of approval may be required for applicators, as certified by states under a program approved by the administrator.

The 1972 act required all pesticide producers to register and to submit information regularly on production and sales volume. It authorized entry, for purposes of inspection and sampling of pesticides and devices, of establishments and other places where pesticides are held for sale or distribution. It authorized stop-sale, stop-use, and removal or seizure orders, to be enforced through civil and criminal penalties. It improved procedures for registering new pesticides and for cancelling permits, by requiring that scientific reviews and public hearings be combined. It established the requirement that all questions must be submitted in writing at the beginning of a hearing. It authorized the administrator to establish pesticide packaging standards, to regulate pesticide and container disposal, to issue experimental use permits, to conduct research on pesticides and alternatives, and to monitor pesticide use and presence in the environment. States were authorized to impose more stringent regulations than those set by the federal government.

Since 1972, as we have noted, the use of pesticides has continued to increase as further technological advances are made in production, marketing, and methods of application. Marked improvements have been made in public understanding of the pesticide problem. Refinements in legislation and administration continue to be made; research goes on. But as long as technological advance continues, the role of pesticides in agricultural production will continue to expand, and the issues in policy related to pesticides will continue to be important.

SUMMARY

Policy analysis of the agribusiness input markets reveals that the industries in these markets are highly concentrated. All markets are characterized by imperfect competition, and most have an oligopsony-oligopoly competitive structure. In spite of this, however, there are few instances where further government intervention is warranted, based simply on a theoretical review of the markets. The industries have continued to grow at a rather steady pace. Together, they are perhaps the leading economic force in further development and growth of agriculture.

The pesticide input market presents a unique problem for policy. This arises out of the generally high productivity of pesticides that is, however, associated with generally high external costs in the use of pesticides. How to control these external costs, while continuing to enjoy results made possible by higher levels of pesticide use, will continue to be an important problem for policy in the future. Recent legislation has helped to define the role of pesticide policy, while allowing for increasing use of pesticide products.

IMPORTANT TERMS AND CONCEPTS

Agribusiness input markets

Imperfect competition in agribusiness input markets

Downward-sloping demand curves faced by firms in imperfect competition

Downward-sloping kinked demand curves faced by oligopolists

High concentration in the farm machinery and equipment input market

Economies of large scale in farm machinery and equipment

Concepts of oligopoly pricing in farm machinery and equipment input markets

Competitive structure of the commercial seed input market

Distribution of fuel-energy input among the economic sectors of agriculture

Impact of energy-saving technologies on use of fuel on farms

Inelastic demand for fuel in agricultural production and marketing

Economic structure of the fertilizer industry

Inelastic demand for fertilizer—implications for policy

Classes of pesticides

Concentration ratios in pesticide manufacturing

Use and productivity of pesticides

The pesticide safety problem

Concept of optimum use of pesticides

Toxicity and persistence of pesticides

Mammalian selectivity ratio (MSR)

Concentration of pesticides in the food chain

Experiences with large-scale pest-control programs

Lessons derived from the poisoning of the food chain

Concepts of irreconcilable conflicts in pesticide control

Experience in making pesticide policy

QUESTIONS AND EXERCISES

1 What are the major policy issues related to competition in the agribusiness industrial-input markets?

2 It has been said that it might be counterproductive to break up the few largest firms in agricultural machinery and equipment to make the industry more purely price-competitive. Do you agree? Explain your answer.

3 The granting of patents in the commercial seed input industry will tend to increase concentration, at least in some instances. On what grounds may this policy be justified? On what grounds can it be criticized?

4 The total fuel-energy used in agricultural production appears to have stabilized, or is declining. If you agree, why is this so? What does the record of fuel use in farming tend to tell us about the elasticity of demand for fuel energy? The elasticity of supply? What are the most important inferences of this for policy?

5 Although some subsectors of the fertilizer industry are highly concentrated, in most subsectors there is little evidence of rigid oligopoly pricing. Why? Are there any important exceptions? Why? What are the inferences for policy?

6 In respect to the pesticide industry, it has been said that the rate of change in the industry's price index is not a very reliable guide to the quality of the industry's market performance. Do you agree? If so, why? If not, why not?

7 What is an optimum use of pesticides? What criteria can be applied to determine optimality? What are the major external costs associated with use of pesticides? What are the major inferences for policy?

RECOMMENDED READINGS

Halcrow, Harold G., *Food Policy for America,* McGraw-Hill Book Company, New York, 1977, pp. 91–126.

Leibenluft, Robert F., *Competition in Farm Inputs: An Examination of Four Industries,* Policy Issues Planning Paper, Office of Policy Planning, Federal Trade Commission, February 1981.

National Academy of Sciences, *Pest Control Strategies for the Future,* Washington, D.C., 1972.

CHAPTER 12

POLICY ANALYSIS OF HUMAN RESOURCE INPUT MARKETS

The modernization of agriculture is characterized by investments in education, skills, and health of people in farming, agribusiness, and economic sectors related to agriculture. Results of such investments are seen in rising rates of productivity of human resources, and in declining labor requirements for given levels of agricultural output. However, some results are also seen in depressed farm incomes, and in a distribution of income from farming that is more skewed than that for most of the rest of the economy. How to get the benefits of increasing productivity without having adverse effects in income is the essence of policy in this area.

IN THIS CHAPTER

1 You can learn how concepts of human resources may be used in policy analysis, especially how to apply supply and demand to concepts of human capital investment and return.

2 You can learn how policy has been developed to apply specifically to human resource investment and development.

3 You can learn how to visualize some of the alternatives in policy for dealing with human resource problems in the future.

CONCEPTS OF HUMAN RESOURCES: SUPPLY AND DEMAND

Human resources may be visualized as a form of capital, which has a supply and a demand function. The supply is created by investment in human beings, and involves

Young people in 4-H clubs, which are a part of the federal-state cooperative extension program, learn to keep records and perform other skilled work. Much of the support comes from volunteer leaders and local funds. How much tax money to invest in the program is an important issue in public policy.

all the processes of life—raising children, investing in training and education, providing for health and happiness. The demand arises out of the results of economic processes to which human beings contribute as laborers and managers. In any market, there is an equilibrium price which appears as a rate of return—a wage, a salary, an annual income, the level of which is determined by the intersection of supply and demand.

In agriculture, as in other industries, the demand for human capital or labor depends on the marginal value of its product, and the supply depends on opportunity cost. Investments that increase the productivity of human capital, such as education and training, increase the demand. Improving opportunities outside of agriculture, which increase the opportunity cost of human capital or labor in agriculture, decrease the supply. These facts lead to the proposition that there are two conditions necessary for economic progress in agriculture, or increasing the real per capita income of people in agriculture, and these conditions can be created by policy in the human resource input markets. What are these conditions?

Two Conditions for Economic Progress

The two necessary and sufficient conditions for economic progress in agriculture are (1) a sufficient rate of investment in human capital to increase the productivity of human beings, and (2) a sufficient level of economic opportunity outside of agriculture to raise the opportunity cost of being in farming or other agricultural sectors. The first condition increases the demand for human capital in agriculture, and the second decreases and controls the supply. Under these conditions, the growth in productivity in agriculture has helped farmers, and it can continue to help them, providing that growth is part of an advance in the economy as a whole, and does not occur at a disproportionate rate. It has been the means of lifting farmers from a well-pumping, kerosene-lamp way of living to the comforts of today.

The desired fruits of agricultural policy in terms of income depend on balancing the increase in human productivity with increasing opportunities outside of agriculture and the farm sector. In a general sense, development and growth occurs in agriculture when new capital inputs and advanced technologies are made available on terms that are attractive to investors. To be attractive for investment, new resources must raise productivity. They must be either yield-increasing, or factor-saving, or both. If they are yield-increasing, output expands; if they are factor-saving, more resources are released for employment elsewhere. Some of the technologies, such as fertilizers and chemical pesticides, may be primarily—or even solely—yield-increasing; other technologies, such as new tractors and mechanized field equipment, may be more factor-saving, while generally resulting in important economies of large scale. The more economically efficient farmers save and invest in their own human capital and in these new technologies, which increases output, and displaces labor in the aggregate. Supply increases as average cost and marginal cost curves shift to the right and, other things being equal, the prices of farm products decline relative to the prices of inputs.

Effects of Technological Advance on the Marginal Rate of Return to Human Capital

The displacement of farm labor by the new inputs and technologies releases labor and, if opportunity cost does not rise, the supply of labor increases relative to its demand. Returns to family farm labor, as well as wage rates for hired farm labor, tend to fall in the presence of new technologies. The farmers who are successful in applying the new technologies continue to save and invest, as their productivity increases; while other farm families, who have not been as successful in applying these new technologies, tend to have lower incomes as a result of the relative decline in prices of farm products.

This sequence of events is typical of agricultural economies in all stages of economic development. As the productivity of capital inputs increases, including, in this case, human capital and all other forms, the supply of agricultural products increases. But, the higher the yield of the new inputs and technologies, the lower will be the *relative* yield of the old capital or technology, including human capital, and the more depressed will be the *relative* return to this capital. The concept of *relative marginal rates of return* must be emphasized because agricultural development and growth is generally marked by a great increase in output per unit of labor employed on farms. For instance, between the mid 1930s and the early 1970s, the output per unit of labor employed in the farm sector increased at least six times.[1] Between just the early 1970s and the beginning of the 1980s, this output increased by about 50 percent, as overall farm output increased by about one-fourth, while the farm population and employment on farms continued to decline (Figures 12-1 and 12-2).

When there is an increase in output per person employed on farms, why does the return to management and labor tend to fall? This is a crucial question for policy analysis. The advances in farm technology resulting from adoption of various innovations tend to increase the demand for the inputs that are most improved by these innovations. Generally, these have been the inputs produced in the agribusiness input industries, and improvements in these inputs tend to displace labor. So the demand for labor on farms tends to drop. In the short run at least, the supply of labor tends to be very inelastic, as opportunity costs of staying in farming are low in the short run. It takes time to develop alternative opportunities for employment, and the labor supply function does not become elastic until a considerable time has elapsed.

If all individuals were equally endowed with human capital and the total supply were fixed, then the marginal rate of return to human capital would fall as new and more productive technologies were introduced, other things being equal. That is, the new technologies would not be employed unless it were profitable to do so, or the marginal rate of return to these technologies must be high enough to make them attractive to investors. Some of the new technologies tend to be labor-saving as well as output-increasing, as farm labor tends to be displaced by the labor and other resources required for the manufacture and delivery of such technologies.

---

[1] John W. Kendrick, *Productivity Trends in the United States: A Study by the National Bureau of Economic Research,* Princeton University Press, Princeton, 1961, pp. 343–367; and Kendrick, *Postwar Productivity Trends in the United States, 1948–1969,* National Bureau of Economic Research, General Series 98, Columbia University Press, New York, 1973.

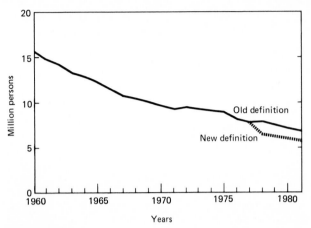

FIGURE 12-1
Farm population of the United States. *(Source: USDA*, 1982 Handbook of Agricultural Charts, *p. 21.)*

Distributional Effects of Human Capital Investment

Individuals are of course not equally endowed with human capital, or with the unique abilities of management and skill to take advantage of the new technologies, and some will be more disadvantaged than others. If their opportunity costs of staying in farming were to exceed their real incomes in farming, then they should be expected to migrate out of farming. But as people grow older, their opportunity costs of staying

FIGURE 12-2
Persons employed on farms in the United States. *(Source: USDA*, 1981 Handbook of Agricultural Charts, *p. 22.)*

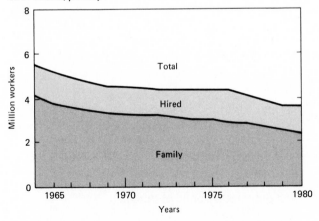

Average number of persons employed in 1 survey week each month
through 1974, the last full calendar week ending at least 1 day before the
end of the month; beginning with 1975, estimates are quarterly and
include the week of the 12th of January, April, July, and October.

The future-farmer organization plays an important role in developing leadership for public policy making in the future. How much public support should be given to this work?

in a given occupation generally fall, and this appears to be especially true in farming. Consequently, the farm population does not decline primarily by the migration of older workers out of farming, but by reductions in the number of young people beginning to farm and by retirement of older farm workers and farm families.

The beginning farmers who are successful generally have made substantial investments in their own human capital in the form of education and training, and they often have additional help from family, relatives, or friends. Some also will take advantage of more educational benefits after entering farming, thus increasing their skills more than others. As they become more efficient and productive, those who have not increased their human and other forms of capital tend to lose relatively, and the skewness in farm income is increased. This skewness in income distribution has led to a number of criticisms of the developmental process in agriculture, and these criticisms can be evaluated for policy analysis, primarily in terms of human capital. Let us consider some of these criticisms.

Criticisms of the Developmental Process in Terms of Human Capital and Farm Income

Since investment in human capital is not equally distributed among individuals, and the farm population declines primarily by reduced entry and retirement, rather than by increased outward migration, there tends to be, as in any developmental situation, a number of individuals and families who are left behind, or disadvantaged. In a highly developed country such as the United States, the numbers in this category are small because the farm population is relatively small, but their income problems may be acute. This sometimes leads to a general criticism of the developmental process, and particularly the educational programs that provide the foundation for it. Jim Hightower, for instance, in the book entitled *Hard Tomatoes, Hard Times*, has appraised the agricultural developmental process in the United States as a failure of the land-grant colleges, and the institutions affiliated with them.[2] His judgment implies a failure to provide social gains in terms of income, or equity in distribution of income, and failures to provide gains in the welfare of the farm and rural populations in spite of their increases in productivity.

This is a general phenomenon, however, of the developmental process in agriculture, in both developed and developing countries. Irma Adelman and Cynthia Taft Morris, in *Economic Growth and Social Equity in Developing Countries,* developed the hypothesis that success in economic growth in developing countries has tended to make the poor poorer and the rich richer in agriculture, paralleling the effects in the economy at large.[3] Bruce F. Johnston and Peter Kilby, in a study of *Agriculture and Structural Transformation,* present the value judgment that agricultural policies for developing countries that emphasize growth must give more attention to income distribution.[4] Although there is a large backlog of modern technology on which these countries can draw, which gives them an advantage in achieving farm productivity advances, there are immense problems of income distribution to be overcome. Generally, the relative size of the farm population is large, and this limits the rate at which labor can be transferred from farming to other sectors. Also, there is generally a relatively large number of small farms for which much of the modern technology is not well suited. Innovations are required that can be used efficiently by small-scale units, so as to complement rather than displace the given country's relatively abundant sources of labor.

A policy that fails to make advances in social equity is more easily criticized than corrected. Developmental programs of the United States Agency for International Development (AID), many of the private foundations and churches, the United Nations Food and Agriculture Organization (FAO), and the World Bank have tried and are continuing to try to move in this direction. But progress comes hard and programs are open to criticism. For instance, Joseph Collins, Frances Moore Lappe, and David Kinley have viewed the operations of the World Bank as creating poverty in developing countries by financing developmental projects, aiding large farms, and failing to provide equivalent help—or any help at all—to the poorer peasants and

---

[2]Jim Hightower, *Hard Tomatoes, Hard Times, The Failure of the Land Grant College Complex,* Preliminary Report of the Task Force of the Land Grant College Complex, 1972, Agribusiness Accountability Project, Washington, D.C.

[3]Irma Adelman and Cynthia Taft Morris, *Economic Growth and Social Equity in Developing Countries,* Stanford University Press, Stanford, California, 1973.

[4]Bruce F. Johnston and Peter Kilby, *Agriculture and Structural Transformation: Economic Strategies in Late-Developing Countries,* Oxford University Press, New York, 1975.

landless laborers.[5] The problem is that the marginal rates of return to investment in developmental capital, whether it be in human or other forms of capital, will tend to be higher if the effects on income distribution can be ignored, or relegated to a secondary position, in deference to that of increasing productivity.

This is the dilemma in designing policy for public investments in human capital. It may be quite correct to say that most developmental programs have not had the desired income-distributional effects. But opportunities have been greatly broadened in most countries as a result of public support for human capital investments. This is especially so in the United States and most other developed countries. But it is important to recognize that improvements have come from two related types of economic adjustment. One is the improvement of the human agent through human capital investment. The other is adjustment of human capital, toward equalization of marginal rates of return, both within agriculture and between agriculture and the rest of the economy. Both of these types of adjustment must be understood in a policy analysis of human resource input markets.

In order to increase our understanding of the process of adjustment, let us turn next to a review of the way in which educational investment has influenced both the development of human capital resources and the adjustment of these resources within agriculture and between agriculture and the rest of society.

EDUCATIONAL POLICY IN HUMAN RESOURCE INPUT MARKETS

Two general values or policy goals have tended to guide investments in education relating to the application of human capital theory to agriculture. One is an extension of the principle, inherent in public education in elementary and secondary schools in the United States, that every child shall have free opportunity for as complete an education as the child's tastes and abilities may warrant. This principle is historic, with its roots in the colonial period in America. The second is that science shall be used to increase the efficiency and progress of industry and agriculture. This is of more recent vintage.

Concepts of Industrial Education Applied to Agriculture

In the early 1800s, an idea began to evolve that education should shift from its traditional literary foundation and become more practical as an aid to commerce and industry by stimulating economic development and growth. The French philosopher, Alexis de Tocqueville, after extensive travels in the United States in the early 1800s, may have expressed this idea the best. "It is evident," he wrote, "that, in democratic communities the interests of individuals, as well as the security of the commonwealth demands that the education of the greater number should be scientific, commercial, and industrial, rather than literary."[6] Others followed this theme. The idea

---

[5]Joseph Collins, Frances Moore Lappe, and David Kinley, "The poverty brokers, The trickle down theory at work in The World Bank," *The Progressive,* December 1980, pp. 40–44.

[6]Alexis de Tocqueville, *Democracy in America,* as quoted by Earle D. Ross, *Democracy's College, The Land-Grant Movement in the Formative Stage,* Iowa State College Press, Ames, 1942, p. 11.

grew and was taken up by some of the active rural societies organized largely to promote agriculture, of which there were an estimated 1,000 by 1858.[7] These societies published magazines, newspapers, journals, almanacs, and books. They promoted fairs, meetings, socials, debates, and various other activities.

In 1851, Jonathan Baldwin Turner, a teacher of rhetoric, Greek, and Latin at Illinois College in Jacksonville, took up the idea and proposed a plan to establish "a University for the Industrial Classes in each of the States. . . ."[8] Turner spoke at great length on this idea to almost any one or group that would listen. In 1852, in a letter published in *The Prairie Farmer,* Turner proposed that if "farmers and their friends" will "exert themselves they can speedily secure for this State, and for each State in the Union, an appropriation of public land adequate to create and endow in the most liberal manner, a general system of popular Industrial Education, more glorious in its design and more beneficent in its results than the world has ever seen before."[9] Such ideas gained influential political support in Illinois; in 1853 the Illinois legislature sent to Congress a set of resolutions declaring that a system of industrial universities, liberally endowed in each state, would develop the people and "tend to intellectualize the rising generation."[10] But it took nine years for Congress to act.

Evolution of Land-Grant Colleges in Agricultural Education and Research[11]

In 1862, Congress passed the Morrill Act, named after Justine Smith Morrill, of Vermont, who introduced the act, which was the founding legislation for the national system of land-grant colleges and universities. The act appropriated 30,000 acres of land for each senator and representative in Congress, based on the census of 1860, and charged each state or territory with the establishment of a college or university according to the principles embodied in the legislation. Teaching of science should be the leading idea and opportunity should be broadly available to the sons and daughters of people in all walks of life. But development came slowly. The grant of land proved to be inadequate as a basis for support. State legislatures were slow to appropriate more money. Farm and rural people generally did not give the idea strong political support, and a full quarter century elapsed before Congress passed another historic act.

In 1887, William Hatch of Missouri introduced a bill to establish an agricultural experiment station in each state in connection with a land-grant college or university. The stations were "to aid in acquiring and diffusing among the people of the United

---

[7]Herman E. Kroos, *American Economic Development,* Prentice-Hall, Englewood Cliffs, N.J., 2d ed., 1968, p. 109.

[8]Mary Turner Carriel, *The Life of Jonathan Baldwin Turner,* as quoted by Richard Gordon Moores, *Fields of Rich Toil, The Development of the University of Illinois College of Agriculture,* University of Illinois Press, Urbana, 1970, p. 5.

[9]*Prairie Farmer,* March 1852, p. 114, as quoted by Moores, ibid., p. 6.

[10]Allen Nivens, *The State Universities and Democracy,* The University of Illinois Press, Urbana, 1962, pp. 15 and 16.

[11]For a summary of laws quoted in this section, see *United States Code, Annotated, Title 7, Agriculture,* chaps. 13 and 14, sections 301–390k. For further discussion, see also Harold G. Halcrow, *Food Policy for America,* McGraw-Hill Book Company, New York, 1977, pp. 451–473.

States useful and practical information on subjects connected with agriculture, and to promote scientific investigation and experiment respecting the principles and applications of agricultural science." In 1890, the Second Morrill Act expanded support for the land-grant colleges. Although it prohibited payment of federal funds to any state or territory "where a distinction of race or color is made in the admission of students," it was determined that compliance could be established by providing separate colleges for white and black students. This led to a dual system in most of the southern states, a situation that prevailed until the Supreme Court ruled in 1954 that such a system was unconstitutional.

The Adams Act of 1906 attempted to lead the experiment stations (there were already 52 at that time) into more fundamental or original scientific research by providing that the funds were "to be applied only to paying the necessary expenses of conducting original researches or experiments bearing directly on the agricultural industry of the United States. . . ." Finally, some 27 years after passage of the Hatch Act and 52 years after the first Morrill Act, Congress passed the Smith-Lever Act in 1914, which authorized federal funds to initiate "agricultural extension work . . . in order to aid in diffusing among the people of the United States useful and practical information on subjects relating to agriculture and home economics, and to encourage the application of the same . . . in such manner as may be mutually agreed upon by the Secretary of Agriculture and the State agricultural college or colleges receiving the benefits of the Act."

The Purnell Act of 1925 authorized more complete endowment of the agricultural experiment stations, and stated, "funds . . . shall be applied to . . . such economic and sociological investigations as have for their purpose the development and improvement of the rural home and rural life. . . ." In 1935, the Bankhead-Jones Act (subsequently amended June 1952 and July 14, 1960) provided additional funds for basic research into the laws and principles relating to agriculture, for further development of cooperative extension work, and for more complete endowment and support of the land-grant colleges.

The Agricultural Marketing Act of 1946 provided for extending research in conjunction with the experiment stations and cooperative extension services on a state matching-fund basis, to provide for "an integrated administration of all laws so that marketing is improved, costs reduced, dietary and nutritional standards improved, and wider markets developed resulting in the full production of American farms being disposed of usefully, economically, profitably, and in an orderly manner."

In 1955, Congress consolidated all the previous laws as an amendment to the Hatch Act,[12] declaring its policy "to continue the agricultural research at the State agricultural experiment stations . . . to promote the efficient production, marketing, distribution, and utilization of products of the farm as essential to the health and welfare of our peoples and to promote a sound and prosperous agriculture and rural life as indispensable to the maintenance of maximum employment and national prosperity and security . . . to assure agriculture a position in research equal to that of industry, which will aid in maintaining an equitable balance between agriculture and

---

[12]*Public Law 352*, 84th Congress, 1st Session, Chapter 790, 1955.

A spectrophotometer is an instrument for comparing the color intensities of different spectra, such as the separate elements in a given food. Learning to operate the instrument is a step in scientific analysis of foods.

other segments of our economy. It shall be the object and duty of the State agricultural experiment stations . . . to conduct original and other researches . . . , including researches basic to the problems of agriculture in its broadest aspects . . ., the development and improvement of the rural home and rural life and the maximum contribution of agriculture to the welfare of the consumer, as may be deemed advisable, having due regard to the varying conditions and needs of the respective states." The 1946 act had required that not less than 20 percent of the research money appropriated to each state be used for marketing. In amendments submitted to Congress by the secretary of agriculture in 1955, it was recommended that the percentage be reduced. But the House Committee on Agriculture reinserted the requirement stating, "the committee believes that the present agricultural situation, with surpluses plaguing the producers of many commodities, is a clear indication of the need for continued emphasis in marketing of agricultural products and the research connected therewith."[13] Since then, with regularity in passing new agricultural acts, extensive hearings have been held, and appropriations authorized to carry on education and research within such policy guidelines. But, in the 1970s and 1980s especially, the federal appropriations have tended to decline in real terms and fall short of the policy goals of most agricultural groups.

[13]*U.S. Code Congressional and Administrative News*, 84th Congress, 1st Session, House Report No. 1298, p. 2977.

Consumer education programs are an important part of public policy designed to improve the efficiency of agricultural marketing and food consumption.

An Appraisal of Policy Based on the Land-Grant College Idea

A discussion of this policy, with emphasis on broadly based industrial education, vocational training, scientific research, and cooperative extension, has described it as a unique system, in which "the essential features of method, of curriculum, of organization, of purpose ... can be identified as American, distinct from those of any other people."[14] The two main features, one emphasizing science and industrial education, and the other extending the opportunity to far greater numbers of students, are strongly developmental on the one hand, and egalitarian on the other, at least as compared with the elitist concepts of traditional higher education. Far greater opportunities have been extended to many more young people, with greater effects on productivity, than even Turner might have imagined.

Yet such a glowing appraisal must be tempered considerably when applied to the

[14]Paul Monroe, "Historic Foundations of American Education," *Essays in Comparative Education,* as quoted by Earle D. Ross, *Democracy's College, The Land-Grant Movement in the Formative Stage,* Iowa State College Press, Ames, 1942, p. 1.

income situation, including the level and distribution of income, in the farm sector. Usually, the average net farm income per capita is only 75 to 80 percent of the average nonfarm income. Typically, the distribution of farm income is more skewed than that in most other industries, and there is a relatively larger number of farm families below the federally defined poverty level. Although the number of families in this category has tended to decline over the long term, as the farm population itself has declined, the numbers are still large as compared with generally accepted policy goals and values. In addition, the hired farm labor force, which is equivalent to almost one-third of the 3.8 million workers employed on farms, contains some 400,000 or more migrant workers, whose earnings and living conditions are among the poorest of any major working group in America.

The decline in the farm population, as shown in Figure 12-1, and the decline in the number of persons employed on farms (Figure 12-2), suggests that advanced technology has been substituted for farm workers, or that there has been a decline in the demand for labor in farming. Also, this suggests that the projected levels of real income in farming, as compared with opportunity costs, are attractive to a declining number of young people. Hence, the farm population continues to decline, mainly as a result of reduced entry, and only secondarily by retirement and migration out of the industry.

The size of the farm population will stabilize in a few years, but important questions for policy remain. What policy in the human resource input markets will best serve the income and welfare goals, and the concerns that people have about the level and distribution of income?

POLICY ALTERNATIVES IN THE HUMAN RESOURCE INPUT MARKETS

According to the generally accepted policy goals, a higher level of farm income, more stable income, and less skewness in income are desired. Let us consider some of the policy alternatives for meeting such goals, with some emphasis on the theoretical concepts.

Equilibrium in the Farm Labor Market

The farm labor market is assumed to conform to the general concept that, in any industry or occupation, the demand curve for labor is downward-sloping and the supply curve is upward-sloping. There is an equilibrium price for labor where the demand and supply curves intersect; this is determined in any competitive market in a manner similar to the way the prices of other goods and services are determined. The demand for labor is derived from the demand for the products to which the labor contributes. If the demand for these products increases (decreases), the demand for labor will increase (decrease), ceteris paribus. The supply of labor depends on its opportunity cost. If its opportunity cost increases (decreases), the supply decreases (increases), ceteris paribus. The general concepts are illustrated in Figure 12-3.

Over the years it appears that the demand for farm labor has decreased as tech-

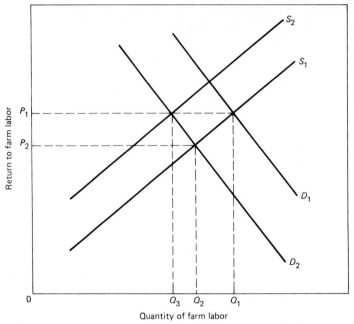

FIGURE 12-3

Given the supply and demand for farm labor, S_1 and D_1, the equilibrium return to labor is P_1 and the equilibrium quantity of labor is Q_1. If the demand for labor falls to D_2, then the equilibrium return will fall to P_2 and the equilibrium quantity of labor will be Q_2.

If farm programs are used to maintain the return to farm labor at P_1 and the supply of labor does not change, then a surplus of farm labor will emerge equal to $Q_1 - Q_3$. The supply of labor must decline from S_1 to S_2 for equilibrium to be maintained at P_1, which may occur as a result of reduced entry, retirement, or outward migration, related to opportunity cost.

nological advance, primarily in the agribusiness input industries, has increased the marginal physical product (MPP) and, correspondingly, the marginal revenue product (MRP) from the agribusiness inputs, relative to the MRP of farm labor. So, we assume that the farm labor demand curve has tended to shift downward and to the left. Then, with a given supply curve, or a constant opportunity cost, the rate of return to farm labor has tended to fall relative to most of the agribusiness inputs, and, in some cases, relative to land.

Policy Alternatives for Raising Farm Income

It may be assumed that the demand for farm labor can increase as a result of human capital investment in farm management or labor skills, the results of which may be conceived as an increase in marginal revenue product (MRP) from a given quantity (hours) of labor. But if the supply of labor is very elastic, which will be the case if there is surplus labor *not* transferable to nonfarm occupations, then increases in farm labor productivity as a result of human capital investment will not increase the return

to labor, as increases in demand are met at a constant supply price (constant opportunity cost) for labor. If the skills *are* transferable to nonfarm occupations, then this
will increase labor's opportunity cost. The supply curve will not be perfectly elastic,
and increases in demand for farm labor will be met at a rising supply price. Hence,
it is the increase in opportunity cost that increases the return to labor, when human
capital investment increases productivity.

   If farm programs are used to control the output of agriculture, with the policy
goal of increasing the return to farm labor, they will be unsuccessful in doing so over
the long term when the labor supply is assumed to be elastic. This may be visualized
as in Figure 12-4, where the supply curve for labor S_1 is drawn as perfectly elastic.
However, in the short term, when the supply of labor S_2 is assumed to be less elastic,
an increase in demand arising out of human capital investment will increase the
return to labor.

   An inference which may be drawn from Figure 12-4 is that human capital investment as well as support prices above competitive market levels can increase the
return to farm labor in the short run when the supply of labor is somewhat inelastic,
but not in the long run when supply is elastic. Moreover, if the control of output is
achieved through restricting the supply of land, then in the short run the return to

FIGURE 12-4
When the long-term supply of farm labor S_1 is assumed to be perfectly elastic, an increase in
demand for labor, from D_1 to D_2, results in a constant price at P_1. However, in the short run,
when the supply S_2 is less elastic, an increase in demand for labor, from D_1 to D_2, results in an
increase in supply price from P_1 to P_2 and an increase in the quantity of labor from Q_1 to Q_3.

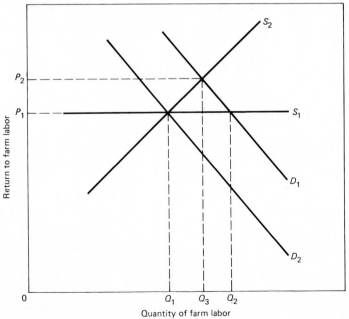

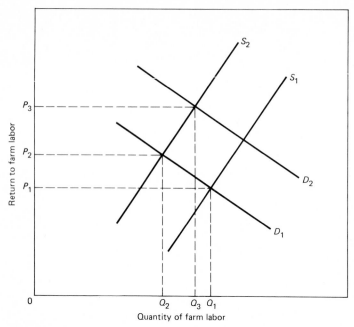

FIGURE 12-5
The effects of shift in supply and demand or returns to farm labor.

land owners will result in windfall gains to them, as a result of the inelastic supply of land. In the longer term, when the labor supply curve becomes increasingly elastic, the initial gains to labor will be dissipated, and no benefit to labor will be retained.

The return to labor can be increased in the short run by restricting the labor supply through increasing labor's opportunity cost, as illustrated in Figure 12-5, when the supply curve shifts from S_1 to S_2. These labor gains may also be retained in the long run, in which case it may be assumed that the supply curve is perfectly elastic at P_2. In addition, if the demand for labor increases from D_1 to D_2, then the return of labor will rise still more to P_3, as the quantity settles at Q_3. An example of this occurred during World War II, when greatly increased demands from war-production industries and the military were reflected in higher farm wages and real farm incomes.

Important Inferences for Policy

Two important inferences for policy may be drawn from this discussion. First, the general level of farm income over a long term of several years will be determined primarily by its opportunity cost. Investments in human capital that improve the opportunities for people in the nonfarm economy will increase the level of return to people in farming because this will tend to decrease the supply of labor for farming. Second, the level of return to farm labor may be increased by human capital investment in the labor that is used in farming, because the investment increases the marginal revenue product from labor, and this increases the derived demand for farm labor.

The results of human capital investment are reflected in comparisons of the labor income from farming as related to years of schooling. For instance, it has been found that two additional years of schooling affect the income of people living on farms as much as does migration of people from farms to urban areas.[15] In other words, improved schooling in rural areas increases the labor income in farming because it increases productivity in farming, although the general level of return to labor in farming will still depend on the opportunity cost of farming. One may conclude that, over several years, investments in education are necessary for solving the farm income problem; and, if carried far enough, with rising employment levels outside of agriculture, such investments can be sufficient.

The Problem of Skewness in Farm Income Distribution

It has been suggested in a number of policy studies that more of the educational and research resources should be programmed to aid the small farm and the low-income groups in the farm sector. Based on a value judgment that the poor should be helped more than they have been, some specifically targeted help for low-income farm families may be socially justified. But it seems unlikely that such efforts can reverse the tide of increasing concentration in the farm sector. The marginal return from a given research and educational effort is generally highly correlated with the level of existing skills and the scale of the farming operation. The progressive well-to-do farm family, in other words, enjoys a higher marginal return from a given effort than does a low-income small-scale farmer. Consequently, if society imposes the value judgment that the low-income family farmer should receive additional educational and research help, it should be understood that a smaller increase in total productivity may be realized than if this help had not been so directed. Nevertheless, such a direction of effort may be justified based on welfare value judgments or social criteria.

The corresponding recommendation that is frequently made, that the poor should receive more aid in getting out of farming, may also be based on a welfare value judgment. But, because low-level managers in farming are not necessarily more underpaid than the high-level managers, programs especially geared for low-level managers to discontinue farming do not necessarily add to the national welfare. Studies of those who have moved out of agriculture reveal that there is a strong positive correlation between their former earnings in agriculture and their subsequent nonfarm earnings.[16] That is, merely moving people from one occupation to another may not solve their problems, unless economically productive investments

---

[15]Finis Welch, "Measurement of the Quality of Schooling," *American Economic Review,* vol. 56, no. 2, May 1966, p. 384.

[16]Dale E. Hathaway and Brian E. Perkins, "Occupational Mobility and Migration from Agriculture," in *Rural Poverty in the United States,* National Advisory Commission on Rural Poverty, Washington, D.C., 1968, p. 207.

are made in the people. Hence, the inference for policy returns to the concept of human capital investment, and its contribution to productivity. Within this concept, the migrant workers in the farm sector present a unique problem for policy analysis. Let us consider this problem.

Migrant Workers in the Hired Farm Work Force

Wages of hired farm workers are generally determined by the interaction of supply and demand. Agriculture was not covered under the first federal minimum-wage law, which was passed in 1938, and since then the efforts to achieve minimum-wage standards to cover farming have always failed in Congress. Except in California and Hawaii, attempts to organize farm workers in labor unions have generally failed, with the result that the hired farm labor force is largely unorganized. The California Agricultural Labor Relations Act of 1975 established an Agricultural Labor Relations Board and extended the privileges and protection of organization to agricultural employees, as generally extended to other workers under the National Labor Relations Act. In Hawaii, the International Longshoremen's and Warehousemen's Union has obtained for sugar workers some of the highest agricultural wages in the world, plus other privileges. But for most of the rest of the states, hired farm workers remain unorganized, and wages are generally low, especially for unskilled field workers. This contributes to the advantages of some large-scale farms over smaller family farms.

The wages of farm labor are probably depressed by minimum-wage standards and successful union bargaining in other industries, because these tend to limit nonfarm employment, and thus increase the supply of labor available for farm employment. There is no doubt that the notoriously low wages of unorganized migrant farm laborers might be improved by unionization, but this would also reduce the number of jobs available on farms. Higher wage rates would tend to encourage more automation. One question is: Would the gains to those who were covered by the union be worth the loss of jobs by those who were thrown out of work?

The policy question for unionization is similar to that faced in the past decades in housing for migrant farm workers. Beginning in the 1960s, a number of television documentaries vividly portrayed the substandard, sometimes squalid living conditions of migrant farm workers. Many of them, who out of necessity lived where they worked, often endured the poorest of housing conditions. Congress responded by holding a large number of hearings, and finally passed legislation to impose higher and stricter housing standards on employers who hire migrants for farm work.[17]

Enforcement of the legislation would have the effect of reducing the employers' demand at a given wage rate, and this would lead to both lower hourly wages and fewer employment opportunities for the migrant workers. Many workers have benefited from the higher housing standards, while some others, who lost their jobs when the higher standards were imposed, may have been made worse off. The reason for this is illustrated in Figure 12-6.

---

[17]For a review of the hearings and further discussion, see Harold G. Halcrow, *Food Policy for America,* McGraw-Hill Book Company, New York, 1977, pp. 473–488.

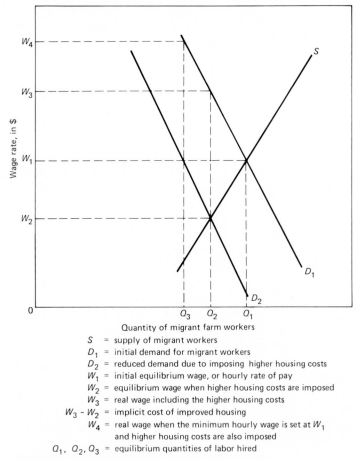

FIGURE 12-6
How higher housing costs reduce the demand for migrant farm workers.

In Figure 12-6, the equilibrium wage for migrant farm workers is W_1 with the supply of S and demand of D_1. Under these conditions, Q_1 workers would be hired. When higher housing standards or costs are imposed, the demand for migrant workers falls vertically by the amount of the implicit cost of the improved housing. The equilibrium hourly wage falls to W_2 and the quantity or number of workers hired falls to Q_2. But the real wages of the workers who keep their jobs rises to W_3, which consists of W_2 received as the hourly wage, and $W_3 - W_2$ as the added value of the improved housing. The policy tradeoff involves gains for some workers and loss of jobs for others. The reduced production implied by there being fewer workers will also be reflected in higher prices in the product market, depending on the elasticity of demand for the product.

If the government attempts to maintain the original hourly wage rate by imposing a minimum wage at W_1, then the quantity of migrant workers employed will fall to Q_3, but their real wage will rise to W_4. Hence, imposing both higher housing standards and a minimum wage would be of further benefit to workers who retained their jobs, but cause still more workers to lose their jobs.

In 1970, when higher housing standards were imposed by the federal government, it was anticipated that there would be a shift from migrant workers to machines by the farmers who had employed migrant workers.[18] But, if we are to judge from the picture presented in Figure 12-2, the apparent switch induced by imposing higher housing standards is modest indeed, if not insignificant, even in the farm labor market, and certainly not of significance in the aggregate national labor market. The added costs are being absorbed by the employers, with perhaps little if any effect on the aggregate national farm output.

One cannot judge from this, however, what would be the effect of unionizing the hired farm labor force, or of imposing a significantly higher minimum hourly wage for migrant workers. The incentives for farm owners to switch to more automation might become much stronger. The effect on aggregate national farm output would tend to be very small in percentage terms, which is to suggest that most of the added cost would be absorbed by employers.

The policy problem in the market for migrant farm labor is an important one because the employers generally sell their products in markets that are purely competitive. A compassionate employer who incurs higher costs as a result of providing more adequate housing and a significantly higher hourly wage for the workers is at a competitive disadvantage. Unless the workers respond by working harder, which they may or may not be able to do, such an employer may be forced to make other cost-saving adjustments. Hence, improvement of the conditions of migrant farm workers requires some type of public action. The California law may be effective in providing this because California dominates the market for many of the products of migrant workers. But other states may not be so successful in coping with the problem individually; therefore, federal legislation is required to cope with the situation. To reach a solution that is optimum for society will require a careful evaluation of the tradeoffs that have been discussed.

SUMMARY

Human capital investment has greatly accelerated the development and growth of agriculture, with output per unit of labor rising rapidly and consistently over several decades. But investment in human capital has expanded the supply of labor in agriculture, while the demand for labor has tended to fall, especially in the farm sector. Hence, there has been a great increase in output per unit of labor employed on farms, while income from farming has tended to be depressed, and more skewed than in most other occupations.

---

[18]See "Housing Dispute Spurs Migrant Farmers to Switch to Machines from Migrant Help," *Wall Street Journal,* June 29, 1970, p. 18. See also Milton Friedman, "Migrant Workers," *Newsweek,* July 27, 1970, p. 60.

Policy analysis, based primarily on supply and demand, has been used to account for the income situation in agriculture, especially in the farm sector. Technological advance does not necessarily result in higher incomes for farm people, nor do higher prices for farm products necessarily have this result. Over several years' time the opportunity cost of farming will be most important in determining the levels of farm income. More education and investment in human capital will increase the opportunity cost, providing there are attractive employment opportunities in the nonfarm economy. The income problem of migrant farm workers has some unique features, and an optimum social solution will require careful appraisal of the possible tradeoffs in national policy.

IMPORTANT TERMS AND CONCEPTS

Human resources viewed as a form of capital

Supply function for human capital

Derived demand for human capital

Human capital investment as a means for increasing supply

Opportunity cost of human capital as related to supply

Process of development and growth related to human capital

Effects of technological advance on the marginal rate of return to human capital

Distributional effects of human capital investment

Criticism of the developmental process in terms of human capital and farm income

Alternatives in structural transformation of agriculture

Concepts of industrial education applied to agriculture

Effects of industrial education on level and distribution of farm income

Concept of equilibrium in the farm labor market

Policy alternatives for raising farm income

The problem of skewness in farm income distribution

Migrant workers as a special problem in human resource input markets

QUESTIONS AND EXERCISES

1 Human resources may be visualized as a unique form of capital. Given this proposition, on what does the demand for human capital depend? On what does the supply depend?

2 What are the two conditions necessary for economic progress in agriculture? How can these two conditions be created?

3 What has been the trend in the number of persons employed on farms in the United States? Is this trend due to a decrease in demand, or a decrease in supply, or both? Explain.

4 How has the developmental process in agriculture tended to affect the distribution of income among farm families? Why has it had this effect? What might be done to change the distribution according to the generally accepted welfare standards? State your assumptions concerning these standards.

5 How has the general concept of industrial education been applied to agriculture? What are the general results in terms of human capital productivity? Income distribution?

6 What are the policy alternatives for raising farm income per capita? What is the role of opportunity cost in determining the level of per capita income? Will increasing the productivity of labor tend to affect its demand, its supply, or both?

7 In general economic terms, explain why there is a continuing skewness in farm income distribution. What is required to decrease the skewness? On what grounds could such a policy be supported? On what grounds could it be criticized?

8 Why are migrant farm workers generally low-paid? In terms of supply and demand, what might be done to raise their incomes? Who might support such a policy? Who might oppose it? Why?

RECOMMENDED READINGS

Adelman, Irma, and Cynthia Taft Morris, *Economic Growth and Social Equity in Developing Countries,* Stanford University Press, Stanford, California, 1973.

Collins, Joseph, Frances Moore Lappe, and David Kinley, "The poverty brokers, The trickle down theory at work in The World Bank," *The Progressive,* December 1980, pp. 40–44.

Hathaway, Dale E., and Brian E. Perkins, "Occupational Mobility and Migration from Agriculture," in *Rural Poverty in the United States,* National Advisory Commission on Rural Poverty, Washington, D.C., 1968, p. 207.

Hightower, Jim, *Hard Tomatoes, Hard Times, The Failure of the Land Grant College Complex,* Preliminary Report of the Task Force of the Land Grant College Complex, 1972, Agribusiness Accountability Project, Washington, D.C.

Johnston, Bruce F., and Peter Kilby, *Agriculture and Structural Transformation: Economic Strategies in Late-Developing Countries,* Oxford University Press, New York, 1975.

Schultz, Theodore W., *Distortions of Agricultural Incentives,* Indiana University Press, Bloomington, 1978.

Schultz, Theodore W., *Economic Growth and Agriculture,* McGraw-Hill Book Company, New York, 1968.

GLOSSARY OF SELECTED TERMS

acreage limitation program   New in the Agriculture and Food Act of 1981, this program (when in effect) requires participants, who may voluntarily comply, to limit the acreage of a crop to a specified portion of their base acreage, and to divert the remainder of the base to a generally nonproductive soil-conserving use.

agribusiness   Agribusiness includes firms and economic enterprises organized to produce and sell services and supplies to farmers for use in farm production and living; it includes firms and industries that buy farm products and process and distribute them through wholesale and retail markets. The first are called *farm service supply industries* and the second *agricultural processing marketing industries.*

agricultural adjustment   A term generally referring to programs designed to regulate or control agricultural production and marketing. The general policy goals of such programs may include: raising and stabilizing prices for farm products; maintaining reserve stocks of grains and other commodities; supplementing incomes of farm families; supplementing exports of agricultural products; contributing to soil conservation; and standardizing quality and grades of farm food products. The Agricultural Adjustment Act of 1933 created the Agricultural Adjustment Administration (AAA) in the Department of Agriculture. Since then adjustment programs have been implemented through similar agencies under various names, such as the Agricultural Stabilization and Conservation Service (see below).

agricultural, or farmers' cooperatives   Agricultural cooperatives—or farmers' cooperatives, as they may be called—are either a federated or a centralized type of organization, although a few cooperatives are a mixture of both. Under a federated organization individual cooperatives join together to create a business superstructure for purposes of more coordinated and efficient operation. The individual cooperatives own and control the federated superstructure rather than vice versa. Members elect the board of directors of the federated cooperatives through the local organizations. Under a centralized organization,

293

the parent cooperative owns or controls various satellite or local cooperatives. Members vote directly for the board of directors, which controls the total organization.

Agricultural Stabilization and Conservation Service (ASCS)   An agency of the United States Department of Agriculture (USDA), it administers farm programs through county ASCS offices.

allocation factor   When applied, it is proclaimed by the secretary of agriculture to be the ratio of national program acreage divided by expected actual planted acreage in the nation. In the 1981 act, it was not less than 80 percent, or more than 100 percent. The factor for an individual farm is equal to the national allocation factor unless that farm reduces its planted acreage by the recommended reduction, below its base acreage, or participates in an acreage limitation program.

authorized acreage   When used in the acreage limitation program, it is the maximum acreage that may be planted with a crop in order to comply with the program. It is always less than the base acreage.

base acreage   The acreage of a crop on the farm used in acreage limitation programs, and to calculate farm program acreage. It is usually the actual planted acreage of the crop on the farm in the previous year, although the previous two-year average could be used. It may be adjusted for disasters, crop rotations, and other factors as necessary to make it fair and equitable.

buffer stocks   Quantities of a product that are stored in order to moderate extreme price fluctuations by assuring a more stable and more adequate supply.

call price   The price level at which farmers with grain in the farmer-owned reserve must repay the nonrecourse loan plus any accumulated interest. Under the 1981 act, the secretary was required to notify the President and Congress 14 days in advance of issuing a call. For wheat the call was automatic when price reached 175 percent of support price. For corn the call price was to be set at "an appropriate level."

capital gains   The difference between the acquisition price and a higher current market value of a capital item such as real estate and equipment. Capital gains may be realized by actual sale, or be an unrealized computation by assuming the capital items were sold at current market value.

cash flow   The total funds generated internally by a firm for covering costs and investment. Farming presents unique cash flow problems when income is generated only at the end of a production cycle; for example, with annual crops and with livestock, where crop failures occur, or if input prices rise faster than product prices.

coefficient of variation   Changes in a variable relative to the average value of the same variable. It permits a valid comparison of the variation in a variable measured in different units, or between variables with different numerical values; for example, variation in the price of corn (in dollars per bushel) versus variation in corn production (in billions of bushels).

Commodity Credit Corporation (CCC)   A quasi-public corporation authorized to borrow funds from the treasury and receive funding to operate the commodity programs.

comparative (absolute) advantages   The condition in which a state or country produces and exports those goods and services which it can produce *relatively* cheaply and imports those which other countries can produce *relatively* cheaply. Absolute advantage implies a country produces goods and services more cheaply than any other country.

Whether or not one of two states is absolutely more efficient in the production of every product than the other, if each specializes in the products in which it has the greatest relative efficiency, trade will be mutually beneficial to both states.

conservation use   An approved use of diverted land that protects it from weeds and from wind and water erosion. If the secretary permits, the land may be used for grazing or for production of certain crops. Under certain circumstances specified by the secretary, the land may be used for wildlife food plots or wildlife habitats and the owner receive a payment.

deficiency payment   Direct government payment to producers when the average price received by farmers falls below the target price. For eligible producers the payment is determined by formula:

$$\frac{\text{deficiency}}{\text{payment}} = \frac{\text{farm program}}{\text{acreage}} \times \frac{\text{farm program}}{\text{payment yield}} \times \frac{\text{payment}}{\text{rate}}$$

The payment rate is usually determined by comparing the target price with the average market price, usually for the first five months of the marketing year. If this price is below the target level, then eligible producers may apply to the ASCS for deficiency payments equal to the lesser of the differences between the target value and either the average market price or the nonrecourse price-support loan.

disaster payment   Payment made to eligible farmers when flood, drought, other natural disaster, or other condition beyond the control of the producers reduces production of a crop by preventing planting or reducing yields. Three kinds of disaster payments were provided for in the 1981 act: preventing planting, reduced yields, and economic emergency. But payments for prevented planting or reduced yield will be made only if federal crop insurance is not available for that crop.

disposable income   Earnings remaining after deductions of all necessary expenses and direct taxes on those earnings, available to be spent, invested, or saved as the receiver chooses.

diverted land   Land that is removed from production of major crops and devoted to approved conservation uses as specified by the secretary of agriculture.

economic costs   Economic costs are payments that a firm must make, or incomes it must provide, to attract and keep resources away from alternative lines of production. These payments or incomes may be either explicit or implicit.

economic emergency disaster payments   Producers of wheat, feed grains, upland cotton, and rice may be eligible for an economic emergency disaster payment if a disaster has reduced production and that loss of production results in an economic emergency. In determining eligibility and payment rates, the secretary of agriculture is directed to take account of other forms of assistance available (including federal crop insurance).

economies (diseconomies) of scale   The reduction in per-unit cost of production associated with an increase in optimal size of operation usually resulting from specialization, division of labor, and technology. Diseconomies are the increase in per-unit cost of production associated with nonoptimal growth in size resulting from inadequate management.

elements of policy   The elements of policy are generally recognized as goals, means, implements, and constraints. *Goals* are based on values and beliefs and express what people want to achieve. *Means* may be visualized as programs to achieve goals. *Implements* are the agencies and organizations used to activate and administer programs. *Constraints* are the general limits put on a policy or program.

emergency compensation   When the support price is set below specified minimum levels, the secretary of agriculture must make emergency compensation deficiency payments at a level that fully compensates producers for the effects of the low support price.

established price   Same as target price.

exogenous variable   Any economic time series that influences, but is not influenced by, a set of economic relationships being studied; a variable that is determined outside the system of equations or relationships.

externality (economic)   An economic impact of any activity by an individual or business on others which is not reflected in the market for that activity. The impact can be positive or negative. Water pollution from farmland erosion and sedimentation of streams and reservoirs can be a cost to the public but is not a part of the farmer's costs of farm production.

farm program acreage   The acreage of a crop on the farm used to calculate deficiency payments. It is equal to the current actual acreage times the allocation factor.

farm program payment yield   The yield used for a farm in calculating deficiency payments and disaster payments. For wheat and feed grains it is equal to the previous year's farm program payment yield adjusted for abnormal factors. For upland cotton and rice it is the average of actual yields on the farm for the previous three years. In no case may the farm program payment yields be less than the yields actually proven by the producer on the farm.

farmer-owned reserve   A program of extended CCC loans for wheat and feed grains. It features extended nonrecourse loans with prepayment penalties unless average prices received reach the release or the call level. Storage payments and low interest rates are authorized. When prices reach the release level, producers are encouraged to pay their interest charges (without penalty). The secretary of agriculture may call the loans in an emergency.

feed grains   Generally, feed grains refers to corn, grain sorghums, oats, barley, and rye. However, some programs may apply only to corn, grain sorghums, and oats; barley programs are optional.

forward contracting   An agreement between a buyer and seller for future delivery of a commodity specifying quantity, quality, place of delivery, price, and date. Exchange of title normally occurs at the time of delivery.

inelastic (elastic) demand as to price   A market demand in which a change in price will evoke a smaller proportional change in the quantity purchased, that is, consumers tend to consume about the same amount regardless of the change in price, with the result that fewer expenditures in the aggregate are made for a "large" production than for a "small" one, and vice versa. An elastic demand exhibits the opposite characteristics.

inelastic (elastic) supply   Supply is inelastic if the increase in production is relatively less in response to a price change. If producers are responsive to a price change by increasing production proportionally more, supply is elastic.

marketing agreements and orders   Marketing agreements and orders have the general purpose of influencing prices by regulating the timing, volume, and sometimes quality of the commodities marketed. They have been used most for milk, fruits, and vegetables. Although most orders are issued under a federal statute, state laws may also apply. In California, for example, the marketing of milk is regulated by a special state law, while the federal law permits the establishment of minimum prices for producers.

marketing orders for fluid milk   Under a milk marketing order, the quantity of grade A milk that is demanded for fluid consumption at the price set and regulated by the order is sold as Class I. Milk that is not bought for fluid use is placed in Class II or Class III for manufacturing butter, cheese, nonfat dry milk powder, and evaporated milk. The price of Class II and Class III milk is supported by the federal government through purchase of products that are not bought by manufacturers or dealers at the level of price support.

marketing orders for fruit and vegetables   Generally, an order applies to a specified production or marketing area and, in contrast to an order for fluid milk, is normally covered by a prior voluntary agreement—a contract entered into by the secretary of agriculture with the handlers of a particular commodity to regulate the marketing of that commodity. Since an agreement is binding only on those who sign it, however, an agreement alone is seldom effective and is useful mainly as a basis for promulgating an order. A marketing order is binding on all handlers of a commodity in the specified production and marketing area regardless of whether they have signed an agreement, provided the order has been approved in referendum by at least two-thirds of the producers or by those who produce at least two-thirds of the total volume of a commodity. The secretary may propose an order without a prior agreement, although, for political reasons, this generally is not done.

marketing quotas   A marketing quota sets the maximum amount of a commodity that a farmer can sell without incurring a penalty. In 1934, the first marketing quotas were authorized in the Bankhead Cotton Control Act and the Kerr-Smith Act for tobacco. The cotton act required approval by referendum by two-thirds of the producers of cotton before a program of quota allotments could go into effect. The tobacco act required agreement from three-fourths of tobacco growers. In the case of an affirmative vote, the quota was introduced by allotting to each producer certificates, which, when accompanying the crop, would exempt the crop from a sales tax that the secretary of agriculture was directed to levy.

national program acreage   The acreage that the secretary of agriculture estimates will produce the desired quantity of a crop, if average farm program yields are realized.

net social income   The gross value of production, including monetary and nonmonetary values, less all costs, including internal costs of the firm, and external monetary and nonmonetary costs.

nonrecourse price-support loan   A price-support loan set by the secretary of agriculture and made by the CCC, usually for a marketing year, to eligible farmers who put up specified storable commodities as collateral. If the product is sold during that period, the loan must be repaid with interest; otherwise, on the due date, the product is transferred to government stocks to satisfy the loan obligation. The government has "no recourse" to force repayment, only to take over the commodity held as collateral. Hence, such a loan is called a "nonrecourse" loan.

opportunity cost   The value of goods and services that must be given up, or sacrificed, to obtain an additional amount of any other good or service. The opportunity cost of a certain amount of a good or service is the value of those resources in an alternative use. Thus, there is an opportunity cost for everything, whether an explicit payment is made or the cost is implicit.

paid diversion program   A program established in specific acts authorizing or mandating the secretary of agriculture to offer voluntary contracts to farmers to divert a specified amount of land from production, thereby balancing supply with demand at a higher price level. In effect, it is in lieu of a rental payment, or a net rent or return, for the resources being held idle. Uses of the remaining land are not limited by the paid diversion programs.

parameter   An assigned constant value based on some type of statistical procedure, which can vary only when there is a structural or behavioral change in the system being studied.

parity price   The current price for a unit of farm commodity that would give it the same relative purchasing power for goods and services that it had in 1910–14, adjusted for the changes in its price over the past 10 years, compared with changes in the prices received by farmers for all farm products during that same period. Prior to January 1, 1950, the parity price for a commodity was determined by multiplying its price in the base period, usually August 1910 to July 1914, by the "parity index" of prices paid by farmers in the given month, with 1910–14 as a base.

On January 1, 1950, a new optional (modernized) method for computing parity was instituted which involved two steps, as follows:

1 Divide the average price received by farmers for a commodity in the previous 10 years by the index of prices received for all farm commodities in the same 10 years, August 1909–July 1914 = 100, the result being the "adjusted base price."

2 Multiply the adjusted base price by the index of prices paid in the given month, the result being the parity price.

Example: Average price of corn 1972–81   = \$2.38/bu
Index of all commodity prices 1972–81   = 505, or 505% of base
Index of prices paid for February 1982 = 1060, or 1,060% of base
Then: \$2.38 ÷ 505% = 47 cents
47 × 1060% = \$4.98 = parity price for a bushel of corn in February 1982

pipeline stock   Quantity of any product needed to perform the normal processing and marketing operations.

prevented planting disaster payment   Producers of wheat, feed grains, rice, and upland cotton who do not have access to federal crop insurance may be eligible for prevented planting disaster payments if a disaster prevents them from planting the intended acreage of their crop. Under the 1981 act, the amount of payment for each acre affected (up to the actual acreage in the previous year) was equal to 75 percent of the farm program payment yield times 33.3 percent of the target price.

price-support program   A program of commodity purchases of nonrecourse loans undertaken by the CCC to raise the average price received by farmers to the support price.

primary (derived) demand   Final consumer or retail demand. Derived demand is primary demand minus processing and marketing charges, and thus can be shifted as a result of changes in either; for example, the demand for corn, an important livestock input, is derived from the retail demand for meat and other livestock products.

protectionism   Usually a reaction by an industry or company to increasing foreign competition. The most common type of protectionism is expressed in policy as an import tariff or quota imposed to reduce imports and shield domestic producers.

recommended reduction   The percentage difference between the national base acreage and the national program acreage for a crop.

reduced acreage   When used in the acreage limitation program, it is the amount of land that must be diverted to conservation uses. The formula is:

$$\frac{\text{reduced}}{\text{acreage}} = \frac{\text{required}}{\text{diversion}} \times \frac{\text{actual acreage}}{\text{authorized acreage}}$$

reduced yield disaster payments   Producers of wheat, feed grains, upland cotton, and rice who do not have access to federal crop insurance may be eligible for reduced yield disaster payments if a disaster has reduced the average yield on a farm below a specified threshold. Under the 1981 act, for wheat and feed grains, the payment per planted acre was calculated as 50 percent of the target price times the deficiency between 60 percent of the farm program payment yield and the actual average yield. For upland cotton and rice, the payment per planted acre was calculated as 33.3 percent of the target price times the deficiency between 75 percent of the farm program payment yield and the actual average yield.

release price The price level at which farmers who have grain stored in the grain reserve may sell it without incurring penalties. Under the 1981 act, it was established by the secretary of agriculture within a range of 140 to 160 percent of the support price for wheat, and at a level defined by the secretary as appropriate for corn.

required diversion When used in the acreage limitation program, it is the minimum portion of a producer's base acreage that must be diverted to conserving use in order to comply with the program.

reserve call The secretary of agriculture may call (demand immediate payment of) reserve loans plus interest if an emergency requires marketing of the commodities pledged as collateral. Same as call price discussed above.

returns to equity The net income or profit of a firm expressed as a percent of its resources that are owned debt-free; that is, the excess of its assets over its liabilities.

salvage value The market price that an owner could receive for any resource already used for some time in production, if it were offered for sale. Such a value is usually less than acquisition cost due to the preference of potential buyers for new, unused resources; due to location disadvantages; or due to deterioration in the quality of the resource for the intended production.

secretary The secretary of agriculture. In practice, many of the functions attributed to the secretary are carried out by the CCC, or by ASCS and other agencies.

set-aside program An acreage reduction program that specifies that an amount of cropland on a participant's farm must be diverted (set aside) if the program crop is planted. The amount of diversion is a fixed percentage of the current year's acreage of the program crop. In a pure set-aside program, the acreage of the program crop is not specifically limited. However, both the 1977 and 1981 acts allowed an additional constraint on the acreage planted.

support price The level of prices received by farmers at which the CCC supports prices through purchase or nonrecourse loan programs. Under the 1981 act, the support price was set by the secretary of agriculture at or above a specified minimum, at a level that balanced quantities supplied and demanded; promoted exports of certain products; and adjusted inventories, taking account of changes in costs of production. For example, in 1982–85 the minimum was $3.55 per bushel for wheat, $2.55 per bushel for corn, and $0.55 per pound for cotton.

target price The price, received by farmers, that the government attempts to achieve through a combination of programs. When prices fall below the target, deficiency payments are made to eligible producers. Under the 1981 act, the secretary was to set target prices for wheat and corn, for example, at a minimum, plus optional adjustments for changes in cost of production per acre. The act established minimum target prices, as follows:

Crop	Wheat	Corn
1982	$4.05/bu	$2.70/bu
1983	4.30	2.86
1984	4.45	3.03
1985	4.65	3.18

trigger price A general term used to refer to the release and call prices.

utility An economic concept that reflects the level of satisfaction an individual derives from the consumption of a particular good or service.

vertical integration The term vertical integration has come into use to describe a situation where two or more firms at different stages of production and processing-marketing combine under a single ownership, or management. An example is a sugar cane plantation having its own sugar-processing plant, and a processing plant taking over one or more plantations. Other examples are a potato processing-marketing firm acquiring potato farms, a citrus-marketing firm merging with one or more citrus plantations, and a firm that markets fresh vegetables acquiring, or merging with, farms that produce vegetables.

Weights, Measures, and Conversion Factors

Bushel weights:
   wheat or soybeans = 60 lbs.
   corn, sorghum, or rye = 56 lbs.
   barley (grain) = 48 lbs., malt = 34 lbs.
   oats = 32 lbs.

Bushels to metric tons:
   wheat or soybeans = bushels × .027216
   barley = bushels × .021772
   corn, sorghum, rye = bushels × .025400
   oats = bushels × .014515

1 metric ton equals:
   2204.622 lbs.
   22.046 hundredweight (cwt)
   10 quintals

1,000 kilograms:
   36.7437 bushels wheat or soybeans
   39.3679 bushels corn, sorghum, or rye
   45.9296 bushels barley
   68.8944 bushels oats

Area:
   1 acre = .404694 hectares
   1 hectare = 2.4710 acres

Yields:
   wheat = bushels per acre × 0.6725 = quintals per hectare
   corn, sorghum, or rye = bushels per acre × 0.6277 = quintals per hectare
   barley = bushels per acre × 0.5380 = quintals per hectare
   oats = bushels per acre × 0.3587 = quintals per hectare

Source: United States Department of Agriculture.

BIBLIOGRAPHY OF BOOKS AND MONOGRAPHS

Abelson, Philip H. (ed.): *Food: Politics, Economics, Nutrition and Research,* American Association for the Advancement of Science, Washington, D.C., 1975.

Adams, F. G., and S. A. Klein (eds.): *Stabilizing World Commodity Markets,* Lexington Books, Lexington, Massachusetts, 1978.

Adelman, Irma, and Cynthia Taft Morris: *Economic Growth and Social Equity in Developing Countries,* Stanford University Press, Stanford, 1973.

Agency for International Development: *War on Hunger,* Washington, D.C., 1975.

Agricultural-Food Policy Review, United States Department of Agriculture, ERS-AFPR-1, January 1977; ESCS-AFPR-2, September 1978, ESCS-AFPR-3, February 1980.

Agriculture: Toward 2000, Food and Agriculture Organization of the United Nations, Rome, 1979.

American Assembly: *The Farm and the City: Rivals or Allies?,* Prentice-Hall, Englewood Cliffs, New Jersey, 1980.

An Adaptive Program for Agriculture, Committee for Economic Development, New York, 1962.

Aronowitz, Stanley: *Food, Shelter, and the American Dream,* Seabury Press, New York, 1974.

Austin, James E.: *Global Malnutrition and Cereal Fortification,* Ballinger Publishing Company, Cambridge, Massachusetts, 1979.

Baldwin, R. L. (ed.): *Animals, Feed, Food and People: An Analysis of the Role of Animals in Food Production,* Westview Press, Boulder, Colorado, 1980.

Ball, Gordon, and Earl O. Heady (eds.): *Size, Structure, and Future of Farms,* Iowa State University Press, Ames, 1972.

Batie, Sandra S., and Robert G. Healy (eds.): *The Future of American Agriculture as a Strategic Resource,* The Conservation Foundation, Washington, D.C., 1980.

Beasley, R. P.: *Erosion and Sediment Pollution Control,* The Iowa State University Press, Ames, 1971.

Becker, Gary S.: *Human Capital: A Theoretical and Empirical Analysis with Special Reference to Education,* published by National Bureau of Economic Research, New York. Distributed by Columbia University Press, New York, 1964.

Benedict, Murray R.: *Can We Solve the Farm Problem? An Analysis of Federal Aid to Agriculture,* The Twentieth Century Fund, New York, 1955.

——: *Farm Policies of the United States, 1790–1950, A Study of Their Origins and Development,* The Twentieth Century Fund, New York, 1953.

Bennett, Merrill K.: *The World's Food: A Study of the Interrelations of World Population, National Diets, and Food Potential,* Harper and Brothers, New York, 1954.

Black, John D.: *Agricultural Reform in the United States,* McGraw-Hill Book Company, New York, 1929.

—— and Maxine E. Kiefer, *Future Food and Agricultural Policy, A Program for the Next Ten Years,* McGraw-Hill Book Company, New York, 1948.

Black, Lloyd D.: *The Strategy of Foreign Aid,* D. Van Nostrand Company, Inc., Princeton, New Jersey, 1968.

Blakeslee, Le Roy: *Post World War II Government Policy Impacts on the U.S. Wheat Sector,* Washington State University College of Agriculture, Technical Bulletin no. 93, 1980.

Block, William J.: *The Separation of the Farm Bureau and the Extension Service, Political Issues in a Federal System,* The University of Illinois Press, Urbana, 1960.

Bogue, Donald J.: *Principles of Demography,* John Wiley & Sons, Inc., New York, 1969.

Bosselman, Fred P., and David Callies: *The Quiet Revolution in Land-Use Control,* U.S. Government Printing Office, Washington, D.C., 1972.

Brandow, George E.: *Interrelationships among Demand for Farm Products and Implications for Control of Market Supply,* Pennsylvania State University, Agricultural Experiment Station Bulletin no. 680, University Park, 1961.

——: "Policy for Commercial Agriculture, 1945–1971," in *A Survey of Agricultural Economics Literature,* vol. 1, University of Minnesota Press for the American Agricultural Economics Association, Minneapolis, 1977.

Brandsberg, George: *The Two Sides of the NFO's Battle,* The Iowa State University Press, Ames, 1964.

Breimyer, Harold F.: *Farm Policy: 13 Essays,* The Iowa State University Press, Ames, 1977.

——: *Individual Freedom and the Economic Organization of Agriculture,* The University of Illinois Press, Urbana, 1965.

Brinkman, George, et al.: *The Development of Rural America,* University Press of Kansas, Manhattan, 1974.

Brown, Lester, R.: *Building a Sustainable Society,* A Worldwatch Institute Book, W. W. Norton and Company, New York, 1981.

——: *Seeds of Change. The Green Revolution and Development in the 1970's,* Praeger Publishers, New York, 1970.

Brown, Peter G., and Henry Shue (eds.): *Food Policy—The Responsibility of the United States in the Life and Death Choices,* The Free Press, A Division of Macmillan Publishing Co., Inc., New York, 1977.

Bryson, Reid A., and Thomas J. Murray: *Climates of Hunger: Mankind and the World's Changing Weather,* The University of Wisconsin Press, Madison, 1977.

Burkitt, Denis P., and H. C. Trowell (eds.): *Refined Carbohydrate Foods and Disease—Some Implications of Dietary Fibre,* Academic Press, London, 1975.

Calef, Wesley: *Private Grazing and Public Lands, Studies of the Local Management of the Taylor Grazing Act,* The University of Chicago Press, Chicago, 1960.

Campbell, Christiana McFadyen: *The Farm Bureau and the New Deal, A Study in the Making of National Policy, 1933–1940,* The University of Illinois Press, Urbana, 1962.

Campbell, Keith O.: *Food for the Future. How Agriculture Can Meet the Challenge,* University of Nebraska Press, Lincoln, 1979.

Carriel, Mary Turner: *The Life of Jonathan Baldwin Turner,* University of Illinois Press, Urbana, 1961.

Chrispeels, Maarten, Jr.: *Plants, Food and People,* W. H. Freeman and Company, San Francisco, 1977.

Clarkson, Kenneth W.: *Food Stamps and Nutrition,* American Enterprise Institute for Public Policy Research, Washington, D.C., 1975.

Clawson, Marion: *The Land System of the United States, An Introduction to the History and Practices of Land Use and Tenure,* University of Nebraska Press, Lincoln, 1968.

———: *The Western Range Livestock Industry,* McGraw-Hill Book Company, New York, 1950.

Cochrane, Willard W.: *Farm Prices: Myth and Reality,* University of Minnesota Press, Minneapolis, 1958.

———: *Reserve Stock Grain Models, The World and the United States, 1975–85,* University of Minnesota, Agricultural Experiment Station, Technical Bulletin 305, 1976.

——— and Mary E. Ryan: *American Farm Policy, 1948–1973.* University of Minnesota Press, Minneapolis, 1976.

Coles, Robert: *Children of Crisis: Migrants, Sharecroppers, Mountaineers,* Little, Brown and Company, Boston, 1971.

Cook, H. L., et al. *The Dairy Subsectors of American Agriculture,* North Central Regional Research publication 257, November 1978.

Cook, M. L.: "The Sources, Limits, and Extent of Cooperative Market Power: Financial Law and Institutions," in *Agricultural Cooperatives and the Public Interest,* B. W. Marion (ed.), North Central Regional Research publication 256. University of Wisconsin-Madison, Madison, September 1978.

Coppock, John O.: *Atlantic Agricultural Unity: Is It Possible?* McGraw-Hill Book Company, New York, 1966.

Council on Environmental Quality: *Global Future: Time to Act: Report to the President on Global Resources, Environment and Population,* U.S. Department of State, Washington, D.C., 1981.

———: *Public Opinion on Environmental Issues: Results of a National Public Opinion Survey,* Washington, D.C., 1980.

Crosson, Pierre, and Kenneth D. Frederick: *The World Food Situation,* Resources for the Future, Washington, D.C., 1977.

Davis, Joseph S.: "The McNary-Haugen Plan as Applied to Wheat," *Wheat Studies of the Food Research Institute,* Stanford University, Palo Alto, February and March 1927, pp. 177–264.

Davis, Kenneth P.: *Land Use,* McGraw-Hill Book Company, New York, 1976.

DeBell, Garrett (ed.): *The Environmental Handbook,* Ballantine Books, New York, 1970.

Gardner, Bruce L.: *The Governing of Agriculture,* The Regents Press of Kansas, Lawrence, 1981.

———: *Optimal Stockpiling of Grain,* Lexington Books, Lexington, Massachusetts, 1979.

Gardner, Charles M.: *The Grange—Friend of the Farmer,* The National Grange, Washington, D.C., 1948.

George, Susan: *How the Other Half Dies: The Real Reasons for World Hunger,* Penguin, New York, 1976.

Good, Darrel L., Thomas A. Hieronymus, and Royce Hinton: *Price Forecasting and Sales Management,* University of Illinois, Urbana, 1980.

Gopalakrishnan, Chennat: *Natural Resources and Energy: Theory and Policy,* Ann Arbor Science Publishers, Ann Arbor, Michigan, 1980.

Grant, Winston, W.: *Bibliography of Regulation of Agricultural and Nonagricultural Industries, 1960–79,* U.S. Department of Agriculture, Economics, Statistics and Cooperatives Service, 1980.

Grennes, T., P. R. Johnson, and M. Thursby, *The Economics of World Grain Trade,* Praeger Publishers, New York, 1978.

Griswold, A. Whitney: *Farming and Democracy,* Harcourt, Brace and Company, New York, 1948.

Guither, Harold D.: *The Food Lobbyists: Behind the Scenes of Food and Agri-Politics,* Lexington Books, D. C. Heath and Company, Lexington, Massachusetts, 1980.

———: *Heritage of Plenty, A Guide to the Economic History and Development of U.S. Agriculture,* The Interstate Printers and Publishers, Danville, Illinois, 2d ed., 1972.

Gunterman, Karl, M. T. Lee, A. S. Narayanan, and E. R. Swanson: *Soil Loss from Illinois Farms, Economic Analysis of Productivity Loss and Sediment Damage,* Illinois Institute for Environmental Quality, Chicago, Document no. 74-62, 1974.

Hadwiger, Don F., and Ross B. Talbot: *Pressures and Protests: The Kennedy Farm Program and the Wheat Referendum of 1963,* Chandler Publishing Company, San Francisco, 1965.

Hady, Thomas I., and Ann Gordon Sibold: *State Programs for the Differential Assessment of Farm and Open-Space Land,* U.S. Department of Agriculture, Economic Research Service, Agricultural Economics report 256, 1974.

Halcrow, Harold G.: *Economics of Agriculture,* McGraw-Hill Book Company, New York, 1980.

———: *Food Policy for America,* McGraw-Hill Book Company, New York, 1977.

———, Earl O. Heady and Melvin L. Cotner (eds.): *Soil Conservation Policies, Institutions, and Incentives,* Soil Conservation Society of America, Ankeny, Iowa, 1982.

Hansen, Roger D., et al.: *The U.S. and World Development—Agenda for Action 1976,* published for the Overseas Development Council by Praeger Publishers, New York, 1976.

Hardin, Charles M.: *Food and Fiber in the Nation's Politics,* National Advisory Commission on Food and Fiber, Technical Papers, Volume III, 1967.

———: *The Politics of Agriculture,* The Free Press, Glencoe, Illinois, 1952.

Headley, J. C., and J. N. Lewis: *The Pesticide Problem: An Economic Approach to Public Policy,* Resources for the Future, Inc., The Johns Hopkins Press, Baltimore, 1967.

Heady, Earl O.: *Agricultural Policy Under Economic Development,* The Iowa State University Press, Ames, 1962.

———: *Economics and Social Conditions Relating to Agriculture and Its Structure to Year 2000,* The Iowa State University Press, Ames, 1980.

———, Leo V. Mayer, and Howard C. Madsen: *Future Farm Programs, Comparative Costs and Consequences,* The Iowa State University Press, Ames, 1972.

Hibbard, Benjamin H.: *A History of Public Land Policies,* The Macmillan Company, New York, 1924.

Hicks, John D.: *The Populist Revolt, A History of the Farmer's Alliance and the People's Party,* University of Nebraska Press, Lincoln, 1968 (first published by University of Minnesota Press, Minneapolis, 1931).

Hightower, Jim: *Hard Tomatoes, Hard Times; The Failure of the Land Grant College Complex,* Agribusiness Accountability Project, Washington, D.C., 1972.

Hildreth, R. J. (ed.): *Readings in Agricultural Policy,* University of Nebraska Press, Lincoln, 1968.

Hillman, Jimmye S.: *Nontariff Agricultural Trade Barriers,* University of Nebraska Press, 1978.

———, and Andrew Schmitz (eds.): *International Trade and Agriculture: Theory and Practice,* Westview Press, Boulder, Colorado, 1979.

Hoos, Sidney (ed.): *Agricultural Marketing Boards, An International Perspective,* Ballinger Publishing Company, Cambridge, Massachusetts, 1979.

Houck, James P., and Mary E. Ryan: *Economic Research on International Grain Reserves: The State of Knowledge,* University of Minnesota, Agricultural Experiment Station Bulletin no. 532, 1979.

Johnson, D. Gale: *Forward Prices for Agriculture,* The University of Chicago Press, Chicago, 1947.

———: *The United States Sugar Program: Large Costs and Small Benefits,* The American Enterprise Institute, Washington, D.C., 1974.

———: *World Agriculture in Disarray,* Macmillan, St. Martin's Press in association with the Trade Policy Research Centre, London, 1973.

———, and John A. Schnittker (eds.): *U.S. Agriculture in a World Context: Policies and Approaches for the Next Decade,* Praeger Publishers, New York, 1974.

Johnson, James, Richard W. Rizzi, Sarah D. Short, and R. Thomas Fulton: *Provisions of the Agriculture and Food Act of 1981,* U.S. Department of Agriculture, Economic Research Service, National Economics Division, Staff report no. AGES 811228, January 1982.

Johnston, Bruce F., and Peter Kilby: *Agriculture and Structural Transformation: Economic Strategies in Late-Developing Countries,* Oxford University Press, New York, 1975.

Kendrick, John W.: *Postwar Productivity Trends in the United States, 1948–1960.* National Bureau of Economic Research, New York, 1975. Columbia University Press, New York and London,

———: *Productivity Trends in the United States,* National Bureau of Economic Research, New York, Princeton University Press, Princeton, New Jersey, 1961.

Kile, Orville M.: *The Farm Bureau Through Three Decades,* The Waverly Press, Baltimore, 1948.

Leibenluft, Robert F.: *Competition in Farm Inputs: An Examination of Four Industries,* Policy Issues Planning Paper, Office of Policy Planning, Federal Trade Commission, Washington, D.C., February 1981.

Leontief, Wassily, Anne P. Carter, and Peter A. Petri: *The Future of the World Economy: A United Nations Study,* Oxford University Press, New York, 1977.

Lin, William, James Johnson, and Linda Calvin: *Farm Commodity Programs: Who Participates and Who Benefits,* U.S. Department of Agriculture, Economic Research Service, Agricultural Economic report no. 474, September 1981.

Madden, J. Patrick, and David E. Brewster (eds.): *A Philosopher Among Economists, Selected Works of John M. Brewster,* J. T. Murphy Co., Inc., Philadelphia, 1970.

Malthus, Thomas Robert: *On Population,* edited and introduced by Gertrude Himmelfarb, The Modern Library of the World's Best Books, New York, 1960.

Manchester, Alden C.: *Market Structure, Institutions, and Performance in the Fluid Milk Industry,* U.S. Department of Agriculture, Economic Research Service, Agricultural Economic report no. 248, 1974.

Marion, Bruce W., et al.: *The Food Retailing Industry,* Praeger Publications, New York, 1979.

Marsh, John S., and Pamela J. Swanney: *Agriculture and the European Community,* Allen and Unwin, London, 1980.

Marshall, Ray: *Rural Workers in Rural Labor Markets,* Olympus Publishing Co., Salt Lake City, 1974.

Matusow, Allen J.: *Farm Policies and Politics in the Truman Years,* Harvard University Press, Cambridge, Massachusetts, 1967.

McClintock, David W.: *U.S. Food, Making the Most of a Global Resource,* Westview Press, Boulder, Colorado, 1978.

McCune, Wesley: *Who's Behind Our Farm Policy,* Frederick A. Praeger, Inc., New York, 1956.

McNicol, D.: *Commodity Agreements and Price Stabilization,* Lexington Books, Lexington, Massachusetts, 1978.

McWilliams, Carey: *Factories in the Field, The Story of Migratory Farm Labor in California,* Little, Brown and Company, Boston, 1939.

——: *Ill Fares the Land, Migrants and Migratory Labor in the United States,* Little, Brown and Company, Boston, 1942.

Meadows, Donella H., Dennis L. Meadows, Jorgen Randers, and William W. Behrens III: *The Limits to Growth: A Report for the Club of Rome's Project on the Predicament of Mankind,* Universe Books, New York, 1972.

Michie, Aruna Nayyar, and Craig Jagger: *Why Farmers Protest: Kansas Farmers, the Farm Problem, and the American Agriculture Movement,* Agricultural Experiment Station, Kansas State University, Manhattan, 1980.

Moores, Richard Gordon: *Fields of Rich Toil—The Development of the University of Illinois College of Agriculture,* University of Illinois Press, Urbana, 1970.

Morgan, Robert J.: *Governing Soil Conservation: Thirty Years of the New Decentralization,* The Johns Hopkins University Press, Baltimore, published for Resources for the Future, 1965.

Mosher, Arthur T.: *Getting Agriculture Moving, Essentials for Development and Modernization,* Frederick A. Praeger, Inc., for the Agricultural Development Council, New York, 1966.

National Academy of Sciences: *Genetic Vulnerability of Major Crops,* Washington, D.C., 1972.

——: *Pest Control Strategies for the Future,* Washington, D.C., 1972.

National Advisory Commission on Food and Fiber: *Food and Fiber for the Future,* U.S. Government Printing Office, Washington, D.C., 1967.

National Agricultural Lands Study, U.S. Department of Agriculture and President's Council on Environmental Quality, Final Report, 1981.

National Commission on Food Marketing: *Food from Farmer to Consumer,* U.S. Government Printing Office, Washington, D.C., 1966.

National Planning Association: *Feast or Famine: The Uncertain World of Food and Agriculture and Its Policy Implications for the United States,* Washington, D.C., 1974.

National Public Policy Education Committee: *Increasing Understanding of Public Problems and Policies,* Farm Foundation, Oakbrook, Illinois, published annually since 1964.

National Research Council: *World Food and Nutrition Study: The Potential Contributions of Research,* National Academy of Sciences, Washington, D.C., 1977.

Nicholls, William H.: *Imperfect Competition Within Agricultural Industries,* The Iowa State College Press, Ames, 1941.

——: *Price Policies of the Cigarette Industry,* The Vanderbilt University Press, Nashville, 1951.

Nivens, Allen: *The State Universities and Democracy,* The University of Illinois Press, Urbana, 1962.

North, Douglass, C.: *Growth and Welfare in the American Past: A New Economic History,* Prentice-Hall, Englewood Cliffs, New Jersey, 1966.

O'Rourke, A. Desmond: *The Changing Dimensions of U.S. Agricultural Policy,* Prentice-Hall, Englewood Cliffs, New Jersey, 1978.

Paarlberg, Don: *American Farm Policy,* John Wiley and Sons, New York, 1964.

————: *Farm and Food Policy,* University of Nebraska Press, Lincoln, 1980.

Padberg, Daniel I.: *Economics of Food Retailing,* Cornell University, Ithaca, New York, 1968.

Paddock, William, and Elizabeth Paddock: *We Don't Know How,* The Iowa State University Press, Ames, 1973.

Paddock, William and Paul Paddock: *Famine—1975: America's Decision: Who Will Survive?* Little, Brown and Company, Boston, 1967.

Paul , Kilmer, Altobello, and Harrington: *The Changing Fertilizer Industry,* National Economic Analysis Division, Economic Research Service, U.S. Department of Agriculture, 1977.

Penn, J. B., David H. Harrington, James D. Johnson, et al.: *Structure Issues of American Agriculture,* U.S. Department of Agriculture, Economics, Statistics, and Cooperatives Service; Agricultural Economics report no. 438, November 1979.

The People Left Behind: A Report by the President's Advisory Commission on Rural Poverty, The Superintendent of Documents, Washington, D.C., 1967.

Perelman, Michael: *Farming for Profit in a Hungry World: Capital and the Crisis in Agriculture,* Universe Books, New York, 1978.

Perspectives on Prime Lands, U.S. Department of Agriculture, Committee on Land Use, Washington, D.C., 1975.

Rasmussen, Wayne D., and Gladys L. Baker: *Price Support and Adjustment Programs from 1932 through 1978: A Short History,* Agricultural Information Bulletin 424, U.S. Department of Agriculture, Washington, D.C., 1979.

Rausser, Gordon C., and Eithan Hochman: *Dynamic Agricultural Systems: Economic Prediction and Control,* North Holland, New York, 1979.

Ray, Susanta K., Ralph W. Cummings, Jr., and Robert W. Herdt: *Policy Planning for Agricultural Development,* Tata McGraw-Hill, New Delhi, 1979.

Resources and Man, Committee on Resources and Man, National Academy of Sciences and National Research Council, W. H. Freeman and Company, San Francisco, 1969.

Response Analysis Corporation: *What the Public Says About Food, Farmers, and Agriculture: A Nationwide Survey,* Response Analysis Corporation, Princeton, New Jersey, 1974.

Review of Agricultural Policies—General Survey, Agricultural Policy Reports, Organization for Economic Cooperation and Development, Paris, 1975.

Rieber, Michael, and Ronald Halcrow: *U.S. Energy and Fuel Demand to 1985: A Composite Projection by Users Within PAD Districts* (Petroleum Administration for Defense Districts), Center for Advanced Computation. University of Illinois, Urbana, 1974.

Rosen, George: *Peasant Society in a Changing Economy: Comparative Development in South East Asia and India,* University of Illinois Press, Urbana, 1975.

Ross, Earle D.: *Democracy's College, The Land-Grant Movement in the Formative Stage,* Iowa State College Press, Ames, 1942.

Rowley, William D.: *M. L. Wilson and the Campaign for the Domestic Allotment,* University of Nebraska Press, Lincoln, 1970.

Ruttan, Vernon W., Arley D. Waldo, and James P. Houck (eds.): *Agricultural Policy in an Affluent Society,* W. W. Norton and Co., New York, 1969.

Saloutos, Theodore, and John D. Hicks: *Agricultural Discontent in the Middle West, 1900–1939,* The University of Wisconsin Press, Madison, 1951.

Salter, Leonard A., Jr.: *A Critical Review of Research in Land Economies,* The University of Minnesota Press, Minneapolis, 1948.

Saulnier, R. J., Harold G. Halcrow, and Neil H. Jacoby: *Federal Lending and Loan Insurance,* National Bureau of Economic Research, New York, Princeton University Press, Princeton, New Jersey, 1968.

Scherer, F.: *Industrial Market Structure and Economic Performance,* Rand McNally and Co., Chicago, 2d ed., 1980.

Schertz, L. P., et al.: *Another Revolution in U.S. Farming,* U.S. Department of Agriculture, Washington, D.C., 1979.

Schmitz, Andrew, Alex F. McCalla, Donald O. Mitchell, and Collin A. Carter: *Grain Export Cartels,* Ballinger Publishing Company, Cambridge, Massachusetts, 1981.

Schrader, Lee F., and Ray A. Goldberg: *Farmers' Cooperatives and Federal Income Taxes,* Ballinger Publishing Company, Cambridge, Massachusetts, 1974.

Schultz, Theodore W.: *Agriculture in an Unstable Economy,* McGraw-Hill Book Company, New York, 1945.

—— (ed.): *Distortions of Agricultural Incentives,* Indiana University Press, Bloomington, 1978.

——: *Economic Crisis in World Agriculture,* The University of Michigan Press, Ann Arbor, 1965.

——: *Economic Growth and Agriculture,* McGraw-Hill Book Company, New York, 1968.

—— *The Economic Organization of Agriculture,* McGraw-Hill Book Company, New York, 1953.

—— (ed.): *Food for the World,* The University of Chicago Press, Chicago, 1945.

——: *Transforming Traditional Agriculture,* Yale University Press, New Haven, Connecticut, 1964.

Schultze, Charles L.: *The Politics and Economics of Public Spending,* The Brookings Institution, Washington, D.C., 1968.

Shannon, Fred A.: *The Farmers' Last Frontier, Agriculture, 1860–1897, The Economic History of the United States,* Farrar and Rinehart, Inc., New York, 1945.

Shover, John L.: *Cornbelt Rebellion: The Farmers' Holiday Association,* The University of Illinois Press, Urbana, 1965.

Schwenke, Karl: *Successful Small-scale Farming,* Garden Way Publishers, Charlotte, Vermont, 1979.

Simon, Julian L.: *The Ultimate Resource,* Princeton University Press, Princeton, New Jersey, 1981.

Soil Conservation Service: *National Resource Inventory,* U.S. Department of Agriculture, 1978.

Speaking of Trade: Its Effect on Agriculture, Agricultural Extension Service, University of Minnesota, Minneapolis, special report 72, 1978.

Spillman, W. J.: *Balancing the Farm Output,* Orange Judd Publishing Co., New York, 1927.

Spitze, R. G. F., and Marshall A. Martin (eds.): *Analysis of Food and Agricultural Policies for the Eighties,* North Central Regional Research Bulletin no. 271, Illinois Bulletin 764, University of Illinois, Urbana, November 1980.

Stein, Walter J.: *California and the Dust Bowl Migration,* Greenwood Press, Inc., Westport, Connecticut, 1973.

Steinhart, John S., and Carol E. Steinhart: "Energy Use in the U.S. Food System," in Philip H. Abelson (ed.), *Food: Politics, Economics, Nutrition and Research,* American Association for the Advancement of Science, Washington, D.C., 1975.

Talbot, Ross B.: *The World Food Problem and U.S. Food Policies: 1972–1976: A Readings Book,* The Iowa State University Press, Ames, 1977.

———, and Don F. Hadwiger: *The Policy Process in American Agriculture,* Chandler Publishing Company, San Francisco, 1968.

Taylor, Carl C.: *The Farmer's Movement,* American Book Company, New York, 1953.

Taylor, Henry C. and Anne Dewess Taylor, *The Story of Agricultural Economics in the United States, 1840–1932,* The Iowa State University Press, Ames, 1952.

Taylor, Ronald B.: *Sweatshops in the Sun, Child Labor on the Farm,* Beacon Press, Boston, 1973.

Thorbecke, Eric (ed.): *The Role of Agriculture in Economic Development,* distributed by Columbia University Press, New York, 1969.

Toffler, Alvin: *Future Shock,* Random House, New York, 1970.

Trager, James: *The Great Grain Robbery,* Ballantine Books, New York, 1975.

Turning the Searchlight on Farm Policy, a Forthright Analysis of Experience, Lessons, Criteria, and Recommendations, The Farm Foundation, Chicago, 1952.

Tweeten, Luther G.: "The Demand for United States Farm Output," *Food Research Institute Studies,* vol. 7, no. 3, Stanford University Press, 1967, pp. 343–369.

———: *Foundations of Farm Policy,* University of Nebraska Press, Lincoln, 2d ed., 1979.

Tydings, Joseph D.: *Born to Starve,* William Morrow and Co., New York, 1970.

Uchtmann, Donald L., et al.: *Agricultural Law: Principles and Cases,* McGraw-Hill Book Company, New York, 1981.

United Nations: *Food and Agriculture in Global Perspective: Discussions in the Committee of the Whole of the United Nations,* Pergamon, New York, 1980.

United Nations, Food and Agriculture Organization: *Agriculture: Toward 2000,* Rome, 1979.

U.S. Congress, Joint Economic Committee, Subcommittee on Economy in Government: *The Analysis and Evaluation of Public Expenditures: The PPB System, A Compendium of Papers,* 91st Cong., 1st Sess., vols. 1–3, 1969.

United States General Accounting Office: *Effects of Tax Policies on Land Use,* CED 78-97, April 28, 1978.

———, Comptroller General: *Grain Reserves: A Potential U.S. Food Policy Tool,* OSP-76-16, Washington, D.C., 1976.

U.S. House of Representatives: *Agriculture and Food Act of 1981,* 97th Cong., 1st Sess., report no. 97-377, Conference Report to accompany S. 894, Dec. 9, 1981.

U.S. Senate: *Agriculture and Food Act of 1981,* 97th Cong., 1st Sess., report no. 97-126, Report of the Committee on Agriculture, Nutrition, and Forestry to accompany S. 894, May 27, 1981.

———: *Proposed Reauthorization of the Food and Agriculture Act of 1977,* 97th Cong., 1st Sess., Hearings before the Committee on Agriculture, Nutrition, and Forestry, March and April 1981, Part I.

Vogeler, Ingolf: *The Myth of the Family Farm: Agribusiness Dominance of U.S. Agriculture,* Westview Press, Boulder, Colorado, 1981.

War on Hunger: A Report from the Agency for International Development, Washington, D.C., 1975.

World Agricultural Supply and Demand Estimates, U.S. Department of Agriculture, Economics and Statistics Service, Foreign Agricultural Service, Washington, D.C., 1980.

BIBLIOGRAPHY OF JOURNAL ARTICLES

(Including published abstracts and substantive excerpts)

Alaouze, Chris M., A. S. Watson, and N. H. Sturgess: "Oligopoly Pricing in the World Wheat Market," *American Journal of Agricultural Economics,* vol. 60, no. 2, May 1978, pp. 173–185.

When the residual demand curve for wheat facing the United States and Canada shifts to the left, or when the exportable surplus of Australia is large, market-shares of these duopolists are reduced. Such circumstances lead to the formation of a market-share triopoly with Australia. The evidence for this proposition is examined and a model of triopoly pricing in the world wheat market is presented. If major exporters continue to be concerned with relative market-shares, the triopoly will reform, stocks will accumulate, and lower prices will prevail; however, prices will be more variable, and possibly higher, than before 1972/73.

Arzac, Enrique: "An Econometric Evaluation of Stabilization Policies for the U.S. Grain Market," *Western Journal of Agricultural Economics,* vol. 4, no. 1, July 1979, pp. 9–22.

This paper evaluates stabilization policies by applying methods of stochastic control and dynamic analysis to an econometric model of the U.S. grain market. Its main results are: (1) the aggregate consumer and producer surplus generated by the model is insensitive to the choice of the market regime; (2) policies directed to stabilize prices at levels compatible with nondecreasing farm revenue require the management of both grain inventories and domestic supply; (3) price fluctuations are significantly less under optimal stabilization than in the unregulated version of the model; and (4) historical policies have destabilizing effects on the market model.

Arzac, Enrique R., and Maurice Wilkinson: "A Quarterly Econometric Model of United States Livestock and Feed Grain Markets and Some of Its Policy Implications," *American Journal of Agricultural Economics,* vol. 61, no. 2, May 1979, pp. 297–308.

This paper discussed the structural equations, forecasting properties, dynamic characteristics, and economic policy implications of a quarterly econometric model of U.S. livestock and feedgrain markets. Quarterly, semi-annual, and annual endogenous variables are incorporated by allowing individual structural equations to be estimated and to enter into the solution of the model with different periodicities. Commodity prices are determined by market equilibrium conditions rather than by autoregressive and other time-series techniques. Dynamic multipliers give the effect of changes in corn exports, beef imports, government grain stocks, corn yield, consumer income, and the support price for corn on producer and retail prices and acreage planted.

Barry, Peter J.: "Rural Banks and Farm Loan Participation," *American Journal of Agricultural Economics,* vol. 60, no. 2, May 1978, pp. 214–224.

Banking theory is used to develop a static, certainty model for evaluating profitability of farm loan participations for rural banks. Techniques are developed and applied to measure empirically the effects of participations on rural bank earnings attributed to farmer customer relationships and costs associated with demand balances required by correspondent banks. Model results show a decline in optimal levels and profits of loan participations for rural banks as correspondent balance requirements increase and as other parameters adjust to levels reflecting tighter monetary conditions. Participation strategies that may enhance the flow of funds into rural areas are also considered.

Bigman, David, and Shlomo Reutlinger: "Food Price and Supply Stabilization: National Buffer Stocks and Trade Policies," *American Journal of Agricultural Economics,* vol. 61, no. 4, November 1979, pp. 657–678.

Trade policies are likely to have a greater impact on the stability of a country's food grain supply than any reasonable size buffer stock. At the margin, countries need to trade off the cost of additional stocks against the cost of unstable foreign exchange balances associated with free trade. A stochastic simulation model is specified to assess the impact of trade and buffer stock policies on the stability of consumption and prices and the expected values and standard deviations of costs and gains to consumers, producers, and the government, and the balance of payments.

Bigman, David, and Shlomo Reutlinger: "National and International Policies Toward Food Security and Price Stabilization," *The American Economic Review,* vol. 69, no. 2, May 1979, pp. 159–163.

At current food production levels, supplies are adequate to feed the world's population even in lean years. A basic premise of our study has been that current food crises are characterized not by overall scarcity but by gross maldistribution of food. With the existing distribution of income and wealth among individuals and nations, the free-market economy is unable to prevent frivolous uses of food at the same time that other people are starving. While trade and buffer stocks can play a major role in stabilizing food grain supplies, effective insurance against hunger will also require special financial measures. Even poor nations can seek to safeguard against their vulnerability to climatic instability by intervening in the market to secure minimally adequate consumption for all, by means of price discrimination or rationing in favor of low-income consumers. Our analysis shows, however, that such national food security measures are very costly, involve substantial transfers of income, and require massive intervention by the government in the free market with possible undesirable consequences in the long run. Alternatively, or at least in addition, we propose an international financial undertaking which would enable developing countries to acquire food in times of need.

Black, J. Roy, and Stanley R. Thompson: "Some Evidence on Western-Crop-Yield Inter-action," *American Journal of Agricultural Economics,* vol. 60, no. 3, August 1978, pp. 540–543.

The empirical findings of this study are consistent with the existence of drought cycles for corn, soybean, and wheat yields. However, not every year within a drought period exhibits below average yield and vice versa. There was no evidence for a two-year cycle.

These findings are relevant for price analysis and have extremely important economic implications given the relatively inelastic nature of demand, particularly for wheat and corn. The implications for price stability analysis and agricultural policy administration, including grain reserves, are evident.

Boehlje, Michael, and Steven Griffin: "Financial Impacts of Government Support Price Pro-grams," *American Journal of Agricultural Economics,* vol. 61, no. 2, May 1979, pp. 285–296.

Recent proposals to index government support prices based on the cost of production will have significant differential impacts on farms with different size and financial character-istics. Simulation analyses indicate that since such proposals result in both increased income and decreased risk and thus capitalization rates, land values could increase dra-matically with the larger, high-equity operator best able to pay the higher price for addi-tional land. Furthermore, the guaranteed cash flow from such a program enables the higher-equity firm to grow more rapidly in terms of net worth and land ownership as well as exhibit higher levels of family living compared with smaller, highly leveraged firms.

Boggess, W. G. and E. O. Heady: "A Sector Analysis of Alternative Income Support and Soil Conservation Policies," *American Journal of Agricultural Economics,* vol. 63, no. 4, November 1981, pp. 618–628.

For nearly five decades Congress has attempted to legislate both higher farm incomes and soil conservation. A national, interregional, demand-endogenous, separable program-ming model is used to analyze the potential of alternative policies to achieve simulta-neously the dual goals of increased farm income and reduced soil erosion. The analysis indicates that a conservation-oriented land retirement policy can be designed to achieve an increase in net farm income equivalent to a traditional general land retirement policy, while simultaneously achieving significant reductions in gross soil erosion, chemical input use, and direct government program costs.

Braden, John B.: "Some Emerging Rights in Agricultural Land," *American Journal of Agri-cultural Economics,* vol. 64, no. 1, February 1982, pp. 19–27.

Agricultural land use rights have become increasingly complex following new policies for soil conservation, nonpoint pollution control, wetlands protection, and farmland preser-vation. When viewed in a framework that distinguishes between ownership and exchange of rights, little change is evident in ownership of rights. The added complexity has come mainly in the rules governing exchanges. Farmers are confronted increasingly with rules which allow specific rights to be limited by government with compensation. These rules retain the flexibility of individual ownership while reflecting a growing awareness that the general welfare depends on wise use of agricultural land.

Bredahl, Maury E., Williams H. Meyers, and Keith J. Collins: "The Elasticity of Foreign Demand for U.S. Agricultural Products: The Importance of the Price Transmission Elasticity," *American Journal of Agricultural Economics,* vol. 61, no. 1, February 1979, pp. 58–63.

A key question that must be resolved in evaluating the elasticity of export demand is the size of the adjustment of foreign prices to U.S. prices, E_{pi}. There is strong evidence that for many major importing and exporting regions internal price is largely insulated from U.S. (and/or world market) prices. Therefore, for many regions E_{pi} approaches zero and these regions do not contribute significantly to the elasticity of U.S. export demand. . . . Consistently empirical estimates of the elasticity of export demand for specific agricultural commodities are either inelastic or slightly greater than one. . . . These estimates may simply reflect the trade restricting behavior of the real world . . ." (pp. 58 and 63).

Burt, Oscar R.: "Farm Level Economics of Soil Conservation in the Palouse Area of the Northwest," *American Journal of Agricultural Economics,* vol. 63, no. 1, February 1981, pp. 83–92.

Control theory is applied to the farm-level economics of soil conservation in a model which uses depth of topsoil and percentage of organic matter therein as the two state variables. An approximately optimal decision rule was tested against the optimal rule and found to be excellent; errors in the decision rule were less than 1 percent within the region in state space of practical consideration. Results suggest that intensive wheat production under modern farming practices and heavy fertilization is the most economic cropping system in both the short and long run in the Palouse Area except under low wheat prices.

Burt, Oscar R., Won W. Koo, and Norman J. Dudley: "Optimal Stochastic Control of U.S. Wheat Stocks and Exports," *American Journal of Agricultural Economics,* vol. 62, no. 2, May 1980, pp. 172–187.

A stochastic dynamic programming model was developed to estimate optimal strategies for U.S. wheat reserves policy using the results of an econometric model which reflects the complex dynamics of supply response. Empirical results indicated that U.S. producers are the beneficiaries of a wheat storage program, while domestic and foreign consumers are relatively small and large losers, respectively. Another result is that wheat storage capacity in excess of 2 billion bushels is difficult to justify economically.

Castle, Emery N., and Irving Hoch: "Farm Real Estate Price Components," *American Journal of Agricultural Economics,* vol. 64, no. 1, February 1982, pp. 8–18.

The research reported demonstrates that farm real estate price involves important components in addition to the capitalized value of rent for the services of land and buildings in farm production, develops an expectations model for the farm real estate market, and compares predictions from the expectations model with farm real estate prices for the 1920–78 period. Capitalized rent explains only about half of real estate values both in the 1970s and over the longer 1920–78 period. The remainder can be explained by the capitalization of capital gains, including real gains or losses from price level changes.

Chambers, Robert G., and Richard E. Just: "Effects of Exchange Rate Changes on U.S. Agriculture: A Dynamic Analysis," *American Journal of Agricultural Economics,* vol. 63, no. 1, February 1981, pp. 32–46.

An econometric model of the wheat, corn, and soybean markets is used to examine the dynamic effects of exchange rate fluctuation on U.S. commodity markets. Exports and agricultural prices are found to be sensitive to movements in the exchange rate, while domestic factors, such as disappearance and inventories, are less sensitive but still responsive. Dramatic short-run adjustments in prices and exports are followed by less dramatic but significant longer-run adjustments. Thus, the hypothesis of elastic response to the exchange rate seems particularly relevant for the short run.

Chambers, Robert G., and Michael W. Woolverton: "Wheat Cartelization and Domestic Markets," *American Journal of Agricultural Economics,* vol. 62, no. 4, November 1980, pp. 629–638.

The effects of cartelization in the international wheat market are analyzed. Particular attention is given to the relationship between the level of cartel profits and the price farmers receive for their wheat. Sufficient conditions are established for a rise in cartel profits to be associated with a rise in the farmgate price of wheat. The potential stability of a cartel formed by the major trading companies also is investigated and a means of preventing cheating is introduced and discussed.

Chowdhury, Ashok, and Earl Heady: "An Analysis of a Marginal Versus the Conventional Land Set-Aside Program," *North Central Journal of Agricultural Economics,* vol. 2, no. 2, July 1980, pp. 95–106.

Excess supplies of farm commodities and the resulting decrease in returns to production factors have been persistent problems in American agriculture over much of the last five decades. Acreage diversion and price-support policies have been enacted for reducing supply and raising agricultural prices to bring improvement in farm income. Two alternatives in acreage diversion directed toward controlling supply to attain higher price levels are analyzed in this article. One assumes the conventional approach of an equal percentage set-aside applied to all regions. The other allows the set-aside to be concentrated by regions according to comparative advantage.

Collins, Keith J., William H. Meyers, and Maury E. Bredahl: "Multiple Exchange Rate Changes and U.S. Commodity Prices," *American Journal of Agricultural Economics,* vol. 62, no. 4, November 1980, pp. 656–665.

A model was developed to assess recent effects of exchange rate changes, and price insulation policies on real U.S. commodity prices. Exchange rate effects are defined so that they can occur and be significant under either fixed or floating rate regimes. The results indicate exchange rate effects on real U.S. commodity prices are smallest under free trade and real commodity price insulation policies but rise substantially as nominal price insulation policies become more prevalent.

Dobson, W. D., and Larry E. Salathe: "The Effects of Federal Milk Orders on the Economic Performance of U.S. Milk Markets," *American Journal of Agricultural Economics,* vol. 61, no. 2, May 1979, pp. 213–227.

Class I price differentials maintained by the U.S. Department of Agriculture and producers during 1965–75 generated Grade A milk supplies in excess of fluid needs and reserves for the federal order system. As required by specified norms, USDA has adopted federal milk order provisions which reduce pronounced seasonality of milk production and lessen certain types of erratic and extreme price variation. If federal milk orders were eliminated and cooperatives and state agencies were barred from replacing the orders, then fluid milk markets characterized by lower Class I differentials, greater milk price variability, and smaller Grade A milk surpluses might emerge.

Eckstein, Albert, and Dale Heier: "The 1973 Food Price Inflation," *American Journal of Agricultural Economics,* vol. 60, no. 2, May 1978, pp. 186–196.

This study analyzes the major causes of the food price inflation of 1973. In the approximate order of their importance, those causes were found to be domestic monetary policy, government acreage restrictions, the Soviet grain deal, world economic conditions, devaluation of the dollar, and price freeze II. Econometric models of the livestock and feed grains and meal economies were used to decompose the price increase in to the various causes given above. The study also details and analyzes events and policy actions taken during the 1971–74 period.

Gardner, Bruce, L.: "Determinants of Supply Elasticity in Interdependent Markets," *American Journal of Agricultural Economics,* vol. 61, no. 3, August 1979, pp. 463–475.

This paper draws out the implications of equilibrium in a two-product, two-factor model for elasticity of product supply, which is found to depend upon input supply elasticities, alternative product demand elasticity, elasticity of substitution between production inputs, relative factor intensity of the product, and relative importance of the product in its use of resources. These factors interact in a complex manner to determine supply elasticity. The author discusses related approaches of Buse, Muth, and Powell and Gruen, and considers several simplified examples in an attempt to provide an intuitive grasp of the workings of the model.

Gardner, Bruce: "Robust Stabilization Policies for International Commodity Agreements," *The American Economic Review,* vol. 69, no. 2, May 1979, pp. 169–172.

The overall results of the experiments to date are that while socially optimal stockpiling rules tend to be fairly robust, some buffer stock regimes are sufficiently robust to be as good as or even preferable to an optimal rule strategy when a plausible range of uncertainty about the parameters used in deriving the optimal policy is taken into account. However, it is important to exercise care in the choice of buffer stock regime. A striking result of the experiments is that the upper limit on the buffer stock tends to be as important as the price band used. The economic reason is that too large a stock can easily run up storage costs which at the margin provide no corresponding benefits, while a small maximum size leaves the system open to large external costs from shortfalls. (p. 171)

Groenewegen, J. R., and W. W. Cochrane: "A Proposal to Further Increase the Stability of the American Grain Sector," *American Journal of Agricultural Economics,* vol. 62, no. 4, November 1980, pp. 806–811.

The viability of United States food and agriculture is dependent on exports to the world grain market. Insulating policies by importers and variable import demands contribute to the instability of the world grain market. As a means to reduce the American grain sector's vulnerability to this instability, this paper proposes that American food and agriculture policy should move in the direction of insulating domestic food and agriculture from world instability and at the same time maintain its position as a dependable supplier of world grains. (p. 811)

Grove, Ernest W.: "Present and Prehistoric Problems of Natural Resources," *American Journal of Agricultural Economics,* vol. 61, no. 4, November 1979, pp. 612–619.

The currently developing crisis in natural resources is put in historical perspective as one stage in the ongoing agricultural-urban revolution. This started after the last ice age, when rising seas covered much land while rising populations needed more. Agriculture was not discovered by hunter-gatherers; it was their last resort when game and wilderness became scarce. The result was conflict and near-slavery for most people. Better conditions came with the fossil-fuel (industrial) revolution, but may prove temporary as the natural resources crunch raises questions not unlike those faced by hunter-gatherers some 10,000 years ago.

Haaland, Carsten, M.: "Availability and Shipment of Grain for Survival of a Nuclear Attack," *American Journal of Agricultural Economics,* vol. 59, no. 2, May 1977, pp. 358–369.

It is assumed that at least 90% of the American population would survive the direct effects (blast, fire, and initial nuclear radiation) of a nuclear attack of 6,000 megatons if about 90 million people were relocated from high-risk areas during a crisis period preceding the attack. If the survivors from the direct effects are protected from radioactive fallout by suitable shelters, the remaining major problem affecting survival will be adequate food. This paper indicates that sufficient grain stocks and transportation will likely be available after the attack to assure survival of the American population.

Hall, Bruce F., and E. Phillip LeVeen: "Farm Size and Economic Efficiency: The Case of California," *American Journal of Agricultural Economics,* vol. 60, no. 4, November 1978, pp. 589–600.

The relationship between farm size and production costs is examined using current data. The analysis indicates that relatively modest-sized farms can achieve a major portion of the possible cost savings associated with size. The sources of efficiency are examined, and it is shown that factors other than labor-saving technology may be important contributors to economic efficiency. The implications of this analysis are developed for the current debate over acreage restrictions in reclamation policy. Strict enforcement of the 160-acre limit could cause a modest overall efficiency loss, but this would be borne by landowners rather than consumers.

Hansen, David E. and S. J. Schwartz, "Landowners' Behavior at the Rural-Urban Fringe in Response to Preferential Property Taxation," *Land Economics,* November 1975, pp. 341–354.

Hansen, Gregory D., and Jerry L. Thompson: "A Simulation Study of Maximum Feasible Farm Debt Burdens by Farm Type," *American Journal of Agricultural Economics,* vol. 62, no. 4, November 1980, pp. 727–733.

Financial leverage, which magnifies the effect of farm income instability upon "bottom line" productivity, becomes less feasible as income fluctuation increases. . . . With a flexible repayment agreement and with land valued at current prices, substantial debt use was feasible for many farm types in the years 1966–75. . . . Management ability appeared to have a greater influence upon debt capacity than farm size. Debt-servicing ability was improved more by becoming a good manager than simply by becoming a large operator. . . . (pp. 727 and 732)

Harris, Duane G.: "Inflation-Indexed Price Supports and Land Values," *American Journal of Agricultural Economics,* vol. 59, no. 3, August 1977, pp. 489–499.

A theoretical model is developed to examine and illustrate some relationships between cost-indexed support prices and land values. The model is developed in the context of a single-commodity, price-uncertain world in which policy makers are allowed to control the percentage of nonland operating costs and the percentage of land costs covered by the support price. The model demonstrates that the time path of land values can be quite sensitive to policy parameters. Attempts by policy makers to guarantee a "fair" rate of return on land may have substantial impact on future land values.

Hathaway, Dale E.: "Government and Agriculture Revisited: A Review of Two Decades of Change," *American Journal of Agricultural Economics,* vol. 63, no. 5, December 1981, Proceedings Issue, pp. 779–787.

Hathaway, Dale E.: "Grain Stocks and Economic Stability: A Policy Perspective," *Analysis of Grain Reserves, A Proceedings,* U.S. Department of Agriculture and National Science Foundation, ERS Rep. 634, 1976.

". . . the use of standard theory to rationalize and determine the size of reserves is inadequate if not irrelevant . . . because it cannot measure the irreversible losses due to inadequate food supplies." (p. 2)

Heady, Earl O., and Stanley A. Schraufnagel: "An Alternative to Land for Supply Control," *North Central Journal of Agricultural Economics,* vol. 3, no. 1, January 1981, pp. 21–27.

This article examines the pattern of production and resource use under two agricultural supply control programs. One is a land set-aside program and the other is a fertilizer reduction program. The study was made in the light of recent changes in energy supplies and prices to determine whether supply control programs resting on inputs other than land might be more consistent with developing conditions of resource endowments. The tool of analysis is a national and interregional programming model. Results indicate that, among other things, less energy would be used and more soil might be lost to erosion under the fertilizer program than under the land program.

Helmberger, Peter, and Rob Weaver: "Welfare Implications of Commodity Storage Under Uncertainty," *American Journal of Agricultural Economics,* vol. 59, no. 4, November 1977, pp. 637–651.

Intertemporal equilibrium is determined for a competitive market when private inventories are held. Production and storage decisions respond to rational expectations of uncertain prices. Algebraic expressions for gains (losses) to buyers and producers are derived in this context. Competitive equilibrium maximizes gains to society. Government programs that stabilize price either completely or partially generate benefits to producers and losses to buyers relative to competitive equilibrium. Welfare effects are quantified assuming an initial period of abundance and various supply and demand elasticities.

Hillman, Jimmye S.: "Nontariff Barriers: Major Problem in Agricultural Trade," *American Journal of Agricultural Economics,* vol. 60, no. 3, August 1978, pp. 491–501.

Nontariff barriers have become one of the key issues in agricultural trade policy and trade negotiations. Laws and regulations of a country, in addition to being directly protective, often give administrators wide leeway for interpretation which results in restrictive trade flows. The domestic agriculture of most developed countries is protected by one or more of the following: quantitative restrictions, licensing requirements, variable levies, export subsidies, minimum import prices, import calendars, state trading, mixing regulations, health and sanitary regulations, and standards and labeling. Ultimately, nontariff barriers must be negotiated like tariffs and other protective devices.

Holland, Forrest: "The Concept and Use of Parity in Agricultural Price and Income Policy," *Agricultural-Food Policy Review,* Economic Research Service, U.S. Department of Agriculture, ERS AFPR-1, January 1977, pp. 54–61.

The historical development of the concept of agricultural parity is reviewed, its components discussed, and the economics of its use analyzed. Parity price formulas are shown, and the relative importance of commodities in the Index of Prices Paid and Index of Prices Received is detailed. Also discussed are the parity ratio as a measure of purchasing power, its shortcomings in accounting for technological change, and other problems related to the rise and use of the parity concept.

Johnson, Paul R., Thomas Greenes, and Marie Thursby: "Devaluation, Foreign Trade Controls, and Domestic Wheat Prices," *American Journal of Agricultural Economics,* vol. 59, no. 4, November 1977, pp. 619–627.

The 1970s have seen sharp fluctuations in grain prices. Several plausible explanations for the unusual severity of these ups and downs have been advanced, including devaluation of the dollar for the upswing in 1972–74. U.S. wheat prices for the year of highest prices, 1973–74, are examined. A trade model that distinguishes wheat by country of origin is used to analyze various events in that year. It is concluded that insulating trade policies by wheat exporters and importers had the largest impact on U.S. wheat prices.

Just, Richard E., Ernst Lutz, Andrew Schmitz, and Stephen Turnovsky: "The Distribution of Welfare Gains from International Price Stabilization under Distortions," *American Journal of Agricultural Economics,* vol. 59, no. 4, November 1977, pp. 652–661.

In a two-country model with distortions and general demand and supply functions, the welfare implications of international price stabilization are analyzed. The degree of nonlinearity of the excess demand function in the free trade exporting country as well as the distortions are found to be of crucial importance in determining who gains from stabilization. With a high degree of nonlinearity, producers in both countries as well as the exporting country as a whole lose from stabilization, whereas consumers in both countries and the importing country gain. This is contrary to previous results with linearity.

Kilmer, Richard L., and David E. Hahn: "Effects of Market Share and Antimerger Policies on the Fluid Milk-Processing Industry," *American Journal of Agricultural Economics,* vol. 60, no. 3, August 1978, pp. 385–392.

The effects of merger restriction policies and market-share restriction policies on the structure of the Ohio fluid milk-processing industry are compared and contrasted within an intertemporal production distribution model. Individual firm size constraints are predicated on the transition probabilities of a Markov Chain. Merger restrictions are found to be less disruptive of industry structure. However, market share is a more effective tool for controlling concentration. The appropriate combination of merger-market share policies must be based on an analysis of market performance on a market-by-market basis.

Konandreas, Panos A., and Andrew Schmitz: "Welfare Implications of Grain Price Stabilization: Some Empirical Evidence for the United States," *American Journal of Agricultural Economics*, vol. 60, no. 1, February 1978, pp. 74–84.

This empirical study demonstrates that, although United States producers and consumers taken together benefit from policies which would stabilize feed graih prices, this is likely not the case for wheat. The model specifies a U.S. domestic demand relationship for food and feed use, a stock relationship, and a foreign demand sector; these are estimated by ordinary and two-stage least squares methods. The key to the analysis is in testing a well-known theoretical model in which the desirability of price stabilization largely depends on the source of instability (i.e., whether instability is generated abroad or is created internally).

Kramer, Randall A., and Rulon D. Pope: "Participation in Farm Commodity Programs: A Stochastic Dominance Analysis," *American Journal of Agricultural Economics,* vol. 63, no. 1, February 1981, pp. 119–128.

The net benefits of participation in farm commodity programs are analyzed with a normative risk model based on stochastic dominance theory. Utilizing entire probability distributions of participation and nonparticipation net returns, the impacts of alternative program features and farm size are investigated. Small changes in program parameters are found to affect participation decisions. It also is demonstrated that farm size can influence participation choices.

Krugman, Paul: "Scale Economies, Product Differentiation and the Pattern of Trade," *The American Economic Review,* vol. 70, no. 5, December 1980, pp. 850–959.

Lamm, R. McFall: "Dynamics of Food Price Inflation," *Western Journal of Agricultural Economics,* vol. 4, no. 2, December 1979, pp. 119–132.

A supply-shift concept of food price inflation is offered as an explanation of why food prices have increased in recent years. This view is consistent with cost-push theories of inflation.

The effects of higher farm product prices on food prices are analyzed using Pascal distributed lag models of the price adjustment process. Estimates are presented for 23 selected food products. The results indicate that higher farm prices are passed through to the retail level most quickly for food products which are not highly processed.

Lane, Sylvia: "Food Distribution and Food Stamp Program Effects on Food Consumption and Nutritional 'Achievement' of Low Income Persons in Kern County, California," *American Journal of Agricultural Economics,* vol. 60, no. 1, February 1978, pp. 108–116.

Participants in the U.S. Department of Agriculture's Food Distribution Program received more food than they would have purchased with food stamps in the market. These participants had slightly higher achievement ratios for some specific nutrients, such as protein, iron, and thiamine, than did nonparticipants. Food stamp recipients also had somewhat similar gains in nutrients, while spending a lower percentage of money income on food than nonparticipants.

Marion, Bruce W., Willard F. Mueller, Ronald Catterill, Frederick E. Geithman, and John R. Schmelzer: "The Price and Profit Performance of Leading Food Chains," *American Journal of Agricultural Economics,* vol. 61, no. 3, August 1979, pp. 420–433.

The net profits and grocery prices of large food chains were found to be positively and significantly related to market concentration and a chain's relative market share. The results refute the notion that higher profits for dominant firms in concentrated markets are due to efficiency and lower costs. Increased profits in noncompetitively structured markets accounted for about one-third of the increase in prices. Higher retailer costs in noncompetitive markets appear to stem from inefficiencies and cost-increasing forms of competition.

Martin, Marshall A., and Joseph Havlicek, Jr.: "Some Welfare Implications of the Adoption of Mechanical Cotton Harvesters in the United States," *American Journal of Agricultural Economics,* vol. 59, no. 4, November 1977, pp. 739–744.

Both consumers and producers in the United States have benefited from the adoption of mechanical cotton harvesters. U.S. consumers received the larger portion of the economic welfare gains, approximatley $230 million or about $1.25 per capita in 1947–49 dollars. The cost savings to the U.S. cotton producers as a result of the adoption of the harvesting technology was approximately 4.5¢ per pound of lint cotton (1.4¢ per pound of seed cotton). This cost savings is about 15% of the average real price received by farmers for lint cotton during 1952–69.

The welfare gains from the adoption of mechanical cotton harvesters reported in this note are based on a partial equilibrium framework and do not reflect the direct impacts on the labor market. Although the benefits to consumers and producers were substantial, the adoption of the labor-saving technology contributed to the disequilibrium in the labor market in the South. Further research on this labor market disequilibrium should provide additional insights into the total magnitude of the social costs and benefits of the adoption of cotton harvesters. (p. 743)

Masson, Robert T., and Philip M. Eisenstat: "Welfare Impacts of Milk Orders and the Antitrust Immunities for Cooperatives," *American Journal of Agricultural Economics,* vol. 62, no. 2, May 1980, pp. 270–278.

Mergers in the late 1960s and early 1970s led to large milk cooperative monopolies. These monopolies have been able to manipulate federal regulation to advantage over competing farmers and regulation continues to protect established power. A social cost analysis model shows that this power cost society at least $70 million a year prior to antitrust action.

Clearly, the antitrust market share standards used to challenge corporate mergers or joint ventures are too stringent for evaluating the anticompetitive impact of cooperative mergers or marketing agreements. But like corporations, cooperatives must be prevented from merger or joint venture where "the effect may be substantially to lessen competition" if society is to be protected from power which far exceeds that originally intended by the Capper-Volstead Act. (p. 277)

Matulich, Scott C.: "Efficiencies in Large-Scale Dairying: Incentives for Future Structural Change," *American Journal of Agricultural Economics,* vol. 60, no. 4, November 1978, pp. 642–647.

The present administered pricing structure could foster inefficiencies by supporting small dairy enterprises while allowing windfall gains to larger producers. A related issue must also be raised concerning the social desirability of widespread structural change in the dairy industry. Though gains in production efficiency are potentially available, they are not without important distributional and social implications. (p. 646)

Meekhof, Ronald L., Wallace E. Tyner, and Forest D. Holland: "U.S. Agricultural Policy and Gasohol: A Policy Simulation," *American Journal of Agricultural Economics,* vol. 62, no. 3, August 1980, pp. 408–415.

This research uses a stochastic simulation model to evaluate the implications of alternative gasohol programs for a large segment of the food and agricultural sector—corn and soybean producers, consumers, and taxpayers. The impacts on corn and soybean prices, production, acreage planted, carryover stocks, exports, and commodity program expenditures are presented. The research findings indicate that alcohol production levels below 2.0 billion gallons do not result in serious dislocations in the agricultural sector. As the level of alcohol production increases and more grain is required, corn prices rise significantly, stocks fall to extremely low levels, exports decline, and government expenditures increase greatly.

Melichar, Emanuel: "Capital Gains versus Current Income in the Farming Sector, *American Journal of Agricultural Economics,* vol. 61, number 5, December 1979, pp. 1085–1092.

Miller, John J., C. Phillip Baumel, and Thomas P. Drinka, "Impact of Rail Abandonment upon Grain Elevator and Rural Community Performance Measures," *American Journal of Agricultural Economics,* vol. 59, no. 4, November 1977, pp. 745–749.

The results indicate that, contrary to popular opinion, cooperatives located on abandoned rail lines do not die but rather continue to grow. When the performance measures were converted to percentages to adjust for elevator size, the data indicate no differences in rate of growth in the performance measures. If additional explanatory variables were considered in the analysis-of-variance model, a larger proportion of the total variation might be explained; however, the raw data suggest that the treatment *F*-statistics would likely show little change. With respect to community measures, no significant *F*-statistics existed for treatment (rail service) or for interaction. The results of this statistical analysis tend to confirm the conclusions of case studies that suggest minor or negligible impacts of rail abandonment on rural towns and elevators. (p. 748)

Morzuch, B. J., R. D. Weaver, and P. G. Helmberger: "Wheat Acreage Supply Response Under Changing Farm Programs," *American Journal of Agricultural Economics,* vol. 62, no. 1, February 1980, pp. 29–37.

Planted wheat acreage supply elasticities are estimated for each of several leading wheat-producing states. Estimates of elasticities for the aggregate of these states are 0.77, 0.45, and 0.52 for spring wheat, winter wheat, and all wheat, respectively, but there is considerable heterogeneity among states. Acreage allotments and marketing quotas appear to have destroyed the role of prices in allocating acreage between wheat and other crops during the years 1950 and 1954–64. Estimates were obtained using multiple regression analysis of time-series data for the period 1948–74. This period was subdivided in order to take account of changing farm programs.

Musser, Wesley N., and Kostos G. Stamoulis: "Evaluating the Food and Agriculture Act of 1977 with Firm Quadratic Risk Programming," *American Journal of Agricultural Economics,* vol. 63, no. 3, August 1981, pp. 447–456.

Federal agricultural commodity programs generally have been assumed to reduce the income risk for farm firms, but limited empirical research exists on this proposition. This paper presents a study of the impact of the Food and Agriculture Act of 1977 on income risk for a representative farm in Georgia. The model is used to derive an E-V frontier for a firm not participating in the program and for the same firm that is participating in the program. Results indicate that participation dominates nonparticipation except for higher levels of expected net income.

Nicholls, William H. and D. Gale Johnson: "The Farm Policy Awards, 1945: A Topical Digest of the Winning Essays," *Journal of Farm Economics,* vol. 28, no. 1, February 1946, pp. 267–293.

Nicuwoudt, W. L., J. B. Bullock, and G. A. Mathia: "An Economic Evaluation of Alternative Peanut Policies," *American Journal of Agricultural Economics,* vol. 58, no. 3, August 1976, pp. 485–495.

Three alternatives to the current peanut-price support, acreage-allotment program are considered. A linear programming framework is used to compare the effects of these policies on geographic location of peanut production, producer and consumer surplus, treasury costs, and value of allotments. Peanut production would expand in all areas except Texas under less restrictive production constraints. The largest expansion would be in Georgia and Alabama. Some version of the target price plan is considered to be a likely compromise program.

Novakovic, Andrew M., and Robert L. Thompson: "The Impact of Imports of Manufactured Milk Products on the U.S. Dairy Industry," *American Journal of Agricultural Economics,* vol. 59, no. 1, August 1977, pp. 507–519.

Recent events have sparked a debate over the effects of increased dairy imports on the U.S. dairy industry. This study attempts to estimate these impacts via an econometric model of the U.S. dairy sector. The time paths of adjustment of consumption, production, and price of specific dairy products and raw milk are estimated under three alternative levels of manufactured milk product imports. The analysis suggests that much larger than historically "normal" import levels are required to bring about a substantial impact upon the dairy industry in the longer run.

Ogg, Clayton and Arnold Miller, "Minimizing Erosion on Cultivated Land: Concentration of Erosion Problems and the Effectiveness of Conservation Practices," *Policy Research Notes,* July 1980–January 1981, Economic Research Service, U.S. Department of Agriculture, August 1981.

Paarlberg, Don: "The Land Grant Colleges and the Structure Issues," *American Journal of Agricultural Economics,* vol. 63, no. 1, February 1981, pp. 129–134.

The alternatives facing the land-grant college system regarding the social consequences of its programs are similar to those related to farm structure: *(a)* continue to imply that technology is socially neutral; *(b)* continue the existing programs and frankly acknowledge that they have social consequences, good and bad; *(c)* modify the existing programs, taking into account their social consequences; or *(d)* a mixture of the three. (p. 133)

Parker, Russell C., and John M. Conner: "Estimates of Consumer Loss Due to Monopoly in the U.S. Food Manufacturing Industries," *American Journal of Agricultural Economics,* vol. 61, no. 4, November 1979, pp. 626–639.

Three independent methodological approaches and data sets are used to estimate the consumer loss due to monopoly in the U.S. food-manufacturing industries for 1975. They include estimates *(a)* built up from previously estimated components of consumer loss, *(b)* derived from a regression analysis of the relationship of market structure to industry price-cost margins, and *(c)* derived from regression analysis of the market structure determinants of national brand-private label price differences. All three estimates converge to the $12 to 14 billion range. Virtually all of the consumer loss is attributed to income transfers; 3% to 6% is due to allocative inefficiency.

Pasour, E. C., Jr.: "Cost of Production: A Defensible Basis for Agricultural Price Supports?," *American Journal of Agricultural Economics,* vol. 62, no. 2, May 1980, pp. 244–248.

This paper has discussed problems related to defining and measuring cost used as a basis for price supports. The cost of producing a commodity is meaningful only in a static equilibrium model and, even then, cost cannot be defined independently of demand when resources are specialized. Under real world conditions, opportunity costs are subjective and vary widely between producers. The preceding analysis does not deny that government can vary output levels by price setting. What is challenged is the contention that such an approach involves the basing of price supports on cost. In view of the problems raised above, attempts to define and estimate "reasonable cost estimates" as a basis for agricultural price supports appear to be foredoomed. (p. 247)

Pindyck, Robert S.: "The Cartelization of World Commodity Markets," *The American Economic Review,* vol. 59, no. 2, May 1979, pp. 254–158.

The measurement of the potential gains from cartelization will require careful analysis on a market-by-market basis. The indications are, however, that there are not many markets where these gains are likely to be large. Undoubtedly more cartel organizations will form, but we should not expect many of them to have a significant impact on commodity markets. (p. 157)

Rasmussen, Wayne D., and Jane M. Porter: "Strategies for Dealing With World Hunger: Post World War II Policies," *American Journal of Agricultural Economics,* vol. 63, no. 5, December 1981, Proceedings Issue, pp. 810–818.

Rausser, Gordon C.: "Active Learning, Control Theory, and Agricultural Policy," *American Journal of Agricultural Economics,* vol. 60, no. 3, August 1978, pp. 476–490.

In the evaluation of key agricultural policies, a number of critical uncertainties arise for which little in the way of empirical evidence has been accumulated. The typical departmentalization within the agricultural economics profession fails to offer any hope of properly assessing these uncertainties. One approach that integrates the separate tasks of system analysis, econometric estimation, optimization, and more pragmatic data collection and summarization efforts is adaptive control. This framework effectively combines the characteristics of dynamic systems, uncertainties, and the active accumulation of information. Implications are drawn for potentially rewarding applications in agricultural and natural resource economics.

Richardson, James W., and Daryll E. Ray: "Commodity Programs and Control Theory," *American Journal of Agricultural Economics,* vol. 64, no. 1, February 1982, pp. 28–38.

The decision-making process for commodity programs in the United States is cast in terms of adaptive control theory, following the control framework outlined by Rausser. It is argued that the actual commodity program decision-making process can be viewed as a sequential multiperiod control problem and that multiple period, open-loop feedback control of a disaggregate policy simulation model can be used to assist agricultural policy makers. The empirical results present the first-round application of a suggested sequential use of control techniques and demonstrate the feasibility of applying control procedures to a multicommodity, agricultural policy simulator.

Runge, Carlisle Ford: "Common Property Externalities: Isolation, Assurance, and Resource Depletion in a Traditional Grazing Context, *American Journal of Agricultural Economics,* vol. 63, no. 4, November 1981, pp. 595–606.

Institutional alternatives to common property externalities are wider than argued by private exclusive property rights advocates. The "tragedy of the commons" is not a prisoners' dilemma, characterized by the strict dominance of individual strategies. The non-separable common property externality is an "assurance problem." The assurance problem provides striking perspectives in analytical and policy terms. It redefines the problem of the commons as one of decision making under uncertainty. Institutional rules innovated by the group to reduce uncertainty and coordinate expectations can solve the problem of overexploitation. Rules come in many forms, and private property is only one.

Salathe, Larry, William D. Dobson and Gustof A. Peterson: "Analysis of the Impact of Alternative U.S. Dairy Import Policies," *American Journal of Agricultural Economics,* vol. 59, no. 3, August 1977, pp. 496–506.

A simulation model is used to measure the impact of four U.S. dairy import plans on Wisconsin farm milk prices and other variables. Estimates for different plans show that each additional billion pounds of milk equivalent in dairy imports would depress Wisconsin farm prices initially by $0.14 to $0.21 per hundredweight. Wisconsin farm milk prices initially would fall by 18% if the milk equivalent of butter and cheese imports rose to 12 billion pounds. Within three years, milk prices would recover. But this recovery would occur only after about 13% of Wisconsin's milk producers had exited from dairying.

Sampson, Gary P., and Alexander J. Yeats: "An Evaluation of the Common Agricultural Policy as a Barrier Facing Agricultural Exports to the European Economic Community," *American Journal of Agricultural Economics,* vol. 59, no. 1, February 1977, pp. 99–106.

The influence of the European Economic Community's Common Agriculture Policy on world agricultural prices and exports of producing nations is analyzed. CAP reduces demand for agricultural imports, imparting more inelasticity into the world demand for them. Increased inelasticity amplifies price fluctuations born by non-EEC producers. Results stress the need for incorporating the subject of agricultural protection into the agenda of the current multilateral trade negotiations. Since CAP can amplify fluctuations in world agricultural prices, the system has a direct detrimental effect on non-EEC producers. CAP's potential for trade restriction, under levies and other protectionist measures, is significant.

Scandizzo, Pasquale L., and Odin K. Knudsen: "The Evaluation of the Benefits of Basic Needs Policies," *American Journal of Agricultural Economics,* vol. 62, no. 1, February 1980, pp. 46–57.

This paper presents a method to quantify social benefits of basic need policies by *(a)* relating their definition to the degree of fulfillment of accepted social standards, and *(b)* recasting the analysis of basic need projects within the general framework of shadow pricing in cost-benefit analysis. An empirical application of this method shows that in poor countries, the attempt at upholding a standard of minimum food consumption for the poor would put substantial premiums on food production over and above world (or domestic supply) prices provided that the increased food supply results in sufficiently higher consumption for the undernourished.

Seckler, David, and Robert A. Young: "Economic and Policy Implications of the 160-Acre Limitation in Federal Reclamation Law," *American Journal of Agricultural Economics,* vol. 60, no. 4, November 1978, pp. 575–588.

Proposals for strict enforcement and, conversely, for relaxation or elimination of acreage limitations in federal irrigation projects have arisen in response to recent court decisions regarding two large California irrigation districts. These proposals are examined against criteria including distributive justice, allocative efficiency, and administrative workability. Empirical evidence is offered which shows that proposed regulations would permit overly generous family incomes in the two areas and brings into question the existence of significant economics associated with larger-size farms. An alternative policy instrument, based on control of the water supply, rather than of the land, is proposed so as to reconcile more effectively conflicting policy objectives.

Sharp, Basil M. H., and Daniel W. Bromley: "Agricultural Pollution: The Economics of Coordination," *American Journal of Agricultural Economics,* vol. 61, no. 4, November 1979, pp. 591–600.

Institutional design is the major obstacle in reducing agricultural pollution. Cost sharing is being proposed for encouraging best management practices. Two models, one representing an agricultural firm and the other a management agency, are used to illustrate the flexibility and analytic capacity that agencies must have in determining the cost-sharing rules that apply to on-farm abatement practices. Off-farm investment opportunities should also be considered. If water quality is to be improved, these institutional arrangements will need the capacity to generate information, adapt to changing conditions, and reconcile the conflicting incentives of other programs.

Sharples, Jerry A., and Ronald Krenz: "Cost of Production: A Replacement for Parity?," *Agricultural-Food Policy Review,* Economic Research Service, U.S. Department of Agriculture, ERS AFPR-1, January 1977, pp. 62–68.

Cost of production could replace parity as the common measure for assessing the equity of returns to agriculture. Parity has been cited as obsolete because of its inability to include productivity as a factor. Inherent difficulties within the cost of production measure, which does include productivity, are discussed, such as defining a basis for assigning costs to land and management. The problems both in measuring costs of production of farm commodities, and in linking target prices and loan rates to such costs are addressed. In particular, a land price spiral can occur when target prices and loan rates are linked to cost of production. The Congress inserted a provision in the Agriculture and Consumer Protection Act of 1973 which directed the secretary of agriculture to conduct a study of the cost of producing feed grains, wheat, cotton, and milk. While the intended use of results is uncertain, such data could provide a basis for future evaluation of loan rates and target prices.

Shei, Shun-Yi, and Robert L. Thompson: "The Impact of Trade Restrictions on Price Stability in the World Wheat Market," *American Journal of Agricultural Economics,* vol. 59, no. 4., November 1977, pp. 628–638.

A 13-region quadratic programming model of world wheat trade is utilized to simulate the effects of unanticipated quantity changes on prices in the world wheat market under different degrees of trade restriction. Three scenarios characterized by different numbers of regions that permit price signals from international markets to be reflected into their domestic markets are specified. As the number of countries whose wheat trade is price-responsive increases in the simulation, the percentage change in world price is smaller in response to a shock such as U.S. export controls or an unanticipated change in Soviet imports.

Sisson, Charles A.: "An Intersectoral Examination of Tax Equity: Farm and Nonfarm Burdens," *Public Finance Quarterly,* vol. 7, no. 4, October 1979, pp. 455–478.

Song, D. Hee, and M. C. Hallberg, "Measuring Producers' Advantage from Classified Pricing of Milk," *American Journal of Agricultural Economics,* vol. 64, no. 1, February 1982, pp. 1–7.

A method of assessing the degree to which classified pricing of milk has favored milk producers over time is outlined, and results of an application of this method to the 1960–79 period are presented. It is found that prices for the different use classes of milk have, over this period, moved closer to consumer "optimal" prices rather than to producer "optimal" prices. Apparently the regulatory authorities in recent years have recognized less the need for farm income enhancement than the voice of consumer representatives.

Spitze, R. G. F.: "The Food and Agriculture Act of 1977: Issues and Decisions," *American Journal of Agricultural Economics,* vol. 60, no. 2, May 1978, pp. 225–235.

While the Food and Agriculture Act of 1977 has much in common with previous legislation and continues the evolution of agricultural and food policy, important changes are made in grain reserves, food stamps, procedures for setting target levels, support prices, acreage bases on individual farms, as well as administration and funding of research and education. Some consequences are evident, but much will depend upon unpredictable events of weather and foreign markets. The results of the act, as compared with no policy, are traced for consumers, producers, foreign trade, and U.S. Treasury payments, under altnerative scenarios. If shortages return, much of the law becomes irrelevant.

Stucker, T. A., J. B. Penn, and R. D. Knutson: "Agricultural-Food Policymaking: Process and Participants," *Agricultural-Food Policy Review,* Economic Research Service, U.S. Department of Agriculture, ERS A-FPR-1, January 1977, pp. 1–11.

Conditions shaping the current environment for agricultural and food policy are sketched. An overall model is presented in which to view the policy process. Participant groups likely to be influential in determining future agricultural and food policy. ... are discussed.

Public policy decisions in large part involve tradeoffs between equity and economic efficiency. Economists can analyze economic impacts of proposed actions that have equity implications. However, the final choices involving the equity and efficiency tradeoffs remain with the body politic.

Subotnik, Abraham, and James P. Houck: "Welfare Implications of Stabilizing Consumption," *American Journal of Agricultural Economics,* vol. 58, no. 1, February 1976, pp. 13–20.

Some economists are now urging the use of buffer stocks to help stabilize farm and food prices. Moreover, price stabilization has been shown to be socially beneficial from a theoretical point of view. Our purpose is to analyze the welfare implications of stabilized consumption and production and to compare them with the known implications of stabilized prices. It is shown that stabilized consumption is the least beneficial in its welfare implications. The relation between the gains from stabilization and the size of buffer stocks necessary to achieve stabilization also is analyzed. Finally, the presentation is extended to cover instability due to fluctuations in export demand.

Svedberg, Peter: "World Food Self Sufficiency and Meat Consumption," *American Journal of Agricultural Economics,* vol. 60, no. 4, November 1978, pp. 661–666.

One of the resolutions adopted at the World Food Conference in Rome urged the rich countries to adhere to simpler and less "calorie-wasting" food-consumption habits. The argument was that in this way large quantities of grain would be released for the benefit of starving people in the Third World.

The objective of this paper is to show that the link between food consumption in the rich countries and the food problem of the poor countries was considered in an erroneous time perspective. Simpler food-consumption habits in rich countries would do very little, if anything, to relieve the long-run food shortage in the poor countries, although a temporary (enforced) cutback of food consumption in the rich countries may under certain circumstances be warranted to solve the short-run problem, i.e., to avert famines in the Third World in years of global crop failures.

. . . altered food habits in the rich countries seem to be an inefficient, if not impossible, means of solving the long-run food problem in the Third World. This is because *(a)* the decrease in food prices on the world market tends to be small because production is also going to fall, *(b)* the effect is not aimed directly at those starving, i.e., the lower prices will not benefit only the starving but also the rich in all countries, and *(c)* there is no guarantee that the governments in the starvation-stricken countries would use the additional incomes to improve the lot of the people suffering from extreme hunger.

Swinbank, Alan: "European Community Agriculture and the World Market," *American Journal of Agricultural Economics,* vol. 62, no. 3, August 1980, pp. 426–433.

The European Communities' common agricultural policy is more complex than some studies would indicate. Not only do the member states succeed in maintaining nationally preferred price-support levels through the use of green currencies and monetary compensatory amounts, but the protective mechanisms applied have a differential impact on some commodities and some supplying countries. The introduction, in 1979, of the European Monetary System had repercussions for the agricultural sector, including the use of a new unit of account.

Taylor, Bernard W., and Ronald M. North: "The Measurement of Economic Uncertainty in Public Water Resource Development," *American Journal of Agricultural Economics,* vol. 58, no. 4, November 1976, pp. 636–643.

The existing benefit-cost criteria for evaluating water resource projects are deterministic and therefore incomplete, since the uncertainty inherent in project outcomes is not considered. A Monte-Carlo simulation approach is used to generate a mean and standard deviation for the benefits, costs, benefit-cost ratio, and net present value for the controversial Spewrell Bluff Project. Subjective estimates defining probability distributions of project benefits and costs were obtained from the Corps of Engineers. A project selection process that includes probability considerations in the benefit-cost criteria is recommended and several approaches for including uncertainty as a variable are suggested.

Taylor, C. Robert, and Hovac Talpaz: "Approximately Optimal Carryover Levels of Wheat in the United States," *American Journal of Agricultural Economics,* vol. 61, no. 1, February 1979, pp. 32–40.

This paper presents results of stochastic simulations of adherence to a first-period first-order certainty equivalence decision rule for approximately optimal wheat stocks in the

United States. The decision rule is obtained by maximizing a first-order approximation of the discounted sum of expected producers' plus consumers' surplus less storage costs over a long-time horizon. For comparative purposes, stochastic simulations of the present system for holding stocks are also given in the paper. Stock levels under the present system were found to be higher than the certainty equivalence stock levels.

Tsui, Amy Ong, and Donald J. Bogue: "Declining World Fertility: Trends, Causes, Implications," *Population Bulletin,* vol. 33, no. 4, 1978.

Tweeten, Luther G.: "Macroeconomics in Crisis: Agriculture in an Underachieving Economy," *American Journal of Agricultural Economics,* vol. 62, no. 4, December 1980, pp. 853–865.

The economic structure of the farming industry in the long run will depend more on federal taxation, spending, money supply, and trade policies in the Federal Reserve System, the Internal Revenue Service, and Department of State than on the commodity programs in the U.S. Department of Agriculture. (p. 864)

Whitacre, R. C., and S. C. Schmidt: "Analysis of a World Grain Reserve Plan Proposed Under a New International Wheat Agreement," *North Central Journal of Agricultural Economics,* vol. 2, no. 2, July 1980, pp. 83–84.

A spatial price allocation model was used to assess the consistency of global wheat reserve stock levels with the stabilization of wheat prices as proposed within the framework of a new International Wheat Agreement. . . . So far, efforts to revise the Wheat Trade Convention and to turn it into an instrument for the moderation of price swings in the world wheat market have not met with success.

White, Fred C.: "State-Financed Property Tax Relief," *American Journal of Agricultural Economics,* vol. 61, no. 3, August 1979, pp. 409–419.

As a result of widespread dissatisfaction with rising property tax burdens, state governments are being called on increasingly to provide property tax relief. Numerous tax reform proposals are being considered by the various states. The purpose of this paper is to develop an analytical framework for evaluating the potential impacts of alternative approaches to property tax relief. Applicability of the fiscal model is demonstrated using three alternative tax relief proposals—increased state funding of elementary and secondary education, revenue transfers for a general reduction in property taxes, and a circuit breaker to ease excessive property tax burdens.

White, Fred C., and Bill R. Miller: "Implications of Public School Finance Reform with Local Control," *American Journal of Agricultural Economics,* vol. 58, no. 3, August 1976, pp. 415–424.

The nation's present interest in school finance reform concerns elimination of inequities in financing and improvement in the delivery of educational services. This paper examines one of the most popular school finance reform proposals that would allow the local school district to select an appropriate tax effort without directly linking quality of education to the district's wealth. Implementation of this reform proposal would result in a slight redistribution of income to poorer districts but would result in further inequities in quality of educational services.

Wonnacott, Paul, and Ronald Wonnacott: "Is Unilateral Tariff Reduction Preferable to a Customs Union? The Curious Case of the Missing Foreign Tariffs," *The American Economic Review,* vol. 71, no. 4, September 1981, pp. 704–713.

Woods, Mike, Luther Tweeten, Daryll E. Ray, and Greg Parvin: "Statistical Tests of the Hypothesis of Reversible Agricultural Supply," *North Central Journal of Agricultural Economics,* vol. 3, no. 1, January 1981, pp. 13–19.

Aggregate supply equations are estimated using four alternative methods to segment the output price variable to measure short-run response of farm output to increasing and decreasing prices. Null hypotheses of equal price response coefficients for falling and rising prices could not be rejected. The four alternative methods used to measure the response to rising and falling prices provided no consistent evidence to reject the null hypothesis of no difference in response. No method of segmentation used appeared to be clearly superior to the others, but shortcomings in application of some of the methods were apparent. . . . Supply response is low in the short run, both for rising *and* falling prices.

Wyckoff, J. B.: "Allocation Problems of Public Lands in the West," *Western Journal of Agricultural Economics,* vol. 2, no. 2, December 1977, pp. 11–20.

Increasing interest in the federally owned lands by individuals and groups representing a broad cross section of society has intensified public land management problems. Pressures for preservation, conservation, and additional nonmarket uses have resulted in management conflicts.

Economic intelligence could contribute to improved decision making by federal agencies charged with public land management. However, inadequate past research attention related to economic problems of public lands presently precludes an optimum input from economists. Articulation of problem areas and economic issues is necessary for developing meaningful research priorities. This article identifies some elements of the problem and suggests some potentially rewarding areas for economic research.

Zwart, A. C., and K. D. Meilke: "The Influence of Domestic Pricing Policies and Buffer Stocks on Price Stability in the World Wheat Industry," *American Journal of Agricultural Economics,* vol. 61, no. 3, August 1979, pp. 434–437.

Domestic pricing policies are a major cause of instability in international commodity markets. The modification of such policies could be a viable alternative to buffer stocks in providing stability. A theoretical model of price intervention is developed to show how common forms of intervention destabilize the world market price. A stochastic econometric model is used to show, first, that most countries in the world wheat market have policies which destabilize the wheat market, and, second, that the modification of such policies would prove as effective as a buffer stock policy in stabilizing the wheat market.

NAME INDEX

Abel, Martin E., 59*n*., 62
Adelman, Irma, 56*n*., 277*n*., 292
Armbruster, Walter J., 174*n*., 184

Babb, E. M., 39*n*.
Backus, H., 36*n*.
Bailey, William C., 108
Baker, Gladys L., 101*n*.
Ball, V. Eldon, 154
Barton, Glen T., 29*n*.
Batie, Sandra S., 218*n*., 248
Benedict, Murray R., 99*n*., 131*n*.
Bhide, Shashanda, 233*n*.
Bigman, David, 134
Black, John D., 93, 96*n*., 99, 108
Blair, William, 261*n*.
Boehlje, Michael, 214
Bogue, Allan G., 191*n*.
Bogue, Donald J., 49*n*.
Bohall, Robert, 39*n*.
Bonnen, James T., 39*n*.
Bowman, John, 191*n*.
Brannan, Charles, 100
Bredahl, Maury E., 79*n*., 83
Breimyer, Harold F., 22, 24*n*., 29*n*., 43,
    131*n*.
Brewster, David E., 10*n*., 22
Brewster, John M., 10*n*., 22

Bryan, William Jennings, 193
Burnette, Mahlon A., III, 177*n*.

Campbell, Keith O., 43, 62
Carlson, Gerald A., 262*n*.
Carman, Hoy F., 128*n*., 214
Carriel, Mary Turner, 279*n*.
Carter, Anne P., 49*n*.
Carter, Colin A., 78*n*.
Castle, Emery N., 262*n*.
Cavin, James Pierce, 99*n*., 112*n*.
Cavin, Linda, 39*n*.
Chambers, Robert G., 81*n*., 84, 134, 154
Chicoine, David L., 207*n*., 214
Clayton, Kenneth, 108
Cochrane, Willard W., 102
Coffman, George W., 38*n*.
Collins, Joseph, 278*n*., 292
Collins, Keith J., 79*n*., 83
Connor, John M., 39*n*., 184
Coolidge, Calvin, 91
Cotner, Melvin L., 33*n*., 239*n*., 240*n*., 248
Cotterill, Ronald W., 169*n*.
Crosson, Pierre R., 59*n*., 218*n*., 248

Davis, Joseph S., 91*n*., 93*n*., 96*n*.
Deiter, Ronald E., 136*n*.

SUBJECT INDEX